Small Group Decision Making

Communication and the Group Process

FOURTH EDITION

Donald G. Ellis
University of Hartford

B. Aubrey Fisher
Late Professor of Communication
University of Utah

McGraw-Hill, Inc.

New York   St. Louis   San Francisco   Auckland   Bogotá   Caracas   Lisbon
London   Madrid   Mexico City   Milan   Montreal   New Delhi   San Juan
Singapore   Sydney   Tokyo   Toronto

SMALL GROUP DECISION MAKING
Communication and the Group Process

Copyright © 1994, 1990, 1980, 1974 by McGraw-Hill, Inc. All rights reserved.
Printed in the United States of America. Except as permitted under the
United States Copyright Act of 1976, no part of this publication may
be reproduced or distributed in any form or by any means, or stored in a
data base or retrieval system, without the prior written permission
of the publisher.

3 4 5 6 7 8 9 0 DOC DOC 9 0 9 8 7

ISBN 0-07-021212-0

This book was set in Palatino by Better Graphics, Inc.
The editors were Hilary Jackson and Tom Holton;
the production supervisor was Kathryn Porzio.
The cover was designed by David Romanoff.
R. R. Donnelley & Sons Company was printer and binder.

Library of Congress Cataloging-in-Publication Data is available:
LC Card #93-27420.

About the Authors

DONALD G. ELLIS holds a Ph.D. from the University of Utah. He has been on the faculty of Purdue University and Michigan State University and is currently Professor of communication at the University of Hartford. He has authored numerous articles on communication theory with particular emphasis on language and interaction processes in interpersonal and group contexts. He and William Donohue edited *Contemporary Issues in Language and Discourse Processes* for Lawrence Erlbaum Associates, and Ellis is the author of *From Language to Communication*. He is also the editor of the journal *Communication Theory*. Professor Ellis participates in various national organizations and lectures and writes in the fields of language behavior, group decision making, interpersonal communication, and related topics.

B. AUBREY FISHER completed his Ph.D. at the University of Minnesota in 1968. From 1971 until his death in 1986 he was Professor of Communication at the University of Utah. Aubrey Fisher was a very respected and accomplished communication scholar and teacher. He wrote many articles and chapters on communication theory and group processes and was the author of *Small Group Decision Making, Perspectives on Human Communication,* and *Interpersonal Communication: Pragmatics of Human Relationships*. He was editor of *Western Journal of Speech Communication* from 1982 to 1984 and was the President of the Western Speech Communication Association in 1985, in addition to holding offices in national organizations.

This book is dedicated to Alex,
who is learning to read.

Contents

Preface

This is the fourth edition of *Small Group Decision Making: Communication and the Group Process*. The book continues to enjoy success. After Professor Fisher's untimely death in 1986 I agreed to take on a revision of his group process text, which resulted in the third edition of this book. At that time I tried to sharpen and update the text in Fisher's tradition. This fourth edition represents a continuation of Aubrey's work in group interaction but with certain changes.

I have completed this revision with the expectation that it might prove useful for a greater variety of instructional purposes. I have tried to write in a clear and engaging manner that makes the ideas in the book accessible to readers without insulting their intelligence by oversimplifying. I have also tried to use theory in the book to inform practice. Practical advice appears throughout the volume. Surely there are no guaranteed "tricks" for managing conflict, making decisions, or leading, but we can apply some intelligence to these problems. I have tried to do that whenever possible.

This book emphasizes communication and decision making. Although it draws from all facets of group life—including training groups, family groups, and therapy groups—decision making is probably the most pervasive group activity, especially in work settings.

Communication is the crux of group behavior. Traditionally, a communication perspective on group behavior has received less attention than psychological or sociological perspectives. This is because communication is typically defined as merely transmitting and receiving messages. Although there is certainly some truth to this definition, communication is actually more fundamental than the mere transmission of messages. Communication is *the* organizing element of groups. Everything that matters in groups—information, relationships, leadership, decisions, effectiveness, understanding—is created by communication. Through communication, group members develop interpersonal relationships and form "groups" from aggregates of individuals.

This book is intended for university students studying group interaction. The readers' primary interests may lie in any number of areas related to group behavior. But the common point of departure is that communication organizes people into an active social system for the purpose of performing some task.

Although I assume full responsibility for this revision, I have benefited from many influences direct and indirect. The work of a number of reviewers was invaluable. They offered insights and suggestions that found their way into many of the chapters that follow. In particular I would like to thank Katherine Adams, California State University at Fresno, who also prepared the instructor's manual; Dan DeStephen, Wright State University; Lloyd Drecksel, University of Utah; Michael Mayer, Arizona State University; Ann Nicotera, University of Oklahoma; Thomas Ruddick, Edison State Community College; and Brant Short, Idaho State University.

I am always grateful to my friends and colleagues in the Department of Communication at the University of Hartford. They are first-rate professionals with contagious interest in communication.

My wife, Karen Beyard, and the kids, Alex and David, are always loving and supportive. They have the patience, humor, and lively sense of family that make these tasks possible.

Donald G. Ellis

Introduction

We must inform you at the outset that we're well aware of many of the jokes concerning decisions made by groups and the process of group decision making generally. We know that the camel is a horse designed by a committee and that a committee is a group of people that keeps minutes and wastes hours. We have also heard that a committee is a group of people who can do nothing individually but, as a group, can meet and decide that nothing can be done. Group decision making has been defined as the confusion of the loudest-talking member multiplied by the number of members present. In regard to the propensity of organizations to appoint committees at every opportunity, it has been said that if several average Americans found themselves on an airplane about to crash, at least one of them would take time to appoint a landing committee.

Occasionally one of the jokes will contain a germ of truth. One of our favorite stories about group decision making involves the *blinder system*. As the story goes, a farmer always plowed his field with a single horse hitched to the plow. Nevertheless, the farmer yelled, "Giddyup, Jack! Giddyup, Casey! Giddyup, Jerry! Giddyup, Tom!" Day after day, his neighbor heard the farmer shouting all those names at the lone horse. One day his curiosity and bewilderment proved too much. He went to the farmer and asked why he called his horse by all the different names. "Oh," replied the farmer, "the horse's name is Jack. But, you see, he doesn't know his own strength. So I put blinders on him, and I yell all those other names. Then he works hard, and he pulls the plow mighty fine. All the time, you see, he thinks he's got all those other horses helping him."

The blinder system may indeed be less of a joke than it appears. Perhaps it is simply another name for the *assembly effect* discussed in Chapter 2. Despite all the witticisms and the alleged limitations of the group process of making decisions, it remains one of the most potent and valuable tools of our society.

The process of decision making in a social setting is vitally important in a democratic society. Nearly every facet of our society—political, legislative, judicial, economic—functions through decisions made by groups. Laws are formulated by large groups of legislators and small groups of legislative committees. National executive decisions come from meetings of the President and the Cabinet or small groups of advisors. The decisions of juries determine the fates of civil and criminal defendants in our courts. Negotiation teams decide the wages and benefits of millions of labor-union members. The functioning of every business, educational, and political organization relies on decisions made by management teams. Group decisions ultimately determine what television programs we are able to view, what products we are available to purchase, what new automobiles will look like, what taxes we will pay, and so forth. Although we are often unaware of the pervasive influence of group decisions, the effects of those decisions on our lives are inescapable.

The small group has been a very common phenomenon in every society from the beginning of civilization. In our society, probably the most common small group is the family. In many respects, the family is a decision-making group that has as its principal task the rearing of children. On the other hand, the family group is little more than a biological accident. Group members do not choose to belong to the family group, nor are they typically free to remove themselves from its confines; runaway children and deserting mothers and fathers are not condoned by our society. Nevertheless, since families do engage in many decision-making activities, they may be considered examples of decision-making groups and included in our study.

Certainly many other types of groups exist in our society, but they are not included in the following discussions of group decision making. The encounter group, the laboratory training group, the consciousness-raising group, the creativity workshop, the awareness group, the assertiveness training group, etc., exist for purposes other than the performance of a group task. Moreover, such groups do not function as bona fide "groups." Rather, they remain collections of individuals, each of whom is pursuing a basically individual goal. The purpose of such groups is to provide individual members with some outcome—perhaps increased sensitivity, increased awareness, increased assertiveness, self-identity, or ventilation of aggressions and feelings. In some respects, these groups are oriented to therapeutic goals; that is, they provide a group context for the behavioral change of individual members.

This book discusses the type of group with a specific identity of the group in which each individual member experiences a sense of membership or loyalty. The group is not merely a convenient context in which individuals make decisions; rather, it is a specific process of making decisions socially. Group decision making, as a process, is quite different from the decision making performed by individuals.

Task-oriented group is a generic term that identifies any one of an enormous variety of groups whose very existence depends on its performing some task. An outside authority often assigns the task to the group, although individuals may, of their own volition, form a group by themselves. They may decide to form a group in order to perform some task that either cannot be accomplished by a single person or cannot be accomplished as effectively by persons acting alone. The nature of what constitutes tasks performed by groups varies widely, ranging from an assembly-line work group whose assigned task is to put bolts *A, B* and *C* through holes 1, 2, and 3 to a group of jury members who ponder the evidence presented at a trial and decide on the guilt or innocence of a defendant. Some tasks, such as that of the jury, obviously require verbal and oral interaction. Others, such as the assembly-line group, require no oral interaction at all.

The task-oriented group is by far the most prevalent group in our society. Every human organization—business, education, service, and political—includes numerous task-oriented groups to carry out the various functions of that organization and other task-oriented groups to coordinate the efforts of all other groups. Perhaps the most interesting of these organizational sub-groups are the management groups—those groups charged with the task of organizing various organizational groups and subgroups into a unitary, effi-ciently functioning organization. Management groups may be the most inter-esting because they deal directly with issues confronting every social system. And much of being a group member is knowing how to work productively with others in a social situation.

Our focus in this book is narrower than the broad variety of purposes implied by the term *task-oriented group*. Specifically, our concern is with one of those purposes, probably the most common group purpose of all—decision making. Decision-making groups make up the bulk of all groups in most human organizations. Groups decide what new products will be manufac-tured, for example, and how they are to be designed, advertised, and sold. Groups decide which laws will govern a society, how those laws will be enforced, how they are to be interpreted, and even how those who violate the laws will be dealt with. Our entire society functions through the organiza-tions that it comprises. And each organization functions through decisions made by groups within that organization. This type of group—the decision-making group—is the primary concern of this book. As later discussions will demonstrate, group decision making differs inherently from individual deci-sion making, both in the process of making decisions and in the nature of the decision-making task. Thus the *group* is considered a decision-making *system*.

Effective decision making is regarded as a natural consequence of the members' abilities to analyze and understand the process of group decision making. But no one can acquire such an ability without active participation in group decision making. Although some people may argue that one cannot effectively experience any phenomenon without thoroughly studying it from the impartial and objective perspective of the observer, others argue just as vehemently that there is no substitute for experience. Both sides of this hackneyed controversy between the values of education and experience are probably at once both right and wrong. Knowledge of anything without experiencing it is as sterile as experiencing it without any knowledge. Stu-dents of group decision making are strongly urged to incorporate their under-standing of group decision making, gained from reading this book and others, with actual participation in groups engaged in decision-making tasks. Combining understanding with experience leads to the most fruitful results and maximizes the effectiveness of group decision making.

Too often overlooked in the study of group decision making is the process of communication—the vitally essential ingredient of any social system. Communication is *the* organizing element of a social system. To highlight the study of group communication, the group is defined in a face-to-face setting that absolutely requires verbal and oral communication as the principle mode of interaction.

WHAT TO EXPECT

Some expectations have probably been established at this point. The first is that the group will be treated as a *whole*. That is, the group is a phenomenon quite distinct from its individual members. In this sense, we are employing the concept of holism, or nonsummativity—a tenet of general systems theory. We shall think of a group as a social system characterized by wholeness and inseparability. In this respect, we can say that the group is different from (and sometimes more than) the sum of its members. The many references to the "group" in the following chapters assume a single entity that, in the context of task performance, is more significant than the specific characteristics (such as the personalities, intelligence, and abilities) of the individual persons who constitute the membership.

A second expectation should also be clear. Our focus will be on decision making, a specific task orientation of the group. The title of this book should make this emphasis clear. Every chapter is oriented to this emphasis. Certainly, aspects of groups other than the specific task are also important in understanding how groups develop and how they make decisions, and the following chapters will include discussions of such aspects. Although these aspects are not unique to decision making, they contribute to understanding the group process; for example, norms and roles exist in all groups, whether they make decisions or not. The book includes discussion of these group concepts because they are characteristics of decision-making groups.

You will find suggestions for improving the effectiveness of communication and the group process, but you will probably be disappointed that these suggestions are rarely specific enough to qualify as surefire principles for ensuring success in group decision making. Some textbooks may make promises to the readers and suggest that if they follow the guidelines in the book, they will know how to "control" or "win" the conference or the group. But this book's perspective on group decision making, viewing the group as a whole and communication as an interactive process, deemphasizes the possibility of an individual member controlling other members. Such control is simply not available in most groups. And when it is available (such as to the "boss" in a group of subordinates), group decision making does not exist. Rather, the boss makes the decision and informs the others, in which case the assumption that a group exists is superficial and misleading.

The primary purpose of this book is to generate in students an understanding of communication and the group process, and hence of group decision making. We shall consistently emphasize understanding rather than mere knowledge. Understanding involves experience—not merely *knowing* what to do, but *understanding* what is going on and then adapting to that experience.

We advocate in this book that each group member should develop the feeling of being both a participant and an observer of group decision making. In other words, the quality of group decision making improves when members are sensitive to the process of communication and group development and thus experience this process while it is occurring. As a result of observing the group during this process, you will be able to participate in the process more effectively. Being a participant-observer—that is, both a participant and an observer—requires you to understand group decision making as well as to be knowledgeable about it. Knowing group decision making is one thing; understanding it is much more significant. We hope that the distinction between understanding and knowledge will become apparent as you continue your reading.

CONVENTIONAL WISDOM: A BARRIER
TO UNDERSTANDING

There was once an instructor of instrumental music who contended that we instructors of communication "have it easy" teaching students the principles of communication because the students are able to benefit from experience. After all, they have spent 10 to 15 years actually communicating every day. But teaching a beginning student how to play the trombone is much more difficult, he maintained, because the student has no benefit of past experience in trombone playing. We maintained that it is precisely for this reason that learning the trombone is probably less difficult. Because the students in our communication classes have vast communicative experience, they possess a large repertoire of alleged "knowledge" gained from this experience—beliefs widely held and tenaciously maintained, whether or not they reflect reality. And this knowledge serves to inhibit, rather than assist, the students' understanding of communication principles.

Nonspecialists' beliefs that are widely (if carelessly) held fall into the genre of "conventional wisdom." Principles from conventional wisdom are considered credible and true, not because they are actually true, but because they are conventional—because many people believe them to be true. The advertising slogan "Fifty million Frenchmen can't be wrong" reflects the simplistic wisdom based on conventionality. If so many people believe it to be true, then it must be true. But if fifty million Frenchmen believed the earth were flat, they would be wrong nevertheless. Conventionality may lead to increased credibility, but it has no direct bearing on reality.

Belief based on conventionality often takes the form of a cliché or an adage believed to possess truth because it is so familiar. We sometimes call such beliefs folk wisdom and fall prey to their influence. How and why conventional wisdom gains credibility through familiarity is a matter of some conjecture. The axiom "Early to bed, early to rise" can be traced to Benjamin Franklin's mother trying to urge her recalcitrant son into bed at the appointed hour. Conventional wisdom is also not necessarily easily identified as conventional wisdom. It is difficult to resist the influence of the familiar antecedent that often precedes a principle from conventional wisdom—"Everyone knows that. . . ." Who wants to be out of step with the rest of the world?

Dangers of Conventional Wisdom

Because conventional wisdom is conventional, it is not necessarily false. On the contrary, many clichés have some basis in fact. But accepting such "wisdom" at face value is nevertheless dangerous. At its worst, conventional wisdom is blatantly false and leads to greater problems than originally existed. At its best, conventional wisdom oversimplifies the situation and desensitizes us to reality. In the case of group decision making, members either create more social problems for themselves because of false "wisdom" or are led to inefficient and unproductive effort by the demands of irrelevant "wisdom."

Most important, axioms based purely on conventionality masquerade as real knowledge and thwart genuine understanding. In the case of group communication, which abounds with folk wisdom, conventional wisdom severely inhibits the improvement of decisional quality and of group communication. In almost no other area of human endeavor do we rely so heavily and so trustingly on conventional wisdom. Although some persons suffering from arthritis continue to wear copper bracelets on their wrists, we generally seek the expert assistance of a physician when illness strikes. Although we may "starve a cold and feed a fever" (or is it the other way around?), we don't seriously believe that eating an apple every day will protect us from illness. We generally don't rely on a pain in the foot to predict bad weather or take delight from a red sky in the evening. When we really want to know what weather is in store, we seek out the forecasts made by expert meteorologists. But when it comes to communication and the group process, everyone seems to be an expert, reverting to the oversimplifications of conventional wisdom.

Conventional Wisdom about Group Decision Making

Representative examples of conventional wisdom about group decision making are listed below. Many of these examples may seem sensible and eminently reasonable, and you will probably discover that you have believed more than a few of them. The examples come from various areas of communication and the group process, represent only a tiny portion of the clichés about group decision making, and have only one trait in common: They are all false.

1. Discussion differs from debate in that members of a group discussion do not advocate argumentative positions but maintain an open mind and a spirit of free inquiry. *Corollary*: The effective decision-making group exhibits a minimum of argument and interpersonal conflict.

2. To be effective, the group should strive for nearly equal participation among group members.
3. Each member of the group should perform certain duties required of group membership. *Corollary*: The duties of the leader differ from the duties of the other group members.
4. In the group context, getting the job done—that is, making the decisions —is more important than getting along with other group members. *Correlative opposite*: In the group context, developing close interpersonal relationships is more important than the actual performance of the decision-making task.
5. Some people are natural-born leaders. *Corollary*: Some people possess the characteristics (or quality) of leadership.
6. The personalities of the members exert the most significant effect on the process of group decision making.
7. In the long run, a group will achieve better results through using democratic methods than through achieving specific results by other means.
8. Almost any job that can be done by a committee can be done better by having one person responsible for it.
9. We talk with one another, but we just don't communicate.
10. Two-way communication is preferable to one-way communication.
11. Compromise is the most effective strategy for resolving social conflicts.

Relying on conventional wisdom is a formidable barrier to the understanding and knowledge of group decision making. By the time you have read the following chapters, you should understand why and how these examples of conventional wisdom are not true. At that time you should also be able to add many other examples to the list. When you are able to do that, you will have taken one giant step forward toward a robust understanding of group decision making.

AN OVERVIEW OF THE BOOK

The preceding pages have established the primary focus of this book—group decision making. There are many ways to approach the study of group decision making. The subtitle of this book provides an insight into the perspective employed in the chapters following; although "communication and the group process" may imply two perspectives, the chapters will illustrate that communication and the group process comprise a single, unified perspective.

Chapters 1 and 2 lay out the framework of the group process, and Chapters 3 and 4 describe the nature of the communicative process. While reading these chapters, you will probably note that both "communication" and "group" are defined as a process—in fact, a single process. As a process, communication and the group are composed of patterned behaviors (or actions) that are constantly in a state of change. Neither communication nor a group should be considered a "thing." Rather, each is a process that is constantly *in process* of continually developing. Both are continually evolving and changing over time.

Chapter 1, The Group Process, describes how to think about group process. This initial chapter emphasizes how individuals organize themselves into a single entity, a group, and thereby develop the social system that is essential to effective group decision making.

Chapter 2, Dimensions of the Group Process, illustrates the interdependence of the social and task dimensions of group decision making. For group members to be effective as a decision-making system, their interpersonal relationships must also be effective. In fact, effectiveness in one dimension is usually tantamount to effectiveness in the other. But groups can be effective only to the extent that they perform tasks that are appropriate to a group. In this way, they take advantage of the uniquely social elements of group decision making.

An analysis of the communicative process reveals both structural (space-oriented) and functional (time-oriented) elements. Chapter 3 (Group Communication: Structural Elements) and Chapter 4 (Group Communication: Functional Elements) discuss these characteristics of the communicative process as they are specifically adapted to the group setting. The structural elements of group communication (e.g., feedback responses, networks, gatekeeping, breakdowns, and barriers) are the most commonly known, but the functional elements may be more significant to understanding the process of group decision making. Chapter 4 illustrates how the communicative process can be viewed from a pragmatic perspective. These functional elements (e.g., feedback sequences, analysis and punctuation of interaction sequences, and the content and relationship dimensions) are vital to our understanding of group decision making.

Chapter 5 emphasizes two of the most important group standards—roles and norms—and discusses them in terms of communicative behaviors. Since roles and norms develop out of communicative exchanges it is sensible to discuss these issues immediately following the discussion of communicative processes.

Chapter 6, The Process of Group Decision Making, traces various approaches and methods used to understand group decision making. The discussion emphasizes phasic development, a process defined in terms of interaction sequences. This model describes decision *emergence* rather than how groups *make* decisions.

Leadership and power are discussed in Chapter 7. This chapter focuses on perhaps the most important role in any group—the leader. The discussion surveys a variety of perspectives on leadership, but settles on a functional perspective, one that is consistent with communication and group process. The chapter clearly identifies the communicative behaviors most associated with leadership, and discusses issues such as leader emergence, power and status, and gender issues.

Chapter 8, Conflict and Deviance, also adopts a functional perspective in explaining conflict which is typically regarded as socially disruptive. The chapter suggests that conflict and deviance are quite normal in groups and should be managed but not necessarily eliminated. The chapter discusses specific techniques for managing conflict.

Chapter 9 is titled Anatomy of Communication in Decision-Making Groups: Improving Effectiveness. The chapter gives a detailed account of how interaction varies during the process of decision emergence that is discussed in Chapter 6. The chapter gives samples of interaction and provides a picture of what decision making looks like. It also provides guidelines to help group members improve their effectiveness; these guidelines center on attitudinal factors, interpersonal factors, and group-identity factors that can improve effectiveness in groups.

Appendix 1, Observing and Analyzing Small Group Communication, is included here to help students learn how information about communication processes in groups is collected. The chapter describes observational methods and techniques for observing group interaction. The chapter is designed to introduce readers to the act of observing and analyzing groups. It is included as an appendix so an instructor may incorporate the material into a course on group communication as she or he sees fit.

Definitions of important concepts and terms in this book are given as they are introduced, and the glossary in Appendix 2 briefly defines most of the book's specialized terms. But keep in mind that while *defining* a concept is easy, *understanding* it is more difficult and infinitely more valuable.

In your classroom study of group decision making, you may well decide to emphasize some chapters more than others, to omit one or more, to rearrange the chapters, and to provide supplemental information. No book's content and organization are sacred; rather, you should adapt them to suit your specific classroom purposes. Each and every chapter of this book emphasizes an understanding of how a group is structured, how it functions, and how it evolves through the process of human communication.

Understanding is the key to effective participation in group decision making. Central to this understanding and to effective participation is human communication in the group. One must always keep in mind that, however members of a small group may differ from one another as human beings with a unique combination of personality and abilities, they all have one thing in common—they are communicating individuals.

But no one can really *teach* effective communication and group process; it can only be *learned*. We hope the truth of this seemingly paradoxical statement will become apparent during your reading of *Small Group Decision Making: Communication and the Group Process*.

Small Group Decision Making
Communication and the Group Process

CHAPTER 1

How to Think About Group Processes

A camel is a horse designed by a committee

We know there are plenty of jokes about groups and committees. We have heard that a committee is a group of people who keeps minutes and wastes hours. The comedian Fred Allen said that a group was a collection of people "who individually can do nothing but as a group decide that nothing can be done." A few other cynics have suggested that most Americans on a plane about to crash would appoint a landing committee.

But think of the other extreme. Think about being a prisoner in solitary confinement enduring years of loneliness. Imagine being a hostage held captive for years, spending days and months with no one to talk to. It is difficult even to imagine the interminable tedium—no one to talk with day after day, no one to laugh with or argue with or just sit in silence with year after year. Most of us can barely stand to be in the house by ourselves for very long.

The effects of isolation are so powerful that it is the technique used for brainwashing. A prisoner is completely separated from all others and cut off from communication with everyone, even the author of a book. The prisoner develops a bond with the jailer or captors; the need for involvement with others is so powerful that it is preferable to insanity, and the prisoner becomes drawn into the jailer's reality.

So all the jokes aside, we require and crave the companionship of others. We need to belong. We need contact with others to accomplish our goals, whether those goals be work-related or psychological. That's why we belong to family groups, friendship groups, community groups, and work groups, ad infinitum. Our membership in work groups is particularly important. These groups exist in order to perform some task within a larger organization. Organizations are complex and they coordinate the work of many people by establishing small groups and asking them to make decisions. The members of these groups are expected to be competent. They are expected to

3

(1) participate; (2) work well with others; (3) often assume leadership responsibilities; (4) present ideas clearly and effectively; (5) disseminate information;
(6) make decisions skillfully; and (7) most importantly, possess good oral and
written communication skills (Hunt, 1980).

We will be mostly concerned with oral communication in this book, but
we will also discuss the influences of new technologies on communication.
The remainder of this chapter is devoted to a perspective on group communication. We will expand our discussion of groups and offer a theory of how
groups work. This theory will provide a framework for helping the reader
learn to think more analytically about groups.

PROCESS DEFINED

According to any good dictionary, four elements are inherent in a process—
action, or acts; a continuous *change in time;* advancement, or *progress* over time;
and a *goal*, or result. Thus, a process clearly implies a time in which action
occurs in a progression toward some goal.

David Berlo (1960, p. 24), an early communication theorist, offered an
excellent and often-quoted definition of *process:*

> If we accept the concept of process, we view events and relationships as
> dynamic, on-going, ever-changing, continuous. When we label something as
> a process, we also mean that it does not have *a* beginning, *an* end, a fixed
> sequence of events. It is not static, at rest. It is moving. The ingredients
> within a process interact; each affects all of the others.

Berlo's definition is richer than the dictionary's and emphasizes the time
dimension. Berlo also provides a clue as to why every process is continually
changing: interaction among the ingredients. Each ingredient affects and is
affected by every other ingredient. The ingredients, then, are interdependent;
that is, any change in one of the ingredients affects all the other ingredients.

The term *process* means that individuals and their groups are continually
changing and modifying themselves. Group members respond to internal
and external stimuli and alter their ideas and behaviors in accordance with the
group's needs and goals. Because a group changes over time, it is misleading
to attempt a complete understanding of a group at any particular point in
time. Rather, the group must be examined as an entity that has developed
over time—where change is a key characteristic.

GROUP DEFINED

A Smorgasbord of Definitions

Marvin E. Shaw (1976, pp. 6–12) summarizes the various approaches to
defining *group.* Most of the definitions cited by him indicate that members of a
group *share* something in common. And it is this common something that

defines the existence of a group. One definition considers a group to be any collection of individuals with shared perceptions; that is, a group is composed of individuals who simply perceive the existence of a group and their membership in it.

Perhaps more familiar is the definition that requires the sharing of a common motivation or goal. Thus, workers unite to form a labor union because they have a common need to satisfy, such as higher wages and better working conditions. The collective strength of the union, then, has the common purpose of securing those goals.

Still another definition based on commonality specifies the sharing of a common fate. For instance, a basketball team or a debate team wins or loses as a group and not as individuals. The outcome affects all members of the group as a whole and not each member individually.

Other definitions look to the structure of the group—the relationships and ties among group members that bind them together into a group. Such a definition perceives the social organization as the "glue" of group structure. Thus, roles, norms, values, status hierarchies, power relationships, etc., govern the behavior of group members and tie them to the group. The presence of these ties defines the nature of the group.

A final category of definitions perceives the central element of a group to be interaction among its members so that the members are interdependent among themselves. It is this type of definition that Shaw (1976) and Gouran and Fisher (1984) find most acceptable; Shaw (1976, p. 11) defines a group as "two or more persons who are interacting with one another in such a manner that each person influences and is influenced by each other person." In this book we use *interaction* and *communication* interchangeably, considering the two terms to be synonymous. The term *interaction* implies the coordination of behavior between two people; *communication*, moreover, implies that symbols are exchanged and shared between two or more people. As you will see later, coordinated behavior has some message (or meaning) value and is therefore communicative. Shaw's definition forms the basis of our definition of *group*.

The Principle of Groupness

Common sense should tell us that not every collection of individuals who talk with one another is a "group" in the strictest sense of the term. Consider several individuals who congregate in an elevator or at a bus stop. They may carry on a conversation, but they do not constitute a real group.

Arguing about whether a particular collection of persons makes up a group is about as worthwhile as arguing about the number of angels who can dance on the head of a pin. But identifying those characteristics that differentiate a group from a collection of individuals does provide insight into a more complete understanding of the nature of a group. Brilhart (1978, pp. 20–21) provides a good definition of the five characteristics of a group.

1. A small enough number of people for each to be aware of and have some reaction to each other.

2. A mutually interdependent purpose in which the success of each is contingent on the success of the others.
3. A sense of belonging or membership felt by each person, with each one identifying with the other members of the group.
4. Oral interaction. (Not all the interaction will be oral, but a significant characteristic of a discussion group is reciprocal influence exercised by talking.)
5. Behavior based on norms and procedures accepted by all members.

Brilhart is concerned with illustrating the principle of *groupness,* which he considers a property that groups possess and collections of individuals do not. According to Brilhart (1978, p. 21):

> "Groupness" emerges from the relationships among the people involved, just as "cubeness" emerges from the image of a set of planes, intersects and angles in specific relationships to each other. One can draw a cube with twelve lines (try it), but only if they are assembled in a definite way. Any other arrangement of the lines gives something other than a cube. Likewise, one can have a collection or set of people without having a group. . . .

Brilhart emphasizes that a group exists as something apart from the persons who constitute the membership. Just as the twelve lines form cubeness when placed in the proper relationship to one another, groupness forms from the relationships among the members. As the individual lines lose their individual identity when cubeness is perceived, so do members lose their identity as individuals when groupness is perceived. Shaw (1976, p. 14) appears to be making a similar observation when he states that "a group is real to the extent that it is perceived as an entity."

A group almost has a "mind" of its own—a way of thinking and a pattern of emotions quite separate from those of the individual members. Though a group does not literally have a "mind," it does have an identity of its own which is separate from the identities of the individuals. In fact, individuals often take on the identity of the groups to which they belong. If you have ever behaved in an odd way or done something you normally would not have just because you wanted the approval and acceptance of a group, then you understand the notion of a group "mind."

THE GROUP AS A SYSTEM

You have probably noticed how the flow of play in a game changes when you change players. You have also probably heard a lot in recent years about ecology and the environment. Each of these illustrates the concept of a *system—a set of component parts that have relationships and are interdependent.* As an example of this concept, let's take the case of the farmer who puts chemicals on his crops to kill insects. Those chemicals seep into the earth and enter the underground water supply. That supply of water drains into the rivers, and, because of the chemicals it contains, it poisons the fish a hundred miles downstream. Bears then eat the poisoned fish and die. When you understand how a farmer using chemicals on his crops can kill bears a hundred miles away, you understand the essence of a system.

We live in a world of systems and subsystems. Your university is a system composed of students, faculty, administration, operations, security, admissions, alumni, and so on. Organizations you might work for are systems made up of parts that interrelate: executive, management, sales, production. Systems can be large or small, simple or complex, organic or inorganic. Small groups are also systems composed of people who spend time communicating in pursuit of a goal. Although it is possible to study small groups from a number of perspectives (see, for example, Lewin, 1951; Bales, 1953; Homans, 1950, 1961; Thibaut and Kelley, 1959; Cragan and Wright, 1990), we will focus on a discussion by Fisher (1978) of how *systems theory* helps us think about small groups. Below are several principles that are important to understanding groups as systems.

Wholeness

The first principle of systems is *wholeness*—that every component of the system affects and is affected by every other component and that a change in one component necessarily effects changes in all other components. A system is composed of interdependent parts that function as a whole unit. Because all the parts are related, focusing on one part to the exclusion of another distorts the functioning of the system. For instance, analyzing the personality traits of each group member is not consistent with the wholeness principle, which would neglect a comprehensive analysis of individual members in favor of a comprehensive analysis of the group as a single entity.

A term related to wholeness and often applied to systems is *nonsummativity*. This means that the whole is different from the sum of the parts. In other words, when parts of a system are related, the result is a collectivity that has an identity separate from the identities of its individual components. We have discussed how groups have an identity and sometimes behave in a way that no individual would; this is an example of the nonsummativity effect. A group's behavior cannot be accounted for by analyzing the individual components of the group. Two adults and three children could be a simple collection of individuals, but if they live and interact together, they constitute a system called a family, and that family is identifiable as a single unit.

A recipe is a good example of nonsummativity. Think about the ingredients of a cake (don't forget heat). Now imagine eating eggs, flour, chocolate, sugar, and so on. Is this the same experience as eating a chocolate cake? Very simply, all the individual ingredients of a chocolate cake interact in such a way as to produce some single entity (the cake) that is different from the individual parts. And if you change any one ingredient it will change the interaction and the outcome.

Nonsystems do not interact in any meaningful way. What if we took everyone in school who was over 6 feet tall and put them in a room. They would not be a system, because they do not relate to each other in any meaningfully interdependent way. A single feature (height) explains what they have in common, but it does not cause them to affect one another. On the other hand, a decision-making group, a labor union, a political party, a family, or a church does function as a whole system in meaningful ways. All of us are part of many systems, and each system is operating meaningfully when we are communicating within the system.

Structure, Function, and Evolution

All systems have a structure, a function, and an evolution. These are quite simple concepts. *Structure* refers to spatial relationships. We talk about things being above, below, beside, face-to-face, and so forth. The organization chart in a company represents structural relationships (see Figure 1-1), it is possible to study the chart and see who is *"above"* whom and who is *"below."* Likewise, the words "superiors" and "subordinates" represent structural relationships between people. Physical objects also have structural relationships. A table can be composed of four legs and a top, but if these component parts are not arranged correctly, the four legs and a top cannot be called a table. Chapter 3 is devoted to the structural elements of communication in groups. It discusses such structural (or spatial) concepts as the *centrality* and communicative *distance* within a network.

 Functional relationships focus on actions rather than on spatial relationships. They pertain to what group members do. They are usually repeatable actions that define how one group member is relating to another; for example, a person may be acting as an information giver, questioner, energizer, or respondent. In a functional relationship, the person is not as important a component as are the actions the person performs in relationship to other

FIGURE 1-1 Acme Electronics organization chart.

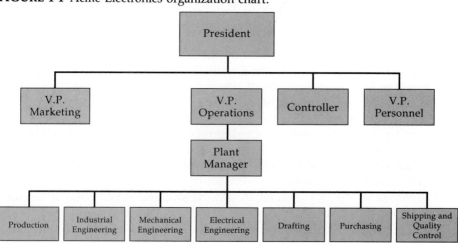

group members. For example, if we say that a group member functions as an information giver, we mean that the person performs actions defined as information-giver behaviors and that these actions serve some purpose in the group.

Evolutionary relationships trace the group's history. In studying the evolution of a group, we are concerned with the changes in structure and function that occur over time. As the term *evolution* implies, change is usually slow and gradual rather than sudden and immediate. And, of course, the evolution includes periods of no change—periods when the relationships in the group are constant.

As an example of the structural, functional, and evolutionary relationships in a social system, consider any rather typical company, such as Acme Electronics in Figure 1-1:

- Structurally, the company might be divided into four components: executive, management, production, and sales. The company might be highly structured, with very strictly defined relationships between people and with clear-cut status relationships and role specializations, or it might be loosely structured, with informal and relaxed relationships between people.
- The functional relationships of the four might be defined as a process of product manufacturing in which the executive component handles the broad policy and decision-making tasks, management deals with the day-to-day operations, production performs the manufacturing duties, and the sales force markets and sells the product to the public. These functions are interdependent (i.e., each is affected by the other). Thus, the salespeople cannot guarantee delivery if the production people cannot meet their quotas, and poor executive decisions will influence all parts of the company's structure.
- The evolutionary relationships trace the history of the company, the changing products, markets, management decisions, people, and economic considerations.

Let's try another example of a system with structure, function, and evolution so you feel comfortable with these concepts. A baseball team is a *system*. Each position is a *structural* element that relates to the other positions in the system. Each structure (position) *functions* in a particular way, such as "pitching," "catching," "throwing," or "covering" certain territory. And a baseball game *evolves* over time: There are innings in which things change and others in which things remain constant. What happens early in the game will influence strategy and functioning later in the game. The game of baseball is *nonsummative*. What if you calculated the earned run average of each pitcher and the batting average of each player on the opposing teams and added them up before betting on a game? There would be plenty of games in which you would lose your bet because each team is a system that plays in ways that cannot be predicted by adding up individual player statistics. There are variables and complexities of a baseball game that cannot be accounted for by individuals alone.

Openness

Group systems are open systems. An *open system* takes in and processes new information; it has a free exchange of information with the environment. A *closed system,* on the other hand, is isolated from the environment and does not accept information from the outside world. Imagine a group that could not gather information from various sources and talk to people outside the group, but was limited to the information and resources of the group members. Such a group would be a closed system, and it would be characterized by retarded development.

Groups are open systems because they have free interchange with the environment; they have inputs and outputs. If a group is trying to decide on a policy toward integrated schools, for example, it will need input from sources other than the group. It will consult specialists, research studies, programs in other communities, and so on. The group's output might be in the form of a report and a series of suggestions; this report would be discussed and analyzed and then used as input. Bona fide groups have permeable but stable boundaries (Putnam and Stohl, 1990). They are dependent on the environment and must interact with it.

To say a group is an open system that communicates with its environment also means that a group will be influenced by the environment. New members come and go and bring new information, perspectives, and resources; the social, economic, and political, environments of groups change. This means that groups must adapt and regulate themselves. The following section discusses one aspect of how groups adapt and regulate themselves—feedback.

FEEDBACK SEQUENCES

Usually, feedback is thought of as a response (or reaction) to a previous action. In a functional, pragmatic view of communication, feedback is not merely a response—it is an entire sequence of actions. This concept of feedback stems directly from the field of cybernetics, which has been credited with coining the term *feedback.*

An analogy may explain this notion of control and the way in which feedback functions to maintain the steady or normal operation of the system. Figure 1-2 depicts a feedback sequence that is often used to illustrate the notion of cybernetic feedback. You will note that feedback, as a sequence, involves a cycle of events, each one of which affects the next event in the sequence. In this way, any change in any one event will precipitate a change in every succeeding event, including itself.

For example, assume that the thermostat of Figure 1-2 is preset at 68°F. Beginning at any arbitrary point on the cycle, we should be able to visualize a change (or deviation) in the normal operation of the thermostatic mechanism. Perhaps the temperature of air in the room falls to 65°F. This change is a deviation from the "normal" functioning of the system, with the "normal"

FIGURE 1-2 The feedback cycle of a thermostat.

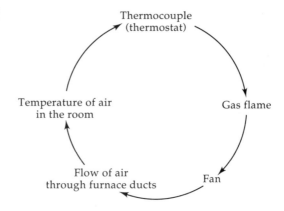

temperature defined by the preset temperature of 68°F. The deviation from the preset temperature causes the thermocouple to close, thus completing the electric circuit and opening the gas jets in the forced-air furnace. The pilot light ignites the gas flame, thereby superheating the air in the furnace chamber, which in turn causes the fan to turn on, which in turn increases the flow of air through the furnace ducts to the room, which in turn raises the air temperature in the room. The feedback cycle is then complete.

Note that the "cause" of the rise in room temperature is the original decrease in room temperature. The effect of feedback is to reflect back on itself by setting in motion a sequence of events. Each of these events affects the next event in the sequence until the cycle is completed by returning to the original event. At this point, the feedback cycle begins again in a never-ending cyclic pattern of self-reflexive regulation of the temperature in the room.

Feedback as a sequence is not simply a knee-jerk reflex to some antecedent stimulus. In fact, feedback is not a single action at all. Rather, it is a process initiated by some action. The action (that is, change in the "normal" state of affairs) sets in motion a sequence of actions, each of which stimulates the next action in the sequence until the sequence closes the cycle by exerting influence on the original source of the action. Feedback is a cycle, or loop, because the action exerts influence on itself through direct influence on each link in the chain of events contained in the cycle.

The urbanization process clearly illustrates feedback loops. In brief, farmers occupy a rural area and create a demand for goods and services, such as groceries, machinery repair, the distribution and sale of agricultural products, a post office, and medical care. Soon a small village blooms in the middle of the rural area, and a company builds a small factory near the town because of the available supply of labor. More people move to the town in order to secure jobs at the factory. With more people available for work, the market for more services is larger, so more stores selling consumer goods are necessary. Shopping centers and more factories are built as more people move to the city. The small town booms and becomes a megalopolis. Each deviation from the originally rural area stimulates more and more deviation, in a classic illustration of feedback.

The international arms race, which is slowing down, is another classic example of feedback loops. The spiraling arms race has brought an extraordinary amplification of innovations in weapons development, from the invention of gunpowder to dynamite and to the atomic bomb, the hydrogen bomb, the cobalt bomb, the ICBM, MIRV, and Star Wars.

Progress, growth, and change in a social system can occur only through feedback cycles. Naturally the social system must devise methods to manage feedback, along with progress, growth, and change, or the deviation gets out of hand. Urbanization may symbolize much progress in our nation, but unmanaged urbanization has created the serious problems we have only recently faced. The severity of these problems, such as air and water pollution, urban decay and blight, urban crime, inadequate civic services, and overpopulation, has prompted the observation that a megalopolis like New York City may be ungovernable. Nations, too, have recently attempted to set limits on the current arms race through treaties and multilateral agreements. And arms-limitation talks among the powerful nations of the world will probably continue for some time.

We will discuss and illustrate feedback cycles again in Chapter 5, but here an example of feedback cycles in groups may help further clarify your understanding. Small groups, as we have said, are self-regulating systems. In other words, there are processes in groups that influence one another and have particular consequences. Let's take the seven group processes illustrated in Figure 1-3. There are of course others but these seven will do for now in illustrating how feedback cycles are established and help regulate the group. These seven processes are defined in the following way:

1. *Likelihood of a good decision*   the simple probability that the group will make a quality decision.
2. *Amount of information*   the amount of facts, knowledge, etc. that the group is working with.
3. *Conflict*   the amount of disagreement within the group.
4. *Agreement*   the amount of consent or uniformity of opinion in the group.

FIGURE 1-3 Feedback in small groups.

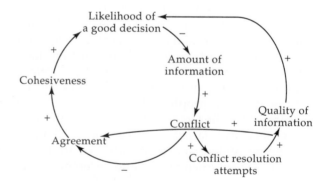

5. *Cohesiveness*   the sense of belonging and caring that the group members have about membership in the group.
6. *Conflict resolution attempts*   the efforts and attempts the group makes to manage and resolve conflict.
7. *Quality of information*   the degree of excellence, accuracy, and value of the group's information. It is separate from the absolute amount of information, which can include information the group is using that is poor, out of date, untrustworthy, and so on.

A plus sign (+) between any two components of this system means that change is in the same direction, with more leading to more and less leading to less. A minus sign (−) means that change in one direction produces change in the opposite direction.

Here is how to read Figure 1-3; if you follow along with the reasoning it should be simple to understand. Figure 1-3 represents actual processes in any group system. The group has a goal, which is to increase its chances of making a good decision. All groups must gather information, so let's enter the system at that point—*Amount of information.* Over time a group gathers information, and as this information accumulates it becomes the subject of conflict because group members inevitably disagree about what information to use. Therefore, as the amount of information in the group system increases, it produces an increase in conflict. (Note the plus sign between *Amount of information* and *Conflict.*) This means that change is in the same direction: A high amount of information means higher conflict as the group grapples with the information. Higher conflict, however, produces less agreement. (A negative sign means change is in the opposite direction.) Less agreement means the group is less cohesive, and less cohesiveness means that the group is less likely to come to a quality decision.

There is a negative sign between *Likelihood of a good decision* and *Amount of information* which means that, as the group becomes less likely to reach a good decision, it goes back to increasing its amount of information. This increase in information causes more conflict and starts the cycle all over again. The group cannot sustain this cycle. If it continues to interact in this way, the group will be caught in constant conflict and significantly lower its chances of making a good decision.

What saves most successful groups is that when conflict increases the group then increases its *Conflict resolution* attempts. (Note the plus sign between *Conflict* and *Conflict resolution attempts*). As groups resolve conflict they improve the quality of their information, and quality information increases the chances of a good decision. High-quality information can take another route. Good information tends to produce agreement around that information. (Note the plus sign between *Quality of information* and *Agreement*). In turn, this increase in agreement among group members stimulates cohesiveness and this, too, increases the likelihood of a good decision.

These feedback cycles are important to the group as a system. We are not talking here about feedback as a response to an individual. (We will discuss feedback to individuals in Chapters 3 and 6.) Group members often think about their own interests and experiences in a group, but more skilled and successful group members understand the relationships among processes in the group as a whole. A skilled group member can alter the processes described in Figure 1-3 to the group's advantage. He or she can make a conscious effort to influence the likelihood of a quality decision by manipulating information, conflict, and so on. As you gain more experience in groups you will improve your ability to do systems analyses.

SYSTEM VARIABLES INFLUENCING THE GROUP

Groups interact with their environments and are constantly making adjustments to environmental influences. Groups are often smaller systems that operate within larger ones, such as communities, organizations, and other groups. A task group in a company must work within the limits and resources of the company. These constant exchanges with the environment increase the demands and stresses on the group. It means that change is a regular occurrence, and there is always potential conflict and difficulty that accompanies change. Probably the simplest and most parsimonious way of thinking about the major variables that influence group systems is to discuss three broad categories: *entry elements, process elements,* and *outcomes.* These are diagrammed in Figure 1-4. The arrows in the diagram represent the feedback

FIGURE 1-4 Variables that influence group systems.

Entry elements

Personalities
Skills
Attitudes
Information
Group resources
Group size
Group charge

Outcomes

Decision quality
Member satisfaction
Solutions
Reports/documents
Personal value
Skills
Relationships
Cohesiveness

Process elements

Communication patterns
Problem behaviors
Cohesiveness
Work norms
Participation norms
Procedures
Leadership

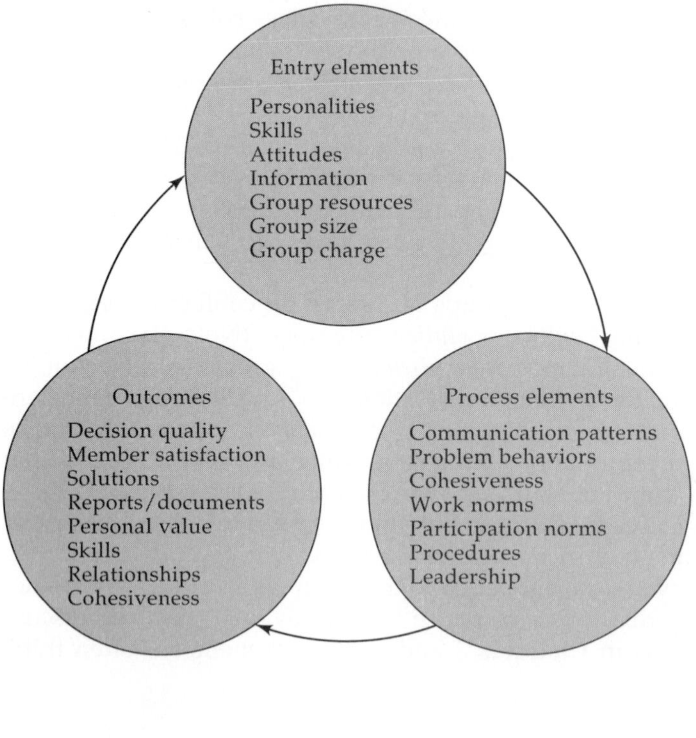

processes through which entry elements influence processes, which in turn influence outcomes, which in turn cycle back to alter the initial influences in the system. This is an *open system model,* representing the groups' regular exchange with the environment and the growth and self-regulation that accompanies such exchanges.

Entry Elements

These are the inputs to the group. They consist of all the features of the group that are present at the outset. Entry elements include all the influences, processes, and resources that help establish the group. Many of the initial elements of a group are individual features of the group members: personalities, skills, attitudes, and information. For example, a member of a group may be very well informed about a subject and exert a lot of influence on the others. But what if another group member has an aggressive personality and does not want others to gain influence and status? This aggressive person might thwart the efforts of the informed group member and the group will not benefit from his expertise.

Other entry-level influences are the group's resources or lack of them. A group might be rich in resources. It might have plenty of money, equipment, and administrative support to help carry out its task. On the other hand, the group might have very little to work with and depend on the energies and good will of the members. Another important influence on a group is its size.

Most authorities recommend that a group consist of five to seven members, although there is no absolute rule about size. When groups have fewer than five members they lose diversity of opinion and develop closer interpersonal relationships that can be detrimental to the decision-making process. In groups of this size, members can also lose a feeling of identification with the larger system. This feeling of belonging to the larger social system is similar to what we have called groupness. Groupness implies a mutually interdependent purpose in that individual success is seen as dependent on the success (or failure) of the entire group. In a group with too few group members it is difficult to distribute work and establish the critical mass of energy that groups thrive on.

Too many members can be equally problematic. In Brilhart's five characteristics of groupness (see pages 5–6), the first necessary characteristic is that the group be small enough for each member to know and be able to react to every other member. If it is difficult for one group member to have a face-to-face conversation with any other group member, then the group is probably too big. When groups get too big, more assertive members tend to dominate others and establish coalitions. This can polarize the group and make the discussion more political and manipulative than deliberative.

Still another important entry element is the group's charge, or purpose. All groups have a charge; that is, they are assigned a task such as making a decision about a new product or planning an event that has particular specifications. This charge is typically imposed on the group by some authority. The precise nature of the charge is an important entry level influence on the group. The group will not be successful if there is confusion about the charge or if some members have goals that are incompatible with the task at hand. It is always helpful for groups to ensure that they clearly understand their charge by seeking clarification.

Process Elements

Process elements are the influences on the group that stem from its actual activities. Communication is at the heart of the group's process. Group members cannot, of course, influence one another without communicating. Communication activates some of the individual qualities discussed above and determines whether or not they will be influential. One person in the group could have an aggressive personality and be a potential source of problems for the group. But if for some reason during actual group interaction that person does not communicate in an aggressive manner, the influence of that entry variable is nil.

Other important process variables are the level of cohesiveness the group develops, work and participation norms, decision-making procedures, and leadership. Good leaders are adept at working the group process to everyone's advantage. For example, one important norm that group leaders can foster is critical thinking and support for open discussion and disagreement. Most people shy away from criticizing others, but group decisions benefit from good criticism. Decisions will be better if part of the group process includes a healthy respect for disagreement. A leader, or any group member for that matter, who encourages group norms that promote critical thinking, disagreement, and active participation is using the group process to influence other variables.

Outcomes

Outcomes are what the group produces and achieves. These include tangible outcomes, such as reports, memos, documents of various types, and specific decision recommendations. But they also include less obvious outcomes, such as decision quality, personal satisfaction, group cohesiveness, and changes in the nature of the group. If a group, for example, has been charged with developing a marketing plan for selling a new line of computers, the actual plan is the tangible output. But other outcomes would include:

1. The personal relationships formed among group members.
2. Any new skills acquired by individuals as a result of working in the group.
3. Group cohesiveness.
4. Member satisfaction or dissatisfaction.
5. The quality of group decisions.

Remember that group outcomes cycle back and become new entry elements. Group members who join a group at one skill level and learn something through the group process, exit the group with new skills. These new skills become entry elements for their future group activities. Member attitudes are often changed by the group experience. Those individuals who begin with skeptical or cynical attitudes about the group but end up valuing their membership in it will be more likely to change their attitudes in the future.

WHY WORK IN GROUPS?

There is little doubt that working in a group can be irritating and frustrating. The act of communicating with other people requires patience and tolerance as the people work to understand one another and accomplish goals. One researcher (Sorensen, 1981) even developed the concept of "grouphate" and found that many people dislike working in groups; but more importantly, Sorensen also discovered that people were more satisfied with groups as they improved their training and the skills associated with effective group operation. Even when groups are maddeningly slow and clumsy, they are important because of the participation and recognition they offer individuals. Our democracy is founded on the principle of the informed citizen who is capable of taking part in decision making. None of us wants others to make our decisons for us. And for that reason alone, it behooves us to understand the subtle workings of communication in groups. In any case, groups are capable of performing functions and achieving some goals more efficiently and accurately than individuals can. Although there is evidence that individuals sometimes perform better than groups (Shaw, 1981), the quality of decision making is enhanced in groups working under certain conditions.

Groups tend to perform best as the complexity of a task increases. The justification for this is that individuals are limited to their intellectual and information-processing capabilities (Abelson and Levi, 1985). Regardless of how hard a person works to solve a problem, he will not succeed if he simply lacks the required knowledge or ability to solve the problem. Individuals tend to simplify problems that are too complex. Groups, on the other hand, can draw on the available pool of information and talent. If you were a member of a student-government committee charged with deciding how much money to allot to the student paper and you were not very knowledgeable about how much money it took to run the newspaper, your decision would benefit from the expertise of others. Working with others would allow you to determine more accurately the needs of the student paper.

Even experts, who have the sophisticated knowledge necessary for some complex tasks, have something to gain from working in groups. A number of researchers have found that experts are not immune to problems in decision making (Alpert and Raiffa, 1982; Tversky and Kahneman, 1983). They found that even experts can (1) become overconfident; (2) misinterpret inconsistent evidence; and (3) engage in reasoning fallacies.

Groups are better at judgment decisions than individuals are. Some decisions require judgment rather than expert knowledge because the nature of the task is more ambiguous or because there is no clear-cut solution to the task. If you were a member of a student group that was asked to develop a student-oriented campaign to attract new students to campus, you would be dealing with a task that had a variety of alternatives, no one of which is necessarily correct. Groups are superior at tasks that require the consideration of a number of judgmental alternatives.

Many of the problems that groups try to solve require the group members to be creative in deciding on possible decisions, to be sensitive to a range of new information, to change beliefs in the face of new information, and to make decisions with incomplete information (Zeev, 1981). The limits to creativity and valuable interpretation of information are extended when individuals have others to stimulate them, and groups have a greater capacity to store and process information. This does not mean that the larger the group, the better the group will perform. On the contrary, there is a point of diminishing returns. But some optimal number of group members will produce more information and decision possibilities, and these factors are characteristic of high-quality decisions (Janis and Mann, 1977).

WHY AVOID GROUPS?

It would certainly be misleading to imply that groups are always advantageous. Some problems are not suitable for groups, and democratic participation is not always the best way to accomplish something. Some of the conventional wisdom discussed in the introduction to this book emerges from stereotypes about groups. We are quick to organize ourselves into groups because we too often believe that such groups can best handle problems. Below are two disadvantages to groups.

Not all problems are suitable for groups. What if you were in a group that had the design of a new bridge as its task and you and the other group members knew nothing about engineering? What good would it do you to work in this group? Would you ever solve the problem of designing a workable bridge? No. Groups are of little value when a problem requires technical expertise and the knowledge of highly trained specialists. There is no need to waste time in groups when one specialist working alone can solve a problem and exceed the decision quality of a collection of less knowledgeable people.

Groups take time. Groups are slow and laborious. There is no escaping the time it takes to include many people in decision making. Group members express opinions, argue, summarize, question, gather information, and evaluate information. They often consider ideas, drop them, and reconsider them. These communication processes are responsible for improving the quality of decisions, but they do slow the system down. It is best not to use group decision making if the group cannot devote the time necessary to capitalize on the group processes.

Many decisions must be made quickly. This is an important issue that you should consider when deciding to work with a group or not. If time is important and a quick decision is essential, then perhaps the decision to rely on a single individual is best. There are a few group situations in which speed is of extreme importance—the military, athletic teams, and disaster and/or emergency situations, to name just a few. Any time the work of several people must be coordinated it is most efficiently done by a single person.

SUMMARY

Understanding the nature of the group process requires an understanding of the nature of *group* and *process*. A process involves the dynamic relationships of events in an ongoing, continuous sequence of time. Each ingredient of the process affects, and is affected by, every other ingredient as changes in the process evolve through time. Although many perspectives have been used to define *group*, this book utilizes the perspective of interdependence and inter-action. A collection of individuals develops groupness over time, so that the identity of a group exists apart from the separate identities of its individual members.

A group is conceived to be a system characterized by its *structure* (the pattern of relationships among its components at any given point in time), its *function* (the relationships among its components through time), and its *evolution* (the changes over a long period). The group is also characterized by *wholeness*, the principle that one part of the system affects and is affected by every part, and by *openness*, which is a free exchange of information with the environment.

Feedback processes are also central to the growth and regulation of the group. *Feedback* is a cycle in which one event produces change in succeeding events. An increase in one group function (e.g., information) can cause either an additional increase or a decrease in another group function (e.g., amount of conflict). And the main variables of the group system are *entry elements*, or inputs to the system; *process elements*, or the actual communicative activities of the group; and *outcomes*, such as group decisions, reports, and member satisfaction.

Finally, there are reasons to work in groups and reasons to avoid groups. Although groups are better at complex tasks and those that require judgments, groups are less effective when problems require a highly trained specialist, or speed of decision making.

CHAPTER OUTLINE

INTERDEPENDENCE OF THE SOCIAL
AND TASK DIMENSIONS

Cohesiveness and Productivity
How to Promote Cohesiveness in
Groups
Defensive and Supportive
Communication

THE SOCIAL DIMENSION

Perspectives on the Socioemotional
Climate
Group Identification
Social Tension

THE TASK DIMENSION: DEFINITION

THE TASK DIMENSION: INDIVIDUAL
VERSUS GROUP DECISION
MAKING

Group Polarization
Persuasive Arguments Theory
Efficiency and Speed
The Group Task

SUMMARY

KEY TERMS

TASK DIMENSION

SOCIAL DIMENSION

PRODUCTIVITY

GROUPTHINK

INTERPERSONAL ATTRACTION

DEFENSIVE AND SUPPORTIVE
COMMUNICATION

MEMBER SATISFACTION

FEEDBACK

INTERACTION MANAGEMENT

SYMBOLIC CONVERGENCE

GROUP POLARIZATION

ASSEMBLY EFFECT

PERSUASIVE ARGUMENT THEORY

GROUP TASK

CHAPTER 2

Social and Task Dimensions of the Group Process

Whistle while you work

People draw rather clear distinctions between allegedly opposing phenomena. For example, we classify a person as a liberal or a conservative, a Democrat or a Republican, a blue-collar worker or a white-collar worker. It is no wonder, then, that we differentiate between two dimensions of group decision making—task and social. Because people are involved in a group, the social dimension is evident. And because the group is expected to come to agreement on a decision, the task dimension is also evident.

It is unfortunate, but true, that the task and social dimensions of group decision making are often viewed as being in conflict with each other. There have been numerous attempts to provide detailed plans and instructions for making a group decision that avoids social or emotional influence. The assumption underlying these proposals is apparently that a decision is better when based on an impersonal and critical evaluation of the facts. We are cautioned against emotional reactions in the apparent belief that such reactions lower the quality of the group decision.

The purpose of this chapter is to provide an insight into the social and task dimensions of the group process. Consistent with the perspective of interdependence involved in group process, these two dimensions will be viewed as different but inseparable. This chapter illustrates how the social dimension affects group decision making and how group decision-making tasks are different from decision-making tasks performed by individuals.

INTERDEPENDENCE OF THE SOCIAL AND TASK DIMENSIONS

Both task and social dimensions are inherent in the process of group decision making. No decision-making group exists without both dimensions. It is important to understand each of them in order to understand effective group decision making and to participate effectively in a decision-making group. *Task dimension* refers to the relationship between group members and the work they are to perform—the job they have to do and how they go about doing it. *Social dimension* refers to the relationships of group members with one another—how they feel toward one another and about their membership in the group.

The task and social areas of the group process have typically been viewed separately. According to one early theorist (Tuckman, 1965), certain comments aid in developing the group's social structure, and other comments are directed toward accomplishing the group's task. Such a total separation is probably unwise. Common sense should tell us that a comment such as "Aw, you don't know what you're talking about!" implies not only an outright rejection of a contributed idea (a task comment) but also an impact on the social relationship of at least two members. The task and social dimensions of group process are highly interdependent—in fact, virtually indistinguishable from each other. That is, one may separate the two from a theoretical perspective, but the interaction between the two makes them virtually inseparable in practice.

There is a reason for using the term *dimension* to refer to the task and social areas of group process. Figure 2-1 illustrates the two-dimensional existence of a plane geometrical figure. A rectangle exists in two dimensions—height and width. Height cannot be separated from width without altering the rectangle itself. Although the height or width may be observed and measured separately, the two dimensions are inseparable within the definition of the rectangle. The same inherent and inseparable relationship is true of the task and social dimensions of a group process. Without either dimension, the group process does not exist.

Cohesiveness and Productivity

You can probably remember being a member of a group you thoroughly enjoyed. There was an esprit de corps among the members, a spirit of camaraderie, a feeling of close personal ties. You undoubtedly felt that the group was worthwhile and rewarding to you, and you felt a sense of loyalty to the group—a personal commitment. In a group such as this, members are proud to be members. Occasionally such groups evolve from classroom

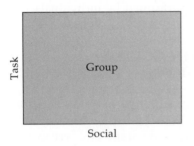

FIGURE 2-1 "Dimensions" of the group process.

groups. The following comments, for example, are selected from the final entries in diaries kept by members of a group formed within a class studying group communication. Their feelings were unanimous:

> "I feel a close bond with the other members of our group and would like to continue working with each one."

> "I am very grateful for this group experience and feel a very close bond of friendship and understanding with each member."

> "What I really want to emphasize is the way that we learned to function as free-thinking people unacquainted, really, with the others (at the beginning of the term) and evolved into an extremely cohesive group."

> "I developed a great amount of respect for and a relationship of oneness or unity with each member individually and the group as a whole."

> "It may sound a little corny, but I feel [list of the other members' names] are good friends and, when this class is over, I will feel, if nothing else, that I have made some friends for life."

On the other side of the coin, you have perhaps been involved with groups that were less than appealing. There may have been bickering among some members, but probably you were more bored than hurt by the group experience. Rather than feeling a sense of commitment or pride in the group, you probably searched for excuses to avoid group meetings. If you had any choice in the matter, you probably dropped out of the group; otherwise, you endured it only as long as you had to. One comment from a final diary of another classroom group illustrates this type of group: "One thing that really affected the development and behavior of our group was not being able to get together for a meeting. It seemed that the five of us could never find one time that was good for everyone. But as they say, you can always find time for the things that are important."

The two types of groups just described illustrate a difference in *cohesiveness*—the ability of group members to get along, the feeling of loyalty, pride, and commitment of members toward the group. It would not be inaccurate to say that cohesiveness is, more than anything else, the degree of liking that members have for one another. To the extent that members like one another, they are committed to the group and feel loyal and proud of their membership status. Cohesiveness may also be viewed as the output of a group's social dimension. That is, cohesiveness is not a process so much as a state of being. As groupness emerges from group interaction, the group may be characterized at some level of cohesiveness. Such a characteristic describes the outcome of the process in the group's social dimension.

In a similar fashion, the output from a group's task dimension may be described as *productivity*. To the extent that a group accomplishes its task, it is productive. As with cohesiveness, the amount of productivity is not always easily determined. Of course, the productivity of a group on a manufacturing assembly line may be measured by counting the number of products its members complete in a given time period. Or the productivity of a basketball team may be determined by the number of games it wins. But what of a decision-making group? The number of decisions is seldom a good indication of productivity. A jury, for example, may have only one decision to make—the guilt or innocence of the defendant. As in most decisions, *quality* rather than quantity is the best determinant of a decision-making group's productivity. And the quality of decisions is exceedingly difficult to measure.

In every group, both cohesiveness and productivity exist to some degree. That is, a group's productivity or cohesiveness should each be visualized as some point along a continuum. For example, in terms of cohesiveness, a group may be low, moderately low, moderately high, high, and so forth. Another analogy may illustrate this point. Height is a characteristic of every person. We measure height conveniently in feet and inches, and everyone has height to some degree. We may describe someone as tall or short, but we would never say that a person has no height. In the same way, we may describe a group as "low" with respect to cohesiveness or productivity, but it is foolish to say that the group is "not productive" or "not cohesive."

Since the interdependence of the task and social dimensions has been established, it seems reasonable that the outputs of these dimensions—cohesiveness and productivity—should also be interdependent. Although we can visualize a group whose members hate one another but are able to be quite productive, this type of group is unusually rare. Common sense would dictate a direct relationship between productivity and cohesiveness—that is, the more cohesive the group, the more productive it is likely to be. And this dictum is true—up to a point. As a group raises its level of cohesiveness, the more likely it is to raise its level of productivity. Conversely, the more productive the group the greater the likelihood that it will be more cohesive. However, the relationship breaks down toward the upper end of the two continuums. Figure 2-2 illustrates this relationship between cohesiveness and productivity. According to this diagram, extremely cohesive groups are more likely to have moderate to low productivity. Although the productivity of highly cohesive groups probably doesn't sink to the level of groups that are extremely low in cohesiveness, such groups are not nearly as likely to be as productive as groups with moderately high cohesiveness.

Several explanations account for this phenomenon. First, the group may have been together so long that its original purpose—its task—has suffered simply because the members enjoy one another's company too much. Many local community service organizations find that over the years the primary purpose of their organization has changed from assisting their community to having a good time. The greater proportion of their activity, then, is socializing rather than working on community service. We are familiar with one group whose purpose, at the time the group was formed, was to raise money for an annual charity drive. The group still raises money annually, but it continues to meet regularly during the year to play cards, eat dinner, and generally entertain itself. The greater proportion of its efforts is social enjoyment, not raising funds.

Another explanation is that a group that is highly cohesive but has low productivity has a great deal of reserve productivity. That is, the group is

FIGURE 2-2 The relationship between cohesiveness and productivity.

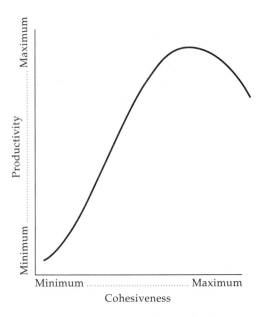

capable of much more productivity but simply does not expend the effort to be productive. Hence, its productivity lies dormant, or in reserve. The classic example is the extremely bright student who does just enough work to earn a passing grade but doesn't earn an A. Teachers, parents, and friends would say that this student isn't working to capacity. Another example is the athletic coach of a losing team who bemoans the fact that the players are capable of winning every game but just aren't playing to the level of their abilities. In both cases, the assumption is that the person/group is capable of superior productivity but actually achieves only average or below-average productivity—hence the term *reserve productivity*.

Whatever the explanation for the relationship between cohesiveness and productivity, the point to remember is that the outputs of the two dimensions of group process affect each other reciprocally. For example, an increase in productivity tends to increase the cohesiveness of a group. The legendary football coach, Vince Lombardi, had all the characteristics that would normally lead to low cohesiveness. He was aloof from his players, highly dictatorial, and a slave driver. The players were forced to do things they would normally have found abhorrent. They were subjected to stringent training rules more appropriate for Little League juveniles than for mature adults. They endured torturous practices above and beyond the normal practice routines. But they won games. They ruled the National Football League during the decade of the 1960s and became famous for their "Packer pride." Apparently the team was a tightly knit, highly cohesive group. We can only wonder how cohesive it would have been had it been a losing football team.

Conversely, an increase in cohesiveness generally precipitates a corresponding increase in productivity. The classic example of this phenomenon is commonly known as the Hawthorne effect. Deriving its name from a series of investigations performed in the Hawthorne plant of the Western Electric Company, the Hawthorne effect generally refers to the increase in productivity that results from an environmental change in the social dimension. Organizational managers may single out a work group within the organization and give that group special attention or special favors, such as enlisting its aid in a research situation. That group is likely to increase its productivity as a result. Athletic coaches talk about getting their teams "psyched up" for the big game with a great deal of group activity: rallies, team dinners, yelling, and so forth. Corporations spend an increasing amount of time and money on facilitating pleasant and positive social relationships. The company picnic, softball game, noon exercise hour, and a host of social activities are all designed to increase a sense of cohesiveness and satisfaction with the organization so that the workers become more productive.

Cohesiveness is how well the group "hangs together" as a unit. The benefits of cohesion are considerable, so it behooves any group to achieve and sustain cohesion. Using the best evidence available, Shaw (1992) summarizes the desirable consequences of cohesion as follows:

1. There is more communication among group members in cohesive groups.
2. Members of cohesive groups are friendlier and more cooperative.
3. Cohesive groups exert more influence over their members.
4. Goals are achieved more effectively by cohesive groups.
5. Cohesion produces more satisfaction in group members.

How to Promote Cohesiveness in Groups

As you will see throughout this book, we offer no magic formulas for the simple and surefire creation of effective groups. The same is true of cohesiveness. You cannot do a few simple things to ensure that a group will be cohesive and therefore productive. Nevertheless, you can apply some intelligence to the problem. Cohesiveness develops when certain conditions exist in the group—and if you can understand and control these conditions, you will have a better chance of producing a cohesive group. Below are six strategies for increasing cohesiveness in groups.

Encourage External Threats This may sound a little harsh, but group members become much more unified when they perceive a threat to their existence or dignity. A threat is indeed one of the most effective cohesiveness devices. Many groups are characterized by argument and dispute, but this all stops when an outsider criticizes the group. Countries have been known to pull together and become much more patriotic and chauvinistic when they are threatened by other countries. Managers use this technique all the time when they set up competitive situations between groups. Forcing groups to compete with one another and then rewarding the winner is one example. Even friendly competition helps. If, for example, a sales group from a company challenges a group from another company to a baseball game, the group members are likely to strengthen their bonds as they work to meet the challenge.

Create History　As time passes and the members of a group share some experiences, they usually draw closer together. This is especially true when the experiences are difficult or trying. Soldiers in combat, work groups that accomplish difficult tasks, and juries that struggle with a decision are examples of groups whose members work hard together and become closer as a result. Often members of an organization will retell stories and humorous incidents pertaining to the company. These stories become part of the historical mythology of the organization and help create a sense of organizational history, and this history contributes to cohesiveness. Some managers arrange special events, such as retreats, parties, or workshops, to discuss the work and problems of group members. These occasions are often used to build cohesiveness because they give group members a common historical experience to refer to.

Establish Interdependent Goals　The goals of a group must be in the interest of all members and, more important, should be goals that require coordination and contribution from everyone in the group. As group members increase their reliance on one another, they increase their need and desire for cohesiveness. There is no need for unity when a job can be done by one person. A factory worker has no incentive to be a positive and productive member of a group when his pay is based on individual work or accomplishment. But if he is a member of a work team that is responsible for an entire project, and if the pay or compensation is based on the quality of the project, then he is much more likely to become a productive member of a group.

Accomplish Something　When members see that they are making progress toward a goal, they feel much better about the group; conversely, there is a decline in cohesiveness when the group stops making progress. The factory worker mentioned above will feel very good about himself and the group if the group makes progress toward its goals. A good strategy for a manager is to set short-term, easily attainable goals for a group so that its members can experience a sense of accomplishment and establish enough cohesiveness to continue their work. Fund-raising committees and capital campaigns often set easily attainable goals in order not only to present an image of success but also to give their committee members a sense of accomplishment in their work.

Develop Relationships and Shared Norms　Obviously, groups are more cohesive when the members like one another; and obviously, group members will like one another more when they are cohesive. It is a "chicken or an egg" issue, because it is impossible to say which comes first. Do people like each other because they are cohesive, or are they cohesive because they like each other? In either case, when group members are friendly and show intimacy and understanding, they are more likely to be cohesive.

The group should also develop common norms and standards of behavior. If group members develop the norms for which they feel a sense of commitment, they will support and accept them. Mutually accepted and understood standards of behavior introduce regularity, making cooperation and coordination easier to achieve. It is true that cohesive groups are able to tolerate some differences in people, even appreciating and taking pride in these differences, but it is also true that too much variation in the norms and values of the group reduces cohesiveness.

Promote Acceptance for Group Members   Secure group members are cohesive group members. When anxiety is reduced and self-esteem is heightened, the members are more likely to perform with energy and enthusiasm. When a person is not threatened by a group and is accepted by its members, the person is much more likely to participate in the group. Group members need to be told that their contributions and behaviors are valued by the group, for group acceptance is of the utmost importance. If a supervisor is more interested in assigning blame to an individual than in solving a problem, the threat of blame will seriously hinder cohesiveness.

All in all, cohesiveness results in a better group, but it has one negative consequence. Janis (1983) discusses a phenomenon called *groupthink*. We will encounter groupthink elsewhere in this book: namely, its influence on decision making (Chapter 6), conformity (Chapter 5) and conflict (Chapter 8). But for now, it is only necessary to know that groupthink is a negative consequence of highly cohesive groups. It is also an interesting example of the interdependence between the task and social dimensions of the group process. Groupthink is related to the quality of decisions by the group rather than to the amount of effort that cohesive group members exert.

One consistent finding about groups is that group consensus changes individuals' opinions and preferences (Moscovici, 1985). In other words, when a group is cohesive and in strong agreement about a decision, the opinions and preferences of the individuals in the group change to conform more to the preferences of the group as a whole. The members are so committed to the group that they use it as a basis for their own opinions, suspending their own critical thinking in favor of the group's opinions. The group exerts both conscious and unconscious pressures on individuals to conform to the group's decisions. And because individuals value their membership in the group and feel a strong sense of commitment, they conform quite easily. When people are very reliant on groups for acceptance and security and have a strong in-group loyalty, they literally conform their opinions and judgments without knowing it. In fact, they will defend what they do.

Groupthink occurs when a group makes an extreme or poor decision because members suspend their critical faculties in favor of consensus. You will see in Chapters 6 and 8 that conflict over ideas is an important part of the group process. Groupthink results when the group short-circuits this process because cohesion and consensus are more important than honest disagreement. The group members usually convince themselves that the judgments and decisions of the group are correct and superior to the opinions of any one member. One person in a classroom group, suffering from what she thought was groupthink, wrote, "Everyone in the group gets along almost *too* well. Ideas that come about, therefore, are shallow and unclear. Members of my group are afraid to challenge or question ideas." Groupthink is a defective and low-quality decision that results when the group is too cohesive and more concerned with agreement and consensus than with quality.

Defensive and Supportive Communication

Building a supportive environment is one of the best ways to develop cohesion in a group. *Supportive communication* occurs when members reinforce, support, and encourage one another. The climate is one of expressing respect for others and indicating that you value their opinions. A supportive climate means that people are free to express themselves and feel comfortable communicating with others. *Defensive communication* occurs when members try to manipulate and control one another. People in the group are made to feel insecure about expressing their feelings and fearful of the opinions of others. The most common defensive and supportive communication behaviors are shown below.

Defensive Communication	Supportive Communication
Evaluation: Judging others and making them feel judged	*Description:* Describing your feelings without making the other person feel wrong
Control: Threatening and dominating others	*Problem oriented:* Focusing on issues and good solutions
Strategizing: Trying to manipulate others for your own ends	*Spontaneity:* Communicating openly and honestly
Neutrality: Communicating disinterest and lack of caring	*Empathy:* Showing your regard for the other person
Distancing: Emphasizing differences in status and roles	*Equality:* Minimizing differences; treating others equally
Certainty: Implying that you are always right; never being unsure or open to suggestion	*Provisionalism:* Communicating tentativeness and openness to others

You should notice that the key element in defensive communication is a judgmental posture. You create defensiveness when you judge and try to control others. This does not mean that group members should not critically evaluate the ideas of other group members. On the contrary, the critical evaluation of ideas is crucial to good decision making. But it does mean that group members must work to keep their criticisms at the ideational level and not at the personal level. People will feel no commitment to the group if they suspect they are going to be frequently criticized. Openness and acceptance of others are the key features of supportive communication. Learn to express yourself firmly but with respect for others. It is particularly important that group members feel they are appreciated and have a rightful place in the group. Supportive communication is certainly the fundamental ingredient of cohesiveness.

THE SOCIAL DIMENSION

Our society has long recognized the worth and dignity of the individual. Advertisements sell products by appealing to the wish to "get away from the crowd" and assert individuality. Laws protect each person's rights to privacy, to earn a living, to gain an education—in short, the right to be an individual. But we also recognize that the human being is a social being. Most human animals seek the company of other humans and apparently need membership in a variety of social systems.

To understand a group is to understand the relationship between the individual and the group. Moreover, to understand this relationship is to understand the individual. This section deals with the reciprocal relationship between the individual and the group. Specifically, the development of the miniculture that constitutes a group entails the development of a climate that socializes the uniqueness of the individual into the social system of the group. The term *socioemotional climate* refers to this merger of the individual into the social system.

Perspectives on the Socioemotional Climate

The most common perspective used to discuss the socioemotional climate of a group is cohesiveness. But cohesiveness is synonymous with the concept of socioemotional climate. Understanding how cohesiveness develops is indeed equivalent to understanding the development of a group's socioemotional climate.

Interpersonal Attraction   One common approach to discussing cohesiveness is to discuss how and why people are attracted to one another: that is, how and why people like one another. The assumption is that people who like one another develop a cohesive group. So a cohesive group is cohesive because members develop interpersonal liking.

Attitudinal similarity is the most frequent reason why people are attracted to other people. As Berger (1973, p. 181) wrote, "one of the most robust relationships in all of the behavioral sciences is that which exists between perceived attitudinal similarity and interpersonal attraction. We like persons whom we perceive to hold attitudes which are similar to ours, especially when these attitudes are concerned with issues which are important to us."

Members of a group will like one another if they perceive that the group is composed of people with similar attitudes and preferences. Even if group members disagree about something, there will be an accompanying pressure to communicate about it, and the increase in communication will usually (but not always) lead to more agreement and therefore to greater interpersonal attraction.

But there are other factors that relate communication to attraction in the group. Certainly group members are attracted to others who have similar attitudes. But group members are also attracted to people who reinforce them. Communication with others can be pleasant or painful and we soon are attracted to those who reward us and repelled by those who punish us. Berger and Calabrese (1975) offer another explanation for interpersonal attraction. They explain that as we get to know one another and acquire more certainty about how others will behave, we become relaxed around them and like them more. Cohesiveness can be the result of interpersonal attraction. The force of interpersonal attraction pulls people toward the group and keeps it together. Though there are no guarantees that group members will like one another, the paragraphs below offer four strategies for increasing their attractiveness to one another.

1. *Increase the Frequency of Interaction* How often people communicate is associated with interpersonal attraction. As people communicate with one another more often, they increase their mutual attraction. One consistent finding in communication (Bochner, 1984) is that there are pressures toward agreement and liking. People basically want to like other people. If members of a group spend time together and talk about anything—tasks or nonrelated social matters—they will increase their attraction to each other. It is possible, of course, to find that you dislike someone after talking to the person for a while, but the odds are that this will not happen. As the frequency of interaction increases, however, it is difficult to know whether this frequency is the cause of the attraction or its effect; that is, are people attracted to each other because they communicate more frequently, or do they communicate more frequently because they like each other? Another "chicken or an egg" question. Nevertheless, increasing the contact time among group members is always a good idea.

2. *Reciprocate Liking and Interaction* A second factor associated wth interpersonal attraction is the perception of reciprocated attraction and interaction. Interpersonal liking is a two-way street. We like people who like us. Moreover, we tend to be attracted to people we think we are going to be working with; even though we have never met them, the natural pressure toward liking and attraction "kicks in" when we think we are going to be communicating with them. Sometimes a few group members are not very interested in other members of the group and can seriously impair the group's progress. If you can communicate to these few members that they will be interacting with others who are interested in them, you can improve the chances of attraction. We begin building perceptions

of others even before we communciate with them, and we will be attracted to those who are attracted to us.

3. *Self-disclose* Self-disclosure may be defined generally as statements made to another about oneself—what one thinks, feels, believes, wants, needs. It is verbally communicated personal information to another person. Rosenfeld (1988) explains the complexities and conditions that make self-disclosure successful, and his fundamental conclusion is that self-disclosure is potentially very beneficial to interpersonal relationships in groups. Self-disclosure does have its risks; group members who choose to self-disclose can meet with rejection or a negative image in other people's eyes. But if disclosive communication is handled properly, group members will experience closer relationships and increased understanding. And the best way to get others to self-disclose is to do it yourself. If your group is experiencing interpersonal tensions, it might behoove you to attempt a disclosure.

It is true that self-disclosure is risky, but so are all strategies for improving relationships. Research indicates that positive disclosures are associated with highly cohesive and successful groups. In task-oriented groups within classrooms or organizations, disclosure can help maintain relationships. Disclosure in task-oriented groups requires some skill. People sitting around in business clothes making decisions do not reveal personal information about themselves very readily. But the presentation of at least slightly disclosive information about yourself presents you as agreeable and nonthreatening. It "humanizes" you to the extent that disclosure makes you appear open, warm, and friendly. Other people will usually respond in kind. Self-disclosure is a very useful way to improve the interpersonal attractiveness among group members.

4. *Develop Bonding Competence* An important aspect of being a capable, competent communicator is developing relationship skills, or what Bochner (1984, p. 588) calls *bonding competence*. There are a number of dimensions to becoming a competent member of a group (see Andersen, 1988), but skill in promoting interpersonal relationships is one of the most important. Skilled group members usually achieve their communication goals by using appropriate social skills and by remaining sensitive to the needs of others. People are attracted to socially competent individuals, ones who not only achieve their own goals but also satisfy the goals of others. Competent relationship bonders show solidarity with others. They communicate in such a way as to indicate to the group that everyone is important and has status. They offer to help, and they make personal sacrifices for the group. Their communication behaviors evidence flexibility and adaptability.

Member Satisfaction Cohesiveness may also be viewed as the extent to which members enjoy, or are satisfied with, their group experiences. Interpersonal attraction can promote cohesion. Member satisfaction is a consequence of cohesion. The term *satisfaction* is used here to refer to morale, loyalty, or any way in which individual members are pleased with their group experience. Marston and Hecht (1988) have written an interesting essay in which they report the results of an intensive study of a small group in which the observers noted the variables that influence group members' satisfaction. How satisfied the group members are with the group is clearly correlated with group consensus, productivity, and general performance and effectiveness (Hecht and Riley, 1985).

Marston and Hecht (1988) report six qualities of groups that are associated with satisfied group members.

The first is the importance of *participation*. Group members get generally grumpy and disaffected when they feel they are not being allowed to participate or that the participation is unequal. Group members are most satisfied when they feel included in the discussion, and they are least satisfied when they feel that others are dominating the discussion. Both the frequency and the duration of the participation are important. Another important factor in participation is bidirectional communication. People are satisfied not only when they are allowed to communicate often but also when others direct messages to them; it is naturally reinforcing to have someone direct questions or information to you. Also, group members must perceive that they have a free, unfettered opportunity to participate. An early study by Heslin and Dunphy (1964) found that actual participation rates were less important than the perception of freedom to interact. You can improve participation rates by controlling group size and making sure that leaders are skilled at including everyone in the discussion.

The *types of messages* are a second important contributor to the group members' satisfaction. There are, of course, many types of messages that influence the group, but the most important are (1) negative communication, (2) ambiguous communication, and (3) orienting communication. Negative communication, which includes personal criticism, decreases members' satisfaction; people must be able to express disagreements, but they must learn to do so in a manner that is not offensive to other individuals. Vague and ambiguous messages also decrease satisfaction; they make for confused meaning, and they generate confusion and equally ambiguous responses from other group members. Orienting communication directs the group discussion by means of clarification, questions, answers, and relevant information; helping the group to keep things organized and focused, orienting communication promotes satisfaction with the group.

Feedback is a third component of satisfaction. Group leaders and other members of the group must do everything they can to provide feedback to other members. Feedback is a statement that is responsive to the behavior of other group members and they should receive both positive and negative feedback. Positive feedback (being told that what you have done is good or helpful to the group) is desirable, but negative feedback is also important. If you can change a group member's behavior so that it becomes more aligned with the group's goals, then you have significantly contributed to satisfaction in the group. The best way to communicate negative feedback is to be performance descriptive; that is, focus on describing the performance of the group member, not the person's emotions or attitudes.

Interaction management is a fourth element of establishing successful group satisfaction. Interaction management refers to one's skill in regulating and coordinating the flow and direction of interaction. The interaction is being poorly managed when people interrupt one another and speak in a confused and uncoordinated manner. One very important factor in interaction management is *turn taking*, a term that refers to the smoothness of the back-and-forth exchanges among speakers. If the group is composed of people who are poor speakers and awkward about who speaks when, there is likely to be confusion and frustration among the group members. The leader should ensure that turn-taking expectations are not violated.

Fifth, satisfaction is highest when group members are comfortable with the *status* hierarchy in the group (discussed in detail in Chapter 7). Status is the prestige or position that a person holds in the group. High-status group members are able to influence other group members because they have some skill or resource that the group values. Group members are very dissatisfied when there is confusion and disagreement over status. If one member acts more important than everyone else, the other members of the group will become irritated. Groups like to think of their members as having equal status, but this is probably impossible to achieve. All groups have some status differences. But agreement on the nature of those differences is important. An individual, say a leader, may have status and power in the group, but there will be no problem if the other group members understand and support that person.

The final source of group members' satisfaction is *motivation*. When everyone in the group has a desire to remain in the group and wants to contribute and devote time to the group, then the members are motivated to perform. There is no substitute for people who really want to be involved in a project. A person will be more motivated when a group is able to reward the person and contribute significantly to the person's sense of identity. Also important is conversational motivation (the motivation to engage in interaction), for satisfaction increases when the members are enthusiastic about taking part in the discussion. Motivated communicators ask questions, seek information, do research, request clarification, and are generally highly involved in and focused on the interaction.

Group Identification

Another perspective from which to view individuals and their relationship with the group is the extent to which they identify themselves with that group. Many scholars discuss group identification as the members' internalization of group goals—the extent to which the group's goals become the goals of the individual members. Group identification here implies a broader meaning. To the extent that each group member feels a part of the group or recognizes membership in the group, group identification may be said to exist.

It is possible to observe group identification even in the classroom, where students will change their classroom seating patterns and begin to sit beside or near their fellow group members. Group members begin to refer to the group in the first person as "my" group or "our" group. When members keep diaries of their reactions after group meetings, the diaries themselves reflect a developing group identification. A diary in the early stages of a group's meetings will include a reference to another member in the third person: for example, "I am having trouble with one of the people in this group. He seems to criticize everything I say." Later, that same member will use first names exclusively in referring to fellow group members—"Steve is still the critic of our group. But I am beginning to realize that he just wants us to think about what we are saying."

Occasionally group members have difficulty establishing group identification, and an impetus is needed to stir their feelings of unity. An example from one such group indicates a possible impetus for increasing group identification. One group member, frustrated by the obvious apathy of his fellow group members, sought help from his instructor. This group, as might be expected, was not very productive and had received a rather low evaluation on a preliminary group project, and the members were naturally disappointed over their low grade. The instructor and the student arranged a group conference. During this conference the entire group, acting as a unit, complained to the instructor about the low grade, and throughout the conference the instructor remained firm and proceeded to justify the low mark, often using rather shaky ground for his justification. The conference proved to be successful in that the group developed much closer ties of group identification. They became united against a common "enemy"—the instructor. At the end of the term, when they were informed of the contrived incident, the group members had almost forgotten it. Group identification, in this instance, was spurred by conflict with some external foe. But more important, the feelings of increased group solidarity were maintained in the absense of the foe.

Symbolic Convergence   "Symbolic convergence" sounds a little daunting, but it is really a pretty clear and interesting concept. Whereas the preceding section discussed some well-established perspectives on the social dimension of the group, symbolic convergence is a special theory of communication that has been evolving in recent years (see Bormann, 1986). It is a realistic picture of the communication in groups and helps explain the social dimension of groups—especially how they come to form a group identity. Moreover, symbolic convergence is significantly correlated with cohesiveness. Groups establish their own culture with information and stories that are unique to the group, and these cultural stories are evidence that the group is forming a special identity that is of value to the group's members.

Symbolic convergence theory is concerned with the evolution of certain patterns of communication in the group. More specifically, it deals with attempts to find recurring communication patterns in the group that are indications of group consciousness. The term *symbolic convergence* refers to the coming together (or unifying) of certain symbols in the group that are important to group members. When group members share and understand symbols in a particular way, they create a common understanding and consciousness with which they can identify; this identification is *symbolic* because it deals with the human tendency to interpret signs and signals and infuse them with meaning. When people participate in a group, they share stories and fantasies and make sense of human action by attributing meaning to human events. When symbolic worlds overlap or come closer together, they are said to *converge*. People are sharing a common consciousness when they understand one another's symbolic worlds.

Bormann (1986) cites *dramatizing messages* as an example of how symbolic themes develop in a group and then the members converge. In 1950, Robert Bales devised categories to code the communication in small groups (see Chapter 6). One of his original categories was "shows tension release," but it was later changed to "dramatizes." A group member dramatizes a message when he or she portrays something in dramatic terms. Bormann (1986, p. 224) wrote that "A dramatizing message is one that contains one or more of the following: a pun or other word play, a double entendre, a figure of speech, analogy, anecdote, allegory, fable, or narrative."

Over the years, small group researchers noticed that some of the dramatizing in groups would cause an explosion of symbolic material that the group became very enamored with. This led to the concept of group fantasy and fantasy-chain analysis. The researchers noted that dramatic messages were not important any time one member made a pun or a joke; rather, they became important when group members became excited, interrupted one another, and showed a lot of emotion.

Sharing Group Fantasies Researchers observed that a group might be working along in a normal manner and then come to a point where the members would get off track and depart from the group's main direction. This might begin with a simple dramatic message. Often the members would lean back in their chairs and get quiet for a while, and then all of a sudden someone would say something completely off the subject and unrelated to the task at hand. She would tell a story about a strange incident or about something that had happened to her. The other group members would join in and add to the story, and the group would get lively and emotional as everyone contributed to the narrative. It was not uncommon to observe group members taking part in these stories and expressing fear, sadness, and joy. Then, just as abruptly as it began, the episode would end, often with one member directing the group back to the task.

These were moments of dramatization. The group had participated in a fantasy. The term *fantasy* does not refer to something unreal or bizarre, but to the act of sharing interpretations of events to satisfy the group's need to organize experience and form communal bonds. Group fantasies often deal with news, television, organizational stories, desires, or things that have actually happened to group members. They serve to achieve an empathic

symbolic convergence. The group members take pleasure in their joint experience of emotions. Group fantasies are also thematic; they have a story with
characters and patterns of action. Group fantasies are not chaotic and confused, but organized. They are composed of characters (sometimes heroes
and villains) that are engaged in human activities that represent themes of
power, control, failure, success, the future, and other common lifescripts.

The example below is from a classroom group. It is a fantasy chain with a
power theme; that is, it illustrates how a group shares fantasies related to
power. The group members are experiencing frustration at their inability to
accomplish the task. After a few moments of silence, Rick begins:

RICK: You know, I'd like to bag this whole project.
PETE: Yeah, screw this guy. Let's just tell 'em we're not going to do this group
    assignment.
SUE: Be serious, we'll all get F's.
RICK: No we won't. We'll get in touch with all the other groups and none of
    us will turn in the assignment. He can't fail the whole class.
BOB: Let's just take over the class, like the students did in the sixties. I mean
    really, what could he or the university do? We'll just insist on not having
    to do this assignment.
RUTH: I read about these kids once who took over a class. They determined
    themselves what they were going to do, what books they would read,
    and who was going to get what grade.
BOB: Sure, I've often thought we should have more say so in what goes on in
    class.
RUTH: There was a movie about it or something.
RICK: It could be done.
SUE: Come on, you guys, we gotta get this done.

This interaction is a power fantasy. It offers the group an exciting way to
discover emotional common ground related to frustrations, attitudes, lines of
action, and opinions. This power fantasy has heroes (the class), villains (the
professor), and scenarios where people carry out behavior. The pattern of
communication allows the group to dramatize its attitudes, and this dramatization becomes an important part of the group's culture. The communication
of an individual or group always reveals attitudes and values. Imagine a
bunch of seniors sitting around talking about looking for jobs, paying loans,
and leaving their friends. The attitudes and values inherent in their culture
are apparent.

Fantasy chains are very important to establishing a common group identity. All new groups must spend time communicating in such a way that they
develop a sense of common identity. Group members succeed at such an
identity creation by recognizing that they are in a group and that this group
has an existence and purpose of its own. They become aware that they are
different in some ways from people who are not members of the group. You
can always tell groups that have a strong identity and are probably very
cohesive because they have fantasies about "outsiders" and "insiders." They

develop a sense of "our group." They use phrases to refer to themselves, such as "our group," "we," or "us." Groups that have pet names for themselves are especially symbolically converged. We have known groups that called themselves the *Testmasters,* the *Bluebirds,* or the *Hawks* (after their school mascot). These names are symbolic of the strong sense of common identity the group has created, and they serve to mark the boundaries for membership in the group.

Social Tension

The feeling of tension is familiar to all of us. A person who feels tense is nervous and irritable. Television commercials have endowed tension with a certain fame, along with its accompanying headache. But tension does indeed have its physiological signs—contracted muscles, the familiar sweaty palms, the averted eye gaze. This is the tension experienced by an individual person. Social tension is not unlike the tension experienced by an individual. Persons in a group suffering from extreme social tension may exhibit many of the signs of individual tension. Extreme social tension is characterized by an electric atmosphere. The very air seems charged. The individual members are uncomfortable. All in all, extreme social tension is not a pleasant experience.

Primary and Secondary Tension   There are two types of social tension— primary and secondary. The difference is one of kind rather than degree. During the initial period of a group's formation, primary tension is inevitable and to be expected as a normal occurrence. One might compare primary social tension to stage fright. Social inhibitions create a lack of assurance about how to behave. Comments are quietly spoken and very tentative. Long pauses occur between comments. Members rarely interrupt one another; and if two members should speak at once, profuse apologies reveal the extent of primary tension present. There can be too much primary tension, as shown in Figure 2-3.

Secondary tension is potentially much more serious. Unlike primary tension, it is not always predictable or easily overcome merely through the passage of time. The hallmark of secondary tension is typically an abrupt departure from group routine. Sometimes a sharp increase in tension begins about an outburst from one of the members. There may be a heated exchange between two or more members. A flurry of verbal activity will be followed by an unbearably long pause. During the heated exchange, members may attempt to shout over one another's comments for extended periods. Usually two or three members will do most of the talking while other members remain rigidly silent, staring at the floor. Extreme secondary tension is definitely an unpleasant sensation and, if uncontrolled, threatens the social health of the group. Figure 2-4 depicts the condition of this group.

The causes of secondary tension are many and varied. Overt interpersonal conflict, occasionally even a personality conflict, may precipitate severe secondary tension. Environmental pressures, such as a shortage of time in

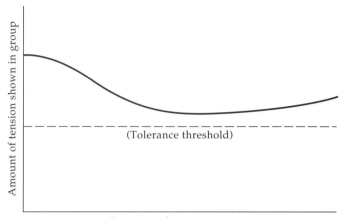

FIGURE 2-3 Tension curve of a hypothetical group:
uncontrolled primary tension.

which to accomplish the task, will cause it to rise sharply. Quite often, a
feeling of frustration among the members foments tension. Such frustration
may stem from an acknowledged lack of success in task accomplishment or
the feeling that the group performance was far short of expectations. A
nonconforming member might cause frustration—particularly one who is
habitually tardy or absent from group meetings or who consistently fails to
fulfill promises made to the group. Whatever the cause, extreme secondary
tension, once experienced, must be brought under control if the group is to
survive.

FIGURE 2-4 Tension curve of a hypothetical group:
uncontrolled secondary tension.

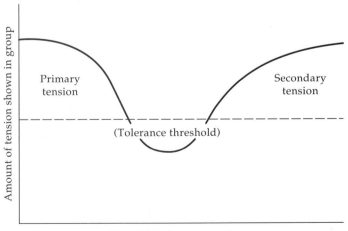

Managing Social Tension   Up to this point we have discussed tension as harmful and destructive to a group's socioemotional climate. Certainly excessive tension is harmful to the group, but some tension is both normal and essential. In fact, some tension is always present in a functioning group. Tension implies activity. An actor, for instance, is not relaxed when performing, but is tense, concentrating on the performance. The successful athletic team is "up for the game." After a group overcomes its natural social inertia in the early stages of group development, the members experience tension. They are alert, on their toes—tense. The functioning group is not at rest, but active, and hence is experiencing some degree of tension.

The problem of social tension, then, is not that it exists, but that it may exceed an optimal level. Every group has a "tolerance threshold" of social tension above which it cannot function effectively. If the tension level is below that threshold, the group is able to function well. But when the tension level rises above the group's tolerance threshold, it becomes the overpowering priority in the group's socioemotional climate. The group must reduce that tension level before it can do anything else.

Of course, the tolerance threshold varies from group to group. Some groups can tolerate a rather high level of tension and function effectively. Another group whose tolerance threshold is lower will find that level of tension intolerable. Just as some individuals can endure more pain than others, some groups can endure more tension that others. The problem for the group, then, is to develop successful mechanisms for reducing tension when it rises above the tolerance threshold.

Some groups overcome the initial primary tension but fail to control the secondary tension. Thus, the secondary tension level remains above the tolerance threshold, and the group is unable to function effectively throughout. For the members of this group, the socioemotional climate is extremely unpleasant. No group can withstand indefinitely the pressures of secondary tension above the tolerance threshold. The life expectancy of such a group will be short. The members will probably disband rather than suffer such social agony much longer.

In another type of group the members are never able to overcome their initial primary tension. They remain a collection of individuals. Members do not identify with the group; they exhibit extraordinary apathy and have virtually no commitment either to the group or to the task at hand. One is reminded of the joke about the community meeting called to protest apathy; no one showed up at the meeting. This group—or, more accurately, this collection of individuals—will not exist long either. If the members do continue to meet (in the event that they are a "captive" aggregation compelled to meet), they will accomplish little.

A third type of group sounds ideal. (See Figure 2-5.) The members overcome primary tension and never suffer from secondary tension above their tolerance threshold. They seem to be a happy, healthy group of contented people. And that may be true. More likely, however, the members of this group are either bored stiff or are suffering from an abnormal fear of

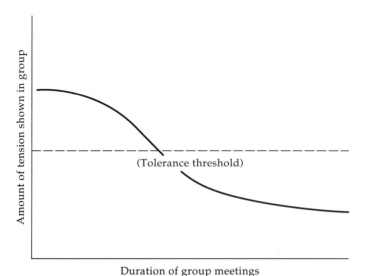

FIGURE 2-5 Tension curve of a hypothetical group: absence of secondary tension.

social tension. It is simply not healthy, perhaps not normal, for group members never to experience secondary tension above their tolerance threshold. One explanation for their never doing so might be that they just don't care enough to get excited about anything. As a result, they do what they are told but have little commitment to the group's activities. Another plausible explanation might be that they are hypochondriacs about social tension. They fear tension so much that they conscientiously avoid any stimulus that would raise the tension level above the tolerance threshold. The members retreat or take flight from any potential source for a social problem. Rather than solving their social problems, they ignore them and hope they will go away.

A fourth type of group is the most likely to enjoy the ideal socioemotional climate. This group has frequent moments of secondary tension above its tolerance threshold, and it consistently dispels the excess of tension. This group successfully manages its social tension and obviously has no fear of secondary tension. Its past behavior is a series of instances of successful management of tension. The members have obviously developed mechanisms for successfully coping with secondary tension and have incorporated them into their system's functional patterns. The social fabric of this group is strengthened with each success in managing social tension. The socioemotional climate is vibrantly healthy, and the members undoubtedly find the group exciting and stimulating. Figure 2-6 illustrates this situation.

The mechanisms developed by successful groups for reducing excessive tension are also many and varied. Moreover, what works in one group may be totally unsuccessful in others. Often one or two persons assume the role of tension relievers, and the group looks to them for help when the time arises. Sometimes a tension reliever is a jokester—a person who is carefree, happy-

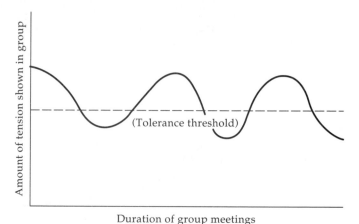

FIGURE 2-6 Tension curve of a hypothetical group: frequent periods of secondary tension.

go-lucky, and makes people laugh. But laughter is not always a clear sign of tension release; it may even signify excessive tension. When members laugh at comments that are really not funny, they are probably exhibiting, rather than releasing, tension. Quick, abrupt, high-pitched laughter is generally a sign of tension rather than of tension release. One group successfully relieved primary tension through a member who constantly told jokes, often at her own expense. But when secondary tension arose, her self-deprecating jokes were unsuccessful. In fact, the other members resented her care-free attitude and finally demanded that she take a more serious attitude toward their task. Thus, the behavior that dispelled primary tension was unsuccessful in coping with secondary tension, even in the same group.

Another tension-relieving role may be that of a mediator between two conflicting members. When secondary tension erupts from such an interpersonal conflict, the conciliator who is respected by both the conflicting members is a tension reliever. Sometimes excessive tension is reduced by finding a scapegoat as a mediating agency. When tension arises from frustration over environmental or task pressures, that frustration must be vented at someone or something. In a classroom group, the instructor serves as a convenient scapegoat (as in the power fantasy in the previous section). In a business organization, the boss becomes the "enemy." The successful scapegoat is generally outside the immediate group membership. Most important to the group, though, is not *how* it manages tension, but *whether* it does.

One strategy for successful tension management is to *confront social problems head on*. More problems are created by avoiding or ignoring potential problems than by facing them squarely. Such overt action is rarely easy, however, and generally requires old-fashioned guts! But the social benefits are worth the momentary and perfectly normal reluctance. One member's diary, written immediately after a particularly productive group meeting, emphasizes the wisdom of confrontation:

> But almost everyone got the preppie stereotype impression of me. It goes to show, first impressions are really terrible, because everyone is so different from what I thought. I told them all exactly what I thought of them and they told me. I thought this would be a total disaster, and everyone would end up hating each other. But it brought us very close together, I think. This meeting was a great accomplishment for our group. Now I think we can start moving.

Whatever the social problem, the importance of confronting it head on cannot be overestimated. Occasionally the group is in for a painful period of agonizing tension during this confrontation. But in the long run the group not only survives, but becomes stronger. One classroom group provides an excellent example of extreme measures used to confront a social problem centered on a single person. This example also demonstrates the constructive effects of confrontation on the group's socioemotional climate. This five-member group was composed of four women and one man. For a variety of reasons, the man was considered a male chauvinist by the women members, a thorn in their side. They deeply resented what they considered his domineering behavior, although they had not directly verbalized their resentment. At one climactic meeting they finally decided to let him know—clearly and forcefully. The following excerpts from the male member's paper analyzing his group most clearly illustrate what happened during the confrontation and its aftermath:

> Then there was the meeting when one of the members hit me with the comment, "Go to hell, you egotistical creep!" It was then that I began to realize the value of this class and how our group reacted. There was, of course, a great deal of tension that day. I was very nervous and uncomfortable. . . . In being blasted I, more than anyone else, I think, felt what a brutal force and what brutal pressure can fall on someone in the social dimension of a group when people begin to attack you.
>
> . . . It was exciting to have each member of the group become confident enough to bare his or her soul to the rest of the group.

A comment from another member of the group corroborates the positive effects of this extreme confrontation:

> My first reaction to Marilyn's "Tom, go to hell" was that it was uncalled for. I thought that that type or degree of honesty was not needed. However, it was exactly what was needed because it opened the door to real communication. We all became very sober and honest with each other. . . . By the end of the meeting my mind was so elated that I felt completely free of anxiety or pressure, and I felt very much at peace with myself and with the world.

Granted, not every confrontation will have such immediate and such positive effects. Nor will every confrontation be centered on a single member or even on a person at all. But avoiding potential social problems will have even fewer immediate effects and many less positive ones. The important point is that the group overtly and conscientiously confronted its problem.

In summary, there is one vitally important point to remember. The successful and socially healthy group is not characterized by an absence of social tension, but by successful management of social tension. No group should expect, or even hope for, an absence of problems caused by social tension. Instead, a group should expect social problems to occur, should confront those problems, and should develop mechanisms for their control. This means that the members must learn to overcome their personal inhibitions, be honest, and require or demand the same behavior from other members. Such "good advice" is, of course, deceptively simple. It is more easily said than done. But a successful group requires not only time for development but also the overt effort of its members to make it a success. One student group encapsulated this good advice in a pithy slogan that may be worth repeating: "The group that fights together stays together." A later version of this slogan may be even better: "The group that fights, unites."

THE TASK DIMENSION: DEFINITION

The nature of the task dimension of the group process has long been a topic of considerable concern among scholars of small group phenomena. In most cases, group tasks are imposed on the group by some external authority— that is, some authority outside the group. For example, the legal system assigns its decision-making task to a jury after a courtroom trial. A group in a business organization that must decide, for example, how to market a specific product is assigned this task by some organizational superior for the purpose of furthering the goals of the larger organization.

Occasionally, however, individuals form a group for the purpose of performing some task that can be accomplished more productively with group effort. For example, political-action groups are often formed by persons who wish to respond as a group to some perceived problem, such as improving environmental quality, lobbying for specific legislation, or electing a candidate to political office.

Certain types of tasks will place different "critical demands" on group members in terms of specifying what behaviors or procedures they need to perform in order to accomplish those tasks adequately. Some scholars have attempted to specify those critical demands by listing the various types of tasks actually performed by groups. Hackman (1968), for example, has identified three types: (1) production tasks, (2) discussion tasks, and (3) problem-solving tasks. A production task calls for the presentation of ideas concerning some stimulus, such as "Write a critical analysis of *Othello*." A problem-solving task requires the group members to specify an action to be taken regarding some pressing need, such as "What should be done to resolve the problem of insufficient housing on campus?" Hackman's discussion task, the most general of his three types, deals with an evaluation of issues that typically have no right or wrong answer. For example, "Is the American economy truly free enterprise?"

The task dimension of the group process central to our interests involves the more comprehensive task of decision making. In virtually any group's decision-making effort, all three of Hackman's tasks (production, discussion, and problem solving) will be involved. Although the discussions in Chapter 6 will indicate some minimal differences between problem solving and decision making, the task efforts of decision-making groups resist any clearly specifiable restrictions as to the nature of the group task.

Much more significant, however, is the tendency to view any task as one that can or even should be performed by a group. We shall take the position that in order to maximize the quality of task performance, certain tasks should be performed by groups, and other tasks are best performed by expert individuals. Our distinction, then, is based less on what types of tasks are given to groups and more on the particular type of task most appropriate to the group process.

THE TASK DIMENSION: INDIVIDUAL VERSUS GROUP DECISION MAKING

Surely the process of making decisions in a group differs from that of one person working alone. This statement should not be too startling. After all, a group is different from a single individual. For one thing, there are more people in a group. This bit of wisdom contains several important implications. A group has a greater variety of resources. There are more minds to contribute to the decision-making effort, more sources of information. Unlike the lone individual, a group is able to divide labor among its members so that, for example, members can work on their own specialties.

On the other hand, a group has potential problems not inherent in individual decision making. The problem of achieving consensus is present in a group. The many examples of hung juries are ample evidence of the existence of this problem. And, with the addition of more people, there is greater opportunity for conflict. At the same time, there are many more sources to generate new ideas. Also, there are more viewpoints from which to evaluate those ideas critically. In other words, a critical exchange of ideas is much more easily accomplished by a group.

Group Polarization

Among the differences discovered when individual and group decision making have been compared is the phenomenon known as group polarization (Moscovici, 1985, pp. 396–399). Simply stated, *group polarization* refers to the tendency of groups to make decisions that are more extreme than the initial opinions of its members. Some early group researchers found that the decisions made by groups rather than individuals tended to be extreme. This was termed the *risky shift*. They found that groups would select an alternative that had a bigger payoff but a lower probability of attainment. If a group and its individual members were to place bets on a horse race, for example, the group would more likely bet on a 100-to-1 shot than would any of the individuals deciding alone. Apparently the group interaction stimulated individuals to take greater risks and be less conservative.

One reason the risky-shift phenomenon generated so much research interest was that it contradicted some prevailing theories of the time. Theories of conformity would predict that groups would avoid deviant opinions because there are interpersonal pressures in groups to accommodate your opinions to those of others. The risky-shift phenomenon also contradicted what was called normalization theory. This theory held that group decisions would reflect an average of opinions and norms. One member of a group might be a risk taker, but another would be more conservative; the result would be an average of the two members and not an extreme decision. There were various explanations of the risky shift, but the most popular explanation attributes group risk to the diffusion among group members of the responsibility for the group decision. Individuals are more willing to take chances because they cannot be blamed. It is the same explanation that accounts for lynch-mob behavior in the old west. No good citizen would think of lynching the man in jail, but in the anonymity of the group, "mob fever" was the result.

Later research concluded that the risky-shift phenomenon should be considered a matter of attitude change. Group polarization means that individuals change attitudes according to the communication and information in the group. Initial involvement in and commitment to the group and its decisions are an important part of any attitude change. When group members hold more extreme opinions, they also tend to be highly committed and to exert more pressure on moderate group members, who find it easier to shift. Communication in a group structures information around group norms, and the norms that a group develops are more polarized (or extreme) than are the norms and opinions of individuals. Myers and Bishop (1971) found that groups composed of racists became more racist after discussion. Polarization effects were found in groups discussing attitudes about women, abortion, and a number of other social issues.

It is also true that group consensus changes individual attitudes and opinions. The groupthink hypothesis discussed earlier is about groups that make faulty (and sometimes extreme) decisions because there are pressures toward uniformity. Our tendency is to be influenced by members of groups who are like us. Groups in organizations are typically composed of people who value their membership in the group and realize that the group has tremendous reward potential. Whenever people are interdependent, as they are in group discussions, there is an attraction toward the majority and there are pressures to conform to the majority. The fact that groups polarize their opinions is the result of highly susceptible group members who establish new norms and then pressure others, often subtly, to be consistent with the prevailing norm, thereby continuing to validate the norm. This spiral leads to riskier decisions. These are the behaviors that lead to polarized opinions, and group members would do well to be aware of them.

Persuasive Arguments Theory

In an effort to learn more about why groups make more polarized decisions than individuals, a group of communication researchers have been working with a theory called *persuasive arguments theory* (PAT) (Meyers, 1989; Meyers and Siebold, 1990). Very simply, the theory states that group members are influenced by the arguments of other group members. In other words, after being exposed to the information in the arguments of other group members they are more likely to shift or move their own decision—sometimes toward the extreme. There are two qualities in the arguments that are most responsible for causing group members to alter their decisions. These two qualities are *novelty* and *persuasiveness*. People are quite likely to be persuaded by arguments from others that are novel or new, arguments that they never thought of before. And they are also likely to be influenced by arguments that are persuasively logical, personally appealing, or well-supported by facts and data.

The theory holds that if all members of the group begin the discussion with the same information and arguments, and if, during the course of the group's interaction, no new arguments emerge, the final decision of the group will not be polarized. It will be the same as it was at the beginning of the group discussion. But if the members are exposed during the group discussion to new and persuasive arguments, they will be stimulated to rethink and reconsider their positions in light of the new information. It is important to remember that what is persuasive or novel for one person will not be for another. What is clear, however, is that novel and persuasive arguments will influence the decision making of some group members. And the more novel and persuasive an argument is the more influence it will have. So if you want to be influential in your group, be sure to work at gathering new information and generating good arguments to persuade the other members.

Efficiency and Speed

Few people have accused a group of being efficient. Referring a proposal to a committee in order to kill it is a well-known parliamentary tactic. Simple arithmetic should illustrate that, in terms of hours expended, groups are destined to be less efficient than individuals. Say that one person can complete a decision-making task in 1 hour. A three-person group would have to complete this task in 20 minutes in order to equal the 1 hour spent by the individual—but the group will probably spend more than 1 hour, thus taking more than 3 times as long *per person* to complete the task.

Compared with individuals, groups are abominably slow. You will recall that it takes time for groupness to evolve. The group must establish a history before it can function effectively as a decision-making system. For a group member, patience is an important virtue. Inevitably, group members become highly frustrated, particularly in the early stages of group development, over the group's apparent lack of progress. Members are anxious to "get the show on the road," to quit wasting so much time and attend to the task at hand. Although these feelings of frustration and discouragement are typical, they should not be considered serious. Progress is not very visible in the early stages of group development, but the seemingly rapid progress later is a direct and cumulative result of the activities that have come before.

There is one possible explanation for the apparent inefficiency and slowness of group decision making. Researchers have discovered that a group's effective attention span is quite small. In fact, the average length of time a group discusses a single theme is only *58 seconds*. In other words, groups tend to jump from topic to topic very quickly without dwelling on any one topic for very long. Groups tend to make decisions in spurts of activity, whereas an individual may be more capable of lengthy periods of sustained effort.

At this point one may be tempted to ask, "If groups are so slow and inefficient as a decision-making system, why bother with them at all? Let individuals make all the decisions." If efficiency and speed were the sole criteria by which decision making were judged, no one would bother with groups. But the *quality* of the decision is infinitely more important than the time expended to make it.

Although it is difficult and often impossible to measure the quality of decisions accurately, there is a deep-seated feeling that in many cases groups will make better decisions than individuals. Our jury system, for example, is based on this premise—that a group of peers is more likely to arrive at a better or more accurate verdict than a single individual, even a judge. The principle of a democracy also operates on this assumption. If it didn't, we would disband the Congress and the Supreme Court and make the President a dictator.

Common sense tells us, then, that in some cases a group, occasionally even a group of nonexperts, will make higher-quality decisions than a single individual—even an expert individual—will. It is this feeling, perhaps, that sustains our interest in group decision making. But it is more than a mere feeling. There is incontrovertible evidence that some situations demand decisions made by groups and not by individuals. Our next problem is to identify those situations.

The Group Task

For years, small group researchers compared individual decision making with group decision making, attempting to determine whether, in fact, two heads are better than one. After numerous studies and conflicting results, researchers revised their perspective. As Collins and Guetzkow (1964, p. 57) pointed out, "It seems more profitable to ask, 'On what kinds of tasks and in what environments will the group perform better than its individual members working separately?' " It seems reasonable to assume that the impact of the social dimension of a group (in terms of more information resources, capacity to divide labor, social conflict, critical analysis, demands of consensus) would give the group a distinct advantage for some decision-making tasks.

James H. Davis (1969, p. 33) distinguishes some characteristics of the group task that are different from those of a task for individuals:

> Some tasks could reasonably be presented either to individuals or to a group. A word puzzle, for example, presents a challenge to an individual person as well as to a set of persons who cooperate in its solution. This type of task is defined in terms of individuals, but the definition remains applicable to groups as well. On the other hand, a number of tasks are impossible, or undefined, for individual persons apart from a group. For example, the major chore facing a group may be reaching agreement on some political issue. An individual subject may have no doubts as to his own position, but be distressed to find others in disagreement. The resolution of this disagreement in order to achieve consensus may represent a formidable task for the group, but there is no counterpart to this task for the isolated individual.

It is clear that some tasks, such as an algebra problem or a crossword puzzle, may be performed by either an individual or a group. But the social dimension of the group process could add nothing to the solution of such a problem. Nevertheless, as Davis points out, some tasks, such as those involving political issues, require the critical exchange of conflicting viewpoints. In such tasks a group has a distinctly superior advantage.

Zaleznik and Moment (1964, p. 143) provide further direction in our search for the group-decision situation. They point out that a group functions under a condition of "psychological interdependence," so that the productivity of the group is more than the sum of the contributions of the individual members. If a group were to perform a task that could be just as easily performed by an individual, the output would be merely the total of the contributions of all the individual members. If one of the members were absent one day and the other members continued working at their same rate, the productivity of the "group" would decrease. In other words, the activity of any of the members would have no influence on the group activity. There would be no interdependence among members. The authors go on to say:

> The output of the problem-solving group is of an entirely different nature. The contributions of the individual members do not accumulate by simple addition to determine the group's output. The output is *more than* the aggregate of individual contributions, or in some instances less. *Such a group deals with the kind of problem that actually requires group activity for its resolution* [emphasis added].

The principle of nonsummativity (that is, that the whole is different than the sum of its parts), which Zaleznik and Moment call *psychological interdependence,* is described by Collins and Guetzkow (1964, p. 58) as the *assembly effect.* According to Collins and Guetzkow:

> *An assembly effect occurs when the group is able to achieve collectively something which could not have been achieved by any member working alone or by a combination of individual efforts.* The assembly effect bonus is productivity which exceeds

the potential of the most capable member and also exceeds the sum of the efforts of the group members working separately.

The importance of the principle of nonsummativity cannot be overestimated. If a group performs a task that an individual could just as easily perform, the group cannot surpass the efforts produced by its most competent individual member. But if group activity is *required* in order to make the decision, the group effort can easily exceed that of its most competent member. The most capable individual in the group is still incapable of producing the critical exchange of ideas developed by the demands on the group to achieve consensus.

We should now be able to define the type of decision situation that is unique to the group process. The distinction is between the type of decision that requires high-quality technical expertise and the type of decision that requires acceptance and commitment from the group. To illustrate this distinction: The solution of a sophisticated mathematics equation requires a person who has considerable expertise in mathematics. We would be at a loss to solve the problem, since we simply do not possess that mathematical expertise. For such an individual task, there exists only one "correct" answer or one "best" answer. On the other hand, if our problem involves deciding who should be the next President of the United States, we are dealing with a very different kind of problem. Experts in political science or economics have no greater voice in this decision than any of us do. Their votes count the same as ours. For such a problem, no single "correct" or "best" answer exists (although each of us is probably convinced that one person would be a better President than any other).

The solution to the group task, moreover, has no external means by which the correctness of the decision can be validated—unlike the mathematics problem, which is wholly determined by the technical laws of mathematics. The sole criterion for validating the group decision is group acceptance or group commitment to the decision once it is made. Thus, the only criterion for validating the decision is whether it achieves consensus. Of course, the passage of time would allow a better judging of the quality of the decision. But remember that the decision situation changes from one point in time to another. What was a "good" decision during the campaign might prove to be less good after the elected candidate has been in office for a few years. Because decision situations change, incumbents are sometimes defeated in bids for reelection.

An important point to remember is that neither groups nor individuals are superior as a decision-making system. One person with expert qualifications should be expected to outperform a group on an individual task, and a group should be expected to outperform a single person on a group task. If the task requires high-quality technical expertise, the available individual who is most expert in that technical specialty should perform the task. If the task requires group commitment or validation by consensus, a group should be expected to perform the task. And unlike individual tasks, group tasks do not have a single "correct" or "best" answer that can be verified by some source external to the group. Many problems arise when groups are asked to perform a task that can just as easily be performed by an individual. Few will deny that there are too many committees in the world. But when the situation warrants it, a committee decision is essential if the decision is to be of the highest quality.

SUMMARY

The group process has two dimensions—the task dimension and the social dimension. Despite numerous attempts to separate them and a pervasive tendency to consider them in conflict with each other, the task and social dimensions of a group process are inseparable and interdependent. Although they may be separated theoretically, the task and social dimensions exert mutual and reciprocal influences on each other and are thus virtually inseparable in practice.

Productivity and cohesiveness may be considered the outputs of the task dimension and social dimension, respectively. A relationship exists between task and productivity, so that as the cohesiveness of a group increases, its productivity also increases to a point of diminishing returns. As a group approaches extremely high cohesiveness, it tends to decrease in productivity. Thus, the group with the highest productivity is generally a group with only moderately high cohesiveness. Consistent with the interdependence of the task and social dimensions, productivity and cohesiveness are also interdependent, each exerting influence simultaneously upon the other.

While it is impossible to guarantee that a group will be cohesive, group members can increase the probability of cohesiveness in the group by encouraging outside threats, creating group history, establishing interdependent goals, making progress toward goals, developing shared norms, promoting acceptance for group members, and encouraging supportive communication.

One result attributable to the interdependence of a group's task and social dimensions is the phenomenon of groupthink. Groupthink occurs in highly cohesive groups and results in a reduced quality of the group's task performance. Members of such a group tend to suspend their individual critical thinking in favor of judgments on which other members appear to concur. Groupthink results in an illusion of unanimity and in less effective decision making.

There are several ways to view the socioemotional climate of a group. All deal in some way with a perception of the cohesiveness of a group. The most common method is to view the extent to which group members like one another. A second perspective involves the degree to which members are satisfied with their group experience. Similar to member satisfaction is group identification—the extent to which members are committed to their membership and exhibit loyalty to the social system. Symbolic convergence is another way to view the socioemotional climate. It is a special theory of communication that explains how groups become unified and form a common identity by sharing symbolic experiences.

The socioemotional climate of a group depends to a great extent on the social tension experienced by the group. Social tension is of two types—primary and secondary. Primary tension refers to the normal period of tension in early stages of group development caused by the absence of a social structure and the normal inhibitions of members new to a developing social system. Secondary tension occurs during group interaction as disruptive periods in group routines of activity. Of the two types of tension, only secondary tension is generally a problem to a group's effective functioning.

A great many researchers have compared individual decision making with group decision making. Although the group process has two dimensions (task and social), the individual process has only the task dimension. The two-dimensional nature of groups results in several points of comparison with individuals. Groups tend to polarize their decisions more than do their individual members making decisions alone. And, compared with individuals, groups are inefficient and slow. But group decisions are necessary for many situations because of the superior quality of the decisions.

There are some tasks that can just as easily be performed by individuals or by groups. For these tasks, group activity adds nothing to the efforts of the most capable member. These tasks are those whose accomplishment requires high-quality technical expertise and for which there is one "correct" or "best" answer validated by the subject matter of the technical specialty.

Other tasks, however, require group acceptance or group commitment for successful performance. For such tasks, no single answer may be externally validated as "best." The sole means of validating this type of decision is whether it achieves consensus. These situations relate to the type of task that may be uniquely labeled the "group task." A group decision, because of the assembly effect, will undoubtedly be superior to the decision made by even the most competent group member working as an individual.

CHAPTER OUTLINE

GROUP STRUCTURATION

FEEDBACK RESPONSES

MESSAGES AS STRUCTURE

NETWORKS

   Characteristics of Networks
   Gatekeeping

SOCIAL STRUCTURE

COMMUNICATION BARRIERS AND
   BREAKDOWNS

NONVERBAL COMMUNICATION
   AND GROUP STRUCTURE

   Proxemic Behavior

SUMMARY

KEY TERMS

STRUCTURATION

COMMUNICATION NETWORKS

FEEDBACK

NETWORK SIZE

REACHABILITY

DENSITY

CENTRALITY

GATEKEEPING

LINKING PIN

STAR

BOUNDARY SPANNING

PROXEMIC

KINESIC

PARALINGUISTIC

PERSONAL SPACE

TERRITORIALITY

SPATIAL ECOLOGY

SOCIOPETAL

SOCIOFUGAL

Structural Elements of Group Communication

This chapter will focus on some important structural elements of groups. Actually, most of this book is devoted to functional elements of groups because communication is so central to group behavior. In Chapter 4 we focus on functions of group communication and downplay the structural dimension. But in this chapter we examine a few topics that are pertinent to group structure.

You should recall from Chapter 1 that we discussed groups as social systems characterized by structure, function, and evolution. At that time we emphasized that structure referred to spatial relationships; in other words, the structure of something is how its component parts are arranged in space. Figure 1-1 depicted the structure of an organization. It illustrated the shape and pattern of an organizational system. Although group structure refers to relatively stable patterns of relationships, this does not mean that these patterns are always the same. It is only realistic to realize that group structures change with the evolution of the group. So we begin the chapter with a brief introduction to a theory about how groups organize their structures, and make use of them to accomplish their goals.

GROUP STRUCTURATION

We know a fair amount about how humans develop individually. We know, for example, that each individual selects and interprets information from the vast quantity of data available in the environment. But some aspects of information processing are unique to the group—that is, to the social process (or social system) of group decision making. Group members control their own behavior, within the constraints of other forces. Groups must work within an environment, deal with internal group rules and structures, and accommodate their members' behavior.

While there are many theories of individual cognitive processing, there are relatively few theories of group social processing. Poole, Siebold, and McPhee (1986) and Poole (1992) have been working out a theory called group *structuration*. This theory is concerned with how groups develop by making use of certain rules and resources. It recognizes that groups are always in the process of changing and processing information and that every act of communication influences the group in some way and thus affects its decision-making process. These influences might be trivial at times, but they are significant at other times. For example, a significant problem frequently encountered by groups is how to deal with inconsistent information. A jury, for instance, must decide which witness to believe when the plaintiff's and defendant's witnesses contradict one another's testimony; even while individual jurors might have a way to resolve the apparent contradictions, the group as a whole must process all the input.

The structurational theory of how groups process and structure information begins by assuming that the decision-making processes in groups are primarily patterns of interaction and relationships (an assumption that we make throughout this book). The theory then examines how group members use rules and resources. *Rules* are statements about how things ought to be done, such as about how to behave in the group, what the group expects, and what certain terminology means; the rules guide and explain the communicative behaviors of the group members (e.g., if one of the group's rules is to behave politely, the members will communicate accordingly). *Resources* are materials and attributes the group can use, such as special knowledge, money, status, equipment, and relationships. The members use the rules and resources as their "tools" of interaction, and each group is unique in that it develops its own rules and resources.

In addition to being guided by its rules and resources, each group is also influenced by its external environment. For example, if a group is assigned a task but is not given enough time or information, it will not be able to structure and process information. Earlier in this chapter we examined some principles of group systems, such as structure, function, and evolution; we also described groups as open systems characterized by feedback processes. As a group evolves over time, it structures itself. In other words, the group employs the rules and resources of interaction that account for its behavior. Each group has its own ways of handling information and using rules and resources, but all groups are also influenced by things they cannot control. Group *structure* is the result of the tension between internal decisions and external constraints.

Let's consider briefly how groups might structure themselves in such a way as to make nonrational decisions. Groups must interpret and utilize a lot of information, and in doing so they make many judgments. Often these judgments are made on nonrational bases; that is, in the language of structuration, groups apply *rules* that lead to nonrational behavior. One rule for group information processing compares a piece of new information with the previously established position of the group. The group's previously established position is a resource; it is something the group uses. One counter-productive rule that groups often employ is that if a new item of information contradicts the group's previously established position, the new information is rejected out of hand. At such times the members consider the information irrelevant or of inferior quality, whether it is or not. Thus, group members treat the information nonrationally. They reject the information first; then they search for a basis for rejecting it (their previously held position) and use that to rationalize a judgment they have already made.

The importance of timing as a resource is also apparent in the above example. The point at which information is introduced is sometimes more important than the quality of the information itself. If the information is introduced after the group has already established an ideational position, the quality of this information might have little impact on the process of group decision making.

Structuration is concerned with how groups develop structures and how these structures change over time. Groups use rules and resources but they also appropriate the structures of other social systems for their own use. Group members take their own information and knowledge about how to work in groups (this information is a resource) and they adapt that information to create their own version of how their group should operate. The principle of majority rule, for example, is well understood by most members of our society. When groups adopt the principle of majority rule, they are appropriating a structure for their own use. Groups make mistakes, however, when they uncritically adopt other structures. If an eleven-member group takes a vote on an issue and the vote is 6 to 5, it can invoke majority rule and implement the decision selected by the majority. But it can count on having problems, because just about half the members disagreed with the decision. Half the group will not be supportive and committed to the decision. The automatic and mechanical acceptance of a majority rule principle will not serve this eleven-member group well. It should continue its discussion and decision-making process until there is an acceptable consensus.

According to Poole (1992) there are three primary factors that influence the process of structuring a group. The first is *member characteristics*. Group members differ in many ways. Those who are well informed and highly motivated will use structures in different ways than others do. Someone who wants to control the group will try to alter the group's procedures to his or her benefit. A group member who wants control, for example, will have different interpretations of how leadership should function in the group. The controlling member will encourage strong leadership if he is the leader, and weaker leadership authority if another group member is the leader.

External factors are a second influence on group structure. These, as mentioned above, are simply factors that the group has less control over: group size, task, resources available, network structure, environmental limitations, etc.

The third influence on group structure is the *dynamics* of the group. In other words, how the group actually uses its rules and resources. For instance, the members might contradict themselves. They might espouse democracy but practice tyranny. This will create a tension that will result in conflict and an assortment of other problems. Groupthink results when group members have the intellectual resources to question information, but fail to do so because of social pressures. Here they are not *using* their resources properly.

The structuration process is interesting and important, and we will encounter it again in Chapter 7.

FEEDBACK RESPONSES

Most of us understand the concept of feedback as a response (or reaction) to a previously transmitted message. You send a message to another person. This message travels along a channel to the other person, who, in turn, receives it and responds to it; that is, the receiver reacts. The receiver "feeds back" information to you, which you then interpret as feedback because you interpret it as response to your previously transmitted message. And the cycle continues indefinitely, or at least as long as you continue to interact with the other person.

We also typically think of feedback responses as very significant during a communicative event. More realistically, however, we should consider feedback as inevitable. Regardless of which perspective is used to understand the nature of communication, one cannot avoid making a feedback response (Haslett and Ogilvie, 1992). For example, if you are waiting in line at a supermarket checkout counter, you are often surrounded by strangers; nevertheless, you and all the other shoppers are involved in a common situation—waiting in line.

Assume that a stranger in front of you turns to you and remarks, "They sure are slow at this time of day, aren't they?" Your response to this statement is inevitably a feedback response. You have numerous responses available to you:

1. You could agree and respond by saying, "They sure are."
2. You could disagree, offering a statement such as "Oh, I don't know. The line seems to be moving rather quickly, even though they are quite busy."
3. You could be noncommittal or perhaps even change the subject—"I hate standing in line" or "I'm in a hurry" or "That other checkout counter seems to be moving faster."
4. You could ignore the original statement by turning or looking away from your new acquaintance.

Whatever you choose to do in responding to the stranger's initial statement, you are engaged in providing a feedback response. Even your attempt to ignore the other person and not engage in communication is a feedback response.

The fact is that you are involved in that communicative event, that common situation, whether you want to be involved or not. Even the fourth response (ignoring the other person) is a feedback response. You have, in essence, said to the stranger, "I'm not interested in continuing this communication. I don't wish to speak with you." Your behavior, both verbal and nonverbal, is a feedback response that conveys information to the other person about yourself, about that other person, and about your relationship to each other. Even your attempt to ignore the other person leads to some interpretation. The stranger may consider you something of a snob, an unfriendly person. The relationship is not likely to be interpreted as a desirable one or to be continued. Furthermore, the other person's self-concept may be damaged to some small extent. He or she may wonder whether body odor or bad breath has provoked your antisocial reaction.

Since a feedback response is inevitable within a communicative event, the common notion of one-way or two-way communication would appear to be of limited usefulness or importance—at least when one is talking about communication in a face-to-face setting. Once two or more people are involved in a common social situation—even strangers who are standing in line together at a supermarket checkout counter—any behavior by any of them is potentially communicative. Furthermore, any behavior by a person after receiving a source's message is naturally interpreted as a feedback response. For purposes of communication and the group process, communication is inevitably and inherently two-way and all behavior following another person's behavior is a feedback response. Thus, feedback responses are constantly occurring throughout the interaction among group members.

One's self-concept, or one's beliefs and attitudes about self, also develop through communicating with others. Every person is constantly receiving new information, which then serves to validate or invalidate one's own beliefs and self-concepts. Every feedback response provides some information to the source of his or her self-concept. Such responses provide information about how others view us.

We do not mean to imply that every statement or feedback response that is received always contains specific information about self. Rather, information that is conveyed to the source must be interpreted. If you disagreed with the person in the checkout line at the supermarket, that may have had an effect on the person's self-concept. For example, that person may have had a friendly, outgoing self-image and taken pride in having the ability to relate to other people very well. Your disagreement (or, even worse, your failure to answer) may have damaged this self-concept or cast it into doubt.

One of the problems in interpreting feedback responses is to determine how honest or authentic those feedback responses are. How sincere is the person who is providing the feedback response? Is the other person merely trying to "make us feel good" while actually masking or hiding true feelings? Some people may believe that all feedback responses should always be honest, genuine, and reflect "true" feelings if the communication is to be effective. If we reflect upon such a belief for a moment, however, we will probably not accept it as a universal principle. In a situation in which a genuine feedback response might be harmful to another person, we often provide a response that is less than authentic—in reality, a lie. Often those dishonest feedback responses occur because we do not wish to hurt anyone's feelings unnecessarily. In other words, we often consider our friendly relationship with the other person more important than the honesty of our feedback responses.

What if a play directed by a friend of yours was terrible? The actors were awful, as was the stage movement, and the pace was agonizingly slow. In short, the play failed miserably. Nevertheless, talking with your friend after the performance, you told him what a fine play it was and how much you enjoyed seeing his production of a well-written drama. If in reply to his "How did you like the performance?" you had given him a truly honest feedback response, his feelings may have been hurt. More important for you, he may have wondered about the future of what was until then a friendly relationship. Your dishonest response may thus have been a compliment, not so much to his directorial abilities as to his status as a friend. You valued the relationship more than you valued the principle of honest and authentic feedback response.

The stronger the relationship, the more valuable the feedback responses. The closer the ties of interpersonal liking (cohesiveness) among members of a group, the more honest and authentic these responses will be. Typically, feedback responses among close friends will include more negative evaluations than will the responses among acquaintances, although many positive responses will also occur during the interaction among friends. One might summarize this discussion by suggesting that the most effective feedback responses occur in groups or social relationships which are strong and in which the interactants like one another. On the other hand, honest and authentic feedback responses do not necessarily cause or lead to interpersonal liking. Rather, because persons like each other, they are more likely to be more authentic. That is, interpersonal liking allows for the probability of more authentic and genuinely honest feedback responses.

Nearly everyone is familiar with the process of response reinforcement in the familiar sense of psychological "conditioning." We are all aware of Pavlov's classical experiments in which the dogs were conditioned to salivate at the ringing of a bell, even without the presence of food. All of us are "conditioned" throughout our lives in the sense that we have been trained to act in ways that are appropriate to our culture. We have been taught to say "Please" and "Thank you," to eat with a fork, etc. This acculturation into our society, in which we learn manners and other appropriate behavior is, in a way, a certain kind of conditioning. After all, we were rewarded when we remembered the appropriate action and were punished when we failed to behave in the socially approved manner.

Conditioning, however, is not the major thrust of this discussion. Rather, we are more concerned with feedback responses. But feedback responses may reinforce the behaviors that precede them. That is, our reactions or responses may or may not be favorable to the preceding comment. We may nod, smile, say "Uh-huh," "I agree," or "Yes," or express approval in some other way. On the other hand, our feedback response may be negative and may express disapproval. We may shake our heads, scowl, or say "No," "I disagree," and so forth. When we express disapproval through our feedback responses, these responses tend to inhibit or extinguish that behavior. In this way, we have punished the other person. When our feedback responses express approval, they tend to enhance or encourage continuation of that behavior—positive reinforcement. Therefore, a feedback response may serve as a positive reinforcement of the preceding behavior, or as a punishment for it, making it less likely in the future.

Many people fear the potential effects of such reinforcement patterns when the power to condition members of a society is in the hands of an unscrupulous leader or tyrant. We fear being manipulated or controlled or even "brainwashed" by a government, an advertising agency, or a group leader. We are all too aware of the fictional accounts of some futuristic society of conformists who are conditioned to accept the will of some "big brother." Books and movies such as *1984* and *Road Warrior* depict the future in depressing and apocalyptic terms. We worry about being "conditioned" by violence on television or by manipulative advertising that will control our buying and even our voting habits. In short, our society suffers from a rather irrational fear of the alleged power of psychological conditioning.

Of course, the human being is not a machine and is not so easily manipulated or so easily conditioned as the writers of fiction would have us believe. Basically, human beings are very obstinate. They can decide what messages to receive, what messages to believe or disbelieve, what messages to remember, and what portions of messages to receive, remember, distort, and revise. In short, the control over the message (and over feedback responses too) lies in the hands of the receiver.

The discussion of group norms in Chapter 7 will emphasize the tremendous power that the social unit of the group has over its individual members. At the same time, however, the discussion will illustrate the capacity of the individual members to shape the formation and the function of the group. Feedback responses certainly do affect our behavior, and through feedback responses we also affect other people's behavior—but we must keep in mind that feedback responses (as attempts to influence) can be, and often are, successfully resisted by the receivers of these responses. In Chapter 4, the discussion of feedback as a more functional (rather than purely structural) aspect of communication will also emphasize feedback as means of "control," although in a much different sense. In both cases, however, we need to keep in mind that feedback as reinforcement is only an *attempt* to control and cannot be an omnipotent influence on defenseless and unsuspecting human beings.

MESSAGES AS STRUCTURE

When people communicate, they exchange messages with one another. One person encodes a message and directs it to another person, who decodes the message, provides some understanding or interpretation of it, and then encodes a message in response. In this way, communication occurs as the messages flow back and forth between the sources and the receivers (i.e., between the members of the group). In this framework of communication, a message is a structural phenomenon; that is, it is conceptualized as some *thing* that is transmitted across space on a channel and received at another point in space. This mechanistic framework emphasizes the structural elements of communication, in which the message and the channel are indeed the central elements.

From such a mechanistic view of communication, it seems reasonable to think of effective, or "good," communication as the exchange of "good" messages. If a lady tells a new acquaintance that she is a faculty member in a university department of communication, the acquaintance is likely to respond with something like "I'd better watch what I say." Conventional wisdom dictates that the messages we transmit and receive carry certain characteristics that render them desirable, effective, or otherwise "good." A structural approach to messages in group communication therefore includes those attributes (or characteristics or qualities) which a "good" message has.

Haslett and Ogilvie (1992, p. 352) offer a list of eight suggestions for giving feedback in group discussions. They offer these eight as desirable characteristics of messages—characteristics that can be used to improve contributions to group interaction. These characteristics are:

1. Be specific and clear
2. Support comments with evidence
3. Separate the issues from the people
4. Soften negative messages
5. Sandwich negative messages between positive ones
6. Pose the situation as a mutual problem
7. Use good timing
8. Use a proper manner of delivery

You should note that not all these characteristics refer to the structural elements of messages themselves. For example, a message is "specific" only if it can be compared with the earlier messages during the group discussion and thus be seen to be more specific. Also, "Pose the situation as a mutual problem" is more an attitude of the people than something contained in a message. Further, a message is "softened" only to the extent that the receiver interprets the message that way; if subsequent discussions continue the train of thought contained in the softened message, one could assume that the message may have provoked it. It is difficult, however, to determine structurally if any message is softened at the time it is first uttered.

The most important of these eight characteristics may be "Use good timing." As later chapters on the group process consistently illustrate, what is said, how it is said, and even who says it may not be nearly as significant to the group process and to effective decision making as *when* it is said. Therefore, it is difficult to determine whether any single message, in isolation, is structurally desirable or undesirable in terms of its characteristics alone. Only when the message is placed within its context of the ongoing group interaction can it be assessed as to its specificity, evidence, softness, and good or bad timing. Learning how to do this takes time.

There is also the matter of the "codability" of messages during group communication. The codability of messages is very similar to Haslett and Ogilvie's "clarity" characteristic. The important characteristic of the message is how easily it can interpreted by the receiver. On the other hand, it is difficult to think of the meaning of a message being contained *in* the message. Rather, we typically tend to think of the meaning of messages as being within people—a property of the process of interpretation. We have even coined clichés which say that meaning is located within the person and not in the message—"Meaning is perception" and "Words don't mean; people do." Phrased another way, the meaning of the message is *assigned* by the human interpreter and does not exist in the coded message itself. Nevertheless, a message may be encoded in such a manner as to increase the likelihood that it will be interpreted quickly, easily, and in a manner similar to the meaning intended by the source.

Messages during group communication are often highly ambiguous or unclear; that is, they have low codability. Members of groups frequently appear to be very tolerant of these ambiguous messages and do not often seek clarification of them. Naturally, ambiguous messages have communicative advantages as well as obvious disadvantages. In terms of the disadvantages, an ambiguous message may drastically affect the efficiency of group conversation in the sense that members may argue at length before discovering that they have been in agreement all along but have been unaware of that fact because they were using messages of low clarity or low codability. The same can be true of a group in apparent agreement on an ambiguous issue, although there may be much disagreement that remains unexposed because of a lack of sufficient clarity.

On the other hand, ambiguous messages often occur early in a group's interaction history and are used by the group members as a means of coping with the group's decision-making task—that is, with the problem to be solved. As Chapter 5 will show, highly ambiguous messages (i.e., messages whose codability or clarity is low) are neither "good" nor "bad" in and of themselves. There are times when such messages are quite typical of, and beneficial to, the making of decisions by a group. At other times during the group process, however, they may be quite inappropriate and detrimental to the group's decision-making efforts.

Eisenberg (1984) makes the very interesting argument that ambiguity can be used strategically and to the benefit of the communicator. In short, it is simply naive to assume that clarity is the norm and the responsibility of the speaker. Some particularly skilled group members are not only unclear, but purposefully so. Sometimes vagueness or lack of clarity can head off conflict; groups often have to juggle many purposes, and there are fewer chances for conflict and tension when some things are vague. Groups can also benefit from general rather than specific goals because they allow for flexibility and change. Pacanowsky and O'Donnel-Trujillo (1983) show that interpersonal relationships in groups and organizations are close, but not too close. Many people in groups form valuable and positive relationships with other group members that facilitate the work they must do, but these same people also keep some distance. Ambiguous messages permit the expression of thoughts and feelings but also allow for deniability. In a very interesting way, ambiguity allows a person both general and specific interpretation. Someone can say, "I don't feel very good about this group," and then deny a specific interpretation of this utterance, such as "You mean you don't like the other group members?" Ambiguity in this case makes for the expression of feelings while at the same time saving face.

NETWORKS

Examining communication networks is the most common structural approach to understanding communication among individuals in the group. Most people are familiar with networks in terms of highways, telephone lines, and water pipes, but interpersonal communication networks in groups are composed of more abstract communicative behavior and are sometimes more difficult to understand. *Communication networks are regular patterns of person-to-person contact that are typically characterized by the exchange of information between humans* (Monge, 1987, p. 243). By observing who talks to whom and what information is connected to which people, we can infer a communication network. Alba (1982) notes that group networks are composed of patterns of contact and communication among people who interact more with each other than with members of larger networks. Groups are very often defined according to what networks emerge.

Since groups typically exist within organizations, it is possible to think of organizations as a collection of connected groups. Figure 3-1 is an example of various subgroups within an organization and how these groups are all interconnected to each other and perhaps to an individual. Each of the groups in Figure 3-1 strives to contribute to a collective goal. Organizations try to develop work networks that make for efficient communication and work, but of course they do not always achieve such efficiency. The messages that flow through the network should facilitate each other's activities and maintain proper information flow. When organizations reorganize and change group structures and reporting lines, they are essentially redefining networks.

All groups and organizations have *formal* networks; that is, clearly stated and established patterns of exchanges. The organizational chart is an example of the formal organizational network structure. This network explains how things are "supposed" to work. But the *informal* networks are equally important and interesting. Two secretaries may have no formal relationship in an organization but they will exchange information over lunch. Person *E* in the subgroup at the far right of Figure 3-1 is formally connected only to person *D*. Perhaps *E* is an employee supervised by *D*. But *E* might live near Person *C* or anyone else in the network system. Their children may be members of the

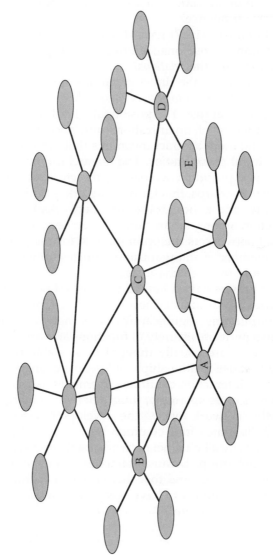

FIGURE 3-1 Interconnected networks in an organization.

same sports team and persons *E* and *C* chat about the company while sitting in the stands. The contents of this conversation might find its way into the company. You have probably heard of the "old boy" network. This is another example of an informal group network that does not appear on the organizational chart. The "old boys" are usually people in influential positions who have been around an organization for a long time. They meet informally and exercise considerable influence.

Monge and Eisenberg (1987) have described three major approaches to networks: the relational, positional, and cultural approaches. Our primary concern, however, is with the *relational* approach. Group networks are relational in that they focus on the direct communicative connections between members of a network; the emphasis is on describing the network and identifiying who is in what role. The positional school is concerned more with the hierarchical structure of organizations and society, while the cultural school focuses on the more abstract meanings that are transmitted throughout society and cultural communities. The hierarchical network of an organization (president, vice president, managers, directors, etc.) exists before the formation of particular groups; this formal network is typically established by an outside authority, and although informal networks may arise during the process of interaction among organizational members, the organization recognizes the formal network as the optimum one for the group's task performances. When a member of an organization utilizes formal channel linkages, it is often called going through channels.

But discussion groups have a limited established network. There may be some members who are designated leaders, for example, but over time the process of communicating significantly alters networks and allows the group's members to perform a variety of functions and occupy many roles. So even though networks are usually thought of as stable relationships, they change over time because relationships and people change. Nevertheless, as the process of group interaction continues, members use some linkages very frequently and others quite sparingly; thus, a network emerges during group interaction, and this network reflects the developing social structure of the group. Figure 3-2 illustrates four common networks that may emerge in a five-member group. (The all-channel network is a theoretical possibility, but it rarely describes actual groups because it implies that every possible interpersonal channel linkage is used and that there is equal channel usage. It is not uncommon for group members to have access to others (links), but it is rare that all links receive equal usage.)

Characteristics of Networks

There are some interesting concepts that apply to group networks. They are relatively easy to understand and to measure, so they can be very useful for beginning group analyses. The most common network measurements are size, reachability, density, and centrality (Tichy, 1981).

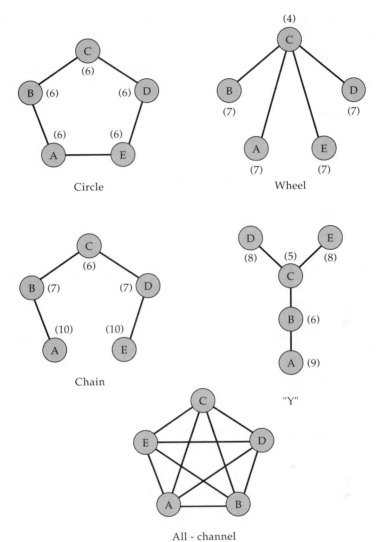

FIGURE 3-2 Common networks in five-member groups.

Network size simply refers to the number of people to which a person is linked. It is possible to establish the size of an individual's network and the size of the network as a whole. In the wheel configuration in Figure 3-2, member *C* is linked directly to four people, so his network size would be 4. Member *B* is linked only to one, so his individual network size is smaller, 1. In terms of the entire network, the wheel is "smaller" than the all-channel network because it has fewer linkages.

Reachability is the number of links it takes to connect one individual to another. In the wheel network, *C* is very "reachable" by *B* because they are directly linked, but *D* is less reachable by *B* because *B* must go through two links. On the network level, reachability is the average number of links separating people. Persons *A* and *E* in the chain network have low reachability because they must go through so many others. The numbers in parentheses in Figure 3-2 refer to the total number of links a person must go through to reach everyone in the network. The number *10* above person *A* in the chain network means that the sum of all the links to everyone in the network is *10*. This may sound momentarily confusing, but if you count up the links you can see where the numbers come from: *A* must go through one link to reach *B*, two links to reach *C*, three links to reach *D*, and four links to reach *E*, and $1 + 2 + 3 + 4 = 10$. Compare that to the reachability of *C* in the wheel; person *C* can reach everyone quite easily. The average reachability in the chain is higher than that in any of the other networks.

Density is related to reachability. It indicates the number of linkages that exist in proportion to the number that would exist if everyone were linked directly. In the all-channel network, everyone has reachability; this network is also dense because of the possible 10 linkages. Your personal network is dense if you are directly connected to a lot of people.

Centrality is a frequently studied concept. Every member of the network is assigned a centrality figure on the basis of how close he or she is to all other members of the network. The most central person is the one with the *fewest* links between everyone else. Thus, the parenthetical numbers in Figure 3-2 indicate centrality; they show which person has the most "betweenness," or lies on the shortest path between others. Person *C* in the wheel network is the most central because everyone else must go through *C* to reach any other member of the network.

Using various points of comparison, studies comparing communication networks have revealed many differences between the types of networks. In terms of speed and efficiency, for example, centralized networks (such as the wheel and the chain) are found to be superior to decentralized networks (such as the circle, the least centralized). But this finding is tempered by a further comparison in terms of problem-solving accuracy: *Centralized networks* solve simple problems most accurately; *decentralized networks* are more accurate in solving complex problems. In terms of group morale, the members of decentralized networks experience greater satisfaction with their group experiences than do members of groups employing a centralized network. In short, whereas centralized networks are considered superior in terms of accomplishing tasks (at least simple ones), decentralized networks foster more cohesive groups and appear to have an advantage in performing more complex tasks.

The structural view of communication networks does contribute to the understanding of the group process in many respects. For instance, the concept of centrality has consistently been related to leadership and status. The most central position in an emergent network is most apt to be the position occupied by the emergent leader, and the various levels of centrality generally reflect the status levels of the group's hierarchy. Figure 3-2 illustrates two status levels (level of centrality) in the wheel network; the relative centrality of C is 4, and the relative centrality of all other positions is 7. Three status levels are reflected in the chain network; C is the apparent leader with a relative centrality of 6, B and D occupy the second status level with relative centralities of 7, and A and E occupy the third status level with centrality figures of 10. The "Y" network illustrates four status levels, a rather uncommon status hierarchy to emerge in a five-member group. Only the circle network has a single status level, and this is an extremely improbable network to emerge in a decision-making group.

The network that finally emerges from extensive group interaction is not the only network employed by the group during the process of decision making. A group may employ one network at one stage of the process and shift to a different network later on as the group enters a new phase of the process. In this respect, centrality does not necessarily reflect leadership or even high status during the intermediate stages of the group process.

For example, the verbally active "problem member" may at some point during interaction be the recipient of influence from every other member verbally attempting to modify the problem behavior. During this period of group interaction, the network would probably show the deviate in position C in the wheel network—a highly central position. This network, showing a problem member in a central position, would undoubtedly be temporary, for a problem member or extreme deviate who does not modify his or her behavior will eventually be ignored by the others and excluded from their interactions. Such action virtually expels the extreme deviate from the network and from effective group membership. Therefore, while centrality is often linked to that leadership and status in the network which finally emerges from group interaction, during intermediate stages in the process of group decision making it may also indicate an extreme deviate under group pressure to conform.

Another stage of network development involves the coalitions or subgroups formed during various phases in the group decision-making process. The network used at that time generally reflects the existence of coalitions. To illustrate, the "Y" network might reflect the presence of two coalitions, one composed of three members (C, D, and E) and the other composed of two members (A and B.) We might hypothesize further that each coalition has formed around its own contender for leadership; the two most central positions, B and C, would then represent these two contenders.

No discussion of the network structures of group communication would be complete without a comment about the limited number of networks described above. There are obviously more possible network combinations than the four (omitting the all-channel network) shown in Figure 3-2, but the other combinations are simply variations of these basic models. For example, the wheel and chain networks can be combined by adding to the wheel network two additional channel linkages between A and B and between D and E. The same network can be formed from the chain network by adding channel links between *A* and *C* and between *A* and *E*. This wheel-chain network is thus a network formed by combining channel linkages included in two of the basic network models.

Further variations should be obvious. The important points are that emergent network structures can be observed in a small group and that these structures provide insight into various aspects of the group's decision-making process.

People working in large organizations usually have strong ties to their primary groups. This means that they are most committed to the people they work with daily, and that they are suspicious of members of other networks in the organization. Often members of different groups are competing for budgets and resources. Even if an entire company is working toward a collective goal, smaller groups within the company protect their own interests and work more vigorously for their group goals than for the more generalized organizational goals. One way for management to foster cooperative relationships between competing groups is to establish policies that structurally require various subgroups to interact. In Figure 3-1 the group at the far right led by person *D* is structurally connected to the group at the far left led by person *B*. Person *C* in the middle is called a *linking pin* because he or she connects one group network to another. This keeps the flow of information moving back and forth and gives at least one person (person *C*) a broad perspective on the issues pertinent to both groups. Like all central individuals in a network, linking pin individuals have status, influence, and of course, "good connections."

A final point to remember about network structures concerns the nature of processes. Interactional patterns change through time as the group moves from one phase to another in the decisional process. Network structures also change. Because changes in structure reflect changes in process, the developing structure of the network can be viewed as an emergent process that changes over time and culminates in the final, emergent network characterizing the group's status hierarchy. Thus, a network's attributes are not purely structural (spatial), but include attributes of action (time).

Gatekeeping

Viewing communication structurally (as the transmission and reception of messages on a channel) reveals a further characteristic of communication. The networks illustrated in Figure 3-2 provide a graphic depiction of the concept of *gatekeeping*. You will note, for example, that some group members in each of those networks (except for the all-channel network) do not communicate directly with every other member of the group. In the wheel network the person occupying position *B* does not communicate directly with the member occupying position *D*. Rather, *B* exchanges messages with the member in position *C*, who, in turn, exchanges messages with *D*. Member *C*, in all networks except the all-channel network, is the intermediary (or link) in a chain of communication channels between members *B* and *D*. That is, *B* communicates with D only through C's intermediation in the circle, wheel, chain, and "Y" networks.

The member who occupies that middle link in the network is in a position of greater centrality. In the "Y" and chain networks, for example, member B is the gatekeeper between A and C. In the chain network, member D is a gatekeeper between C and E. In the wheel network, member C is the gate-keeper between every possible pair of members—A and B, A and D, A and E, B and D, B and E, and D and E. In other words, all messages sent and received in the wheel network are transmitted either to or by the group member who occupies position C. For this reason, the wheel network is the most centralized network of all.

It seems reasonable, then, that a gatekeeper is a person who occupies a position of considerable potential influence. This member receives more mes-sages from more different sources than members who are in less central positions in the network. Given this informational advantage over other group members, a gatekeeper (in the sense of a centralized position in a small group network) often becomes a group leader or at least a member with above-average influence. The concept of leadership will be discussed in more detail in Chapter 8.

The gatekeeping role in classroom groups may also be a factor in activities that occur outside the face-to-face situation. Therefore, gatekeeping is not readily apparent in the actual group meetings during the performance of its decision-making task. One classroom group, in particular, contained one member—Marilyn—who performed an important gatekeeping role, but this role was apparent only in situations outside the face-to-face meetings of the group. Marilyn was neither a leader nor a particularly high contributor during the group's discussions at its meetings. Nevertheless, she, probably more than any other single member, was responsible for the group's successful decision-making performance.

Marilyn's group had a problem. The problem was Carol. Carol proved to be quite irresponsible in her interactions with the group. She was often absent from the meetings, usually with a legitimate excuse (employment and other classroom pressures). But reasons for absences from group meetings are of little concern to a functioning group. Quite reasonably, the other group members resented Carol's absences because she was not doing her part to help the group do its work—a task that placed it under considerable time pressure. Regardless of the legitimacy of Carol's absences, the other group members found themselves having to assume a heavier burden in the group's task efforts. Carol just didn't accept her share of the group's responsibility. Moreover, she also had what appeared to be a personality conflict with a few of the group members, a conflict that probably stemmed from a disagreement over proper social behavior.

During the meetings that Carol did attend, her contributions were not frequent and were not directed to any one member of the group more than others. When she was unable to attend the meetings, she consistently con-tacted Marilyn outside class meetings, often giving her material to bring to the meetings. Soon Marilyn was the person who spoke for Carol during group meetings and who explained Carol's absences or reported on her progress. In other words, Marilyn became the gatekeeper between Carol and the group members. While the others resented Carol's lack of commitment to the group, they considered Marilyn to be a valuable member. Through Marilyn, they came to accept Carol as a member of what developed into a rather cohesive group.

When gatekeeping occurs in the exchange of messages in a group, communication is mediated in the sense that communication between a source and a receiver "goes through" a mediator. On the level of an entire society, we often refer to this phenomenon of mediated communication when thinking of the mass media—radio, television, newspapers. Our mass media serve as the go-between for informational sources and the larger society—us, the consumers of information. Mediated communication is thus rather efficient in terms of mass information processing. Too many data are available in our informational environment for us to process or consume them all—that is, to interpret all the data as meaningful information. The gatekeeper plays a structural role that reduces considerably the quantity of data available. By relaying information to the receiver, the gatekeeper converts much data into a manageable amount of information and typically conveys this information in a more understandable form.

Gatekeepers have an awesome responsibility. They must make many crucial decisions before relaying or retransmitting the messages. For example, should information be transmitted in the same manner and the same form in which it is received? Often, relaying identical information is quite impossible. There is simply too much of it to be relayed. The gatekeeper must then reclassify the information into larger "chunks." At this point, the selectivity of the gatekeeper becomes highly significant. The mass media, and particularly newspaper and television news reporters, have often been accused of allowing their biases to dictate what information they select and retransmit to the public.

Gatekeepers have no choice but to exercise their selective processes. They must recognize, interpret, and then retransmit information. The gatekeeper who uses the selective processes adequately is called objective—as in the "objective news reporter." More often, however, the objectivity of a news reporter is determined by the extent to which the information received is consistent with the biases of the reporter in the gatekeeping position. But before we hasten to condemn, keep in mind that this use of the selectivity processes in information processing is quite normal.

When the person in a gatekeeping position must deal with information that exceeds his or her capacity to store and retrieve information, the result is called *information overload*. Information overload is more of a problem in a large-scale organization (which would involve many more people and much more information in various forms—for example, written memoranda, oral conversations, formal letters, market reports, sales reports) than it is in a small group. The face-to-face interaction of a decision-making group would normally use information in the same limited forms—verbal and nonverbal speech.

Furthermore, as Chapter 5 will discuss, groups soon develop methods of coping with too much information. They handle many different pieces of information for very brief periods of time rather than simultaneously discussing the same items over a long period. Information overload, then, is rarely a problem during small-group decision making, although it may be a significant problem within a large organization. Most important, overload occurs not throughout the entire group or organization, but at a specific point or position in the network, and this position must be relatively central—that is, a gatekeeping position.

An interesting concept related to the gatekeeping process is *boundary spanning*. A boundary spanner is a person who communicates and processes information *between* networks. In organizations, it is the person within the organization who communicates with the environment and influences the flow of information from the organization to the environment and back again (Adams, 1980). The chief executive officer of a company is often a boundary spanner, and his or her skill in representing the company to the community, and the community to the company, is an important part of the job. Marilyn in the above example was a boundary spanner; she could move between the network boundaries of the group and the environment. Boundary spanners act like gatekeepers because they have access to information that is usually unavailable to other members of their group. Like a media gatekeeper, they select and transmit information that less well-informed people should have.

There are three types of highly connected individuals, but only one of the three is a boundary spanner (Tuchman and Scanlan, 1981). The first is called an *internal star*. This person is well-connected within an organization or group. This might be a person in your group who knows everyone well and can reach the right person at the right time; he or she is well-connected , but not a boundary spanner. The second type of well-connected person is an *external star*. This person has primary contact with people who are external to a group. The third type, a *boundary spanner*, is well-connected both internally and externally and translates knowledge from one network to the other. If you are a member of a group that must deal with other groups, and if one person in your group communicates with the other group and then carries that information back to your group, this person is spanning the boundaries of the two networks.

Boundary spanners are very important people in corporations. Because they work in a multitude of information environments, they have access to many ideas and types of data. Moreover, they are the people an organization turns to when it needs influence with some component of the environment.

SOCIAL STRUCTURE

The social structure of roles and status levels in a group also affects the communication among the group members. The members communicate with one another in different patterns and networks, depending to some extent on the status levels (such as leader and followers) in their group's social structure.

It is clear that the social structure in a group affects the structural aspects of its communication. Leaders and other high-status persons, for example, are major participators during group interaction, both as initiators and respondents of messages. Low-status members communicate a disproportionately large amount of their time with high-status members, thus affirming that network centrality is associated with leadership and status. The typical explanation for this structural phenomenon in the group's use of networks involves the individual member's desire to aspire to higher status. An individual who finds it impossible to rise to high status through his or her own achievements will substitute for actual status a vicarious membership in a higher status by communicating upward in the status hierarchy.

Certainly the status of the group member affects the messages that he or she initiates and receives. *Who* says it is as important to perceiving the relative importance of the message as *what* is said. Status endows a message with value. In the study of persuasion and attitude change, the credibility (or "ethos") of the communicator appears to be a significant factor in how people attend and react to persuasive messages. Thus, the communicative structure in a small group affects, and is affected by, the social structure of the group members. Communicative structure and social structure exert a mutual and reciprocal influence on each other and may therefore be considered interdependent.

COMMUNICATION BARRIERS AND BREAKDOWNS

If we describe communication as messages traveling through space from one person (a sender) to another (a receiver), then a *communication barrier* is a "dam" that blocks the flow of messages so the receiver cannot receive an initiated message. A *communication breakdown* assumes that the connecting link between communicating individuals ceases to exist—in the same sense as a broken telephone line. In any case, the concept of barriers and breakdowns depends on the idea that a linear flow of messages across space is the central feature of communication. The basic analogy of communication barriers and breakdowns is the machine in which a barrier (e.g., a clogged fuel line) or a breakdown (e.g., a broken fuel line) could certainly be said to exist. But keep in mind that communicators don't send and receive isolated messages; they engage in a process—the development and maintenance of relationships. And these relationships are defined by the recurrent, sequential patterns of messages in the context of the entire interaction. Communication as an interaction process does not really get blocked, nor does it break down. Can an interpersonal relationship be blocked or break down? In group communication the interpersonal relationship is groupness, interdependent with the process of group communication. As long as any vestige of groupness exists, communication continues to exist. A barrier or breakdown ignores the more important problem of ineffective communication.

Furthermore, Chapter 9 will demonstrate the normality of social conflict and deviance. If the flow of messages is central to group communication, social conflict and deviance must by definition be inherently disruptive. That is, conflict will lead to closed channels and communication barriers or breakdowns. But as we will see, that conflict is a positive force in groups.

Occasionally, members of an unsuccessful group believe that conflict is harmful and disruptive. Because of their belief, the members overtly avoid conflict until their tension level and suppressed hostility become so extreme that communication barriers and breakdowns do seem to exist. Such a group illustrates a classic example of the self-fulfilling prophecy in action. If group members believe that conflict is disruptive and harmful, they tend to behave as if it were and eventually succeed in disrupting effective group communication and harming the group process. To take too seriously the notion of communication barriers and breakdowns is to miss the point that all communication can be problematic. Emphasizing effective and ineffective communication is a much more valuable and beneficial way to think about communication.

Subsequent discussions in this book will emphasize the improvement of communicative effectiveness and the effectiveness of the group process. What you might otherwise have considered to be a communication breakdown, at least in terms of conventional wisdom will be treated as communication, but ineffective communication. Try to reconceptualize barriers and breakdowns and see them as a communicative process that is not operating adequately or effectively, but is working nevertheless.

NONVERBAL COMMUNICATION AND GROUP STRUCTURE

Members of groups usually attend to the words and intentional meanings of other group members. But the meanings of words and messages are also influenced by *nonverbal* communication—eye contact, pauses, gestures, intonation, spatial relationships, and the like. In this section we will consider the structural and functional aspects of nonverbal behavior. The next chapter will consider those aspects of nonverbal behavior which are part of the functional nature of communication. A functional approach to communication emphasizes what communication does, how it affects other people, and how messages function in groups, whereas a structural approach examines the physical and spatial forms that influence meanings and perceptions.

One way to describe the variety of possible nonverbal behaviors is to categorize them into three types:

1. *Proxemic behavior*   This how people are affected by spatial and distance orientations.
2. *Kinesic behavior (body motion)*   This includes gestures, body shifts, eye movements, facial expressions, and posture. These physical movements can be described structurally, but they are more usefully discussed as motions that accompany spoken words and modify verbal meanings.
3. *Paralinguistic qualities*   These include loudness, pitch, tone, and rate of speech. They are vocal qualities which have no dictionary meaning but which add to the interpretation of words.

We will now examine the fundamental structural issue in nonverbal communication in groups—proxemic behavior. Then, in Chapter 4, we will examine how the other two types of nonverbal communication help to clarify messages, orient speakers, and signal power and emotional states.

Proxemic Behavior

Proxemics is the study of the communicative use of space—the ways in which we use, arrange, and perceive physical space.

Have you ever had somebody stand too close to you and make you feel uncomfortable?

Have you ever been even slightly intimidated by someone who was taller than you, or have you intimidated someone who was smaller?

Have you ever noticed the difference between the arrangement of furniture in your living room and the organization of a classroom?

Have you ever placed your books or coat on a table to "save" a seat for yourself in the cafeteria or library?

If you have experienced any of these things, you have experienced the influence of proxemic patterns on your behavior. The spatial and distance orientations that group members maintain exert considerable influence on the flow and patterns of communication in the group. Communication is facilitated when the distances between people are comfortable, and it is hindered when we deviate from these comfortable distances, because the organization of space relates to some of our most fundamental human needs.

Territoriality and Personal Space   The possession of one's own territory is an example of a fundamental human need with respect to proxemics. *Territory* is space that you feel ownership toward; it is an area or object that you have rights to and defend accordingly. If you place your books and coat on a cafeteria table and then go off to get lunch, you will be surprised—and feel that your territory has been violated—if someone moves your books and sits down. Group members often claim territory for themselves. A chair or position at a table might be the territory of a particular group member, and tension can result if someone else invades this territory. Such tension is usually subtle and may appear as aggression later in the group discussion. But the very subtlety of such influences makes them more insidious, because they are less apparent and it is more difficult to identify the source of the problem.

In an interesting study, Taylor and Lanni (1981) wrote about what they called the "resident advantage." This is the advantage that accrues to the group or group member who is using space that he or she owns. You have undoubtedly heard of the "home-court advantage" in basketball and other sports. Individuals and teams simply perform better in space that they "own." The same is true for groups and their members. If a group has a favorite place to meet, such as a dorm room or library study room, then it will perform better if it continues to meet in its own "territory." Taylor and Lanni also found that individuals who host the group in their home or some other private location are more likely to communicate in a dominant manner; this is even true for group members who are not predisposed toward dominance. So the nature of physical space influences how group members feel about the group and themselves.

An idea related to territory is personal space. *Personal space* is that psychological outline of space around your body which you define as your own. If people or objects get too close and "violate" your personal space, you feel strange or uncomfortable. For instance, if a group member moves his or her chair too close to you and you feel awkward, then that group member has violated your personal space; as a result, you might feel anxious and withdraw from the discussion. The area around our bodies that constitutes personal space expands and contracts to meet the social needs of a situation; we keep this area wide in the presence of strangers, for example, but narrow it for intimate relationships. The anthropologist Edward T. Hall (1959) identified four categories of personal space and their corresponding social functions, and all four categories have implications for group behavior:

1. *Intimate distance* (0 to 8 inches) is for body contact and intimate relationships. Your group will probably not use this distance unless the group is composed of people who have very well developed, perhaps intimate, relationships. Children, who have yet to become socialized about personal distance, will often penetrate your intimate space. If some group members interact at such personal distances, they will probably make the other members nervous.
2. *Personal distance* ($1\frac{1}{2}$ to 4 feet) is the most typical interactional distance for friends and acquaintances. Touch is a little more difficult and less expected at this distance. Most groups interact within this zone.
3. *Social distance* (4 to 12 feet) is clearly out of the range of touch but allows us to recognize the other person. This distance is used for casual contact with strangers and for some business functions.
4. *Public distance* (12 feet and beyond) is for formal encounters, speeches,

platform presentations, and encounters with public officials. This is the distance at which groups can break up into smaller groups if they are not careful; people feel as if they cannot make contact with others at the outer edge of this zone, so they turn their attention to those around them.

These distance zones are useful and generally accurate, but other factors also influence how group members use personal space. Women, for example, sit closer to one another than men do because women are typically more involved in personal relationships and more receptive to symbolizing closeness. Groups consisting mostly of women interact differently than groups consisting mostly of men. The topic of conversation also influences the use of personal space; group members who are in a serious conversation about an important, impersonal topic related to the group's task tend to sit far apart, whereas they tend to sit to close together for intimate discussions.

Group Spatial Ecology   The area of proxemics that relates to the influences of physical space (such as furniture arrangements, architecture, doors, and walls) is called *group spatial ecology*. We seldom think about the influence of the physical environment, but it can dictate patterns of communication; it has a strong impact on which people we communicate with and on how we communicate. For instance, the living room in your family home is probably arranged for conversation and relaxation; there are comfortable chairs facing one another so that people can talk. A classroom, on the other hand, where the seats are arranged in rows, is designed so that everyone focuses attention on one place (the teacher) and conversation between students is more difficult (although they manage it). For the most part, groups should be concerned about arrangements that bring people together and facilitate face-to-face communication.

Environmental psychologists and communication theorists have been studying how various arrangements of space influence communication. Two basic types of arrangements are shown in Figure 3-3. Environmental arrangements that encourage contact and communication are called *sociopetal* arrangements. Living rooms and restaurants, for example, are designed to bring people together and to foster interaction; you can see in Figure 3-3 that the furniture forces people to face one another and limits the physical barriers between people. The tables in a restaurant or bar are the only space for food and drinks; the customers are therefore environmentally "pressured" to make contact with one another. Arrangements that keep people away from one another, discouraging communication, are called *sociofugal* arrangements. They separate people by turning them away from one another (e.g., back-to-back seating), placing greater distances between them, and using physical barriers to make contact difficult.

The effects of proxemics on small-group behavior have been examined in a number of studies, which find that it is possible to discourage or facilitate good group communication by manipulating proxemic variables. The physical environment either limits or extends the options and types of communica-

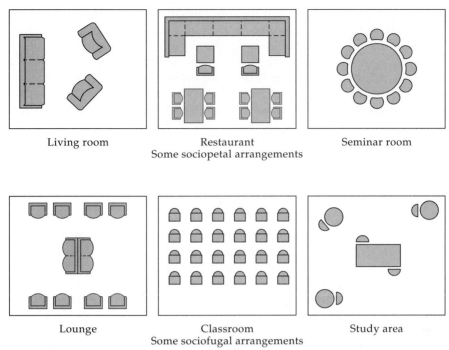

Living room   Restaurant   Seminar room
Some sociopetal arrangements

Lounge   Classroom   Study area
Some sociofugal arrangements

FIGURE 3-3 Some environmental arrangements. *(Source: Burgoon, 1988.)*

tion available to people. For instance, it is easier to interact with people who are opposite you than with those on either side; also, individuals at the corners of a table will contribute the least to discussions, while those at the head or in central positions will contribute the most. Knapp (1978) concluded that people would prefer to sit in adjacent seats around a table or face-to-face and that these arrangements are the most conducive to cooperation. Groups should choose seating arrangements that encourage eye contact and face-to-face interaction.

People in high-status and leadership positions are granted special places. In groups, they will occupy *high-interaction* positions; these are locations that offer the most contact with people. Leaders and dominant people gravitate toward the end of rectangular tables and choose to sit opposite other people. Holding a dominant seating position in a group enables the person to monitor and influence other persons in the group. It is pretty obvious what you have to do if you want to be a leader or to exert influence in the group: Sit in a place that makes you the symbolic leader of the group. Likewise, if you want to increase the participation of a particular group member, you might succeed by placing the person in a centralized seating position, for a central position in a seating arrangement confers status and authority on an individual.

Spatial arrangements are also related to interpersonal relationships in the group. The members use each other's distance orientations as signals of how involved each person is, in what the other has to say, and of what each thinks of the other. When people like each other and are involved in their relationship, they lessen the distance between themselves. When people are angry or displeased with each other, they choose an extreme proximity. They might withdraw and move away, or if they are especially irate, they might move very close in order to shout. Group members can use their knowledge of proxemic choices to their advantage. If you want to communicate exclusion to certain group members, you can physically distance them from other group members, whereas moving closer to them will indicate your interest and interpersonal acceptance.

SUMMARY

Viewed as a process, communication has both structural and functional dimensions. Groups organize people and resources and structure themselves. One structural element of communication is feedback; feedback responses are unavoidable and occur continuously during the give-and-take of group interaction. Effective feedback responses during group interaction depend on the cohesiveness of the group members and on the interpretations of the feedback responses by the persons who receive them.

Certain characteristics of the messages that constitute the group interaction are important to decision making. For effective group decision making, the timing of the messages may be more significant than their content.

Viewed structurally, group communication can be seen as a network—a pattern of channels that link members of the group. Networks are distinguished from one another by size, reachability, density, and centrality. The most central position in a network is apt to be occupied by a leader or by a deviant who is under extreme social pressure to conform. During the process of group decision making, several networks generally emerge from the group's interactive patterns; these networks reflect the coalition formation and leadership at various stages in the group process.

The gatekeeper in a network is someone who is responsible for receiving, transforming, and retransmitting information to other members of the group. Because gatekeepers are usually in central and pivotal positions, they possess much authority and responsibility. A boundary spanner is someone who acts like a gatekeeper but transmits information between networks. Who says what to whom is also influenced by the social structure of the group; high-status members and leaders of a group initiate more communication than low-status members do, and this fact confirms that status is linked to network centrality. The concept of communication barriers and breakdowns is best thought of as ineffective communication.

Proxemic behavior is also part of the structure of communication in groups. Proxemics is the study of the communicative use of space. All of us have personal space and territoriality needs; that is, we have a sense of ownership about the objects and space around us. Group members often claim territory (such as chairs and tables) for themselves. Spatial distance can be either intimate, personal, social, or public. The physical environment can be arranged to encourage communication (in sociopetal arrangements) or to keep people away (in sociofugal arrangements). The use of personal space is related to a number of other variables, such as sex, leadership, and interpersonal relationships.

CHAPTER OUTLINE

THE NATURE OF COMMUNICATION

Communication Defined
Some Myths about Communication
The Content and Relationship
  Dimensions
Analyzing Interaction
The Organization of Interaction

DIMENSIONS OF COMMUNICATIVE
BEHAVIOR

The Content Dimension
The Relationship Dimension

LISTENING AND QUESTIONING

Critical Listening
Critical Questioning

NONVERBAL FUNCTIONS AND
GROUP INTERACTION

Clarification
Control
Emotional States
Interpersonal Relationships

SUMMARY

KEY TERMS

COMMUNICATION AND
  INTERACTION

PROCESS

CODE

MESSAGE

COMMUNICATION MYTHS

CONTENT DIMENSION

RELATIONSHIP DIMENSION

ACT

INTERACT

DOUBLE INTERACT

DECISION PROPOSALS

CONTROL MODES

SYMMETRY

COMPLEMENTARITY

SUBMISSIVE SYMMETRY

COMPETITIVE SYMMETRY

CRITICAL LISTENING

CRITICAL QUESTIONING

NONVERBAL FUNCTIONS

Communication in Groups

You have undoubtedly been trained in various aspects of communication throughout your experience in elementary and secondary schools and in college. You have probably mastered its grammar. For example, you know about nouns and verbs, agreement between subject and predicate, etc. The semantic dimension is also emphasized in our schools, generally in the sense of finding a referent for a word in order to decipher its meaning. That is, a word stands for something. Early in your educational career, you learned to use the dictionary and provide definitions for words—semantics. The dimension of communication that rarely appears in our schools' curricula, however, is the pragmatic dimension.

The pragmatic dimension of communication deals with the relationship between words and people. Another way of understanding the pragmatic dimension of communication is to think of the functions performed by a message or a unit of communication. That is, what does the action *do* in the communicative process? Beyond the grammar of the sentences and the meanings of the words is the pragmatic notion of how the action functions in the communicative situation as, for example, a bluff, a threat, a plea, or an expression of intimacy. Anytime someone in the group utters a sentence or phrase, he or she performs a type of action that has some meaning for and influence on the hearer of the action. In the following example, Jim is talking to another group member (Ben):

JIM: You know, Ben, if you don't have that information from the Department of Transportation by Monday, I'm going to ask someone else to get it and give you a poor evaluation.

Whenever you speak, you perform actions with your words. The words in Jim's sentence perform some *communicative* function. If you were asked what Jim was doing in that utterance, you might say he was *threatening* Ben, telling Ben that there would be negative consequences if he did not get the necessary information. You could say that Jim was "performing" a threat.

Now in Jim's utterance we took the words at their face value. Jim threatened Ben with a loss of status and a poor evaluation if he did not get the information the group needed. It was a genuine and serious threat. But what if Jim had said in a rather playful manner, "Ben, old boy, you'd best get that information we need or I'm gonna kill you." Obviously, these words are not to be taken literally. This would not be a genuine threat. It is still a statement indicating what Jim wants Ben to do, but its *effect* is different; its pragmatic function is different. An emphasis on the pragmatic functioning of human communication is an emphasis on the functions of communication. Later in this chapter it will become apparent that the same comment (even using the same words) may perform different functions, depending on the intent of the speaker and on when it occurs in a sequence of interaction. The function of any particular communicative act often depends on what precedes or follows it during the normal course of human communication.

THE NATURE OF COMMUNICATION

Our approach to the study of communication in groups is only one approach among others (see Shaw, 1981, and Hirokawa and Poole, 1986), but it leads us to consider a number of important issues. For example, we must take into account the context in which communication takes place; we must know who the speaker and the hearer are at least, and we should know when and where the communication takes place.

Many people think of communication as synonymous with the ways people make contact; thus, communication is easily equated with telephones, computers, radio, and television, and these perspectives emphasize the channels for transmitting and receiving messages. However, we are using the terms *communication* and *interaction* interchangeably in this book. When a speaker utters words that have some message value and does so in a particular social situation and at a point in the unfolding stream of talk, the speaker is both communicating and interacting: *communicating* because the language carries meaning and content, and *interacting* because the language functions to express social relationships. It is impossible to do one without the other.

Communication Defined

Our definition of *group* in Chapter 1 emphasized that a group is a system of communicative behaviors composed of identifiable patterns of interaction. Our definition of *communication* closely parallels this definition of *group* because we consider the group process and the communicative process to be related. (Thus this book's subtitle, *Communication and the Group Process*, indeed refers to a single process.) At the same time, because small group decision making is the focus of attention in this book, we are viewing the communicative process in terms of the group—and particularly in terms of the group as a holistic decision-making system.

The analysis of communication in groups is the analysis of language in use. We will define *communication* simply as *the process of people exchanging messages, which are formulated according to the principles of a code, in a context*. The important words in this definition are "process," "messages," "code," and "context." The definition simply says that people use language to create messages and that these messages acquire their meaning both in a situation and in relation to previous and subsequent messages. Figure 4-1 illustrates the components of communication.

Your language is a code (or set of principles) for organizing symbols. Readers of this book are competent users of the English-language code, but there are other ways to organize symbols. There are other languages (e.g., French and Swahili) and other ways to express the code (e.g., sign language and mathematics). All of the above are linguistic codes; that is, they are governed by formal rules about how sounds and words can be organized. Linguistic codes have a grammar. There is a grammar of French, of Swahili, and of sign language. Sign language is not nonverbal communication just because the symbols are not spoken; even though it expresses linguistic meaning through the use of hand and body movements, it still functions according to linguistic principles. Nonlinguistic codes are what we often call nonverbal communication, which includes body movements, facial expressions, physical features, and much of what passes for "animal communication."

We are concerned with the social-interaction aspect of language, not with the formal grammatical and linguistic properties of language. We want to know how an utterance in the group (such as a threat, promise, or piece of information) counts as social action. The meaning and significance of what people say in groups is not based on the grammar or strict content of a statement by a group member; rather, it is based on the coherence of conversational sequences and on the actions performed by those sequences. A pragmatic approach to communication locates the action and meaning of utterances *in the interaction*. That is, meaning results from applying one's knowledge of the contexts and the people in them to the words that group members utter. In the following example, Sue and Howard use their shared knowledge to accomplish communication:

SUE: What time is it?
HOWARD: Kelly's class just ended.

FIGURE 4-1. The components of communication.

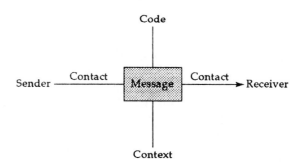

Howard's response is not a literal answer to the question because he never states what time it is. But the relationship between Sue and Howard is such that they share knowledge of a Professor Kelly and when her class ends. Howard's utterance is perfectly sensible and responsive to the question, but only in relationship to what preceded it and the context of his relationship with Sue as a member of his group.

Communication is the major vehicle for accomplishing tasks, and it soon becomes clear that many concepts in groups are apparent in the communication. The following example is of a group argument. The group has been discussing case studies of a business that behaved unlawfully in order to reap a small profit. The group's goal is to analyze the cases and decide what it would do, given the conditions of the case. Only a portion of the entire argument appears here:

JOY: Well, I finished the case. It was interesting but disgusting.
ANN: Uh hum.
JOY: It was so dumb. I'm a business major, and real businesses don't do those things, I mean, you know, it was so dumb to cheat.
PETE: Just cuz you're honest doesn't mean these things don't happen.
JOY: I know, but . . .
PETE: I think it's very common. That's exactly how lots of millionaires got started. I've even known companies like that.
JOY: That was some time ago. I don't think it relates any more.
PETE: Sure it does. My friend had trouble with a company like that.
JOY: Yes, but . . . (The argument continues.)

The group members are providing valuable information that will be important when they make their final decision. Pete and Joy are interrelating their personal experiences with the subject matter the group is discussing. Their differing opinions are being worked out in the interaction that characterizes the group's decision-making processes. All communicative utterances are interpreted by the participants in the communication, and each participant assumes that a message "counts as" a type of social action. Pete's statement, for example, that just because Joy is honest does not mean that others are might be counted as a put-down. Joy can choose to treat it as nonthreatening and unimportant—or she might take offense at the statement, and at some point her argument with Pete could get emotional and begin to have negative consequences for the group. It is important to underscore that actual communication consists of the data that people use to conduct the business of the group.

When the focus of communication shifts from the individual human being to the social system (the group), the most significant elements of communication become the *relationships* between group members rather than the internalized feelings, attitudes, emotions, or beliefs of individual members. The only way two persons can establish a relationship with one another is to act toward one another, to engage in communicative actions. How Pete "feels" about Joy cannot affect their social relationship unless and until this feeling becomes observable to Joy and to other group members—that is, until this feeling is expressed in the form of action, a communicative behavior. Although the internalized feeling may be highly important to Pete, it is significant to Joy and to other group members only to the extent that they are able to become aware of it. In other words, private elements of a person's self can be important to the group system (and to group decision making) only if they become public and knowable or if they affect behaviors that are then public and observable. In either case, the focus is on the communicative actions, the behaviors.

Why do we choose to engage in some behaviors and not others in any given situation? Although we are capable of free choice and free will, this fact does not imply that our choice is random, that we choose to behave in a purely happenstance or capricious manner. Rather, we choose to behave on the basis of what we consider to be appropriate to a given situation. Stated another way, our choices are limited in the sense that many alternatives are eliminated and are thus not available to be chosen in any given situation. We have the capacity to choose among behaviors at the same time that our communicative choices are subject to numerous constraints that limit the range of alternatives available to us. In many instances, we are only vaguely aware, or actually unaware, of any of these constraints, but we submit to them nevertheless. For example, we wear clothing in public rather than appear nude. We speak in a language that contains specific rules of syntax and meaning and conform to those rules even though we may not be aware of the rules that operate to constrain our choices.

Often constraints occur as a result of a particular social situation in which we find ourselves. For example, in your family group the constraints that fellow family members place on your behavior are quite different from the constraints present when you are in a group of close personal friends. Furthermore, either of these situations will place constraints on your actions that will be different from those evident in a group of strangers or new acquaintances. We will communicate in one way with a boss or an employer and in a different way with a close friend or fellow family member. The social environment places many constraints on our behavioral repertoire and significantly influences the communicative process.

The principal origin of the constraints on our behavior is the previous interaction itself. That is, constraints result from our past communicative choices during interaction as well as from the past behavior of others. When communicating with someone, you *must choose* to enact some communicative behavior; that is, you have no alternative but to choose and thereby enact some behavior. Regardless of what your initial choice is, your subsequent behavior in the situation is thus constrained as a result of what you and the other communicators have elected to perform in past communicative behavior. Watzlawick, Beavin, and Jackson (1967, pp. 131–134) refer to this phenomenon as the "limiting effect of communication" and describe it as follows: "In a communicational sequence, every exchange of messages narrows down the number of possible next moves" (emphasis deleted).

An example may illustrate this limitation principle of communication more clearly. A man was riding on a city transit bus when an elderly woman boarded the bus and sat beside him. After a few minutes, she remarked that it was shameful that the city had cut down so many of the big trees along the street on which they were riding. Without really thinking, he responded, "Yes, it sure is." This single exchange of messages functioned to place both of them in a communicative situation that limited the man's subsequent behavioral choices. At the very least, he experienced some degree of involvement in this casual relationship. This involvement proceeded directly from his agreeable response to the woman's initial attempt to make conversation. They continued the conversation and became more involved.

A communicative relationship develops during the process of interacting with others. Each communicator soon learns which behaviors are appropriate to the situation and which behaviors are inappropriate. The interaction then stabilizes over time. Stated another way, each person in every communicative situation learns how "to play the game"; learns what the rules are that govern the communication. As a result, the individual communicators shape their behavioral choices into identifiable patterns.

Communication is understandable as certain sequences of acts become familiar. That is, certain acts tend to follow other acts so frequently and are repeated so often that we come to expect the next act in the sequence even before it occurs. The interaction becomes familiar because it has been repeated so often in the past. In this way, past sequences of interaction constrain future interaction, even though the communicators themselves may be unaware that their actions are being constrained. Communicative relationships are thus characterized by what sorts of actions are performed by communicators who are familiar with the appropriate sequence.

Some people have certain friends with whom they engage in mutually insulting behaviors. Either one will insult the other, and this insult is a clear sign that the next act in the sequence will be another insult in response. And some interpersonal relationships are characterized by argumentative interaction; that is, virtually anything that one person says will be followed by the other's disagreement. Both sequences of interaction are symptoms of very close interpersonal friendships. These particular people would never have dreamed of insulting or disagreeing with the woman on the bus, however; that sequence was characteristic of a casual first acquaintance. Insults and disagreement would have been quite inappropriate in such an early stage of interaction. The close relationships characterized by mutual insults and argument have developed over a long period and are based on frequent exchanges of similar behavior in the past. Those past sequences are now familiar and constrain the present interaction.

Communication, then, is a series of events, each one following the other in a stream of ongoing actions, or behavior. These actions engaged in by the communicators are "connected" with one another within this ongoing stream. Therefore, we think of the "connectedness" among the various actions rather than of each individual action in isolation. We talk about *interac-*

tion or communication to signify the entire conversation, the entire process of communication.

Group communication, then, involves a sequence of the actions that are contributed by individual members. As a sequence, each action follows after or precedes another action. The person, when engaging in, or becoming part of, communication, contributes actions (or behavior) to the overall process of communication. For some period of time, any individual group member gets the floor and later relinquishes his or her turn to another member, who then has the floor for some additional period of time. Each person's action is connected in some manner to the action that precedes it and to the action that follows it. An example of such connectedness occurs when we say that a comment following a question may be regarded as an answer. Rather than think of each individual action separately, we think of the *connections* between actions and thus view the communicative process as a *system* of communication rather than as actions and reactions by individual persons.

Some Myths about Communication

Because communication is so commonplace, many myths have been perpetuated about it. Communication is something all of us do every day and there are plenty of people who try to tell us how to do it better. It is inevitable that some confusions and outright falsehoods emerge. Here are a few of the most common myths about communication.

Problems Result from Communication Breakdowns   When something goes wrong or someone doesn't understand you, it's easy to think it must be a communication problem. This is one reason why there are so many popular books written about communication. But interpersonal problems have many causes, including social and personal difficulties that cannot always be solved so easily. One member of a relationship might want more independence and the other more togetherness. One member of a group might prefer one decision and another member a different decision. The people in these situations might understand each other very well, but just have different opinions and values. Communication is certainly necessary in solving these problems, but the problems themselves are not the result of communication "breakdowns."

More Communication Is Always Better   Perhaps you have heard people say, "What we need here is more communication." But sometimes the more people communicate the more they realize how little they have in common or how differently they really feel about things. All relationships, even the more well-developed and stable, depend on a balance of involvement and detachment. Simply increasing the amount of communication in a group can have the result of merely increasing the existing amount of confusion, misinformation, and repetition—and lead to boredom. Again, there is a fine line here between when to approach and when to avoid someone that experienced communicators have learned to draw. But the assumption that all you need is more communication is usually wrong.

Complete Understanding Is the Goal of All Communication   You must never forget that much, perhaps most, of the communication you experience is designed to persuade, convince, manipulate, or influence you in a particular way. Television, advertising, politicians, intimates, and other group members usually want you to agree with them rather than simply "understand" them. Suppose a friend asks your opinion about a new piece of clothing and you tell him you like it, when in fact you don't like it or think it's just "okay." In this case you are not communicating to "achieve understanding" in the strict sense. Your answer reveals that you probably care more about your relationship with your friend than you do about your own honesty. This is fine, but you are still communicating so as to manipulate his feelings. Complimenting a group member when he or she doesn't deserve it achieves a similar purpose.

There Are Some Tricks to Communication   Even the most skilled and experienced communicator fails. It is certainly possible to improve communication skills and increase your likelihood of success, but there are no guarantees. Communication cannot be reduced to a few skills or tricks that always work, because there are too many factors involved. The same communication skill that works in one situation will fail in another because the conditions and participants are different. Moreover, the success of any communication depends on both parties: however skilled the initiator of the communication may be, he or she can never completely control the response. The recipient of the message must respond appropriately for the communication to be a complete success.

Communication Is Easy Because We All Do It   In the "conventional wisdom" section of the introduction to this book we told the story of the music teacher who thought teaching communication was easy because it is something we do all the time. But just because we do something frequently doesn't necessarily mean we do it well. In fact, most people just practice bad habits. Just because you practice a sport or musical instrument doesn't mean you will improve at it—unless you are practicing the right things. True, we communicate every day, but it is a myth to think that we automatically get better at it.

The Onus of Communication Is on One Person   It takes two to tango; in other words, poor communication and misunderstanding are never the responsibility of a single person. Communication is a cooperative activity, in that the speaker needs to fashion messages in such a way that the listener can understand them, and the listener must at the same time work to understand the speaker. It is easy to blame others for communication failures, and

sometimes such blame is appealing, but the fact remains that both participants in an interaction share the responsibility for understanding.

The Content and Relationship Dimensions

To this point, our discussion has focused on actions performed by individual
communicators. We have said little or nothing concerning the interpretation
of these actions or what they might contain. Assume that any communication
engaged in by any person during a communicative event can be called a
message. As such, it contains information. This information involves two
dimensions—a content dimension and a relationship dimension. As dimensions, the content and relationship aspects of communication are inseparable
and are always present in every communicative behavior. We will illustrate
the content and relationship dimensions of communication in more detail
later on in this chapter. Here we will simply introduce the subject. The
content dimension of communication refers to the aspect of behavior that
deals with specific data. The content is the topic of conversation, the subject
matter. The relationship dimension refers to the way the message's content is
to be interpreted. It enables the members of the communicative situation to
develop some definition of their social relationship.

The content and relationship dimensions of communication may be compared, respectively, with the *information* contained in a message and the *style*
in which the information is expressed. To express a message that contains
some information is to express that message *in some way*. Stylizing a message
is unavoidable. In other words, a message will contain some content, and it
will also be stylized. We teach children early in their formative years to stylize
messages in order to develop satisfactory relationships. We call such training
in stylizing messages "being polite" or "having good manners." The child
soon learns not to say, "Gimme the potatoes." Instead, we teach children to
ask, "Please pass the potatoes," along with other stylizations, including
"Thank you," "You're welcome," and "Excuse me." The *content* of the two
messages requesting potatoes is precisely the same, but the relationship
dimension within the two messages differs significantly. In every exchange of
messages in a sequence of interaction, the content and relationship dimensions of communication are present. Within group decision making, the two
dimensions are even more apparent and probably more meaningful than in
normal everyday conversation.

It is important to remember that whenever communication occurs, the
communicators are dealing with information at the same time that they are
developing a social relationship. This relationship dimension of the communication may develop into one of friendship, enmity, cooperation, equality,
superior-subordinate, or any of many possible social relationships. Moreover,
these relationships develop during the sequence of interactive behaviors and
may or may not be consistent with the expectations arising from the situation.
For example, you have probably had communicative relationships with some

"bosses" who interacted with you as though they were indeed superior to you; another boss, however, may have been more of a colleague or an equal in your interactions. Many husband-wife pairs interact in the form of a superior-subordinate relationship, while others have developed a more equal relationship. Inevitably, the relationship (together with the content) is an inherent part of, and is reflected in, the communicative behaviors exchanged by the participants during group communication.

Group decision making is clearly a social enterprise. While members are communicating with one another, they are simultaneously attempting to achieve consensus on decisions and establishing a social relationship that unites individuals into a functioning group. Thus, group members perform their decision-making task at the same time that they are developing their group relationship. Every act of communication performs a content (informational) function as well as a relational function.

Consider the following excerpt from the interaction of a classroom decision-making group. The students are discussing the pros and cons of establishing a coal-burning plant to generate electricity in southwestern Utah.

TIM: Well, the environmental groups are certainly opposed to a power plant so close to the national park.
JACK: Frankly, I think that the environmentalists are all a bunch of nuts.
MIKE: I don't think I understand. What do you mean?
JACK: They just don't seem to care about the people who live in that area. The residents want the plant.
MIKE: Don't care? You've got to be kidding. They care more about the future of those people than lining the pockets of a few utility companies.
JACK: But look at all the jobs that will be created.
MIKE: And look at all the pollution that will float into the park.
JACK: What *are* you? Some kind of environmental freak?
MIKE: What are *you*? A polluting developer?
TIM: Does anybody know what time it is?

This brief excerpt illustrates the interplay of the content and relationship functions within the interaction. Jack and Mike are engaged in an argument over specific information related to the topic at hand. Apparently their argument includes relational overtones as well. Their conflict over the content issues leads to a rather competitive relational conflict. Their final comments are as much a personal attack at the relationship level as they are inquiries into the ideational basis of each other's opinion.

Tim's last comment illustrates clearly that the content and relationship dimensions are simultaneously functioning during the interaction. In terms of the content of his final comment, Tim is asking a question that seeks information concerning the time of day. The question changes the subject matter of the discussion on the content level. In fact, one of the other group members responds and tells him the time according to her watch. More important to the relationship dimension of the interaction, however, Tim's request breaks the tension that has been developing in the group as a result of the informational and interpersonal conflict between Jack and Mike. Tim's abrupt change of topic leads to the release of relational tension created by Jack and Mike's interpersonal rivalry.

Similar to the social and task dimensions of group process, in every act the content and the relationship functions of communication always operate simultaneously during the process. Every act of communication contains information in the content dimension as well as some additional indicators as to how that information should be interpreted (that is, the relationship dimension). Sometimes the relationship dimension is reflected in the manner in which the words are said (in the inflection, vocal emphasis, etc.), or perhaps in the choice of words used to express the information, or even in the movements, gestures, or facial expressions during the utterance of the words. Under all circumstances, then, the content and relationship functions of communication occur simultaneously.

Analyzing Interaction

One method that attempts to understand the ongoing stream of interaction during group decision making involves categorizing each communicator's utterances. In this way, any action contributed by an individual member is perceived to be of a certain type. Chapter 5 includes this method of understanding group communication in order to facilitate a fuller understanding of how group members make decisions (task dimension) and relate to one another (social dimension). The practice of interaction analysis, in which categories of communication are used to analyze the ongoing process of group communication, is also the subject of a more detailed discussion in the Appendix.

Of course, any action performed by an individual group member fulfills different functions. For example, the above conversation between Tim, Jack, and Mike about the power plant provides several examples of multifunctional comments. Tim's final remark, for instance, serves several functions. He is not only requesting information, but he is also releasing the social tension that has developed because of the increasingly personalized conflict between Jack and Mike. Also, Tim's comment serves to change the topic of conversation.

Keep in mind that it is always difficult to interpret the communicative behavior of others and feel confident about the interpretation. Some communication scholars have spent considerable time studying how it is that we can know what others mean by their communication (Folger and Poole, 1982). But there is always the question of whose interpretation is more useful. If you ask any participants in communication what they meant by a particular utterance, they are certainly biased according to their perceptions of the situation and of other people. In the example above it may appear as though Mike is attacking Jack, yet Mike might not see it that way at all. But on the other hand, an outsider may not know as much about a speaker's intentions. Participants in interaction are usually preoccupied with their own intentions, as are observers of interaction. Communication in the group not only performs many functions but also serves the interests of many people.

The point of understanding group communication, then, is not to identify which function is the most important one served by any given action. We should recognize that each individual action performs several functions in the communicative and group process. The categories used to analyze interaction focus on specific classes of functions in order to let us understand the interaction from a certain perspective. Another list of categories, however, may focus on other functions and lead to an understanding of the interaction from the perspective of a different set of functions. Therefore, one can regard the interaction of the same decision-making group from the viewpoints of several different category systems. Combining the results from such analyses will provide a more complete description, explanation, and understanding of the process of group decision making.

Using different category systems to understand the ongoing interaction appears to be quite sensible. We wouldn't think of looking at a painting in only one way in order to understand it completely. A study of the colors and the artist's combinations of them in the painting would provide only one way of understanding the work of art. Concentrating on the composition of figures and objects in the frame would be another way of looking at the painting. We might also consider such factors as the mood or impression created in the painting, the artist's purpose and style, the school of art the painting represents, the reactions of critics and the public, and so forth. Communication is understandably a complex phenomenon. It is multifaceted and involves many different functions. Thus, different categories of human actions are necessary in order to achieve the fullest possible understanding of communication and the group process. Later in this chapter (and in Appendix 1), we will discuss specific lists of categories (or functions) of communication that have been used to analyze ongoing interaction in group decision making.

The Organization of Interaction

An analogy may best illustrate how one can organize, and thus derive meaning from, a sequence of communicative acts. Consider a stream of letters of the English alphabet strung together, unorganized and ongoing such as the following: *aneatdeskisasignofasickmind*. These letters come from an office wall sign, but the sign presents the letters in organized groups of words. That is, the letters are *punctuated* (organized) into words by placing spaces between the letters. The groups of letters are more understandable, more meaningful, than the letters by themselves. Properly punctuated, the sign reads, "A neat desk is a sign of a sick mind."

Punctuating is nothing more than organizing or grouping elements in order to enable one to interpret their meaning more easily and more meaningfully. Unpunctuated letters themselves have no intrinsic meaning or significance. But words (punctuated groups of letters) do endow the letters, in combination with other elements, with an interpretable meaning and hence with significance. Furthermore, if you change the punctuation rules, you tend to change the possible interpretations of the sequence of elements. Several years ago, after discussing the organization of interaction sequences, a student attended the next class meeting with a hand-lettered sign on his shirt. The sign consisted of the "words" *toti emul esto*. He asked us to interpret the phrase. Not one of us was sure, but we all felt that the phrase was vaguely Latin. Since none of us knew Latin, we were unable to decipher the three words. His response was to punctuate the apparently Latin phrase into four English words. He did not change the sequence of the letters. He merely revised the punctuation rules of the sequence and got *to tie mules to*. The punctuation, then, allows for a meaningful interpretation of the meaning (or significance) of communication. We are all familiar with the famous experiments of Pavlov, who conditioned dogs to salivate at the ringing of a bell even without the presence of food. On the other hand, *that* organization of the sequence of events was the scientist's interpretation. If one of Pavlov's dogs had been able to speak, it might have said, "See how I have this dumb human trained! Every time I feel hungry, I just salivate. Then he rings the bell and gives me food." Pavlov himself, the dumb human, punctuated the sequence of events quite differently. He thought Fido was the one who was conditioned.

If a single behavior of an individual group member is an act, then groupings of acts result from punctuating the interaction sequence. At this point it is necessary to introduce *interact* and *double interact*, two terms used to denote specific groups of acts. We already have terms to designate the grouping of letters of the alphabet in the written mode of communication. We call these groupings *words*. Groupings of words are called *sentences*, and groupings of sentences are called *paragraphs*. Our present purpose requires similar terms to designate groupings of actions (or behaviors) within an ongoing sequence of interaction during group decision making.

The *act*, then, is the contribution to the discussion of a single individual. One act following another act (that is, a pair of acts) is called an *interact*. Thus, an interact is composed of two contiguous acts. A *double interact* is a combination of three contiguous acts in the interaction sequence. Member *A* performs an act (a single act), which is followed by an act from member *B* (thus forming an interact), which is followed by a third act from member *A* (a double interact). Because our emphasis is on communication, or *inter*action, the most important units of analysis are the interact and the double interact—that is, the connectedness of acts to form interaction. In this way, the individual acts are always within the context of the communicative process—the preceding and succeeding acts.

The earlier excerpt of interaction from the group composed of Tim, Jack, and Mike comprises a total of ten acts (count them). Those ten acts also contain nine interacts (or possible combinations of two contiguous acts); Tim's first remark followed by Jack's comment is one interact, Jack's comment followed by Mike's subsequent comment forms another interact, and so on. If one numbers those ten acts from 1 through 10, then the nine interacts are 1-2,

2-3, 3-4, 4-5, 5-6, 6-7, 7-8, 8-9, and 9-10. Each individual act, then, is the second act of one interact (in combination with the preceding comment) and the first act of another interact (in combination with the following comment); note that because the first act has no antecedent and the last act has no subsequent act, there are always fewer interacts than there are acts. The same is true in forming eight double interacts from the same list of ten acts. The eight double interacts are 1-2-3, 2-3-4, 3-4-5, 4-5-6, 5-6-7, 6-7-8, 7-8-9, and 8-9-10.

The question remains as to which groupings of acts (interacts and double interacts) are to be regarded as the appropriate ones. The rules for punctuating acts within the interaction sequences are less explicit and less readily identifiable than the punctuation rules for grouping letters into words, phrases, and sentences. The punctuation of the sequence of letters, discussed earlier, into *toti emul esto* does not conform to those familiar punctuation rules. The alternative punctuation (*to tie mules to*), however, does conform to those rules. The latter punctuation reveals four recognizable English words. The former punctuation produces no recognizable English words among the three. And why are the words recognizable? One reason is that they are familiar in common usage. That is, we have used these words so often in the past that they become recognizable when we use them again.

Although the rules are not quite so specific in punctuating acts into interacts and double interacts, some sequences of interaction are recognizable as sequences. Consider the following list of three acts that are scrambled (that is, out of sequence) in terms of a recognizable double-interact pattern:

"Fine."

"Fine, thank you. How are you?"

"Hi. How are you?"

Clearly this double interact is in reverse order. The sequence is recognizable as the greeting ritual of our American culture. The sequence is so familiar, so patterned, and has appeared so often in the past (and is thus familiar) that we respond to the question as a ritualistic greeting and not as a realistic inquiry into the state of our health.

How, then, are interaction sequences punctuated into interacts and double interacts? The most common method of punctuating them is to organize the sequences into interacts and double interacts that are familiar—and they become familiar, of course, to the extent that they have been repeated often in the past. The punctuation of interaction sequences is therefore typically a matter of sheer redundancy. The more often the interacts and double interacts have occurred in sequence in the past, the more we are able to expect them to occur again in the future, and the more we will tend to punctuate them as recognizable sequences in the present. In Chapter 6 and Appendix 1 you will find that the discussions of the decision-making process and of the development of social relationships are based on the punctuation of interaction sequences in terms of their past frequency of occurrence: that is, in terms of how their repetitiveness (or redundancy) makes them recognizable as sequences of interacts and double interacts. We will see more examples of this in the following section.

DIMENSIONS OF COMMUNICATIVE BEHAVIOR

Earlier in this chapter we discussed the two dimensions of communication—content and relationship. As you will recall, *content* refers to the specific subject matter, or information, of communication, while *relationship* indicates how the information is to be interpreted. That is, every communication serves to establish some identifiable social relationship between the communicators, regardless of the content or the subject matter of the communication. From the previous discussion of interaction analysis in this chapter, you will recall that any category system used to analyze communication focuses on specific functions performed by communicative actions. Thus, it is possible to focus on the content or the relationship aspect of communication with a given category system while still recognizing the fact that the content and relationship dimensions are both present in each communicative act. In this section we will examine how the ongoing interaction of decision-making groups can be viewed in terms of either the content dimension or the relationship dimension, or both. Such analyses, of course, involve using different category systems to analyze communicative behavior.

In referring to content and relationship as "dimensions" of communication, we have adopted the view that *every* act contains both a content aspect and a relationship aspect, although we may focus on only one of the dimensions in a given category system to analyze interaction. Therefore, any attempt to separate acts into those which are primarily oriented to either content or relationship is quite impossible.

Viewing the content and relationship dimensions of communication pragmatically, we are able to examine different lists of interaction categories that emphasize one or the other dimension. Some of these lists of categories will be discussed in this chapter, with the purpose of providing an example of the specific category systems—specific lists of functions performed by communication during the process of group decision making. A more detailed explanation of interaction analysis appears in Appendix 1. The results obtained from actually observing the interaction of decision-making groups will be discussed in Chapter 6.

The Content Dimension

One way to view the interaction of decision-making groups is to consider each act in terms of how it functions to influence the opinions of other group members toward a specific issue being discussed. Central to such a category system is the concept of *decision proposal*. Each issue or topic of discussion during group decision making is potentially a decision that the group can make. In other words, each topic of conversation is a proposed decision which may be incorporated in the final consensus or which must be resolved as a preliminary step to achieving consensus on a final decision.

For example, a jury whose decision-making task is to determine the guilt or innocence of a defendant undoubtedly discusses many issues preliminary to that final verdict. That is, the jury members may need to determine whether a specific eyewitness is credible, whether the prosecution proved beyond a reasonable doubt the existence of motive, whether extenuating circumstances were sufficient to excuse the defendant from a crime, and so forth. In this way, each individual act during the jury's deliberations functions on a given proposal in such a way that it attempts to influence the perceptions of other members toward that proposal.

Once a decision proposal is identified, the categories of interaction provide a list of functions performed on that potential decision. This coding system, based on decision proposals, includes the following categories:

1. Interpretation
   f. Favorable toward the decision proposal
   u. Unfavorable toward the decision proposal
   ab. Ambiguous toward the decision proposal, containing a bivalued (both favorable and unfavorable) evaluation
   an. Ambiguous toward the decision proposal, containing a neutral evaluation
2. Substantiation
   f. Favorable toward the decision proposal
   u. Unfavorable toward the decision proposal
   ab. Ambiguous toward the decision proposal, containing a bivalued (both favorable and unfavorable) evaluation
   an. Ambiguous toward the decision proposal, containing a neutral evaluation
3. Clarification
4. Modification
5. Agreement
6. Disagreement

Even the act that initiates the decision or introduces a topic for discussion functions on the proposal in some way. It may *interpret* favorably, unfavorably, or ambiguously, with or without substantiation. But under any circumstances, every act functions on a decision proposal in terms of how that idea should be viewed by the group members. This category system, based on the concept of decision proposals and used to observe the interaction of actual decision-making groups in real life, provides the categories for the model of decision emergence that will be discussed extensively in Chapters 6 and 9.

Significant to this category system are the favorable, unfavorable, and ambiguous categories of interpretation and substantiation. A comment that is classified as favorable is a comment that functions on the decision proposal by expressing a favorable attitude toward it, thereby implicitly attempting to influence the perceptions or opinions of other members toward a favorable position regarding the proposal. Similarly, a comment that is unfavorable toward the proposal attempts to influence other members to reject the proposed idea.

It is possible to interpret or substantiate (that is, to interpret with evidence) a decision proposal ambiguously. An ambiguous comment is one in which the speaker's attitude or opinion is not explicit in the act itself, either because it is neutral (for example, "That's interesting") or because it contains both a favorable and an unfavorable evaluation (for example, "That's a good idea, but it needs a lot of work before it is acceptable").

Using this category system to observe the earlier excerpt showing the interaction of Tim, Jack, and Mike provides some indication of what that interaction is like. Even without being thoroughly familiar with these interaction categories, one can clearly see that the interaction between Jack and Mike reflects a sequence of favorable and unfavorable interpretations or substantiations of the decision proposal regarding the establishment of the power plant so near a national park. Their resulting interaction is a sequence of favorable-unfavorable-favorable (*f-u-f*) interaction—a clear indication of conflict over ideas or over the subject matter of the discussion. This conflict arises over a decision proposal—a conflict in the content dimension of communication. Whereas Tim's comments may reflect a neutral or ambiguous attitude toward the proposal, the comments of Jack and Mike are definitely not ambiguous.

Mike's first comment, in which he asks for clarification of Jack's preceding act, is the only act of either member that reflects neither a favorable nor an unfavorable interpretation or substantiation of the decision proposal. Mike is merely asking for more information in order to determine "where Jack is coming from." When Mike gets this information from Jack's subsequent comment, he solidifies his position and takes a clear ideational stance on the decision proposal.

This category system for analyzing decision-making interaction is specifically related to the content dimension of decision-making tasks. Although the system may not be entirely appropriate for examining the interaction in other types of tasks, it is altogether appropriate for examining group decision making, our focus in this book.

Later chapters will discuss the categories of decision-making interaction listed above. Appendix 1 shows how they are applied, and Chapters 6 and 9 will refer to them explicitly.

The Relationship Dimension

There are many ways to view the possible relationships that can unite the individual members within a group. Such relationships may be defined in terms of one or more previously discussed interpersonal factors. For example, we can define a relationship in terms of its level of intimacy, how much interpersonal trust is present, or how much self-disclosure occurs and is reciprocated among members. The category system of social relationship to be discussed in this section, however, defines the relationship in yet another manner.

The present category system has been used more extensively than any other to show the nature of social relationships in groups. It is presented here not necessarily because it is the best way to view a social relationship, but because it has been used often.

Gregory Bateson, a social anthropologist, was an important scholar in the content and relationship dimensions of communication. He defined *relationship* (1972) in terms of what he called *control modes* of communicative actions. We often use this same concept of control-mode relationships in everyday conversation when we describe the game of one-upsmanship. We often characterize a conversation, for example, by suggesting that someone is trying to one-up the other. *One-upsmanship* means an attempt by one person to control the other, to achieve a higher social status than the other, and in some respects to be dominant over the other.

Viewing communication in terms of control modes involves three basic categories:

↑ One up: An attempt to restrict the behavioral options of the other person

→ One across: An attempt at mutual identification

↓ One down: An attempt to relinquish one's own behavioral options to the other person

At the risk of oversimplifying these categories, we can look at certain examples of how an individual may contribute a one-up, a one-down, or a one-across act. Actually, however, the only way to define a comment as either one up, one down, or one across is to consider that comment in relation to the interaction sequence, particularly the comment preceding it. For example, returning to the Tim-Jack-Mike interaction, Mike's comment "You've got to be kidding!" is probably a one-up act. Mike is relationally saying to Jack, "I am not going to allow you any behavioral options other than the one of agreeing with me." His statement is highly imperative; it is didactic. Mike commands Jack to change his mind and conform to Mike's own opinion.

Jack might have responded by saying to Mike, "Yes, I guess you're right. You've convinced me." If he had done so, he would have clearly relinquished his behavioral options to Mike in making this one-down comment. In reality, however, Jack responded by arguing with Mike. That is, he refused to relinquish his behavioral options to Mike and responded with another one-up comment.

A one-across comment does not attempt to control the other person. Nor does such a comment acquiesce to the other person's control. Such an act serves to define the relationship as one of equal status. It may function to restate, repeat, or clarify the previous act. Some group interactions, particularly in encounter or training groups, encourage one-across actions. Often such a comment is preceded by the ritualistic and explicit declaration that the comment is restating a previous act for the sake of clarification: "What I hear you saying is . . ."

Obviously a single utterance by one person cannot hope to establish a social relationship. The relationship is definable only by a sequence of individual acts. A one-up comment does not establish a social relationship, but in the context of other acts it can be part of a relationship. In this sense of a social relationship, it becomes apparent that a person "engages in," or "becomes part of," the communication (that is, the relationship). No one individual can unilaterally define a communicative relationship. Rather, it is defined by individual actions in concert with the actions of other persons.

There are two identifiable social relationships under the general headings of "symmetry" and "complementarity." The minimal instance of one of these relationships is, of course, an interact. A *symmetrical* relationship is an interact in which the antecedent and subsequent (first and second) acts in the sequence are the same function—either ↑ ↑, ↓ ↓, or → →.

A *complementary* relationship is an interact in which the antecedent and subsequent acts "fit together" to form a complete relationship. In the same sense that two angles that together form a right angle (90°) are called complementary angles in geometry, two acts that fit together to form a complete social relationship are called a complementary social relationship. Thus, a complementary relationship involves one person's attempt to assert control over the other and the other person's acceptance of that control: ↑ ↓ and ↓ ↑. A complementary relationship may take the form of any of the following common social relationships: dominant-submissive, question-answer, buying-selling, giving-receiving, employee-employer, parent-son or parent-daughter, superior-subordinate, husband-wife, teacher-learner, sender-receiver, etc. These social relationships are complementary in the sense that they fit together.

The two forms of complementary relationships (↑ ↓ and ↓ ↑) are essentially the same. One is a mirror image of the other—that is, the reverse of the other. Member *A* is dominant and member *B* is submissive, or member *A* is submissive and member *B* is dominant. The three forms of symmetry (↑ ↑, ↓ ↓, and → →), however, are quite different from one another. The ↑ ↑ symmetrical relationship is one of competition—competitive symmetry. Each person is trying to one-up the other. They are competing with each other, as shown in Mike and Jack's interaction.

Submissive symmetry (↓ ↓) is not so overtly competitive, but it may reflect an underlying competition, nevertheless, in the sense that each person is attempting to force the other person to take the initiative. If you have ever played chess, you will know that it is sometimes to your advantage to force your opponent to attack or to make the initiating moves. A boxer who is a strong counterpuncher may want the opponent to lead with the punches. Submissive symmetry is also apparent in an interaction familiar to all of us. It is the conversation that occurs in situations that involve such decisions as how to spend the evening. The conversation may go something like this:

"What do you want to do tonight?"

"I don't know. What do *you* want to do?"

"I don't care. It's up to you."

"No. Really, you decide."

"But I really don't care."

"Neither do I."

Relationships characterized by submissive symmetry are often the most difficult and frustrating of all.

Equivalent symmetry ($\rightarrow$ $\rightarrow$) is characterized by the establishment of a peer relationship—equal partners. Equivalent symmetry, according to a commonsense interpretation, would probably characterize a democratic relationship, such as a decision-making group composed of equals and led by a democratic leader. We must be careful, however, to avoid thinking of any relationship, including equivalent symmetry, as the most desirable type of social relationship. In certain contexts, one kind may be more valuable than another. We doubt, for example, that a relationship of equivalent symmetry would be highly desirable in a group of soldiers in combat or in an orchestra or a flight crew. Such situations probably call for a highly complementary relationship between officer and enlisted personnel, between conductor and players, and between captain and crew.

It should be obvious that not all these relationships can be sustained for an indefinite period. For example, competitive symmetry ($\uparrow$ $\uparrow$) must be resolved in some manner, or the relationship will be highly uncomfortable. Mike and Jack's competition was apparently so unpleasant that Tim found it necessary to relieve the social tension with his innocuous comment asking for the time. Submissive symmetry ($\downarrow$ $\downarrow$) is also not likely to be sustained for any long period. The participants simply won't get anywhere. No progress will be made. It is a relationship that is temporary at best.

The complementary relationships ($\uparrow$ $\downarrow$) and ($\downarrow$ $\uparrow$) and equivalent symmetry ($\rightarrow$ $\rightarrow$) are, on the surface at least, relatively stable. They appear to be those that can characterize a relationship over a longer period of time. Although such a conclusion seems consistent with common sense, it is probably not the case.

A "healthy" relationship contains some symptoms of several kinds of relationships—competitive symmetry, submissive symmetry, complementarity, etc.—at various times during the course of the interaction. As we shall see later, the healthiest and most cohesive social relationship is often characterized by periods of conflict. A decision-making group without conflict is not very productive. Equivalent symmetry is by no means the most desirable social relationship in every circumstance if "most desirable" implies the exclusion of other kinds of symmetry or complementarity.

LISTENING AND QUESTIONING

Listening and questioning are two of the most important communication skills you can develop in your group. Listening and questioning are interdependent and necessary for engaging group members and discovering what they are thinking. They are necessary for establishing a dialogue and creating a climate of analysis and understanding in the group.

Communication may be a matter of exchanging messages, but "good" communication requires lively, active, and cooperative exchanges that result in analysis and argumentation. Good communication means many things, but at the very least it means sharing ideas, analyzing, questioning, paraphrasing the comments of others, and building on the ideas of others. Ideally, group members should be working through ideas together. Asking questions and listening to others helps increase involvement and builds a sense of mutuality; that is, everyone is working as a system and immersing themselves in the task at hand.

In Chapter 2 we described defensive and supportive communication. Groups must maintain a balance between cooperation and conflict. Conflict is good for the group, but at some eventual point the members must cooperate and create a supportive atmosphere. Conflict and disagreement can help clarify ideas and positions, but no group succeeds unless its members support one another. Listening to other group members and asking questions that draw out the opinions and perspectives of others are the best ways to develop supportive and cooperative environments. Defensive and uncooperative groups rarely listen to one another. Usually the group members are competing to win points or arguments, and information is not developed mutually.

Critical Listening

Although it is difficult to teach people how to listen better, one can improve their skills. There are a few prevailing myths about listening: (1) listening is related to intelligence; (2) listening cannot be learned; (3) listening is the same as hearing; (4) listening is automatic and so it can't be learned; (5) the speaker is responsible for communication; and (6) listening to someone means agreeing with him or her. But none of these myths is true.

We listen in different ways. Sometimes we listen *appreciatively*. This is the easy listening that comes when we are relaxing or enjoying ourselves. You listen to music or an enjoyable lecture appreciatively. Sometimes we listen *empathically* when we are working hard to understand and identify with another person. A therapist or intimate friend often listens empathically. When we are listening to purposively be judgmental we are listening *evaluatively*. Evaluative listening occurs when the listener is analyzing and passing judgement on the comments of other group members. Often we listen evaluatively to a politician who holds different views than we do. Evaluative listening is characteristic of a defensive group environment.

Group members should learn to listen critically. *Critical listening* refers to the active mental process of engaging the speaker intellectually. In other words, you do not just sit there and let the speaker's words wash over you. You analyze and interpret what the speaker is saying. You question his or her utterances but you also question yourself as you listen. The critical listener is silent but very active. Below are four strategies that will help you to listen critically.

1. *Eliminate distractions* Focus on the other person. Do not let your eyes wander so that you begin to think about the room or other people. Convince yourself that what you are hearing is important, so pay attention! Control the physical environment as best you can. Reposition yourself if you need to and maintain eye contact.

2. *Listen for concepts and ideas* Try to figure out the main point the person is making. Don't get hung up on minor points or irrelevances. Also, think about what the speaker is *not* saying. Manipulative group members can leave out information and change topics to distract the listener. When listening to other group members it's useful to ask yourself if there is some additional information you should be hearing and thinking about.

3. *Organize what you hear* Work to associate ideas and make logical connections. If you listen for a main idea or concept, use this main idea as an organizational tool. In other words, if you understand the main topic of the other person's comments, you can take other ideas and details and interpret them within the framework of the main idea. The main idea can help you understand the importance and relevance of other ideas. When a speaker offers evidence or data to support a statement, think about the relationship between the evidence and the claim.

4. *Evaluate what you hear* After listening to the ideas of the speaker and organizing what you have heard, evaluate what the speaker said. It is helpful to withhold judgment as long as possible because you do not want to discount an idea before you fully understand it. But at some point the good critical listener must decide on the quality of what he has heard. Evaluate the evidence the speaker has presented. Ask yourself if there is contrary evidence or if the evidence is logical and appropriate. Think about the arguments the speaker has made and judge their cogency. Try to note any inconsistencies or discrepancies.

Critical Questioning

Question asking is the single most effective way to extract and examine ideas and information. Even though we ask questions of others every day, most people are poor at it. *Critical questioning* occurs when a group member asks another group member to add to, clarify, and/or justify the information already given. It means being probing and analyzing what they have said. It does not mean being critical of people or their opinions. It does not mean being cynical or impolite toward others. By asking questions, you improve the quality of discussion and make progress toward group goals. You make information specific, expand information, and make people think. Below are some suggestions for critical question asking.

1. *Request clarification* Do not hesitate to ask a speaker to say more. Ask such questions as, "Would you say that again, please?" or, "I'm sorry, but the second point you made is not clear to me. Would you explain it again

please?" It is easy not to fully understand someone, and requesting clarification is important. Make sure you know what another group member has said before you criticize or ask for a justification of it.

2. *Ask analytical questions* Direct questions to causes and consequences. Simply ask, "What is the reason for this?" or "What are the implications?" Over time you will learn to do this so as not to put the speaker on the defensive. Assume you are in a group that is charged with budget reduction in your company and one group member has just reported how much it costs to produce a product the company makes. If you explore the reasons for the cost of the product it will help you begin to formulate ways to reduce those costs. Asking analytical questions means asking questions that break things down into component parts so that you can understand how they work. These questions will help others think critically.

3. *Ask the tough questions* Groups are usually doing important work. Their decisions make a difference, so they must be made with care and professionalism. It is necessary to ask difficult questions. Don't be afraid to ask about ethical issues and values. If you are on a budget-cutting committee then you should ask about the implications for the people who might lose their jobs, or have their lives affected in some way. Ask ethical questions by relating information to the decisions and not to individual ethical motives.

4. *Ask group members to develop and extend their thoughts* Sometimes when a speaker finishes it is useful to just ask them to "say more." Speakers will necessarily be brief or not say too much for fear of violating norms about taking too much time. But if you encourage them with such questions as, "Would you say more?" or "Can you provide additional information or examples?" you can get more detail and insight into what they are saying. These questions also stimulate speakers to think more deeply and elaborate their ideas.

5. *Learn tact strategies* People occasionally feel that they are on the spot when asked questions, so it's useful to learn how to be tactful. The most common tact strategy is to precondition your questions with polite references to your own needs and feelings. Saying, for example, "I'm sorry, but can I ask a question?" before actually asking the question requires the speaker to give you permission to ask. This then justifies your question, and of course communicates that you realize the imposition you are causing. And, of course, everyday norms such as "please" and "thank you" never hurt.

NONVERBAL FUNCTIONS
AND GROUP INTERACTION

In Chapter 3 we discussed some structural elements of nonverbal communication, showing how spatial arrangements and territoriality influence communication and group behavior. In this section we focus on the functional elements of nonverbal communication. Nonverbal communication is part of a functional approach to communication that emphasizes meaning that is communicated in a context. It is usually very difficult to separate nonverbal communication from verbal behavior; in most communicative situations, body motions and vocal qualities are used in conjunction with language (i.e., nonverbal behavior usually "accompanies" words). If, for example, someone makes a fist, it would be very difficult to attach meaning (at least very specific meaning) to such behavior. But if he makes a fist while saying, "You've just got to listen to me!" then the fist is a body movement that functions to intensify his verbal message. It makes sense only in the context of his language. Nonverbal communication signals listeners about how to interpret a message. We will now discuss the functional nature of nonverbal communication by examining how nonverbal displays signal (1) clarification, (2) control, (3) emotional states, and (4) interpersonal relationships.

Clarification

As you know, *how* something is said can be more important than what is said. This is an overstatement (since you must say something in order to say it in a certain way), but it is true that tone of voice helps us clarify and interpret messages. There are many ways to say a word or utter a sentence. If someone says, "Do we want to meet tomorrow?" and you say, "Yes," the "yes" can be said in many ways. It can signal excitement and enthusiasm about meeting again so soon, or you can say it in such a way as to communicate that you are not happy about meeting.

People tend to believe vocal cues and body movement whenever these contradict verbal messages, because they think that nonverbal qualities are more difficult to hide. A group member can look you right in the eye and say whatever she wants. But if her body or voice contradicts what she says you will tend not to believe her words.

Most message clarification is accomplished by vocal qualities, and while it is impossible to be precise about how a group member is using his or her voice, there are some typical patterns of nonverbal communication. Generally, increased loudness is a signal of anger, hostility, or alarm; when accompanied by waving arms or violent body movements, loudness is a pretty good sign that someone is angry. Softening the voice conveys feelings of sympathy, powerlessness, and grief. Pitch is another important vocal feature. A high-pitched voice usually indicates alarm, anxiety, and fear; a low-pitched voice typically indicates emphasis on a certain point the speaker is making. Gestures are also used to clarify and add meaning to messages. Comedians raise their eyebrows or move their bodies in certain ways to emphasize suggestive or humorous remarks. Members of a group who are trying to emphasize what they say will use their arms, head, shoulders, and torso to add meaning to their words.

Control

Some people can exert considerable control without being obvious about it. And others are simply very effective and persuasive people either individually or in a group. Both types of people are very good at using nonverbal control signals. Certain nonverbal cues are positively reinforcing for other group members. In other words, when a member of the group is talking and accompanying his communication with smiles, nods, eye contact, gestures, facial expressions, body leans, etc., these not only help clarify his meaning but are also reinforcing to the listeners. And positive reinforcement is a fundamental way to control others. The converse is also true. Negative reinforcement will diminish the likelihood of certain behaviors. So if someone yells, threatens, reduces eye contact, and uses cold vocal cues, these are not reinforcing and can also signal attempts to control the communicative behavior of other group members.

Consider the example of someone in the group who talks too much. What are some ways you can use to control the person's voluminous verbal output? Sure, you can tell the person to "shut up" (i.e., resort to direct verbal confrontation), but most of us are uncomfortable with such techniques and prefer to communicate in a more polite manner. There are ways to accomplish this. You can deny the person the customary eye contact by shifting your gaze in another direction and by establishing eye contact for a prolonged period with another group member. This can be accompanied by turning your body away from the person and focusing your attention elsewhere. Neutral facial gestures and cold vocal cues will also negatively reinforce the talkative group member. In this way you can withhold the signals of approval that a communicator generally needs. On the other hand, you may want to encourage a group member who is presenting valuable information. Encouraging the person with head nods, eye contact, and approving vocal cues will reinforce a speaker and prompt him or her to continue talking.

Many group members also signal dominance and status in the group as a way to exert control. Dress is an important signal of power. People in organizations wear suits and ties or expensive women's clothing to communicate that they are to be taken seriously.

Body and vocal cues are the most typical signals of control when a group member must state his or her ideas in a credible manner. The following list summarizes some of the techniques for exerting control in this manner:

1. Present yourself physically with a solid presence of steady eyes, calm hands, and a comfortable body position. Try to look like you belong where you are.
2. Be animated when necessary, but do not overdo it. If you feel passionately about a point you are making, communicate your ideas with force and confidence; however, you will lose your impact if you communicate this way too often.
3. Speak in a low or hushed voice to make a sensitive or emotional point.
4. Learn to speak fluently. This increases your credibility with listeners.
5. Use an authoritative tone. Speak slightly more loudly and rapidly than you might normally. Vary your intonation so that you emphasize points you want to make and provide some tonal variability; this helps you maintain your listeners' attention.

6. Use your voice and body to signal confidence and authority. Cues that communicate liking and approval are also effective control devices, for listeners are influenced by people they like.

Emotional States

Nonverbal behaviors are key indicators of emotional states and feelings. Again, the most significant cues are vocal cues and body movements, but the area of the face is the most important sector of the body for communicating emotion. We use the face to signal anger, disgust, fear, pleasantness, happiness, surprise, anger, and boredom. Different parts of the face display different emotions, and group members can learn to control these expressions. Cultures vary with respect to emotional expressions, but of all the areas of nonverbal communication the face is probably the most conventional in any given culture. There are relatively standard ways of signaling fear, interest, pain, surprise, and disgust. We express interest with eyebrows that move downward and eyes that have an intentional focus. Enjoyment is manifested by wide eyes and broad smiles. Surprise or startlement sends the eyebrows upward, and our eyes blink as if they are trying to focus. Anguish and distress make our mouths turn down and eyebrows arch. Fear causes our eyes to fix in a frozen position, the body trembles, the face turns pale, we sweat, and our hair bristles. The face is a source of emotional leakage. That is, even when we are trying not to express emotions, certain feelings leak out of the face. The eyes, mouth, and forehead portray people's responses and inner feelings. Even when people are trying to control their emotions, their faces often give them away.

The second most predominant emotional channel is the voice. Anger is most easily identified by the tone of voice alone, but people have a little more trouble identifying other emotions from the voice. They often confuse such emotions as fear, sadness, and nervousness. That is why it is important to become sensitive to a variety of nonverbal channels; group members will use their voice in conjunction with facial expressions, body movements, and other microcues. Individuals vary in their ability to interpret vocal cues, and this ability is directly related to one's amount of experience. Individuals with more group experience simply do better at interpreting nonverbal cues in the group.

Interpersonal Relationships

Group members use many channels of nonverbal communication to signal their attitudes about interpersonal relationships. In a broad sense, relational messages involve anything that has to do with how two or more people regard each other, themselves, and their relationship. Interpersonal attraction and liking are a part of any group process. People decide that they like or dislike other members of the group, and the relationships they form are crucial to the group's performance.

There are basically four types of information about relationships carried by nonverbal communication. The first is inclusion or exclusion: that is, whether a person is considered to be a part of an interaction or not. The second is confirmation or disconfirmation: whether messages are supportive of others or negative. The third and fourth are control messages and emotional messages, respectively, both of which have been discussed above.

Certainly eye contact functions to orient two people toward one another. Sustained eye contact has always been associated with people who like one another. Eye contact is confirming and inclusive. Group members who make direct and serious eye contact with the rest of the group will communicate to others that they respect them and want to include them in their relationship. And, as we said above, eye contact is a way of communicating emotions and control.

The face and the body are also carriers of relational messages. Smiling while leaning toward other group members is a pretty clear sign of empathy and concern. People who like each other usually nod their heads as the others speak, lean toward them, maintain similar postures, and generally orient their bodies toward the others. People who like each other mirror each other's nonverbal behavior. Some studies have shown that doctors and nurses achieve the most rapport with their patients when their bodies mirror their patients' expressions and gestures (Mansfield, 1973). Next time you are in a group, see if those group members who have good interpersonal relationships fall into the same postures.

SUMMARY

Communication is viewed as a pattern of behaviors in which the acts of each communicator constrain and are constrained by the pattern created by his or her own and others' behaviors. All people who engage in communication develop to some degree an interdependent relationship with one another, a relationship that embodies both the structural and actional (functional) attributes of a process. This interdependent relationship is the process of communication.

Although there are myths about communication, all communication is behavior, and the understanding of communication focuses on the social system—the connectedness of actions performed by individual group members in an ongoing, turn-taking sequence. Furthermore, every communicative action contains both a content dimension (information) and a relationship dimension (how the information is to be interpreted), analogous to the interdependence of the task and social dimensions of a group process. Thus, communication and the group process are defined similarly and may be said to constitute a single process.

The ongoing stream of communicative behaviors can be understood by analyzing each action as being of a certain type of function performed. Every communicative act can then be analyzed within a category of communicative functions. All the categories for analysis thus constitute a list of functions that can be performed by communication. To understand the ongoing process of communication, one must focus on the connectedness of those categorized actions. Acts are thus punctuated (organized, or grouped) into recognizable sequences of interacts or double interacts on the basis of their familiarity, or recognizability. And certain sequences become recognizable as interacts or double interacts on the basis of their frequency of occurrence during the history of past interaction. Listening and questioning are two important communication skills for group members to develop.

Nonverbal communication is also a part of pragmatic group functioning. Group members use the various channels of nonverbal communication (e.g., face, voice, and body movements) to signal communicative functions. The nonverbal channels function predominantly to indicate message clarification, control, emotional states, and interpersonal relationships.

CHAPTER OUTLINE

ROLES

Role Defined
Role Performance
Role Conflict
Role Differences
High-Performance Groups

NORMS

Norms Defined

DEVELOPMENT OF GROUP NORMS

Pressures to Conform
The Norm of Reciprocity

SUMMARY

KEY TERMS

ROLE

ROLE PERFORMANCE

Region
Partial Inclusion

ROLE CONFLICT

Intrarole Conflict
Interrole Conflict
Interpersonal Role Conflict

POLITICAL MODEL OF ROLES

TASK ROLES

MAINTENANCE ROLES

INDIVIDUAL ROLES

GROUP PRODUCTIVITY OBSERVER

HIGH PERFORMANCE GROUPS

Work Roles

NORMS

Explicit
Implicit

TOLERANCE REGION

CONFORMITY PRESSURES

GROUPTHINK

PREMATURE CONSENSUS

RECIPROCITY

Behavioral Standards:

Roles and Norms

Developing the socioemotional climate of the group is essentially a process of acculturation. Typically, the process of acculturation implies a new member's joining an already established culture, in the sense of a Vietnamese immigrant's coming to the United States to live, a midwesterner's moving to New York, or a southerner's relocating in the north. Certain modes of behavior are acceptable within a given culture, and others are unacceptable. Previous members of a culture have established certain expected patterns of doing and thinking. These patterns must be learned by the newcomer.

One familiar example of the impact of cultural differences on behavioral expectations is that of the North American in a Latin American country who arrives at 2:30 for a 2:30 appointment. The North American, considering the arrival to be "on time," is unable to comprehend why the Latin American should consider it rude to arrive so "early." Each culture develops its own rules for guiding behavior, and these rules may be quite different from those in another culture. The alien newcomer, then, must adapt to the new behavioral patterns or face the consequences of culture shock.

Members of every group soon realize that their membership in the group constrains, to some extent, their freedom to choose their own behaviors. That is, each member has a range of behavioral choices available to him or her. But the process of group development narrows this range of acceptable behaviors, so that some behaviors are appropriate and others are inappropriate within the group context. Each member soon learns what is expected of him or her and what is expected of others. In regard to the informal rules, at least, every member has had a voice in formulating those expectations.

You will recall that the discussion of groupness in Chapter 1 states that one of the characteristics of groupness is the development of behavioral standards. That is, one of the characteristics of groupness is "behavior based on norms and procedures accepted by all group members" (Brilhart, 1978, pp. 20–21). Although the rules that guide the behaviors of group members are seldom formalized in the sense of a written code, the members of groups soon

113

develop expectations of how each member is to behave during group interaction. The normal process of group development leads to these expectations and the developing groupness.

This chapter will discuss the two most common standards for group members' behavior—roles and norms. Some roles and norms may be beyond the control of the group members themselves. That is, external standards may, in some respects, be stronger than the group's ability to devise informal norms and roles. Nevertheless, the development of informal roles and norms creates an extremely potent force that guides group interaction. The primary emphasis of this chapter, then, is on the development of these informal roles and norms.

ROLES

Comparing the concept of a social role to the dramatic role portrayed by an actor on stage is all too familiar. Even Shakespeare believed that all the world is a stage and life is just acting out one part after another. But we must not conform too closely to this analogy if we are to capture the richer meaning of the social role. The stage actor does create a role but is limited by the playwright's lines and the foreknowledge of the play's conclusion. The actor must also divorce the self, to a large extent, from the character portrayed. One's social role, on the other hand, is a direct reflection of one's self, and the specific behaviors that constitute the social role are much more spontaneous. And, of course, one cannot rehearse most of these behaviors beforehand.

Role Defined

The famed sociologist Erving Goffman (1961, p. 87) refers to a role as "the basic unit of socialization." As each individual member of any social system (a group, a culture, a society, etc.) identifies with and becomes identified with that system, the member assumes a role in that system. Goffman suggests that "It is through roles that tasks in society are allocated and arrangements made to enforce their performance."

A *role*, for our purposes, may be defined as a position in an interlocking network of roles that make up the group. But to define a role solely in terms of its "position" relative to the "positions" of other members of a group is to fail to comprehend fully how members function in their performance of roles and, ultimately, how the group functions as a decision-making system. A fuller definition, then, is that a *role is a set of communicative behaviors performed by an individual and that it involves the behaviors performed by one member in light of the expectations that other members hold toward those behaviors.* This definition also includes the behavioral tendencies that emanate from the person's own personality but which may or may not be expressed in actual role behaviors.

Considering a group member's role in terms of the expectations of other members, we can understand that the behavior of each individual member can be either consistent or inconsistent with what the other members expect that individual member's role to be. In other words, if the behavior of the member is similar to what other members expect, that behavior can be considered to be role behavior. Surely you know certain persons who create within you certain expectations that they will behave in a specific way. But if one of those persons were to do something that you didn't expect, you would probably describe such behavior as being "out of character." In other words, the behavior was not consistent with your expectations of that person's role.

To think of one's role solely in terms of one's "position" in a group network of roles is to provide only a partial picture of a group's social structure. Often a group that is subject to external pressures (e.g., a group within a larger organization) is also subject to a network of roles (within the larger organization) that is imposed on the group. A leader may be designated because of the status, seniority, or position which that member holds within the larger organization (for example, the company president and a group of advisors, or a supervisor and a group of subordinate workers). In this formal structure, each role position exists somewhat independently from the person who occupies that role. That is, when the person leaves the group, the position (or role) remains unfilled.

Furthermore, the person's behavior in such a formal role may not be consistent with the other members' expectations of the behaviors that should be performed by a person occupying such a role. Then we say that the person occupying the position is not fulfilling the role obligations; for example, the leader is not doing the leading. Defined in terms of behaviors and position, a role becomes an inherently behavioral concept. Furthermore, a behavioral role exists only when a person is communicating within a role. And those behaviors, in combination with the expectations of other group members, constitute our working definition of the role in a decision-making group.

Each role must be defined, to some extent, in terms of the communicative behaviors engaged in by the member occupying that role. The definition of a role solely as some preordained position that exists apart from the identity of the person occupying the position is incomplete. If we were to view a role in its broader sense, we might consider "president" of a government or a large organization to be a role. This type of role, defined solely as a position with attendant duties and privileges, exists independently of the person who actually serves as the president. Such a role definition governs many of the behavioral choices of the person filling that position. In addition, the position exists within the organization's structure despite the identity of the person who occupies it and continues to exist whether or not any person occupies it. Later in this chapter we will see how such positions influence relationships.

The role of "father" in a family group is also determined by factors other than behavior. The role of father is determined biologically (or legally, in the case of adoption) rather than simply by the actual behaviors performed. On the other hand, we also refer to the behavioral functions of the role "parent," regardless of who performs them. Therefore, an older child, for example, may perform "parenting" functions (that is, behaviors identifiable with the parent's role) even though that child does not occupy the formal position of parent, determined legally or biologically. The role, determined by behavior, is the informal role of parent.

To the extent that each group is capable of developing its own roles, norms, and social system, the members develop a system of informal roles. Such a system is created in addition to any preestablished network of roles that is "passed out" to the members by some external authority. Thus, each member (together with the other group members) works out his or her role through performing communicative behaviors. Each member's role, along with that role's relationships with the roles of other members, must be defined principally in terms of the behaviors performed by that member in combination with fellow group members. No role appears to be universally present in all (or even most) groups, with the probable exception of the role of leader. But because the leadership role is unique and so significant to the group process, Chapter 7 is devoted entirely to it.

Bormann and Bormann (1988, pp. 101–104) provide one possible explanation for the idiosyncracy of informal roles in decision-making groups. Their discussion of role emergence suggests that roles develop over time, out of a pattern of response reinforcement during group interaction. As a member performs a given behavior, other members either encourage or discourage its continued performance through their reactions. They postulate that if the other members encourage this role function, the member will be likely to repeat that behavior until it becomes a full-fledged role function. If the other members discourage the behavior, however, the person will probably cease engaging in such a behavior during subsequent interaction. Thus, each individual member develops a role by consistently performing those behaviors that receive positive reinforcement from other group members. Furthermore, the other group members develop a set of expectations concerning a given member's role behavior on the basis of that person's repeated performance of similar behaviors.

One member of a classroom decision-making group was informed by her fellow group members that they believed her role to be that of "blocker." She responded in her report of the group meeting, "I was considered a blocker. I can't figure out why." Her role behaviors during past group meetings, even though she was apparently unaware of them, were consistently critical of the group's directions and its potential decisions. She consistently characterized the progress made during previous meetings as "Not much." Hence, a role consists not only of the behaviors performed by each individual, but of those behaviors in conjunction with other group members' behaviors and expectations. After the fact, then, the members are able to discern the behaviors that are "typical" (that is, consistent with the role) and come to expect them.

Another member of a classroom group, in her diary of group meetings, wrote the following about her own role: "It is really nice to know that I have a role now, so that I can play it. Everyone says that I am a supporter and harmonizer. . . . I really enjoy my group, and this has really helped me to understand people in groups. Before, I have been so scared of interacting.

This class [group] has helped me come out of my shell more than usual."
While one's private tendencies will affect one's behavior to some extent,
every person's behavior in a group is more the product of the group interaction, taken as a whole, than it is a product of the person's own tendency to
behave in a certain way.

Each individual member develops that pattern of behaviors which constitutes his or her role in conjuction with fellow group members. Thus, the
role—the behavior pattern—that a person develops in one group may be
quite different from that same person's role in another group. A role, then, is
not wholly determined by someone's innate personality traits. The human
being does not carry a role from one group to another. A role is more like a
suit of clothes that is put on or taken off to suit the occasion. The group's
demand on the individual member's behaviors change because the group
itself changes.

Role Performance

Role performance is the actual behavior of an individual while in the group. If
we think of a role as a formal position in a network, the performance of that
role by the person who occupies it is determined largely by the informal
development of role behaviors in conjunction with the other members of the
social system. Moreover, each person has an implicit notion of being "on
duty" when performing that role. When on duty, the person is likely to engage in certain role behaviors. But when a person is "off duty," his or her behaviors are less likely to conform to the expectations of other members of the
social system.

We recall one classroom group in which the members recognized one of
their group as their leader. At the same time, they resented somewhat his
overbearing and arrogant approach to performing that leadership role. He
talked constantly and tended to override any objections by other members to
his directions. That same person rarely spoke during the meetings of the
entire class. He never volunteered a contribution to classroom discussions.
When called upon, he was very soft-spoken and acquiescent. Apparently he
considered himself to be "on duty" as a "leader" only in his smaller group. In
the larger classroom, he was "off duty" and felt no need to conform to the
group's expectations of what a leader should do.

Goffman (1959, pp. 106-140) distinguishes role performance in terms of
"regions" of behavior. In other words, a person performs a role when he or
she is before the audience appropriate to that role (the "front region"). On the
other hand, when the person is "backstage" (in the "back region"), there is
apparently no perceived need to perform the role. Consequently, role performance is quite inconsistent with other people's expectations when the
performer is in the back region; it is consistent with the expectations of others
only when the performer is in the front region.

The noted psychologist Karl Weick adds an important insight to the
notion of role performance when he talks about partial inclusion (Weick,

1979, pp. 95–97). *Partial inclusion* simply means that a person does not invest (or include) all his or her behaviors in a single role. The various behaviors you are capable of are dispersed among the several groups of which you are a member. You might be a leader in one group, a follower in another, aggressive at one time, and passive later. You can behave as a friend, a colleague, a son, a daughter, a husband, a father, and so on. All of us are capable of performing many roles, and it is important to remember that your role in a group is consistent with your own willingness to behave in a certain way in light of the expectations of the other group members. It is a mistake to equate personality with role behavior. The group needs only certain types of communicative behavior from you; you may have skills and ways of behaving that are simply not wanted or needed from the group. You do not invest your entire personality in the group. Group members perform certain roles because they are using particular patterns of talents or behaviors that the group and the individual desire or need. Their entire personhood is only partially included in the group.

Role Conflict

Occasionally role strain or role conflict occurs in a group in which a member finds that the demands of the group on his or her behavior are more than can be performed (*role strain*) or that the role behavior in that group is contradictory to her or his role performances in other groups (*role conflict*). Typically, the informal role structure is free from patterns of role strain, since every member works out a certain role performance in combination with other group members. Rarely does a person become committed to an emerging pattern of role behaviors which that person is unable to perform adequately.

Occasionally, an individual member will perceive a conflict between role performance in the group and role performance consistent with the member's own personality or self-concept. One such member expressed just such a conflict in her reactions to a classroom group meeting. She wrote, "I started out with the feeling that I was going to remain passive and not contribute to the group—just to see if anyone would try to get things going. I was tired of trying to spark everyone and get them moving. I couldn't do it. I guess my personality is not suited for that role." Another individual expressed a similar role conflict when she confided, "I became very embarrassed when the group described my role (as they saw it) in the group. . . . I guess I'm not too 'big' on confrontations as well as tension. I can't confront others unless it's positively."

One student in a classroom group apparently experienced a similar feeling. She was the member delegated by her group to confront another frequently absent member with the group's ultimatum: "Put up or shut up." She wrote in her diary of her reaction to the group's decision to appoint her as the confronter. She considered herself a friendly and amiable person—one who was unable to perform such an aggressive task. Nevertheless, she did just that during the next group meeting. Her diary, written at the conclusion of that meeting, included the following comment: "I felt that my role [as confronter] in the group meeting had a stifling effect on me, but I felt that we accomplished a lot." Her successful performance, then, evidently compensated for her internal struggle with the role.

A more likely and perhaps more typical strategy of a person who is placed in an incongruent role is to modify perceptions of that role. Such a strategy may result in perceiving the role as something it is not or in perceiving the self in a different role. Another classroom group may provide a classic example of role self-perceptions that were quite unrealistic and quite inaccurate in terms of the individual member's perception of his role in the group. Bob, as we shall call him, perceived himself to be a natural leader and certainly the leader of his classroom group. After one meeting he wrote his personal reactions to that meeting in his diary (a class requirement): "I sort of felt insecure in my role as leader. I let John take it mostly, and he finally came to terms with the task and analyzed it well. However, everyone was unanimous in their support of me, so I guess they feel good about me as leader."

John's reactions to that same meeting appeared in his diary: "I do not object to Bob's trying to control every meeting. But if he slips or does something I do not agree with, I jump in and take control." Another member, after that same group meeting, wrote, "Bob tried to dictate to us again today, but I thought John handled him very well, under the circumstances." A meeting two weeks later brought the following comments from two other group members. One member wrote, "The meeting was short, but we accomplished everything we needed. I guess I'm feeling a little less annoyed with Bob." The other member wrote, "I was especially pleased with this meeting because Bob and I did not conflict as we did in the past. Perhaps this is due to two factors. First, he realized my right to have an opinion and respected my opinions more. Second, though, I might have been too tired to assert myself." Bob's reaction to that same meeting reflected quite a different perception of the situation: "My position as leader was more firmly established." Incidentally, at the end of the class when the group members voted on who they thought had led the group, John received every vote except one—probably Bob's.

A more typical variety of role conflict is the inconsistency between a person's behaviors in the role of group member and a role in another group. One member of a classroom group, an older woman who described herself as "old enough to be the mother of any of my fellow members," found herself in role conflict in her group. The particular role conflict she perceived might have been something of a "generation gap." During one meeting especially, she found this role conflict to be virtually unbearable and described her reactions in her diary: "Because of the subject of the discussion [premarital sex], I am still reacting as a parent rather than a 'free-thinking' individual. I shall try to 'cure' this habit. Carefully taught and long-ingrained standards make it hard to compromise. They never change completely."

This particular member was quite committed to both groups (her family and her classroom decision-making group) and to the ideals of the two groups. She earnestly wanted to engage in appropriate role performances in both groups but found the carryover from one to be in conflict with the other. Consequently, she wanted to believe in opposite sides of the same issue. She never did completely resolve this role conflict.

One reason for the different roles developed by the same person in different groups is the interdependence of the social dimensions. The nature of the task stimulates certain expectations or requirements so that the network of roles is affected along with all elements of the social dimension. Another example from a classroom group may illustrate this phenomenon. One woman, whom we shall identify as Margie, felt that her contribution to a group was limited to that of follower and information giver. Although bright, Margie was extremely shy and found it difficult to assert herself in any social setting. In a classroom group discussing problems of educationally disadvantaged children in urban ghettos, she found her behavior pattern quite different from what her personality traits might have predicted. Her fellow members discovered that she had had summer experience in social work and consistently turned to her for critical advice. They recognized her expertise based on personal experiences. Margie became a critic-evaluator and by far the most frequent contributor to her group. Rather than being a follower, Margie found herself in a role of dominance because of the nature of the task and her relationship with it. Of course, her personality was unchanged. She remained shy and nonassertive. But in the role network of this particular group working on this particular task, Margie's behavior pattern was assertive and her role was quite dominant.

In contrast to Margie, Steve was a "big man on campus"—a starting member of the football team, an officer in his fraternity, handsome, and loaded with personal charm. It was impossible to dislike Steve. Everyone liked him from the first meeting, including his fellow classroom-group members. Steve was used to being a leader and seemed to have the knack of exerting the forcefulness of his personality on whomever he came in contact with. But as the pressure of time to complete their task impinged upon the group members, they became increasingly disenchanted with Steve's role behaviors. He discovered that his personality and charm were insufficient to meet the demands of task accomplishment. Bewildered by the social ostracism from his fellow group members and frustrated because his contributions were consistently rejected or ignored, he uncharacteristically remained silent and became a habitual absentee. For Steve, the experience of being in that group was obviously socially painful.

Role conflict can certainly occur, as it did in Steve's case. Generally, however, a person is able to keep the role in one group fairly distinct from that in another group. At a commonsense level, your behavior at home with your family group is different from your behavior with a group of your close friends. And both behavior patterns are different from your behavior in a classroom. You behave differently at a football game from the way you behave at a fancy restaurant. Implicitly, and often without consciously doing so, we make changes in our role patterns and performances as we move from group to group. And we do so as easily as we change shirts. This is the nature of social roles.

Baird and Weinberg (1977, pp. 164–168) summarize three different types of role conflict: "intrarole conflict, where someone experiences conflict while playing a single role; interrole conflict, where one person is simultaneously required to play two different roles; and interpersonal role conflict, where two or more individuals compete for the same role." The problems of role conflict, particularly those of intrarole and interrole conflict, are most pronounced in the network of formal role positions imposed by external sources on a group. The informal network of roles typically avoids intense role conflicts. The individual person and the group are able to devise their own role network and expectations in a form that is comfortable for most group members. In other words, role conflict is rarely a problem, except in the structure of formal roles. Any problems of role conflict that are evident in the formal structure are often ameliorated in the informal role structure worked out by the group members during the process of group development.

A political model of group interaction is another way to look at role performances and role conflicts. This perspective underscores how complex role conflicts can be. A political perspective on groups is different from our normal notions of group interaction. Most group members assume that others will be rational, motivated, participatory, and work in good faith. But a political perspective warns that power relationships between group members leads to alliances, coalitions, conformity, and wheeling and dealing. A political perspective on groups recognizes that status differences and personal agendas influence group interaction in such a way that group members spend much of their time affirming power relationships; communication becomes an act of maneuvering for position.

A high-status person's membership in a group will influence the other members' role behavior in particular ways. Often in organizations groups are led by vice presidents or managers who bring their titles, prestige, and power into the group. The presence of these people often inhibits critical discussions of diverse viewpoints and alters the way people communicate. The following is a typical example:

There is a meeting of a group in a large corporation. The senior vice president chairs this group, which is charged with making decisions about how to cut the operating budget by 10 percent. After about an hour it is obvious that the vice president has made up his mind about the cuts and disagrees with a few other group members. At the group's next meeting, most of the other members remain silent and allow the vice president's opinions to shape the group decision. It is obvious that the other members have concluded that, given the vice president's strongly held opinions, the political benefits of not confronting the vice president outweigh any concerns for active participation and critical discussion.

Group members serve in overlapping and sometimes incompatible roles. In the above example the group members had their role behaviors influenced by political considerations in the organization. Usually these conflicts lead to ineffective role performance. We cannot blame the group members in the example for considering their self interest, but such conformity leads to weaker decisions and the neglect of important behaviors. In Chapter 7 we will discuss the development of leadership roles, an area in which conflict between people is more common.

Role Differences

As individual group members work out their own roles in cooperation with other group members, each member takes on a role that differentiates him or her from the other group members. That is, even though each member's role behaviors depend on the behaviors of other members, the resulting pattern of interactive behaviors distinguishes each member's role from those of other members. The group is thus composed of a network of roles, but each group member individually possesses an identity that distinguishes that member from other members. Group members therefore come to expect an identifiable set of certain behaviors from one person and a different set of behaviors from another person. In this way, each member maintains an identity as an individual, and the network composed of all individual identities becomes identifiable as the group.

It is impossible to identify a complete list of all the roles in a group, but some common classifications are listed below. This classification scheme is still one of the best descriptions of the various types of roles performed in groups (Benne and Sheats, 1948). The scheme includes three types of roles: group task roles, group building and maintenance roles, and individual roles. Although it is difficult to make a clear distinction among all roles, it is surely the case that the three role types indicate that some roles are not oriented toward group goals, but apparently fulfill some purely individual needs. Below, each role is described and then defined with a sample communication representative of the role. All the communication examples come from transcripts and recordings of actual group interactions.

1. Task Roles These roles are task-oriented and move the group toward its goal.

> *Initiator-Contributor* Presents lots of new ideas; initiates new ideas and directions. "Let's examine the social consequences of these taxes."

> *Information Seeker* Seeks information, clarification, and evidence. "Has anyone found research supporting this program?"

> *Opinion Seeker* Checks the opinion and agreement or disagreement of other group members. "How do the rest of you feel about this way of doing things?"

> *Information Giver* Provides and contributes important and relevant information. "The program was funded by property taxes in New York. There was a tax increase of 3 percent."

Elaborator Explains, extends, and clarifies the ideas of others. "John was probably thinking about the magnet school programs in Boston. That was state-supported rather than locally supported."

Coordinator Shows relationships between ideas and facts. "The Boston program can't be compared to the New York program because of the different ways in which the programs were funded."

Orienter Keeps the group on track and moving toward the goal. "We are straying from the point. Let's get back to the issue on the floor."

Evaluator-Critic Comments on group information and applies critical standards. "That proposal might work if we had an income tax in Connecticut, but we generate revenue by sales tax only."

Energizer Stimulates the group to action. "Okay, let's go. Who'd like to handle the research on magnet schools?"

Procedural Technician Deals with procedural tasks, such as scheduling, copying, and handouts. "I have reserved Room 233 and a slide projector for next week."

Recorder Takes the minutes and keeps the group's records and history. "Last week we decided to have a long meeting this time."

2. Group Building and Maintenance Roles   These roles are communicative behaviors that focus on interpersonal relations in the group and on the general quality of the socioemotional environment.

Encourager Accepts and reinforces the ideas of other group members. "Good idea, Bill. That really helps."

Harmonizer Keeps the peace and resolves tensions in the group; often uses humor or sarcasm. "Nothing like a little friendly communication" (immediately following an argument).

Compromiser Tries to offer ideas and solutions that satisfy everyone. "Okay, if the tax information is too difficult to find, I'll get the information about the tax laws, and you find the community stuff."

Gatekeeper and Expediter Tries to encourage even participation. "Let Sarah talk. She usually has good ideas."

Group Observer Makes generalized comments about the behavior of the group as a whole. "It seems as though we're stuck."

Follower Goes along easily with the trends in the group. "Sounds okay to me if it's okay with you guys."

3. Individual Roles   These roles are self-centered and satisfy personal needs rather than the goals of the group.

Aggressor Criticizes and attacks other group members in order to enhance his or her own status. "I am not impressed with this solution. I think we should do it the way I suggested earlier."

Blocker Does not cooperate, and opposes much of what the group tries to do. "I don't like any of these ideas."

Recognition Seeker Seeks to enhance his or her own status by citing past accomplishments. "Last year the group I led was very successful because we were organized."

Self-Confessor Talks about himself or herself and offers irrelevant information about his or her own feelings and attitudes. "You know I always do that. I really have to try to change my habits."

Playboy Behaves in a nonserious manner, always fooling around and joking. "Hey, let's bag this and go have a beer. We can talk more there if you want."

Dominator Tries to monopolize the group with long speeches and suggestions on how to do everything. "Well, I think we should [etc., etc., etc.]." "My opinion is. . . ."

Help Seeker Tries to elicit sympathy and help from everyone; expresses insecurity a lot. "I am not good at writing. I think someone else should do it, or at least we should do it together."

Special-Interest Pleader Has a private agenda and ideas, and pleads for these. "I still think the magnet school idea is a good one. Let's read this report and then talk about it again."

This list of roles certainly does not exhaust the list of all possible roles that can occur in groups performing decision-making tasks. An additional role, common to many groups, is that of "joker." Depending on the specific interaction, a joker may be a harmonizer, a follower, a tension reliever, a playboy, or even an information giver (although the joker's information is typically phrased in a humorous way). In cloaking information in humor, the joker may allow the group to accept information that would otherwise be unacceptable.

People tend to associate the joker's role primarily with the socioemotional dimension, rather than with the task dimension, and this association may possibly be valid. When the joker's role as the group clown arouses a set of expectations that the joker is not serious about the task or is disinterested in helping the group achieve consensus, however, the role is probably more disruptive than beneficial to the group process. Every role is inevitably relevant to both the task and socioemotional dimensions of the group process. In a decision-making group, any role performance (such as that of the joker) that leads group members to believe that the member is not serious about completing the task is likely to be detrimental to the most efficient functioning of the group process.

The "silent member," or low participator, is another role that may have important functions in the group process. If a member is characterized by other group members as a silent member, these others often come to believe that the silent one is not fully committed to the group or the group task. On the other hand, a silent member may develop into an important contributor to the group process if the group members do not perceive low participation as a symptom of low commitment.

One classroom group contained a silent member who later played an important role in that group's development, even though the total amount of talk he generated remained well below the average of all group members. His later contributions, though infrequent, consisted of volunteering to do the group's outside activities, to research materials, and generally to perform the less desirable legwork of the group. Not only did the other group members come to view his role as quite valuable, but the member himself became much more satisfied with the group and his membership in it. One of his reactions to a group meeting late in the class expressed his increased satisfaction: "I felt I made some very important, objective contributions. I have moved from being a low participator to an important, candid one. Meetings are more fun now."

When a group is sincerely and seriously interested in self-improvement, one assigned role that may well enhance the group's progress is that of "group productivity observer." The member assigned this role, while still carrying out his or her informal role developed through normal group interaction, takes on the additional responsibility of reporting at the end of each meeting on the progress that the group appears to have made during the meeeting.

To benefit from the possibility that a group productivity observer may be beneficial to the group process, the other group members must be open to the observer's criticisms and observations. Moreover, they must have faith in the objectivity of the member they choose to be the observer and must be willing to trust that member. Of course, the person who is assigned the role of group productivity observer must be frank, candid, and honest in observing the group interaction and must give the group an accurate assessment of its productivity. If your group wishes to assign this role to one of your group members, you may find such a role performance quite helpful. But the group productivity observer is beneficial only to the extent that you are all willing to accept the member's observations and strive actively for self-analysis. On the other hand, if your group appears to be functioning quite normally and acceptably, you will find little reason for assigning such a role to anyone.

Because of the changing roles of women in society, there has recently been a great deal of interest in the roles played by males and females in the group process. Much attention has been directed at the influence of sex-role stereotypes on group functions, but some investigations have attempted to discover potential role differences between males and females in terms of their role performance and their influence on the overall group process; for example, Coates (1986, pp. 151–155) reports differences between all-female and all-male groups in terms of their role differentiation and communication. The findings suggest that all-female groups exhibit less differentiation between their members' roles than do all-male groups; at the same time, since female groups often outperform male groups in performing their assigned tasks, it appears that role differentiation does not necessarily lead to greater productivity.

There are a number of classification schemes to describe roles in small groups. One scheme simplifies matters by considering only the two main functions discussed earlier—the task and social functions. Figure 5-1 locates various roles on these two major dimensions. Even though it is impossible to completely distinguish between task and social roles, it is possible to consider behaviors as predominantly one or the other. Sector 1 includes silent members and low participators who have little influence, either on the task or on social relations within the group. Sector 2 includes group members who are very task-oriented but who ignore the group's social dimensions. Sector 3 includes group members who strongly influence the group's social dimensions, but who contribute little to the task requirements of the group. Sector 4 includes the group's leaders—those who have a high impact both on the group's progress toward its goals and on social relations within the group.

High-Performance Groups

As a student you are learning about your own skills, abilities, and preferences. In this book we have encouraged you to learn new behaviors and practice new roles and communication patterns. But over time, and as you work more in groups, you will develop a work style preference. Two researchers (McCann and Margerison, 1989) have developed some principles of

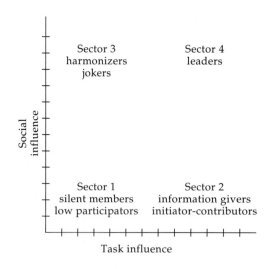

FIGURE 5-1 Types of task and social roles.

groups based on determining individual work styles. Group members usually have different ways of working and leaders can capitalize on these differences. High-performance groups have members play roles that are most suited for them. They do not try to turn followers into leaders or information specialists into innovators. Below are nine "types of work" that McCann and Margerison have identified. These result from the analysis of countless groups in business, industry, consulting, planning, and engineering. They are "work roles" that group members play and the key is to compose groups by having the "right" individual perform the "right" role for him or her.

Advisers   These people gather information and make it available to others. They gather data from reports and other people and then interpret the data for others in the group. Planners and information officers are examples of people in some organizations who fit into this category.

Innovators   These are creative people who think up new ideas, products, and ways of doing things. After advisers gather information and make it available, the innovators use the information to create new and successful products and services.

Promoters   Ideas have to be marketed and sold. It does not matter how good an idea is if you cannot convince others. The need for promoters is often neglected by groups whose members fail to understand that their ideas must be presented effectively to other people (or to other departments within an organization). Group leaders must have the ability to promote ideas.

Developers   These people work on implementating decisions and putting plans into practice. After an idea is "sold," the group must confront the practical realities of developing the idea and making it work. At this point a group must work its way through the practical constraints that an organizational environment can impose.

Organizers   These are the people who are good at making plans and getting things done. Organizers work well with people and help them meet deadlines. Again, managers spend most of their time organizing.

Producers   Once plans, schedules, and organizing are complete, products and services must be produced. Producers are the people who do the repetitive work of the group. In a classroom group a producer might be the one who makes charts or types a paper. In a large organization producers work with "production managers" to ensure the production of a product or service.

Inspectors   Inspection is a quality-control function and another group role that is often neglected. Inspectors keep surveillance and control over things. They make sure that products, documents, and group activities are of sufficient quality.

Maintainers Maintenance is an administrative function that supports the infrastructure of the group or organization. Maintainers in a large organization that has an infrastructure (building) to "maintain" will include janitorial and service workers. This role is important to groups working within organizations. But it is less relevant to classroom groups.

Linking This is the primary role of a leader. A linker is at the hub of the group and responsible for coordinating and integrating all functions. Good linkers are like the boundary spanners discussed in Chapter 3 and can connect the group to the outside environment. They also coordinate people within the group to ensure that team members are cohesive. Finally, linkers facilitate social relations among group members. They harmonize and promote good feelings.

These groups are called *high-performance* because they capitalize on the unique skills of group members. Research on successful groups indicates that groups succeed when people enjoy their work and perform successfully. A leader can increase the chances for success by organizing highly specified groups based on work preferences. McCann and Margerison also found that people who enjoyed their work in groups displayed some common characteristics. Promoters are creative; producers are practical, and so on. High-performance groups are well-balanced with respect to group roles and have excellent linking skills. When group members' job functions match their work preferences, they are far more likely to be motivated and perform at high efficiency and quality. Leaders should aim to balance group roles as much as possible.

NORMS

Conformity by members to certain behaviorial patterns is a normal and consistent phenomenon of every social system. The punishment for nonconformity is often not clear, but the pressure to conform is strong nevertheless. We consistently follow the changing fashions of dress and music, for example. What was conformist yesterday may be nonconformist today, but we continue to heed the changing social whims in an overt drive to avoid being abnormal.

The human animal apparently has a strong desire to follow the herd. At one time or another, you have probably proved this point with some variation of the "emperor's new clothes" prank. In one variation, for example, a group of people stops at a busy street corner and stares upward at a purely arbitrary point in the sky. They engage in totally meaningless, animated conversation about this imaginary phenomenon they are allegedly observing. They point to it, "oohing" and "aahing" over the magnificence of the sight. Within minutes a crowd gathers, and everyone stares, pointing at the sky. When the people in the orginal group feel that the crowd is large enough, they quietly slip away and congratulate themselves on their remarkable ability to manipulate human behavior.

As standards for behavior, norms vary considerably in the extent to which they are known. Some norms, such as the laws or bylaws of a formal organization, are very explicit; the organization's members know what its laws are and what the punishments are for violating them. Laws are easily recognized and understood. Other norms, however, are less explicit. Members of the social system may not realize what norms exist until having violated them. Newcomers to a group often learn the group's norms only by accidentally breaking them and experiencing the consequences.

Also, even while some social norms apply to all members of a group, other norms apply only to one or another role; that is, a specific behavior considered normal in one role is not necessarily considered normal in another. For example, a superior can walk directly into the office of a subordinate, but entering a superior's office without permission would violate a norm. This illustrates that not all of a social system's norms apply equally to all members of the system. Rather, each role has its own limits of acceptable (or normal) behavior. Thus, playing golf and joining a high-class country club would be considered normal behavior for a business executive, but drinking beer with the "hard-hats" in a saloon after work would be considered abnormal behavior for this executive.

Norms Defined

The most obvious definition of *norm* includes some characteristic of necessity or obligation—"oughtness." Norms describe how common behavioral and intellectual standards have developed in the group (Moscovici, 1985, p. 373). The degree of oughtness may vary from situation to situation and from role to role, and it may also determine the extent of the punishment to be meted out for deviating from the norms. That is, when one belches at a party, one is behaving contrary to some norm, but the punishment for this deviation is not going to be as severe as the punishment for violating some codified norm, such as robbing a bank. Under any circumstances, however, to behave contrary to a norm is to do something that the system decrees ought not to be done.

Andrews (1988) distinguishes between explicit norms and implicit norms, a differentiation that is particularly relevant to our study of group decision making. *Explicit norms* include those which are formal and which are intentionally adopted by the group, such as the procedures the group adopts or the rules it abides by in its meetings; Robert's *Rules of Order*, for example, is a set of explicit norms. *Implicit norms*, on the other hand, emerge during the interaction of the group members and become "knowable" as the interaction continues. Group members may be aware of both explicit and implicit norms, but the implicit norms are more changeable as the members continue to interact with one another.

Some norms, which may be either explicit or implicit, also originate from the values of members. Davis (1969) refers to a *value* as "a basic belief or assumption about what is good, right, or proper." Such values probably originate in a larger culture or society to which the specific group members

belong. The values of a business organization, for example, would be imposed on the members of subgroups within that organization. After all, the
group members are also members of the larger organization. Members may
also have values that they bring to the group from the larger society to which
they all belong—the university community, a church, a national culture, etc.

Norms may thus originate in a larger society, in the group's interaction,
or in the procedural rules officially adopted by the group. In this way, they
may be imposed on the group as well as created or formulated during the
process of group interaction. Like other behavioral standards (such as roles),
norms may be formal or informal. In summary, norms may be imposed on the
group from an external authority or may be developed by the group members
during the actual process of group interaction.

DEVELOPMENT OF GROUP NORMS

Norms develop slowly in groups and are always a reflection of the values and
information shared by the group members. As the members repeat behaviors
over time, the developing patterns become norms. Even something as simple
as seating habits are subject to norms. After a few weeks in most classes, you
will notice the students (including yourself) seated in approximately the same
seat every day. If you come to class late and find someone else sitting in
"your" seat, you probably feel slightly irritated.

But the development of norms in decision-making groups is more complex than the simple repetition of behaviors. Norms develop through feedback loops and interaction. When an individual is in a group, he or she has
some ideas about the subject matter under discussion. In a sense, individuals
have norms of their own. But group membership means that the individual
must exchange ideas (communicate) with others. Eventually people notice
that their views on things do not coincide; they meet with disagreement.
People become a little uncertain of their own opinions and information and
work to reduce the differences by finding a consensus satisfactory to all.
Thus, groups establish norms in order to reduce tension. Even the choice of
where to sit in the example above is based on simplicity and consistency,
which reduce tension. It is simply easier to sit in the same seat and allow
others to do so.

Moscovici (1985) explains that groups do not establish norms as much as
they transform individual norms into a single one. People come to the group
with attitudes and opinions, and these are transformed by the process of
interacting with others. Individual attitudes and opinions converge toward
agreement with others, and the group transforms individual attitudes into
group-held norms. There is a classic research study by Sherif (1935) that
demonstrates this point with great insight. Sherif had subjects look at a
stationary light shown in total darkness. This stationary light produces the
autokinetic phenomenon, which means that the light appears to move; the
light is actually stationary but creates the impression of motion. In the first

phase of the experiment, people estimated how much the light was moving and established a personal norm. In the second phase, two or three people who had different personal norms were brought together for discussion, and in the course of the group discussion their judgments developed toward a common norm. The study showed that individual norms were transformed into a single one.

Some members of a group in an organization, observed by one of the authors, had established the norm of verbally forceful argument. Early in the group's history some new members were presenting documented evidence in a calm and professional manner, but they were attacked quite harshly by the other members. Their evidence was questioned and their arguments criticized. The new members tried to remain composed and to respond in a dispassionate manner, but they were almost shouted down. Soon the new members, too, adopted the norm of assertiveness and forcefulness to support their views. The group had now established predictable communication sequences that established a norm of verbal forcefulness.

Norms develop because group members establish expectations about what ought to occur. As a result of feedback and patterns of reinforcement, group members establish a psychological ideal for a specified behavior and then patterns that fall above or below expectations. Figure 5-2 illustrates this process. Each group establishes expectations for member participation. As the group evolves, people are reinforced or punished for verbal participation. If one member perceives that his or her contributions are valued by the group then they are likely to increase their participation. The opposite is true for a member who is not reinforced for communicating. Over time participation norms will develop. The dashed line on Figure 5-2 represents a hypothetical midpoint for expected amount of participation, and then there is a tolerance

FIGURE 5-2 Model of member participation norms.

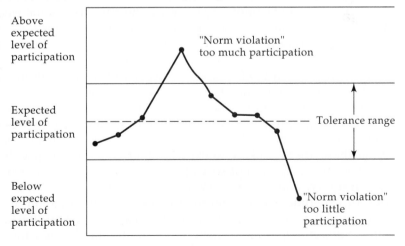

Amount of participation

range around that midpoint. You will note that group members who go above or below the tolerance range have committed a "norm violation." They are talking too much or too little. Norm violators will be negatively judged. They need to identify the tolerance range for acceptable behavior.

Norms "belong" to the group and not to the individual member. Everyone, moving from one group to another, is subject to different norms because of the differences between the groups, not because of a new internalization of a different set of norms. We shall consistently refer to group norms with the full implication that the norms do indeed "belong" to the group.

As classroom instructors, we strive to encourage a classroom norm of argument—a free exchange of conflicting opinions and ideas. Students engage in verbal conflict with other students and with the instructor. Many students and instructors are uncomfortable with this norm and consider it inappropriate, disrespectful, and disruptive. The point is that no norm is more "correct" than another. Rather, social norms vary from one social system to another and may even conflict with one another. Therefore, a norm developed in one social system is appropriate within that social system but may be quite inappropriate in another.

Pressures to Conform

Although deviance from norms is the subject of Chapter 8, it is important at this point to provide some discussion of conformity pressures exerted by a group on its own members. We shall take the position that not all conformity is alike. Nor is all deviation alike. The typical reaction to conformity (and, paradoxically enough, to deviance) is rather negative. That is, people often feel that conformists have no minds of their own. They merely succumb to the will of some unnamed majority. Also, deviance is typically regarded as distasteful, and a deviant is regarded as a criminal or an immoral person. We maintain that neither conformity nor deviance is harmful or beneficial in principle. Some element of conformity is socially healthy, as is some element of deviation from group norms. The important principle is not *whether* conformity or deviance is good or bad, but *what* conformity or deviance is good or bad.

Few will disagree with the fact that groups, societies, and cultures exert enormous pressures on their members to conform to the norms established by the social system. Conformity and its counterpart, deviation from norms, will be present in all groups and in all societies. Furthermore, group pressures to conform to social norms and to sanction negatively those members who deviate from them are also likely to exist in all groups, both explicitly and implicitly. Even the suggestion of social pressure causes people to conform. Hocking, Margreiter, and Hylton (1977), in a very interesting study, gave subjects in an experiment either positive or negative information about a band. They found that positive information increased the positive evaluation of the band. Subjects were more likely to enjoy the band when they had previous positive information.

On the other hand, all norms (particularly those which develop informally through group interaction) are not consistently enforced to the letter of the law. A certain range of behaviors is expected, and a certain range of deviation from norms is expected. In this sense, members will interact and behave within a certain range of allowable behaviors without being perceived as deviants. But behaviors beyond those limits will be labeled as deviant, and group pressures toward conformity will be brought to bear on those members performing such behaviors.

Typically, informal norms are accepted by group members, so that members will generally conform to those norms. When members accept a norm, they not only acknowledge that the norm exists and that they understand it, but also that the norm applies to the behaviors of members within that group. Because norms develop as a product of the group interaction, rather than through an internalizing process of each individual member, informal norms are enforced by the group. Without enforcement of norms and punishment of deviants, the norms will cease to exist.

Certainly some of us are more likely than others to accept norms. For example, a person with a poor self-concept, a need for social acceptance, or a submissive personality trait will be more likely to conform with minimal group pressure. When conformity results from the personality characteristics of individual group members, however, the significance of those social norms to the group process decreases accordingly. More important are those norms that members accept because of the nature of the group process. That is, members who are committed to the group are engaged in active participation in the group deliberations. They feel that the group is important and are loyal to it.

Groupthink   Perhaps the most dramatic consequence of pressures to conform to group norms, especially in cohesive groups, is the groupthink phenomenon. *Groupthink* is what happens when a group avoids conflict and reaches consensus without criticizing and evaluating ideas. When the members of a group are very attracted to the group and reap many rewards from their membership in the group, they are especially vulnerable to the groupthink phenomenon. These groups have developed strong norms about not "rocking the boat," and they encourage almost blind loyalty to the group by discouraging conflict and independent opinions.

The following is an example of a groupthink situation: Robert Lynne, chairman of Regal Airlines, is meeting with his board of directors to decide whether or not to purchase a small ground transportation company. Lynne organized the meeting and opens with a few words in support of the purchase. As soon as he finishes, the rest of the board members begin nodding their heads in approval and supporting the idea. No one disagrees. The conversation that follows is light, supportive, and sprinkled with positive predictions about what this will mean for Regal Airlines. The group votes to approve the purchase and comments, "This was a great meeting and an important moment in the history of our company."

"Bob Lynne is taking us in new and productive directions," states another board member. "He certainly has my support."

This may appear to be a smooth and effective meeting, but the group is not really functioning well. The decision was made quickly and on the basis of normative pressures to "go along." It was a groupthink decision. Irving Janis, the sociologist who first wrote about groupthink, has observed these types of decisions in government policies. Janis studied documents and transcripts of meetings in the Kennedy administration during the 1962 Bay of Pigs invasion and concluded that the administration's decision to attack Cuba was a groupthink decision. It was the result of a cohesive group's reluctance to express private doubts about the decision. Janis has discovered groupthink tendencies in a number of government fiascoes (Janis, 1983).

Groupthink occurs because of the presence of certain group norms. And there are always pressures to conform to norms. Here are four norms that establish conditions for groupthink to occur:

1. *Mindless cohesion*   This is when a group feels that it can do no wrong because it is extremely optimistic and committed. While cohesion is, of course, important, it becomes counterproductive when the members dismiss anything that might threaten the group. The people in the Regal Airline example are more interested in conforming to the norm of cohesion than in critically examining their decisions.

2. *Pressuring nonconformists*   Group members are pressured into going along with the group. The pressure can be subtle, such as rolling one's eyes or frowning, or more direct, such as expulsion from the group. In time this leads to what Janis calls self-censorship, which is a tendency for group members to avoid expressing opinions.

3. *Failing to reward critical thinking*   Sometimes people give in to the pressures of high-status individuals. Very often groups that do not encourage critical thinking are those with strong leaders who demand support, not conflict. The group and its leader feel invulnerable. This feeling of invulnerability is a classic symptom of groupthink. Groups are ideal places for discussion and disagreement, and the quality of decisions suffers when honest opposition is not encouraged.

4. *Tendency to justify what they have done*   Groups make poor decisions when they discount information because it is inconsistent with an established position. Groupthink decisions emerge from rationalizations. The group blindly believes that what it has done in the past is best. They reject new information and reaffirm the inherent "correctness" of their own group. This leads to a false sense of consensus. The group is unified and spirited, so it appears that everything is fine. The members of the Regal Airline board of directors are congratulating themselves and feel very good about the decision; nevertheless, they have not reached a true consensus, one that emerges from discussion and critical evaluation.

More recent work on groupthink focuses on this matter of false and premature consensus. Cline (1990) essentially defines groupthink as premature consensus and then identifies communication patterns that are responsible for this defective decision making. Rather than blame flawed communication in a group on the presence of groupthink, Cline describes the type of communication that *leads* to groupthink. In short, groups that experience groupthink are in a rush to agree with one another. They fail to analyze issues critically and have an unhealthy fear of argument. Cline (1990) finds that groupthink groups will maintain harmony at all costs and have an unusually high percentage of agreement statements. Moreover, groupthink groups have relatively little disagreement and conflict and thereby strengthen the impact of agreements and accelerate the group's sense of unanimity.

Groupthink creates a very powerful vision of unanimity. It leads a group to believe that it has achieved consensus when, in fact, the group has not engaged in critical analysis. Members of groupthink groups use three strategies to produce a vision of unanimity. First, discussions are characterized by numerous statements of agreement without any clarification. Often members do little more than agree with themselves. Second, these groups use simple head nods or verbal regulators as indicators of agreement. The words "right," "yeah," or "okay," uttered in response to statements by another group member are understood to be agreements when they are actually merely part of the normal coordination of communication. A third way that groupthink groups create illusory unanimity is by actively soliciting agreements. Members will end their utterances with statements like "right?" or "Don't you think that's true?" Very simply, groupthink results from an overriding concern with harmony and conformity at the expense of critical thinking.

Conformity, when healthy or beneficial, is linked closely with the level of cohesiveness developed by a group during its interaction. Lacking cohesiveness, the members are unlikely to produce strong pressures for conformity on deviant members; they probably don't care whether deviant members conform to the group norms, since they are also less committed to the group process. In order to avoid groupthink, it is necessary to find the right balance between conformity and critical analysis.

The Norm of Reciprocity

Chapter 2 discussed the phenomenon of reciprocity, specifically the reciprocity of self-disclosing communication. This human phenomenon is so pervasive in groups that reciprocity has even been labeled a social "norm" (Gouldner, 1960). Humans tend to react to other humans in a manner similar to the way in which those humans behave toward them. Furthermore, humans apparently reciprocate the behaviors of others in a sense that they feel they "ought" to do so. The human value leading to reciprocal behaviors is embodied in the golden rule and even in the golden rule in reverse. When attacked, we tend to fight back. A small boy will justify his aggressive behavior by saying, "He hit me first!" Apparently this norm of reciprocity justifies reciprocal fighting.

Probably no one social norm is present in all groups. But if any social norm is nearly universal among social systems, it may be the norm of reciprocity. In its state as a do-unto-others norm, reciprocity functions as a member's tendency to reciprocate similar behaviors in response to the behaviors of others. That is, if *A* helps *B*, *B* feels compelled to reciprocate that assistance. If *A* likes *B* (and *B* perceives that liking), *B* feels compelled to reciprocate. Consistent with previous discussions, if *A* confides some rather intimate self-disclosing information to *B*, *B* will tend to respond with intimate self-disclosing statements. The norm of reciprocity creates something of a snowball effect as each person's behavior reinforces the similar behaviors of the others. For this reason, perhaps, a norm embodying a pattern of communicative behaviors develops rather quickly in the continuing interaction of the group.

Perhaps the most important principle in understanding norms as they function in the group process is that group norms "belong to" the group and not to its individual members. Moreover, in the presence of high cohesiveness and high levels of member commitment to the group, those group norms become very powerful forces in shaping the behaviors of the individual members, even sometimes to the detriment of the group.

Group norms are significant and potent forces in groups. There are studies that have found that preventing people from fulfilling group expectations is one of the most fundamental sources of frustration for people. Often, and perhaps typically, people will sacrifice their own individuality and individual needs (even physical ones) for the purpose of furthering and realizing group goals and conforming to social norms. And this is perfectly normal social behavior. The important principle remains: Social norms are group norms, rather than merely norms that are internalized by individual persons.

SUMMARY

The two most common standards for group members' behaviors are roles and norms. A role may be defined as the set of behaviors performed by a member in light of the expectations of other group members toward those behaviors. Each person's role often varies from group to group. Role performance, however, encapsulates each set of role behaviors within the region of performance—that specific group.

Some persons may experience role strain or conflict when a role performance places too great a demand on the group member or is incongruent with role performances in other groups. Occasionally, role conflict occurs when the expected role performance is incongruent with the person's personality traits. In that case, a person typically employs one of several strategies in order to reduce the role conflict (short of leaving the group). Every group member typically performs a role that differentiates him or her from other group members. High-performance groups take advantage of different work preferences. The number of available roles is very large and is typically idiosyncratic to each group, probably because of the fact that each member develops his or her role in conjunction with other group members during the process of group interaction.

Group norms provide standards for how each member ought to behave in the group. The members typically apply pressures on deviant members to conform. Those pressures are strongest and healthiest in a successful and cohesive group and sometimes lead to a phenomenon called groupthink, whereby groups make poor decisions because they discourage critical thinking. The most common norm of group interaction is reciprocity, the tendency to behave toward other people as they behave toward you.

CHAPTER OUTLINE

AN OVERVIEW OF KEY TERMS

PRESCRIPTIVE APPROACHES TO DECISION MAKING

Generating Ideas
Decision-Making Strategies
Implementing Solutions
Regulating Meetings

DESCRIPTIVE APPROACHES TO DECISION MAKING

Early Models of Development

THE PROCESS OF DECISION EMERGENCE

PHASES OF DECISION EMERGENCE

OTHER MODELS OF DECISION MAKING

The Spiral Model
Functional Communication
Using Communication to Modify Decisions
Multiple Sequence Models of Decision Making

INDIVIDUALS AND DECISION MAKING

Thinking Abilities of Members

SUMMARY

KEY TERMS

DECISION MAKING

PROBLEM SOLVING

NEGOTIATION

VOTING

CONSENSUS

PRESCRIPTIVE APPROACHES

Rational Reflection
Brainstorming
Buzz Groups
Focus Groups
Nominal Group Technique (NGT)
PERT
Robert's Rules

DESCRIPTIVE APPROACHES

Equilibrium Models
Phase Models
Spiral Model
Functional Communication

DECISION MODIFICATION

MULTIPLE SEQUENCE MODELS

Decision Paths
Routing Statements
Breakpoints

CONVERGENT THINKING

DIVERGENT THINKING

The Process of Group Decision Making

The past several decades have witnessed a growing concern over the allegedly clandestine nature of some decision-making groups in our society. The specter of a decision-making group in the proverbial smoke-filled back room is familiar to all of us. More often, the group making vital decisions is quite visible, but entrance into the group is highly restricted. Thus, concern has been concentrated on gaining a voice in the group decisions. For example, the "student power" movement of the 1960s resulted in student representation on most university committees, faculty senates, and even boards of regents. Now that a voice in the decision-making process has been, or is being secured by previously powerless minorities, the problem might appear to be solved. Unfortunately, nothing could be further from reality.

The sentiment of one newly named student member of a university's governing board aptly described the persistent problem. He stated that he had worked long and hard for student representation on that board, but now that the students' voice could be heard he didn't know how best to use it. The fact is that membership in the decision-making group is necessary but not sufficient for effective decision making. A knowledge and an understanding of the process of group decision making are absolutely essential for effective membership. Hundreds of business organizations seek assistance from professional consultants so that their management personnel can function effectively in decision-making groups. Being a member of a group is simply not enough. An understanding of how groups actually make decisions—the process of group decision making—is necessary for effective participation in group decision making.

The purpose of this chapter is to describe the process that characterizes group decision making. But there is one thing that must be emphasized. There is no simple formula that will ensure good decisions. Groups are complex entities and they belie simple and sure answers. We have two general goals for this chapter. First, we want you to understand the natural and emergent process of group decision making; that is, what groups do when they are left on their own to establish their own patterns and produce decisions based on true consensus. But secondly we are going to present some standard, or commonly accepted, group procedures. These are designed to help beginning students of group interaction get started. It is important to emphasize that forcing a group to go through a set of standard steps and procedures can often lead to problems. The group can become more concerned with the procedures than with the quality of the decision. Nevertheless, our guiding principle throughout this book has been to equip the student with intelligent choices about performing in groups. We present standard prescriptions for group success in that light. We want you to become sensitive to, and aware of, all aspects of what is occurring during group interaction. And while awareness of the group process is no guarantee of group success, it will certainly increase the chances for success.

AN OVERVIEW OF KEY TERMS

Preliminary to reading the ensuing discussion of the group decision-making process, one should have a full understanding of several key terms that will be used extensively in this chapter. All these terms are familiar and prompt immediate definitions. But in a sense these terms are jargon. That is, each of them specifies a rather precise meaning, probably narrower than the meaning used in everyday conversation. It is for the sake of precision, then, that the following definitions are included.

The relationship between *decision making* and *problem solving* is not a source of universal agreement. Some view the two terms as virtually synonymous; others draw rather clear distinctions between them. Our concern is with all decision making, which includes some types of problem solving while excluding others. Recall the earlier distinction between tasks more appropriately performed by individuals and those uniquely adapted to the group process. The basis for that distinction also differentiates between two types of problem solving. One kind of problem possesses a "best" or "correct" solution, which is determined by external and objective means. Such problems may be typified by a mathematical problem for which only one solution is acceptable, by a logic puzzle governed by the invariable rules of induction and deduction, or by a crossword puzzle. Certainly these problem-solving tasks are not within the province of group decision making. They are best handled by a trained individual.

On the other hand, some problems have no solution that is subject to external validation. The solutions to these problems can be discovered only through group acceptance—the willingness of the members to commit themselves to implementing the solution. Thus, the only possible check of the validity of the solution is whether it achieves group consensus. Such problems would include determining how to combat pollution or crime most effectively, questions of penal reform, the rising costs from inflation, and so forth. The value of such solutions may ultimately be determined by how well they work after they have been put into practice. But at the time of their achieving consensus in the group, only validation through group consensus determines their worth.

Some decision-making tasks, of course, are not strictly within the scope of problems to be solved. Juries make a single decision on questions of value and unverifiable facts. Voters make decisions on candidates for political office. Such decisional situations do not stem directly from problems that require solving, and they include even such prosaic decisions as what clothing to wear tomorrow, what the theme for homecoming should be, what color to paint the house, and what brand of toothpaste to buy. Certainly decision making includes some types of problem solving and much more.

A *decision* resulting from group interaction is inevitably a choice made by group members from among alternative proposals available to them. Rarely does a group make a single decision in isolation. Although only one decision is sometimes apparent, such as a jury's decision of guilty or not guilty, many preliminary decisions are essential to that final decision and are made by the group on its way to achieving consensus on the final decision. The jury, for example, must decide which witness to believe, which piece of evidence is stronger, whether there is a reasonable doubt, and so forth. Group members, then, focus their attention on various proposals during their interaction and choose from among those alternative proposals which ones they will accept or reject. The sum of the accepted proposals constitutes the productivity of the group.

A group reaches a decision as its members achieve consensus on a proposal. The term *consensus* implies a variety of differing meanings. Some think of consensus as the will of the majority that results from democratic voting procedures. Some believe that unanimous agreement is necessary for consensus. Often consensus implies the absence of a formal vote but implicit agreement not necessarily verbalized by the group members. Obviously a consensus decision is one on which members typically agree, but agreement, while often necessary, is not a sufficient condition for consensus. That is, members may agree with a decision, even unanimously, but may not achieve consensus.

For our purposes, consensus implies not just agreement with the decision reached, but commitment to it. In fact, members may be committed to a decision to the extent that they work to put it into effect without ever fully agreeing with it. Zaleznik and Moment (1964, p. 142) clarify the nature of consensus as commitment:

> Our meaning of consensus lies in the degree of personal commitment the members feel toward the group decision after it is reached. This means, for example, that even though some members might disagree with the decision on principle, they will accept it and personally carry out their part. Their emotional commitment to the group is measured by willingness to put the plan decided on into effect, in their own personal behavior.

Simple agreement on a decision proposal, then, does not necessarily guarantee that the decision has achieved group consensus. In fact, group members who submit to pressures or external authority might express agreement without really accepting the proposal itself. In such instances the decision achieves false or superficial consensus: that is, agreement masquerading as consensus. The phenomenon of consensus without real agreement is not extraordinarily rare. For example, unsuccessful candidates for their party's nomination for political office often campaign strongly for the winning candidate. People may disagree on a new law or new tax passed by their elected representatives, but they generally obey those laws and pay those taxes.

The prime requisite for consensus, then, is not agreement with the decision, although agreement is highly common and even typical. The essential ingredient of consensus is the extent of group loyalty shared by members. To the extent that the members are cohesive or have developed groupness, the decision reached by that group are most likely to achieve consensus as well as agreement. Thus, the rather cohesive group is more likely to be effective as a decision-making body.

There are three modes of decision making, of which consensus is one (Wood, 1992). As stated above, consensus means that all members take part in shaping a decision and, most important, that all members are committed to the decision. But consensus is not always possible. Consensual decision making means that individual goals have either been met or are overshadowed by group goals. Moreover, consensus is most possible in groups in which (1) members share objectives, (2) members are status equals, (3) participation is balanced, and (4) opinions are not strong and unwavering.

Although consensus is highly desirable, there are two other common decision-making techniques: negotiation and voting.

Negotiation describes decision making when all members of the group do not share common goals or cannot reach agreement. Negotiation works best when people have competing goals, and when it is less important that all members share a commitment to the decision. The communication is often more aggressive and competitive in negotiation because of the operating perception that one person's gain is another's loss. This is why the resolution of a dispute between labor and management or between the two parties in a divorce is typically considered a negotiated decision. Negotiated decisions are complex because the multiple concerns of often incompatible positions need to be safeguarded. Unlike consensus, group members only need a minimal investment in negotiation. They communicate in such a way as to get the most, give up the least, and maintain enough goodwill to stay in the discussions. Negotiations are pragmatic. Group members may not develop the spirit and commitment of consensual decisions, but they reach conclusions born of practical necessity.

Voting is the third means of reaching decisions, and it is probably the least satisfying. When groups vote they do not reach agreement or even acceptance. Voting simply involves the establishment of some predetermined criterion (e.g., majority, two-thirds) and then a count of those who support or do not support a resolution to determine whether the criterion has been met.

Voting is quite different from consensus or negotiation because there is the clear expectation of winners and losers. Voting accomplishes closure. It completes a task with little or no concern for harmony, commitment, or equal representation. When voting is the mode of decision making, the communication is much more egocentric and persuasive because of the necessity of winning allies and the knowledge that there will be winners and losers. Implementation and future commitment to a decision are difficult in the case of voted decisions because minorities may not have a stake in the decision. Inexperienced groups are sometimes too quick to vote. They naïvely think that everyone will be satisfied with a majority. When groups must continue to work together, voting contributes little to cohesiveness.

This chapter is most concerned with questions of *how*—how groups achieve consensus on decisions over time; how members try to exert influence on one another during various periods of group interaction; how members' communicative behaviors occur in interstructured patterns during interaction. In short, the process perspective emphasizes how members actually interact during discussion of decision proposals and how certain proposals achieve consensus during group interaction; it is a descriptive approach to decision making. But first we will examine a prescriptive approach to decision making.

PRESCRIPTIVE APPROACHES TO DECISION MAKING

A prescriptive approach to decision making is one in which the group adopts a standard set of steps based on theories about how groups *should* make decisions. These are prescriptions for good decision making in the same way that a doctor's prescription is a prescription for good health. Prescriptive decision making is based on an "ideal" process; it implies a "best" way to make a decision. Below we will describe a prescriptive model for good decision making based on a rational approach to problem solving. The steps in this model are useful and can be applied in many situations; they offer a reasonable and intelligent way to approach group decision-making problems.

Nevertheless, we must once again offer a caveat. It is unwise to force groups to go through a process that they are unwilling or unprepared to experience. All groups should examine their composition, resources, time, energy, commitment, goals, and problems before deciding on a particular approach.

There are essentially three criticisms of prescriptive approaches to decision making. First, while following a standard approach can be practical, it can also stifle creativity; groups usually get through the task, but they accomplish it with little imagination or true excellence. Second, prescriptions typically assume that group members will act rationally and unemotionally, but we all know that not all members will. In fact, some nonrational (not irrational!) behavior is often good for the group. And third, there is simply conflicting evidence about whether prescriptive procedures improve the quality of groups' outcomes.

On the other hand, prescriptive procedures do help avoid inefficiency, redundancy, and delay. They often succeed in coordinating group members and focusing their attention on common isues. Moreover, prescriptive procedures gather the attention of the group around a jointly agreed-upon activity; for example, if the group declares itself in the "problem analysis" stage, then each group member is focused on the same activity.

In this section we present a variety of group techniques, each designed to accomplish specific objectives. We have organized these according to their specific functions, but the techniques can be modified or combined with others depending on your needs. The functions addressed are (1) generating ideas, (2) decision-making strategies, and (3) implementing solutions.

Generating Ideas

All groups must produce information and ideas that members can use. It is a mistake to think that ideas will simply "emerge." The group must make a concentrated effort to increase its supply of useable information. Below are three techniques.

Brainstorming   This technique is designed to stimulate the group's creativity by eliminating some of the constraints of problem solving—especially criticism and evaluation. The essential technique is to disallow any criticism or evaluation of an idea presented by a group member. The group begins with a problem to solve that is stated either specifically or generally, depending on how the group is phrasing the problem. The group leader explains that all criticism and evaluation must be withheld. This is crucial to brainstorming because it is fear of criticism that hampers people's creativity. The leader also tells everyone to contribute as many ideas as possible. Wild ideas are encouraged and not criticized, because they can be tamed later.

The group records the ideas so they are available to everyone. It is best to write them on a large pad that is posted and clearly visible. The group members will relax when there is no criticism or discussion of ideas. Their contributions will increase and they will feel invigorated as ideas flow forth. Brainstorming can be used at the beginning of decision making or at any later point. Evaluation of ideas is reserved for a later time. After the members have produced many ideas they go back to the list and begin paring it down to the best ideas. This is when the group applies critical thinking analysis so as to eliminate weak or unworkable ideas and focus on the best ones.

Buzz Groups   Like brainstorming, buzz groups are good for encouraging ideas, but they also stimulate participation and involvement. Buzz groups are more appropriate for large groups because they involve breaking groups into smaller units for discussion. These smaller groups should have no more than six people and no fewer than four. Each subgroup is given a question under consideration and then instructed to maximize the number of ideas and record them. First the subgroup generates ideas and then it evaluates them, deciding which to eliminate and which are the best. These smaller groups make it easier to involve more people and help establish the more relaxed environment that is conducive to idea generation.

After the buzz groups have pared down their lists they report back to the main assembly. Usually each group chooses one person to report for the buzz group. Duplicated ideas are removed and the remainder are distributed to the whole group for discussion. Buzz groups combine the advantage of people working in small groups to produce ideas with that of getting feedback from a larger assembly.

Focus Groups   Discussion in focus groups is used to analyze and determine people's interests, values, and habits. Focus groups are very popular in market research when companies want to determine the purchasing practices of consumers. Political campaigns also use focus groups to determine how voters feel about issues. Focus groups usually have eight to ten people, but there can be more. The leader of a focus group introduces a topic and then instructs the members to discuss the topic in any way they feel comfortable. For a while the leader says nothing and offers no direction. The discussion is tape-recorded and observed through a one-way mirror. Later the leader analyzes notes or tapes of the discussion and then returns to the group and asks the members to develop certain ideas.

One of the authors of this book took part in a focus group aimed at discovering what services people would use 900 telephone numbers for and how much they would be willing to pay. The leader asked the group to talk for a while and then returned with follow-up questions. He asked us to offer more detail and expand on our discussion. The group generated many ideas with respect to cost, possible uses of 900 numbers (e.g., sports scores, theater information, news, and so forth), and service requirements.

Decision-Making Strategies

After a group generates ideas and information it must begin the process of making decisions. No single decision-making approach necessarily guarantees quality decisions, but using some orderly approach to decision making usually improves the likelihood that the group will be successful. Below we describe the two most common decision-making techniques. The first capitalizes on the advantages of group interaction and is the most popular and well-understood model of decision making. It is called the Rational Reflection Model (Siebold, 1992) and is based, in part, on Dewey's (1910) reflective thinking model, but contains major additions from current research. Hirokawa (1983a) found that groups were more successful when they used a rational and systematic approach to problem solving. The second decision-making technique we'll describe takes advantage of the fact that people sometimes work better individually. It is called the Nominal Group Technique and is designed to avoid the inhibiting effects of groups (e.g., powerful members, status differences, and so forth).

Rational Reflection   In this approach group members work through a series of steps designed to force them to "reflect" on certain dimensions of a problem in a "rational" manner. The group proceeds through each step and communication is limited to the dimensions of the problem under consideration.

Define and Limit the Problem   The group begins by defining and limiting the problem. The members discuss only the definition of terms and how the problem relates to other issues. Limiting the problem is crucial. It is important not to define a problem so broadly that it generates never-ending discussion and does not lend itself to concrete solutions. Ideally, everyone in the group should agree about what the problem includes and what it excludes. The following are some tips for how to proceed and what to talk about during this step:

1. Define the problem specifically. Try to phrase the problem as a question.
2. Discuss the group's goals.
3. Identify the resources available to the group.
4. Determine the relevance and importance of the problem to the group.
5. Clarify all procedural constraints, such as meeting times and places and when the final report is due.

Analyze the Problem and Gather Information   This is the essence of the decision-making process. It is important to spend time on this step before suggesting solutions. Hirokawa (1983b) found that successful groups do not jump quickly into the solution phase; they spend much time analyzing the problem and gathering information. The purpose of this step is to collect evidence and information that will help you explore and clarify the problem. Think about your audience; who will be reading the final report? For example, if you are discussing the rising cost of tuition on your campus, your group report must reflect your primary audience; the university administration will be interested in one sort of evidence and information, and students will perhaps be interested in another. In either case you must always know who you are working for. The following are important issues for the problem analysis stage:

1. Determine your audience.
2. Research and establish the history and causes of the problem.
3. Discuss how the problem relates to other issues.
4. Collect relevant information.
5. Discuss this information in your group.
6. Critically examine the facts and information. This means challenging the facts and assumptions to make sure that they stand the test of scrutiny.
7. Make sure you have enough information.

Establish Decision Criteria   The group now decides what criteria (standards, or requirements) an acceptable decision must meet. The group should agree on specific criteria, and these criteria should provide methods of evaluation. If the decision criteria are properly developed, they will help the group recognize acceptable decision proposals and reject inappropriate ones. During this stage the group's discussion should focus on the following:

1. What an ideal decision would look like, and what it would include and exclude.
2. What a reasonable, but less than ideal, solution would be. This is important because it is not always possible to reach an ideal decision.
3. What standards the group should use to judge the decision.
4. What the group would consider valid and feasible about the decision.

The group should try to develop criteria as specific as possible. The following are some examples of decision criteria. They are responsive to the problem that one group was discussing concerning "What the role of the state should be in integrating public schools."

1. Maintain the quality of education.
2. Ensure a balanced racial environment.
3. Guarantee no increase in taxes or costs to families.
4. Do not displace only minority groups.
5. Generate simple and workable transportation facilities, including options for extracurricular activities.
6. Design a phase-in program for a smooth transition.

Discuss Possible Solutions   Now it is time to discuss and explore the most useful solutions. It is important to wait until now, because premature discussion of solutions is associated with poor decision making. Now that you have defined the problem, gathered information so that you can discuss it intelligently, and established some ground rules for what is acceptable, you are in a much better position to examine solutions. The goal is to come up with as many ideas as possible. You should seek quantity before quality. During this stage you should not be afraid to propose as many alternatives as possible; record every suggestion, regardless of how absurd it might seem. Some questions to be considered are:

1. Have all possible solutions been considered?
2. What is the evidence in support of each alternative?
3. Has the group used brainstorming techniques to produce ideas?

Determine the Best Solution   This is the point where the group agrees on a final solution. The group does this by testing the possible solutions against the decision criteria it established. The goal is to find the best solution relative to the original issue and the decision criteria; the method is to discuss each decision possibility in light of the decision criteria, including feasibility and desirability. The group should discard the unsatisfactory solutions, concentrate its discussion on the remaining alternatives, and make sure that the discussion includes the following:

1. Does the solution minimize the problem?
2. Is it workable?
3. What are its limitations?
4. Are there more advantages to the solution than disadvantages?
5. How does the solution compare to the decision criteria?
6. Are the facts and the information gathered consistent with the proposed solution?

Determine How the Final Decision Should Be Implemented   It must be possible to implement a solution. The group should begin to discuss plans for implementing a decision. Implementation is often not possible in classroom groups, but in other groups it is a very important component of the group's decision making. Sometimes only a final report is due; when this is the case, the group should assign individuals to the various tasks of report preparation.

Normal Group Technique (NGT)   This is a decision-making technique for increasing participation in the group. In conventional groups some members may be inhibited and limit their contributions to the group. The word *nominal* means "in name only" and is appropriate for this technique because members work individually. After the problem has been identified there are four steps to the NGT.

1. *Individual idea generation* Each person brainstorms individually and writes down his or her ideas. Group members should work silently for about fifteen minutes.
2. *Recording ideas* A group leader has each person contribute one or more ideas that are recorded on a flip-chart visible to all members. Ideas are recorded until everyone agrees that a sufficient number has been produced. This idea-contributing step is handled in round-robin fashion and there is no discussion or evaluation of ideas.
3. *Clarification of ideas* The group discusses each item on the list but only to elaborate or clarify each idea. There is no arguing or criticizing until all the members are satisfied that they fully understand each idea. It is also possible to rank the ideas in order of their importance during this step.
4. *Discussion and decision* Now there is an open and thorough discussion and evaluation of the top-rated ideas. This is the time for critical thinking and argument. If this discussion produces consensus, the group's work is complete. If not, the group members may continue the discussion or have a series of votes until one idea emerges.

The Nominal Group Technique tries to avoid the disadvantages of working in groups. This technique works best in groups of twelve to fifteen members but can work with groups of varying sizes. It is important during the first stage for everyone to work silently because independent and thoughtful ideas are the goal. During the discussion stage it is helpful to have the originator of the idea begin, and then ask the others to contribute. The group leader should be skilled at drawing out ideas and opinions from others. The NGT can contribute to group productivity and cohesiveness by stimulating greater commitment on the part of group members to continue working on the problem.

Implementing Solutions

After a group has posed a solution, it must consider the details of implementing the solution. This can often be a complex process and involve the coordination of activities among many people. In fact, many groups and organizations fail at this point. They meet, discuss, and come up with solutions but never put them into practice. To help a group move its conclusions forward toward actual implementation, a technique called PERT can be very helpful.

PERT stands for the Program Evaluation and Review Technique and is a procedure very well suited for tracking and coordinating all the steps necessary to carry out a plan. It details what steps are necessary, how long they should take, who is responsible, and what materials are needed.

1. Decide what the solution should look like when you finish. How will the solution appear when it is implemented and operational?
2. Enumerate everything that must occur before the final solution is realized. Write down everything you must do before you can reach your goal.
3. Now list these activities in chronological order. What must you do first, second, and so on.
4. When the solution is complex and involves numerous steps, develop a flow chart. This will help you keep track of your progress toward the goal.
5. List the necessary materials and resources for each thing you must accomplish.
6. How much time will all this take? Estimate the time needed to complete each step in the process. Establish a time requirement for each step and then add these up to determine the total time needed to implement the solution.
7. Go back over the deadlines for each step and compare them to the total time. Make sure that your deadlines are reasonable. If not, alter the deadlines or increase the number of people working on the task.
8. Finally, decide which group members will be responsible for which tasks. Make sure everyone is clear as to their responsibilities, resources, and deadlines.

Regulating Meetings

You have probably heard of *Robert's Rules of Order*. These are a set of rules that regulate the conduct of groups so that fair participation is ensured. *Robert's Rules* codifies procedures for protecting the participation rights of majorities, minorities, individuals, and absentees. Most large groups must be run by formal rules to guarantee order and fairness. But any group can adopt Robert's rules for committees. We encourage you to become familiar with Robert's rules because they govern most assemblies in the United States. But you cannot learn Robert's rules by reading about them. To learn parliamentary procedure you must take part in groups that practice it, just as you must actually take part in a game to learn how it's played. Below is a summary of Robert's rules for committees so that you can begin to learn how they work. Whereas parliamentary law governing large assemblies is detailed and complex in order to protect the rights of multiple constituencies, the rules of order for committees and small groups are fairly simple and straightforward.

1. A chairperson can be named by an organization, or the committee can elect its own chairperson.
2. The chairperson calls a meeting of the group, or if the chair does not call a meeting, any two members can request a meeting unless policies of the larger group prohibit such a meeting.
3. The majority of the committee constitutes a quorum unless otherwise stated in the committee's bylaws.
4. The committee typically appoints a secretary to keep the minutes. If no secretary is appointed, keeping the minutes is the chairperson's responsibility.
5. Committees are typically governed by the policies of the full assembly unless otherwise stipulated.
6. Members of committees do not need to request the floor to speak as long as they do not interrupt one another. Moreover, the chairperson may take a more active role in the debate. In larger assemblies the chair often votes only to break a tie, and refrains from active discussion of a motion.
7. Motions to close debate are not allowed in committees.
8. In larger assemblies discussion must be directed toward a stated motion. In committees there are no limits as to when or how much discussion may take place.
9. Decisions are usually arrived at by majority vote. The chairperson can ask for a straw (unofficial) vote to determine whether consensus exists before a binding vote.
10. Members do not need to make a motion to state a proposal and request a vote.
11. In small groups you can ask to reconsider a vote as many times as you like.
12. Most of what is considered parliamentary procedure is a hindrance to small group committees. There is no need to make points of order, table motions, or request personal privilege. Virtually anything can be discussed informally.
13. Committees make formal reports on the basis of their own requirements or those of the larger assembly of which they are a part. If a minority group disagrees with the decision of the majority, they are permitted to submit a separate opinion.

DESCRIPTIVE APPROACHES TO DECISION MAKING

The section above presents prescriptions for various phases of decision making. It is based on the assumption that groups can benefit by going through the steps we outline. But the approach that we will concentrate on for the remainder of this chapter is a descriptive approach. A *descriptive* approach does not say how groups *should* make decisions, but how research indicates they *do* make decisions. These are "descriptions," based on observations of groups, of what interactive processes are common to groups. Whereas a prescriptive approach is based on an "ideal" process, the crux of the descriptive approach is the "reality" of observation.

There are several assumptions of the descriptive approach to decision-making groups. The most basic is that a "natural" process of group decision making does indeed exist. That is, groups develop their own interdependent task and socioemotional dimensions in a normal and fairly consistent interactive pattern that leads to validation of decisions by consensus. The process is assumed to be natural because it occurs in most effective and successful decision-making groups. This natural process can be disrupted to the extent that the group is influenced by outside forces. For example, a group that adheres strictly to a prescriptive method will not experience this natural process. External authorities, resource constraints, special instructions, and many other factors will also interfere with the process to various degrees.

The perspective of communication and the group process is best served by emphasizing descriptive approaches to group decision making. We will focus on the pragmatic interaction patterns of group members—their interlocked communicative behaviors—as they occur and change over time. We will trace these patterns throughout the group's history. Poole and Doelger (1986, p. 35) state that "The essence of group decision-making is interaction." Our concern, therefore, will be the patterns of interaction that characterize decision development in groups.

Early Models of Group Development

Although formal instruction in group decision making is a twentieth-century phenomenon, the historical roots of group communication date back to the classical age of Greece and the philosophical origins of dialectic. The ancient Greek philosophers viewed the practice of dialectic as the search for truth through the exchange of opinions or arguments in free discussion. While the classical philosophers regarded dialectic as a branch of philosophy (specifically, logic), the contemporary view of group decision making is more closely aligned with the social sciences.

Sociologists, psychologists, and psychotherapists, as well as communication scholars, have long been concerned with studying how groups develop over time from a mere aggregate (or collection) of individuals into full-fledged groups. A few of those early models of group development are described in the following paragraphs in order to provide some background and perspective for the models that constitute the major thrust of this chapter.

Equilibrium Models   One approach to the study of groups is to explain the group process in terms of a balance, or equilibrium, between two opposing forces. An equilibrium model is popular in many social-psychological explanations in the sense of an approach-avoidance conflict (opposing forces favoring and disfavoring some course of action), cognitive dissonance (simultaneous knowledge of positive and negative information concerning a course of action), along with numerous other explanatory models.

Such equilibrium models are popular perhaps because they are consistent with physical phenomena. That is, the equilibrium principle is evident in the axiom that actions have equal and opposite reactions, the balance scale, in the positive and negative forces of magnetic energy, etc. Furthermore, such models of group decision making implicity assume the rationality of human beings, an assumption difficult to sustain in explanations of human behavior.

Although Robert F. Bales is known for his development of the categories for interaction process analysis, or IPA (Bales, 1950), he also developed an equilibrium model to explain group behavior. His IPA categories were probably developed as a way of observing actual interactional behavior in terms of an equilibrium between task and social forces. Bales (1953) hypothesized that every group has a problem of adapting to its environment. During this adaptation, it develops social mechanisms that serve to differentiate members from one another—for example, differences of roles, differences of status, and the development of a leadership structure. As a result of this emphasis on differences between group members, the social dimension of the group (in terms of its cohesiveness and interpersonal solidarity) suffers.

According to Bales's equilibrium hypothesis, then, the work that the group performs in accomplishing its task leads to a deterioration of the group's social structure. Conversely, as the group attempts to increase the interpersonal ties between its members and to perform work in the social dimension (that is, to raise the level of cohesiveness), its work on the task suffers. Groups tend to fluctuate back and forth between task and socioemotional activities: that is, between attempting to solve their task problems and maintaining group solidarity.

Bales's IPA categories (see Figure 6-1) are consistent with the equilibrium hypothesis. You will note that the twelve categories are divided equally between the task dimension and the socioemotional dimension—six categories each. Note further that the twelve categories are also divided equally between polarized (or mutually opposed) categories oriented to specific problems in either the task or the social dimension. Bales thus conceptualizes each and every act as directed toward solving some task or social problem confronting the group. Furthermore, every action that a member contributes to the group discussion is oriented to either a task problem or a social problem, but not both. Bales's categories are still very popular.

Phase Models   The most popular approach to understanding the developmental process of groups over time is to describe group activity moving through a sequence of different kinds of interaction. This sequence develops into stages, or phases, of group interaction from the beginning of a group's

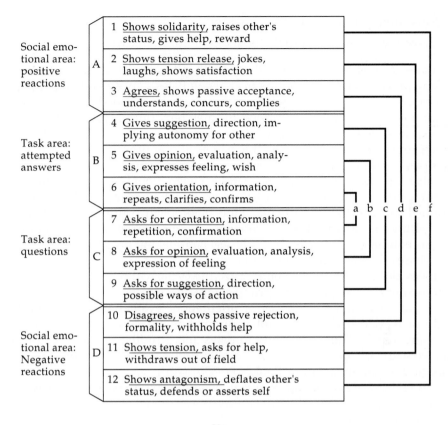

Key:

a Problems of orientation   d Problems of decision
b Problems of evaluation   e Problems of tension-management
c Problems of control   f Problems of integration

FIGURE 6-1 Bales's categories for "interaction process analysis."

activity as an aggregate to its eventual maturation as a group and the establishment of full-fledged groupness. From a task-oriented perspective, the phases of group development chronicle the group's interaction from the beginning of a group's task performance to the achievement of consensus on decisions.

The most familiar of all descriptive models of the group process is the three-phase model advanced by Bales (1950) and Bales and Strodtbeck (1951). These authors discovered that decision-making groups, most of which were problem-solving groups, tend to discuss different kinds of task-related problems at different periods of time in their group interaction. Their three phases may be briefly described as follows:

Stage 1 Emphasis on problems of *orientation* (deciding what the situation is like)

Stage 2 Emphasis on problems of *evaluation* (deciding what attitudes should be taken toward the situation)

Stage 3 Emphasis on problems of *control* (deciding what to do about it)

Bales and Strodtbeck base their three phases of the group decision-making process on data compiled from using Bales's (1950) system of interaction process analysis. Figure 6-1 illustrates this system. The IPA classifies each communicative behavior performed by members during group interaction. The classes of behavior include twelve categories—in reality, six bipolar pairs of categories. Each category in the pair is the antithesis of the other: for example, "agrees—disagrees," "shows solidarity—shows antagonism." The IPA also separates the group's task and socioemotional dimensions by labeling three pairs of categories in each area. And each bipolar pair of categories is assumed to deal with a particular kind of problem confronting the group. Each of the first three types of problems—orientation, evaluation, and control—is emphasized in order by each decision-making group in three successive phases during group interaction.

Bales and Strodtbeck also emphasize the cyclic nature of the three phases of group decision making. As a group completes one decision-making task by progressing through the phases of orientation, evaluation, and control, it tends to recycle back to the initial orientation phase as it performs each subsequent task. Thus, according to Bales and Strodtbeck, the three phases characterize each performance of a single group decision-making task. We will see this activity again in Poole's (1983b) work.

An early study by Dunphy (1964) also depicted a sequential analysis of group development. He advanced a four-phase model of group development in terms of emotionality cultures:

Stage 1 Dependency (group members look to the leader for direction of their activity)

Stage 2 Fight-flight (group members resist the leader's direction and develop their ability to work independently of a leader's guidance)

Stage 3 Pairing (group members demonstrate a marked increase in group cohesiveness)

Stage 4. Work (little emotionality of any type appears during the final stage of group activity)

You will note that Dunphy's developmental model is similar to Bennis and Shepard's (1956) model of levels of work, which will be discussed in the following paragraphs. Dunphy also emphasizes the socioemotional dimension of the group process. This emphasis clearly reflects his interest in training groups (or T groups) rather than in groups specifically oriented to decision-making tasks.

Bennis and Shepard developed a four-phase model to describe group development. Their observations were much more subjective and interpretive than the direct observational method of interaction analysis (see Appendix 1). They derived their description from the reactions of nonparticipant observers. Their findings, according to the authors, also reflect their interpretations over a five-year period of teaching classes in group dynamics. The following four phases of group development are labeled according to the level of work the group is able to accomplish:

Phase 1 One-level work. Personally need-oriented—not group-oriented (Dependence and Authority Relations).

Phase 2 Two-level work. Maintaining the group task. Group-oriented and necessary—but routine (Resolution-Catharsis and beginnings of feeling of interdependence).

Phase 3 Three-level work. Group-focused work with new methods of attack, goal establishment, idea-testing (Interdependence with group focus and sense of direction).

Phase 4 Four-level work. Creative and integrative interpretation with immediate relevance to present problems of group task (Consensual Validation and Maximum Productivity). (1956, pp. 753-755)

Several interesting observations emerge from Bennis and Shepard's model. For example, it illustrates a group's progressive ability to do more sophisticated work. This ability is apparently gained in successively progressive stages as the group develops interdependence among its members. As the group begins its process of development, it is dependent on some external authority responsible for the group task. In a T group, that authority is the trainer; in an organization, it is the boss; in a classroom, it is the instructor. The group can do two-level work only as the members begin to reject the external source of authority. By the time the members are able to do three-level work, they have completely rejected their dependence on the external authority.

Tuckman (1965) employed still another method for observing groups as he devised his four-phase model for group decision making. In fact, he himself did not observe any groups but synthesized the results of other published observations. He notes that groups simultaneously confront two kinds of problems in each phase of decision making. He labels these two problem types (a) group structure (how to get along) and (b) task activity (how to proceed). Essentially, these two types of problems are "social problems" and "task problems," thereby denying the inseparable interdependence of the two dimensions of the group process. Tuckman characterizes his four phases and their corresponding social and task problems with a catchy rhythm of four rhyming words:

Phase 1 "Forming." (a) Testing and independence; (b) attempting to identify the task.

Phase 2 "Storming." (a) Development of intragroup conflicts; (b) emotional response to task demands.

Phase 3 "Norming." (a) Development of group cohesion; (b) expression of opinions.

Phase 4 "Performing." (a) Functional role-relatedness; (b) emergence of solutions.

Tuckman's point of departure, like Bales and Strodtbeck's, is the type of problem under discussion at various stages in group interaction. He also clearly separates the members' communicative behavior into task and socio-emotional areas. And, like Bennis and Shepard, Tuckman assumes that the group accomplishes most of its productive output in the latter stages of the decision-making process.

Although the descriptive models do not reflect identical characteristics of each phase, several phases include characteristics common to all three models. That is, the first stage of group decision making in all three models is a period of orientation—a period in which members adjust their individualities to group membership and accustom themselves to the task at hand. This orienting period generally involves a search process in which members search for ways to view their task with no particular focus or established opinion toward the task.

One of the middle phases in each of the models includes a period of social conflict among members, differences of opinion on task ideas and social norms. This similarity seems to confirm that social conflict and deviance are indeed a normal part of the group process. Moreover, social conflict and deviance are normal during only one period of group interaction. And this period of normal conflict is near the middle of the process and not near the beginning or the end of group task performance. Thus, the norm of social conflict and deviance characterizes a specific intermediate phase in the process of group interaction that ultimately leads to validation of decisions through consensus.

A final stage of interaction in which members apparently accomplish most of their work on their task is common to all models, although the exact nature of this stage is not abundantly clear. Bales and Strodtbeck indicate that the final stage is characterized by a maximum number of positive reactions. The other two models indicate that the group becomes capable of creative and effective task performance. But all models agree that the group members achieve consensus and thereby validate their decisions during this last phase.

THE PROCESS OF DECISION EMERGENCE

Chapter 7 will discuss the phenomenon of leader emergence—the fact that groups do not "select" leaders so much as the leader and other roles "emerge" during group interaction. If the task and socioemotional dimensions of group process are truly interdependent, it seems logical that the decision-making process should be similar to the leadership process. Moreover, group decision making, like leadership, possesses no single "best" or "correct" answer to be discovered in a "Eureka!" or "Aha!" manner. It is reasonable to conclude that groups do not *make* decisions. Decisions *emerge* from group interaction.

If you were to observe a decision-making group as a participant or as a nonparticipant attempting to determine the point at which the group makes its decision, you would find such a task extraordinary difficult, if not impossible. During some period of the group's interaction, the decision is probably apparent to you even though the group members continue their discussion. Even groups following prescriptions don't know exactly when they have made a decision.

Phases of Decision Emergence

Using interaction analysis (see Chapter 9 and Appendix 1) as the method for observing group decision making, Fisher (1970a) discovered four phases in the process of group decision making. Unlike other observational schema, Fisher's method identified each alternative decision proposal suggested during group interaction and attempted to observe the process whereby preliminary ideas are transformed into consensus decisions. Thus, each member's communicative act functions on the decision proposal under discussion by expressing some opinion (favorable, unfavorable, or ambiguous) toward that proposal, providing evidence to support that opinion, modifying the proposal, clarifying it, and agreeing or disagreeing with another member's opinion. The group interaction is thus anchored to the subject matter of the group interaction—the decision proposals—and to members' attempts to influence the perceptions of other members toward these proposals.

The observed pattern of communicative behaviors indicates four rather distinct phases of group decision making, each characterized by a different pattern of interaction. These phases are (1) orientation, (2) conflict, (3) emergence, and (4) reinforcement.

Orientation Phase   A group's early problems of socializing and excessive primary tension affect the interaction patterns in this phase. Members clarify and agree most often at this time. Because the members are unaware of their social position initially and not sure of how to handle the task, they do not quickly or strongly assert themselves or their opinions. Consequently, they make assertions tentatively in order to test the group, and they agree with virtually everything. For example, a member states an ambiguous opinion about the decision proposal, a second member agrees with that ambiguous opinion, and this is followed in turn by another ambiguous opinion. Since members even agree with comments serving only to clarify points of information, agreeing with another member's comment seems to function in the orientation phase not so much to reinforce other members' beliefs and opinions as to avoid disrupting the developing social climate.

Group members in the orientation phase search tentatively for ideas and directions to aid their decision-making efforts. They are unaware of the direction the group will eventually take, so they don't commit themselves, favorably or unfavorably, to the newly introduced decision proposals. Rather, they express attitudes that are ambiguous toward proposals—fence-sitting attitudes that could go one way or another.

Many of the ambiguous opinions expressed in the first phase probably reflect favorable attitudes in the making. That is, since members assert opinions and arguments favoring the proposals with increasing intensity as the discussion progresses, these opinions must be in the preliminary stages of formation during this orientation phase. As the issues become clarified and as the social climate becomes more conducive to the honest statement of one's true position, many members apparently change their ambiguous opinions to opinions favoring the decision proposals.

Characteristic of the orientation phase, then, is getting acquainted, clarifying, and tentatively expressing attitudes. This stage is a period of forming opinions, not rocking the boat, and getting rid of social inhibitions—in short, the orientation phase.

Conflict Phase   The second phase of group decision making is characterized by dispute—ideational conflict over decision proposals. In the orientation phase, members only tentatively express their opinions, which are typically ambiguous. In the conflict phase they appear to have made up their minds. Members are now aware of the direction the group is taking toward the decision-making task and of the relevant decision proposals emerging from the group deliberations. Thus, members typically express either a favorable or an unfavorable attitude toward these proposals. Gone is the tentativeness of ambiguity. Gone, too, is tentativeness due to social inhibitions.

Polarization of attitudes means disagreement and conflict. In the conflict phase, expressing a favorable attitude is generally followed by another member's expressing an unfavorable attitude (and vice versa). Members have different opinions and express them in argument with one another. Not only do members express less ambiguous attitudes, but they also express them more tenaciously. They now provide data and evidence to substantiate their beliefs and engage in full-fledged debate with other members.

The interaction patterns of the conflict phase reflect the formation of two coalitions resulting from polarization of beliefs. That is, two coalitions are present in this phase—one favoring and one opposing those decision proposals that ultimately achieve group consensus. To illustrate, members A and B favor the proposals and reinforce each other's favorable opinions; C and D oppose the proposals and reinforce each other's unfavorable opinions. Expression of ambiguous attitudes or the presence of a "mugwump" (independent) member is not normal in the conflict phase. The norm is dissent, controversy, social conflict, and innovative deviance. In fact, mugwumps are deviates in the conflict phase in that they do not participate in the debate over ideas and opinions.

It is quite probable that the coalitions centered around leader contenders are the same coalitions formed by polarization of ideas during the conflict phase. The interdependence of the task and socioemotional dimensions seems to confirm this explanation.

Emergence Phase   Social conflict and dissent dissipate during the third phase. Members express fewer unfavorable opinions toward decision proposals. The coalition of individuals who have opposed those proposals which eventually achieve consensus also weakens in this phase. The interaction patterns in the emergence phase reflect significantly less positive reinforcement of one another's unfavorable attitudes. A few residues of overt social conflict remain, but they are not significant. Comments expressing unfavorable attitudes are not only not reinforced by subsequent agreement or more unfavorable attitudes from other members in the coalition; they are not expressed so tenaciously either. That is, opposing members typically assert unfavorable opinions without including supporting evidence or reason to substantiate them.

The hallmark of the emergence phase is the recurrence of ambiguity. As in the orientation phase, some members express opinions ambiguous toward the decision proposals and tend to reinforce them by responding with further expressions of attitudes ambiguous toward the proposals. Thus, ambiguity toward decision proposals is prominent in the orientation phase, declines significantly in the conflict phase, and rises again during the emergence phase.

But although the proportionate number of comments expressing ambiguous opinions and interacts reflecting reinforcement of ambiguous comments does not differ substantially from the orientation phase, the function performed by ambiguity in the interact patterns of the emergence phase is significantly different. During orientation, members express opinions tentatively in the form of ambiguous attitudes toward the decision proposals. Some of these ambiguous comments are undoubtedly the initial expression of favorable or unfavorable opinions in a rudimentary form of development. But group members have no reason to be tentative in the emergence phase. They are certainly no longer searching for attitude direction. They have plotted that direction in the orientation phase and debated it during the conflict phase. In the emergence phase, task direction is obviously no longer at issue. It is quite unreasonable to conclude that expressing an ambiguous opinion at this late point in the discussion reflects a tentative expression of a developing opinion.

The key to the function of ambiguity in the patterns of group interaction lies in associating the emergence phase with the conflict phase. Ambiguous communicative behavior functions in the third phase as a form of modified dissent. In the conflict phase, members either favor or disfavor the decision proposals. In the emergence phase, the bimodal distribution has shifted to favorable or ambiguous attitudes toward these same proposals. That is, the group member who expresses opposition to decision proposals in the conflict phase is in the process of changing from disfavor to favor through the mediating step of expressing ambiguous opinions.

Members expressing ambiguous opinions in the emergence phase have already committed themselves to a stand of opposition in the conflict phase and cannot be expected to change their opinions so abruptly. Thus, their dissent changes to assent by way of ambiguity. A dissenting member in the conflict phase responds to another member's comment favoring a proposal with an opinion disfavoring it. In the same situation during the emergence phase, the response will be an opinion ambiguous toward the proposal. Opposition to the proposal is still being expressed, but opposition is dissipating as attitudes are modified.

The two coalitions present in the conflict phase also dissipate during the emergence phase. The coalition of dissenting members opposing the decision proposals does not immediately disintegrate but turns to ambiguous comments as a final form of dissent. Just as the exact point in time at which a leader or a decision emerges cannot be pinpointed, neither can one determine the exact moment of the death of the dissenting coalition. The dissipation of dissent and the dissipation of the coalition are gradual and mediated by ambiguity. In the absence of outright social conflict, decisions may appear to have been reached. But the expression of ambiguous opinions, while not totally unfavorable, is not yet favorable. As disfavor dissipates to ambiguity, however, favorable opinions toward the decision proposals increase concomitantly.

The third phase is probably the crucial stage in the group process of decision making. During this third phase the eventual outcome of group interaction becomes increasingly more apparent. Therefore, this third phase is called the emergence phase.

Reinforcement Phase   While group members tend to reach decisions during the emergence phase, they achieve consensus on these decisions during the reinforcement phase. Substantiating one's opinion toward the decision proposal is no longer necessary. After all, the ideas were thoroughly tested during the conflict phase, but members continue to provide evidence and reasons to support their opinions favoring the decision proposals, thus adding additional fuel to the fire of emerging consensus. Members constantly and consistently express opinions favorable to the proposals and positively reinforce one another's favorable opinions with expressions of agreement and additional social support. This overwhelming preponderance of interaction patterns that favor the decision proposals and positively reinforce the favorable opinions clearly identifies the final phase of group deliberations.

Dissent has all but vanished in the reinforcement phase. This phase includes the lowest number of comments opposed to the decision proposals and virtually no interacts of social conflict—that is, a favorable comment followed or preceded by an unfavorable comment. Of course the orientation phase contains few interacts of social conflict too. But whereas the low level of conflict during orientation reflects the members' conscious avoidance of conflict due to social inhibitions, the reinforcement phase reflects unity of opinion among group members. The dissipation of dissent, both direct (unfavorable opinions) and modified (ambiguous opinions), is virtually complete in this phase of group interaction.

Pervading this final phase in group decision making is a spirit of unity. All members seem to agree and strive to show this agreement by positively reinforcing one another. Their interaction patterns reflect virtually no tension; rather, the members are jovial, loud, boisterous, laughing, and verbally backslapping each other. This is the phase of developing members' commitment to those decisions which were the object of conflict in the second phase and which emerged during the third phase. This is the reinforcement phase.

Orientation, conflict, emergence, and reinforcement, then, are the four phases of decision emergence. They have been described here in terms of characteristic patterns of interaction. The descriptions of the four phases are rather general and provide no examples of group interaction. In order to illustrate the phases more clearly and reveal the "flavor" of group decision making from the viewpoint of members' communicative behaviors, Chapter 9 provides detailed examples of interaction patterns from an actual decision-making group.

OTHER MODELS OF DECISION MAKING

Although the prescriptive and descriptive models described earlier are different in many significant respects, they are all based on a step-by-step progression toward the completion of task objectives. The steps in these models assume a given order; a group completes discussion of one set of problems before moving to the next. Each model assumes that solving one set of problems is prerequisite to solving the next set of problems; that is, the group is incapable of solving the second set of problems until it solves the first, and so on. Groups cannot or should not deal with problems out of sequence. Any step out of sequence would be considered a lack of group progress and an error of that group. In this section we describe some other models of decision making that rely on different assumptions.

The Spiral Model

Thomas M. Scheidel and Laura Crowell (1964) discovered that group interaction aimed at developing ideas does not correspond to a linear model. Using a system of interaction analysis as their observational scheme (Crowell and Scheidel, 1961), these authors describe the group process of idea development as a spiral model (Figure 6-2). One member introduces an idea, and other members respond with agreement or disagreement, extension or revision. The idea is the object of discussion, and it develops over time to reflect the group's viewpoint. When an idea is developed to the point that it is an object of agreement by all group members, the group anchors its position on that idea and introduces new preliminary ideas progressing from that anchor point of agreement. The spiral process, then, involves "reach-testing" forward from an anchored position of agreement. If the reach-tested idea is affirmed by the group, a new anchored position is established, and reach-testing proceeds from there. If the new idea is rejected, the group returns to its anchored position and reach-tests another new idea from that same anchor point.

The spiral process of anchoring and reach-testing is not linear in that the group constantly retraces its path of idea development. Groups develop new ideas not in linear sequence, but cumulatively. One idea leads to another. One idea is progressively modified and remodified during the course of

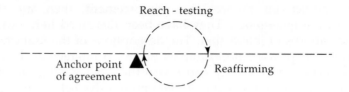

Reach - testing

Anchor point
of agreement

Reaffirming

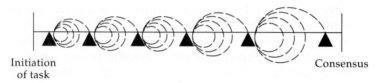

Initiation
of task

Consensus

FIGURE 6-2 The spiral model of decision making.

group interaction until the group achieves validation of its final decisions by consensus. The spiral process is cumulative and progressive, reflecting continuous modification of ideas and backtracking to agreed-upon ideas as members reconfirm positions.

As noted earlier, several descriptive models indicate that the bulk of the group's task activity occurs in the final stages of interaction. The spiral model denies this allegation, but it explains the fact that groups appear to accomplish more work during the final stages. The spiral process is cumulative, and all ideas developed in the latter stages of interaction are the result of earlier agreements and anchored positions. But in the final stages, the group has acquired a vast background of many agreed-upon positions. Reach-testing in the final phase therefore proceeds from a broader base of agreement with increasingly diminishing need to backtrack to earlier anchor positions.

The spiral model also accounts for the apparent inefficiency of group decision making regarding the use of time. Every beginning geometry student knows that the shortest distance between two points on the same plane is a straight line. But group decision making does not conform to the straight line of a linear model. Rather, the group process is more like a spiral of anchoring and reach-testing.

Functional Communication

Hirokawa (1992) has been interested in why groups succeed or fail. He finds that the amount and accuracy of information is the most important factor. The group's interaction and decision making are based on its discussion of such information; that is, the group engages in reasoning and critical thinking to arrive at a collective decision. Hirokawa is less concerned about the phasic development of the group, and argues that the interaction can be more or less organized, but that all groups attend to the same functional requirements.

A group begins the decision-making process by ensuring that it *understands the situation and the nature of the problem to be solved*. The members' individual knowledge and the complexity of the problem will determine how much time they spend on this. They plunge in by discussing the current state of affairs and asking: What exactly is the problem? What caused it? What harmful results have developed?

Once the members understand the problem they have two courses of action available to them. First, they can *examine the alternatives available* by talking about what they might do to approach the problem. Alternatively, the group can *discuss its goals and potential accomplishments* and try to come to an understanding about its objectives. At this point the members will also assess the amount of work ahead of them and try to minimize their efforts. Most groups spend time detailing their resources and obligations at this stage so as to maximize their efforts.

Next, according to Hirokawa's functional approach, a group tries to *determine the positive and negative aspects of its goals and alternatives*. This is an important step because decision quality is directly related to recognition of the positive features of available choices. A group can make a faulty decision if it miscalculates the positive and negative qualities available to it. To illustrate, imagine a group trying to decide whether to purchase an expensive computer or a cheaper one. If the members fail to fully understand the positive features of the expensive computer and how it can save the group money in the long run, they may make a faulty decision. On the other hand, if they fail to fully understand the financial impact of purchasing the expensive computer, they might make an equally faulty decision.

Gathering and using information is a fourth factor that influences the group's decision making. Information is always important to the decision-making process. Groups process and use information during all phases of group interaction. Quality information is probably the most significant factor affecting group decision making. Data will come from many sources and all of it must be evaluated. But in assessing information, the group may make some errors. It might simply accept and act on invalid information, for example. (A company might simply have inaccurate financial or marketing data and make decisions on this basis.) Rejecting good information is another error a group may make. Sometimes the power and status of certain individuals will establish a preferred course of action, and the group will reject everything that does not support the preferred course of action. This can lead to the false consensus and groupthink discussed in Chapter 5.

Hirokawa's functional model of decision making illustrates how (1) understanding the problem, (2) establishing an objective, (3) evaluating choices, and (4) using quality information can determine the reasoning processes of groups and result in higher or lower quality decisions. In the next section we will examine even more closely how groups use communication to modify decisions.

Using Communication to Modify Decisions

The spiral model of idea development, described by Scheidel and Crowell (1964) and affirmed in the phases of decision emergence, reveals that group decision making is a process of cumulative development of consensus decisions. Groups achieve consensus on decisions through interaction patterns that modify, reject, accept, or combine previously introduced decision proposals. Below, we present the specific nature of the interaction patterns that cumulatively modify decision proposals until they appear in consensus form.

Studying the interaction patterns of decision-making groups, Fisher (1970b) discerned a pattern of cumulative, step-by-step modification of decision proposals. That is, groups do not typically modify preliminary decision proposals by clear and direct amendments, but in sudden jumps to different formulations of the same root proposals. Consistent with Berg's (1967) discovery of a group's rather brief attention span, Fisher found that groups apparently do not discuss each proposal for an extended period. Rather, a group member introduces a specific decision proposal, and then members discuss it for some length of time, drop it in favor of discussing another decision proposal, and reintroduce the first proposal later during the group deliberations.

An example may illustrate this pattern of modification more clearly. A corporate management training group (four men, here called *A*, *B*, *C*, and *D*) was engaged in making decisions regarding the management of a hypothetical corporation. One of their consensus decisions was to concentrate their sales and advertising campaigns for their business in two market areas—one urban and one rural. Member *B* initially introduced this decision proposal in its rudimentary form—to withhold all attempts to sell their products until after the results of a market analysis had become available. The following excerpt is from the group's interaction at that point:

B: This is going to be our plan initially, to get this market analysis. I feel we should consider holding our market in inventory and not sell the first quarter until you find out where the market is.
A: What would you do with the sales representatives, then? Just let them sit around?
B: Pay their salary—$8,000 for the quarter.
A: But you're not getting any return on your money.
D: You've got to put them out in the field.
C: Put them out. It wouldn't cost us anything.
A: All right. What should we do about advertising?

The group members did not respond favorably to *B*'s proposal, and they quickly moved to another, as yet unrelated, proposal concerning advertising. Later, *C* reintroduced a substitute decision proposal regarding how to allocate the company's sales representatives:

C: As a matter of fact, if we were to take one area and blanket it with our sales reps and take another area for our market analysis, we might be able to calculate a second area based on the result of our sales.

A: We might be able to. At least it's a better possibility than . . .
D: It's an indicator.
C: An indicator. You've got more information.
B: We need to get a job description of the chairperson.

The group members responded favorably to the substitute proposal. Yet they dropped the second proposal, too, before coming to a final decision and before exhausting their discussion of it.

The decision proposal to concentrate their sales representatives in two market areas came closest to the form of a direct amendment to the decision proposal while it was being discussed:

C: Our first shot at sales is really to obtain a market coverage.
B: What do you mean by "market coverage"?
C: I'm sorry. A market forecast.
B: That's what we were saying. Get a forecast on each region and try to cover sales in each.
C: But I don't think we can do that. I think we can blanket only one area.
B: If you put two sales reps in each area, you use six sales reps. But I don't think you want to do that.
D: No. We can't reallocate. If we put two in each one of those areas and reallocate one of them to the other area, then we cover it.
B: You're covered if the first guy gets a sale.
A: You've got to gamble a little bit, but I don't think you want to throw your whole sales staff into one area. I think we ought to distribute three and three. [By allocating the six sales representatives "three and three," A proposes to distribute them equally in two market areas. He appears to amend the earlier proposal to concentrate them in a single area.]
C: Three and three?
A: Three and three. And then see what the results of our market analysis are. On the basis of this knowledge, we can better reallocate.
D: Where are we going to do our market analysis anyway?

Member A initiated a new decision proposal largely by amending the proposal under discussion—to concentrate all six sales representatives in one area—and introducing it in amended form—to distribute them equally in two areas. But, without exhaustively deliberating this proposal, the members quickly shifted to another decision proposal regarding the area of market analysis.

Earlier the group had discussed the decision proposal of whether the company should advertise:

B: How much for advertising?
C: Mr. Marketing, would you recommend two pages of advertising for each of the areas we are going to cover?
D: Yes. I think that's the least we can do. If we are going to put sales reps in an area, we ought to support them.
B: Remember, we haven't got much cost there.
C: You can't make money unless you spend it.

B: No. But we are just finding out where the market is right now. Why spend it for advertising?

C: But what if the other people spend? We'll find out, of course, if we lose a sale to the competitors.

B: Let's not advertise.

C: We ought to advertise something.

D: I think we should have one page.

C: One page, at least.

B: But we don't have the money.

A: How are we doing in formulating our long-range objectives?

Unlike the previous examples of decision proposals dropped after initiation and brief discussion, members responded to this proposal with a direct conflict of opinions. But without resolving the conflict, the group again shifted to a totally different proposal—formulating the company's long-range objectives.

The two decision proposals to concentrate their sales force in two areas and advertise in both areas were combined later in a further reformulation of the decision proposals:

A: With the marketing advantage you have getting this information, you'd better spend as much as you can on advertising and sales in that place and ignore the rest.

B: I don't know if we want to go into two areas or not. We aren't going to have enough to cover.

C: I would suggest that we take a shot at two areas. If we hit area four, which is urban, and pick area two right above it, which is . . .

A: Strictly rural.

C: If we hit area four and area two, we can draw conclusions and see if there really is a difference between the urban and rural markets.

Member C's addition of "urban" and "rural" to differentiate the two market areas is not so much a modification of the proposal as it is an observation on the advantage of concentrating advertising and sales representatives in two areas. This point seemed to win over the obviously reluctant member B. And this configuration was the decision proposal that eventually achieved group consensus.

Each of the reformulations of the initial decision proposal is introduced, discussed, and dropped several times. The excerpts included above illustrate only those moments in the group's interaction in which members initiated the proposal in a modified form and does not include other reintroductions of the same proposal. Thus, members modify decision proposals by leaps, or jumps, rather than continuously by direct amendment and prolonged discussion.

In short, reformulations or modifications of the initial decision proposal do not typically emerge from direct criticisms of the proposal while it is being discussed. Rather, group members appear to wrestle with the proposal, sometimes with conflict and sometimes without, and then to put it aside temporarily until one of the members experiences an insight and suggests a reformulation that seems closer to what the group really wants. This can be frustrating for the group. One group's self-analysis reveals just such frustration:

> We would be talking about one subject and then all of a sudden in midstream change and start talking about something else. Our group has the trait of going around in circles.

This perceptive comment reflects the concern of a group member who considered this "going around in circles" as indicating some failure in group interaction. Unfortunately, the members of this group never realized during their interaction that they were behaving quite normally. The only disruptive factor was their frustration.

Conflict and Decision Modification   Although the evidence is not conclusive, there is a justifiable basis for believing that the patterns of decision modification do reflect the influence of conflict over decision proposals. That is, when members consistently respond to initiated proposals with a conflict of opinions, the successive reintroduction of those decision proposals follows a distinctive pattern. And when members experience little conflict of opinions toward initiated proposals, the successive reintroduction of those proposals corresponds to a different pattern.

The pattern of decision modification characterized by little conflict is generally a process of lowering the level of abstraction of the language phrasing the decision proposal. That is, each successive reintroduction of a substitute proposal is slightly more concrete than the previous one. The example of the corporate management training group corresponds to this essential pattern. Another example of this pattern of lowered abstraction appears in the interaction of a group of nursing experts planning a workshop-conference for educators in public health nursing.

Early in the nursing group's weeklong deliberations, the members discussed the present status of public health nurses and observed that public health nurses felt they were downgraded by the rest of the nursing profession. The group then felt that the public health nurses attending the conference would be defensive and would resist new proposals. Later, a member initiated a substitute proposal to begin the conference with "a nonthreatening something." After being discussed and dropped, the substitute proposal was reintroduced, proposing to "get the conference feeling good and then change them." A later substitute proposal suggested that they begin the conference "on common ground." Eventually the proposal was reintroduced in the form that achieved consensus—"Begin the conference with a history of the contributions that public health has made to the field of nursing."

Each reformulated decision proposal follows from the previous one, and none elicited much dissent from the members. Furthermore, each succeeding decision proposal was more concrete or specific than the previous one. Thus, without conflict, group members modify decision proposals in an evolutionary and methodical process of lowering the level of abstraction of each successive proposal. This pattern might be illustrated in the following methodical sequence:

Statement of the problem. "Public health nurses feel their lack of status and will therefore be defensive and resistant to change."

Criteria for the solution. "Begin the conference with a nonthreatening something." "Get the conference feeling good and then change them."

Abstract statement of solution. "Start the conference on common ground."

Concrete statement of solution. "Begin the conference with a history of the contributions that public health has made to the field of nursing."

In the absence of conflict or significant dissent, the lowering-of-abstraction pattern of decision modification seems to be painless, systematic, and eminently reasonable. But not all emergent decisions follow such a methodical route to consensus

The presence of conflict and dissent stimulates a different pattern of decision modification in which members introduce successive decision proposals at essentially the same level of abstraction. The same nursing group proceeded through the following reformulations of another initial proposal. The final reformulation achieved group consensus and was prerequisite to several other decisions to include specific programs in the conference:

1. "The public health nurse is engaged in treatment of pathology."
2. "Public health nurses should have more clinical work with patients."
3. "Public health nurses do perform tasks that require clinical nursing skills."
4. "Clinical skills are required for working with patients in the home as well as in the hospital."
5. "Public health nursing is a clinical nursing specialty."

This second pattern reflects the characteristic start-and-stop cumulative development of a consensus decision. But unlike the lowering-of-abstraction pattern associated with minimal conflict and dissent, this pattern reflects substitute decision proposals that are virtually restatements of each other. Each proposal is essentially the equivalent level of abstraction of every other.

The lowering-of-abstraction pattern is methodical in that members express little disagreement about the credibility of each decision proposal. In the absence of conflict, group members apparently perceive their task as one of seeking, or "discovery"—in this case, discovering what to include in the conference that would solve their problem and meet their established criteria.

The second pattern including conflict seems to reflect a different task for the members. To some members of the nursing group, public health nursing is a form of community social work or civil service in a government-sponsored clinic. To others, public health nursing is a clinical nursing specialty equivalent to, for example, psychiatric nursing. The issue produced disagreement and significant social tension between group members. Rather than being perceived as a task of discovery, the task in the presence of significant conflict was perceived to be "persuasion," or attitude change, in order to secure intragroup agreement. Whereas creativity is required to perform a task of discovery, persuasion is required to secure agreement.

Conflict, then, does not affect the basic start-and-stop process of decision modification, but it apparently does result in a distinctive pattern of that decision modification. When there is little substantive conflict, members methodically reintroduce substitute proposals in a pattern that consistently lowers the level of abstraction of that proposal. When a decision proposal precipitates conflict between members, the proposal is typically introduced at essentially the same level of abstraction in successive restatements of the root proposal.

Multiple-Sequence Models of Decision Making

All of the phase and development models of group process discussed above are useful for understanding how groups actually make decisions. You might have noticed that as these ideas developed there was increasing attention to the various cycles that groups experience. But all the phase models discussed above are single-sequence phase models; they generally posit a rather unitary and direct sequence of phases and these phases are assumed to describe most groups. More recently Poole (1981, 1983a, 1983b) has questioned these single-sequence phase models and presented data in support of what he calls multiple-sequence models.

Multiple-sequence models suggest that groups can take different developmental paths depending on such factors as the nature of the tasks, group procedures, and relationships between members. Poole argues that groups do not evolve from single phasic units, but interweave different patterns over time. This perspective on groups builds on the spiral model and the process of decision modification discussed above. Poole (see also Poole and Doelger, 1986) proposes three fundamental group threads:

1. *Task process activities* These are about how the group structures its procedures. Introducing subject matter, analyzing problems, and comparing solutions are all examples of task process activities.
2. *Relational character* This is concerned with the working relationships between group members at a particular point in time. Are they currently in harmony and integrated? Are they in conflict? Are they focusing on work, or are they socializing?
3. *Topical focus* This is the substantive issue being dealt with in the group. What is the group talking about at a given point in time?

These three threads can be coherent or incoherent. Consider the following coherent thread: Task activity = problem analysis; relational character = focused work; topical focus = subject matter X. Assume that a student group, talking about how to stop theft from the library, is discussing the extent of the problem. The topical focus (or subject matter) is: the extent of theft in the library. Their relational character is focused attention, energy, and work on the topic. The group's members are not currently in conflict. The task activity is problem analysis. This configuration corresponds to the problem analysis stage of the prescriptive model presented early in this chapter. Poole shows how these three threads vary and how the group goes through many sequences. At any time, for example, the members might shift their relational character to conflict, such as continuing to talk about the same problem but experiencing conflict over their analysis.

The three threads can change at different rates and at different times. Poole (1983a, 1983b) and Fisher and Stutman (1987) show how the group develops along different trajectories that can be identified by breakpoints. A *breakpoint* is the point in the flow of communication at which one group sequence ends and another one begins. Some typical breakpoints are delays, disruptions, adjournments, topic shifts, and planning periods. One way for a group member to "manipulate" the work of the group is to inject breakpoints artificially. Fisher and Stutman describe *routing statements*, or statements that signal the group to follow a new or potentially different path. These can be procedural statements, such as "I think someone should take notes," or they can suggest a future direction such as "Why don't we talk about the fundraising issues?" Statements that summarize the group's position also function as routing statements (for example, "I think most of us agree that we will take the following three steps").

The work of Poole and Roth (1989) is helpful because it accounts for some of the more complicated aspects of decision making by invoking a few rules and processes. Poole and Roth explain that there are really three major decision paths that groups can take.

The first of the three decision paths they describe is a *unitary path* such as the Fisher model, in which the groups go through standard periods of unified activity. They found that this path (which is not very frequently taken) is most characteristic of groups that are cohesive and have unclear goals. Under these conditions, groups generally orient toward a problem, analyze it, and then go through reinforcement in a manner consistent with the Fisher model.

Complex decision paths comprise the second type of paths used by groups to make decisions. A repeated problem/solution cycle is the hallmark of complex decision paths. Some groups fixate on problem/solution discussions. They do not orient themselves or reinforce their decisions. Other groups have enough orientation and reinforcement during their problem analysis. Poole and Roth found that questions of value that have moral implications and are laden with potential opinions stimulate groups to use complex cyclic paths.

In the third decision path, the groups studied by Poole and Roth move immediately to *solution-oriented* discussion. They spend very little time defining the problem and focus their attention on confirming a solution. Groups with clear goals and a task requiring little creativity are most likely to use a solution-oriented decision path.

INDIVIDUALS AND DECISION MAKING

There has always been some disagreement about whether the results of a group decision are directly associated with the individual members of the group—their attitudes and abilities—or whether the communicative process in the group alters and counteracts the individuals' abilities. Most current thinking (Allison and Messick, 1987; Jarboe, 1988) holds that individuals' abilities and attitudes are significantly influenced by the communicative process in the group.

Many early studies tried to associate demographic qualities (age, sex, education, race, etc.) with group performance (see Shaw, 1981, for a review), but these approaches usually do not explain very much. Jarboe (1988) found that you cannot understand very much about a group's decisions by considering only "input" variables related to group members; it is imperative to examine the communicative process during the group's deliberations. This process apparently mediates the effects of individual members' personalities and abilities.

But group members can improve their thinking ability. Certain ways of thinking that individuals bring with them to the group can be an important input factor.

Thinking Abilities of Members

It would be foolish to say that the members' abilities have no impact on group decision making. Certainly, groups composed of intelligent members will make more intelligent decisions than will groups of less intelligent persons. Similarly, groups of more capable or more expert members will make more capable or more expert decisions than will less qualified groups. It would also be foolish to attempt to discuss in any definitive sense the possible combinations of different abilities among members of decision-making groups. Shaw's (1981) discussion is the place to look for a more comprehensive discussion. Our present purpose includes discussing only a few abilities which members may possess and which are relatively important to the process of group decision making. These abilities are not necessarily more important than others, but they are influential in terms of their potential impact on the outcome of group decision making.

Some research has supported Dewey's (1910) model of reflective thinking as it is typically used—as an agenda to guide group deliberations. Indeed, this is the typical and traditional use of reflective thinking in group decision making. The ability to think rationally can help the group. Group members who rank high in reflective-thinking ability are perceived by their fellow members as more capable and as contributing more to the group's decisions than do members who are low on this ability. Moreover, groups of members with high reflective-thinking ability make higher-quality decisions.

Scheidel (1986) has discussed another personal ability that may be directly related to improving the quality of group decisions. Scheidel differentiates between two different types of thinking, which he calls convergent thinking and divergent thinking. He describes convergent thinking as comparing and evaluating ideas; it is consistent with logic, rationality, and reason. Mr. Spock of *Star Trek* is probably the fictional archetype of the ideal convergent thinker. Divergent thinking, on the other hand, deals with new and quite arbitrary ways of looking at problems; it is highly creative in the sense that it explores new and unorthodox views of familiar situations, and it is less rational and logical than covergent thinking. Whereas convergent thinking deals with a step-by-step approach to problem solving, with emphasis on the greatest probability of success, divergent thinking involves leaps of the imagination and a lack of concern with probabilities of success.

To illustrate the difference between convergent and divergent thinking, here is an example. You may be familiar with the puzzle concerning the cannibals and the missionaries crossing the river in a single boat. It goes something like this: Three missionaries and three cannibals must cross a river. They have but one boat, which will carry only two people. Since the river is filled with crocodiles and piranhas, no one can swim the river. The problem, however, concerns the cannibals' latent tendency to eat people. The missionaries are safe as long as their number is equal to or greater than that of the cannibals. But if the cannibals outnumber the missionaries on either side of the river, it's good-bye, missionaries. How can all six people safely cross the river in the single two-person boat?

The exclusively convergent thinker may find this puzzle somewhat difficult to solve without numerous trials. The more divergent thinker, however, experiences little difficulty and typically uncovers the solution immediately. In case you have not discovered the answer, the step-by-step solution follows:

1. One cannibal and one missionary cross the river. The missionary returns with the boat.
2. Two cannibals cross the river. One of them returns with the boat.
3. Two missionaries cross the river. *Both a missionary and a cannibal return with the boat.*
4. Both remaining missionaries cross the river. One of the cannibals returns with the boat.
5. Two cannibals cross the river. One of them returns for the remaining cannibal.

The key to solving this little problem lies in step 3. The convergent thinker, concerned with efficiency and achieving the goal in the most direct manner, is apt to overlook the possibility of having *two* people return with the boat. But such a step is necessary if you are to keep the cannibals from outnumbering the missionaries on one or the other side of the river. The divergent thinker, on the other hand, is not blinded by the constraints of efficiency and "rationality at all costs." Such a thinker quickly sees the key to the solution and solves the puzzle with little difficulty.

You may be tempted to believe that divergent thinking is superior to convergent thinking, or vice versa. Such a conclusion, however, would be quite mistaken. Both types are complementary modes of thought. In some situations one will be superior, but at other times the other will prove to be more useful in solving problems. It would be wise, then, for everyone to develop abilities of both divergent and convergent thinking. Unfortunately, while convergent thinking can be (and is) taught and learned in contemporary classrooms, divergent thinking can be learned only through experience and revelation. It defies any formalized description or instruction and can be acquired only through experiences with the novel, the creative, and the unexpected.

SUMMARY

Decision making includes problem solving, which requires the group's high acceptance of the solution. Decision making also includes other types of activities that are not clearly classified as problem solving: A decision is a choice made from among alternative proposals, and the consideration of these proposals constitutes all or part of the group's task performance. Consensus signifies the members' commitment to a decision reached by the group, and this commitment is measured by the members' degree of willingness to implement the decision. Negotiation and voting are other modes of decision making.

Prescriptive views of the group decision-making process attempt to illustrate how groups *should* make decisions. They assume rationality on the part of the group members, assume that there is an ideal process of decision making, and are assumed to improve the quality of group decisions. We presented an example of a rational problem-solving technique in addition to other techniques for generating ideas and implementing solutions.

Descriptive models of the group decision-making process attempt to illustrate how groups *do* solve problems and assume the presence of a natural (or normal) development of consensus decisions. Such models differ in terms of the observer's perspective and of the tools used to observe the group process. The most commonly used descriptive model is the three-phase model from Bales's IPA. Other descriptive models using different observational techniques reveal significant similarities to the three-phase model, but few models employ the perspective of group interaction patterns.

Unlike linear models of group decision making, the spiral model, the functional model, and the multiple-sequence model assume a pattern of anchored group positions of agreement and of reach-testing forward to develop new ideas. In this way group members refine, accept, reject, modify, and combine ideas progressively and cumulatively until the idea reflects the group's consensus. The spiral process, normal to the group process, accounts for the apparent inefficiency of group decision making as well as for the influence of the social dimension in achieving higher-quality decisions.

Decisions are not so much *made* by a group as *emergent* from the members' interaction. This emergence of decisions is illustrated in the four-phase model of orientation, conflict, emergence, and reinforcement, each phase characterized by a distinctively different communication pattern.

Group decisions achieve consensus in a spasmodic and cumulative modification of decision proposals in which proposals are introduced, discussed, dropped, and reintroduced in slightly modified versions until the proposal appears in a form that achieves group consensus. Although this start-and-stop process of decision modfication is typical of all introduced decision proposals, the presence of social conflict affects the pattern of reintroduced decision proposals and the members' perception of their group task. In every case, the spasmodic process of decision modification reflects the normal interaction patterns of group members and influences both the task and socioemotional dimensions of the group. Poole and Roth describe three possible decision paths for groups.

The individual characteristics of the members of the decision-making group may also affect the group's task performance. For example, a higher ability level of the group members will probably lead to a higher-quality group decision.

Leadership and Power

Probably the most familiar of all social phenomena is the concept of leadership. Although not studied extensively until the last three or four decades, leadership has intrigued philosophers for centuries. How and why do people come to power? Why do people so zealously follow leaders like Adolf Hitler? What do leaders do that nonleaders don't? What constitutes good or effective leadership?

It is amazing that so many people could study one phenomenon and gain such little understanding of it. The number of unanswered questions concerning leadership is staggering. The purpose of this chapter is to shed some light on leadership in a small group. Consistent with the perspective of communication and the group process, this chapter deals with leadership as an emerging process precipitated by the interstructured communicative behaviors of all group members.

POWER AND INFLUENCE

Some form of power is universal in human groups. It exists in small groups, organizations, families, and nations. Power and leadership are not uniquely human phenomena. Indeed, a leadership structure and power relations are present in all forms of animal life. The female lion dominates the pride. Usually the largest male ape is dominant in the colony. And insects of all sorts display power and status relations.

When an individual has power, he or she is in a position to demand compliance. It is best to consider power as a continuum: on the high-power end, a person is able to coerce one or more other people to behave as the powerful person wishes or suffer the consequences.

Power is the ability to exert control over others—and it is different from influence, because influence suggests persuasion rather than control. The two concepts—power and influence—are really quite distinct because it is possible to exercise one without the other. Power is not required for influence. A group member can be persuasive and influential without "possessing" power; some other group member can be powerful because he or she can control the behavior or resources of other people, but he or she might not be personally influential (Hollander, 1985). But even though power and influence are different processes, they are typically interrelated because group leaders are able to use both, depending on the situation and other group members. In many respects, influence is a more important concept because most leaders, even the very powerful, must use influence (or be persuasive) more often than they use raw power. Because unrestrained and bold power can be so disruptive and counterproductive, most leaders rely on persuasion more than on the full power at their disposal.

Discussions of power and leadership begin with a very basic premise, which is that a leader usually has power over others. The more fundamental sources of power in groups are structural and personal (Pfeffer, 1981). *Structural power* simply means that a person is in a position or place that has power attached to it. If you are a member of a five-person group and one person is designated as the "leader," then the person in that position has power even if he or she is incapable or unwilling to use it. People hired into such positions as vice president, dean, director, or foreman all acquire a certain amount of power simply because the position is a validated power position. A leader in one of these positions has "legitimate" power because the position has been sanctioned by some appropriate group or agency.

Personal power, on the other hand, refers to individual qualities that make a person powerful. Some people have personal characteristics that make them powerful. But personal power also refers to *resource dependency*, which means that if person A controls something that person B needs or wants, then person A has power. For example, if a friend of yours has to sign for every one of your financial transactions, you would be dependent on that friend for a resource: signatory authority. Your friend would have personal power over you. Anyone who has special knowledge or competence, regardless of his or her position, has personal power.

STATUS

Status comes with leadership and power. Status is the "prestige of the position" that is afforded an individual (Shaw, 1981, p. 271). A person newly appointed to a vice presidential position of an organization will not only be in a position of leadership where she can exercise power but will also acquire status. All social organizations (such as small groups, corporations, and societies) have status hierarchies. People acquire status from social class, background, professional membership, or the possession of certain objects, such as money, cars, and clothes. But the status hierarchy of a small group is more dependent on the ability to influence other group members. High-status members in most groups are perceived by other members as having provided the greatest assistance to the group's task accomplishment. If the raison d'être of the group is to accomplish some goal, whoever helps the group make progress toward that goal is rewarded with a high-status position. Social groups award status on the basis of the person's past behavior in the group, and achieved status is the most important status concern when there is no external authority that awards status to group members.

All organizations have *formal* and *informal* structures. When two status hierarchies exist side by side—one based on ascribed status and one based on achieved status—you have formal and informal structures. A business organization, for example, has its own status hierarchy ascribed by the organization, but the workers in that organization may have developed their own status hierarchy, which may not conform to that sanctioned by the organization. When the authority of the two hierarchies is in conflict, the resultant tension can be very great. Many organizational problems arise over a conflict between structural power and personal power. This sort of conflict emerges in classroom groups when an instructor designates one group member as leader. This ascribed leader has status only because he or she has been appointed to the position, and the person's success or failure as a leader now depends wholly on the behavior of the group. Since group members award the highest status to the person who has helped them progress toward the goal, the appointed leader might be in for a surprise if he or she fails to meet the group's expectations. In fact, groups that have reached full agreement on the status hierarchy perform better than groups that are democratic but unsure of the status hierarchy.

A status hierarchy exists in every group and organization. It is impossible to avoid. But it does not mean that members who have less status than others are of little value to the group. Productive groups value the contributions of everyone. Nevertheless, it is natural for people to attribute importance and value to the behavior of others; some members are therefore assigned a higher status. But the attribution of status to group members is a rank ordering of members' communicative behaviors relative to one another, not a judgment according to an absolute standard. Status, then, is something that is achieved in a particular group according to its goals and communication patterns. It is not a reward that a person can transfer easily from one group to another.

LEADERSHIP AND POWER

Several years ago one of us served on a committee charged with the task of selecting a chairperson for a university department. Several of the initial meetings were devoted to defining the role. We were unanimous in agreeing that we wanted a "chair" rather than a departmental "head." In other words, we agreed that we wanted leadership but that we did not want a dictator. The essential difference between "chair" and "head" was apparently the degree of power at the disposal of the leader.

The concept of extreme power in the hands of a leader is not novel. Indeed, nearly five centuries ago Machiavelli conceived of a political power so strong that rulers could use any means at their disposal to control the behavior of their followers. In fact, he believed that such power is essential for a centralized government. Machiavelli's name today refers to the unscrupulous exercise of political power. And the term *Machiavellianism* has been employed in reference to a person's ability or desire to dominate or control the behavior of another person during interaction.

It is important to distinguish between a *head* (for lack of a better term) and a *leader*. A head possesses the power to control the fate of others and thus has considerable power to coerce those under his or her leadership. A small group head would determine the goal of the group, give directions that must be obeyed willingly or unwillingly, and levy direct sanctions against non-followers. There would be considerable social distance between the head and the followers. In short, the relationship between head and followers is unidirectional: the head can influence followers but is less susceptible to any influence from them.

Instead of a head, many groups have a leader who is determined by the group members themselves and not imposed by an authority *outside* the group. But a leader has power too. The difference between headship and leadership is not the amount of power, but the basis from which the power is derived. As we saw earlier, one common basis of power is the control of resources that are needed or desired by others. Saudi Arabia, for example, possesses much more power than its size warrants because the country controls a vast quantity of oil needed and desired by all industrialized countries of the world. And when we think of powerful countries, we immediately think of those countries with the capacity of nuclear weapons. In short, power resides in the possession of some relatively scarce resource needed or desired by others. Such a concept of power is expressed in conventional wisdom by the adage "In a country of the blind, the one-eyed man is king."

Most groups do not typically provide such a basis of power. While intelligence, for example, might be considered a personal resource, it is not something that can be transferred from one person to another or acquired by a person in the same sense that the resources in the examples above can be acquired. Unlike the unidirectional relationship between a head and the followers, the relationship between a leader and followers is reciprocal. Consistent with the doctrine of interdependence, a leader leads at the discretion of the followers. That is, the basis for a leader's power is "consent of the governed." A leader may be deposed at any time. When a leader fails to satisfy the followers, his or her basis of power is undermined. Hence, the leader ceases to lead. A basis of power, such as the control of scarce resources, defines a leader in isolation, regardless of the will of other group members. Such a definition is contrary to the elements of process and interdependence inherent in groups. For our purposes, then, a leader is defined only in terms of followers. To discuss leadership is to discuss followership. One cannot exist without the other.

A leader is, of course, recognized by group members as the leader. Their recognition takes the form of deferential behavior. That is, members accede to the leadership moves made by the leader. They accord the leader respect and, generally, liking. (We shall return later in this chapter to the subject of the leader as an object of liking.) Members perceive the leader to be aiding the group in making progress toward their group goals. Normally, such progress implies the leader's activity in aiding the group in accomplishing its task. Perhaps more important than any other definitive characteristic, the leader is the person who consistently acts like a leader by performing leadership acts.

TRADITIONAL PERSPECTIVES ON LEADERSHIP

The vast quantity of research and philosophical writing about leadership reveals considerable confusion. The reason for the confusion stems from the many perspectives used to view leadership. People commonly consider leadership to be embodied in a person occupying a given position in the group; therefore, a leader is a person first and position in a role network second. While this viewpoint is a common one, it may have hindered progress in discovering the nature of leadership. In order to provide the basis for this book's perspective on leadership and to enrich our understanding of this elusive phenomenon, and evaluative survey of the most common perspectives on leadership follows. Hollander (1985) also provides a concise summary of some recognized perspectives on group leadership.

Traits

Letters of reference to employers, universities, and scholarship or loan agencies often ask for evaluations of the applicant on selected personality characteristics. A characteristic often included in such lists is "leadership ability." The assumption underlying this characteristic is the belief that a leader is a unique person possessing some innate ability that allows him or her to assume a leadership position in any social system. Further assumed is the belief that leaders are born, not made. Our conventional wisdom contains this same assumption in such well-worn phrases as "a natural leader" and "born to be a leader." It is not surprising, then, that the early approach to leadership searched for those individual characteristics or traits that leaders possess. The traits approach still influences contemporary views on leadership.

The traits approach attempts to distinguish leaders from nonleaders on the basis of how they differ in terms of personal characteristics. The very earliest research using the traits approach highlighted physical characteristics, consistent with the notion that the childhood leader is the biggest bully on the block. Because of consistently fruitless efforts to discover distinctive physical characteristics of leaders, this perspective soon focused on the distinctive traits of a leader's personality. The results from the traits approach have been contradictory and disappointing, however. Many personality traits have, at one time or another, been linked to leadership, including such traits as dependability, intelligence, self-confidence, enthusiasm or dynamism, originality, responsibility, verbal facility, critical thinking ability, and creativity.

A list of such traits appears consistent with common sense. One would normally think that a leader should have all these traits. But the traits approach to observing leadership has failed to achieve consistent results. Indeed, a leader of one group does not consistently achieve leadership in other groups. In fact, the leader of one group often cannot maintain leadership even in the same group. The traits approach plainly cannot account for the change of leadership in the same group.

It is probably impossible to assume that leadership can be explained simply by referring to the personality traits of individuals. Hollander (1985) explains that there have been two persistent questions about the qualities of leaders. The first asks what qualities *distinguish* leaders from followers. This is essentially the traits approach to leadership, where one assumes that leaders "possess" certain characteristics that cause them to be successful leaders. And, as Hollander argues, "this effort has not been very productive" (p. 492).

The second concern is what makes *effective* leaders. This is a very pragmatic question and can be studied by evaluating leaders in situations and noting effectiveness with respect to outcome criteria. This second approach is still concerned with leadership qualities, but only to the extent that situation-specific conditions are accounted for. Followers perceive leaders to have certain qualities, whether these qualities are apparent or not. There is currently considerable interest in leadership qualities with respect to how a leader's qualities are related to task demands (Boyatzis, 1982). This approach (discussed in more detail below) recognizes that the problem of assessing leaders in different situations is more complicated than simply identifying who is the leader.

In short, a strict traits approach to leadership is unsatisfactory. Personality traits are difficult to measure and people often disagree about personalities. Moreover, there are different traits required for different activities. The traits approach cannot differentiate between a good leader and a bad one, and it fails to explain the difference between achieving leadership and maintaining it. The variations in leadership qualities and requirements are so great that any list of traits would surely exclude some successful leaders and include some unsuccessful ones. The styles approach to leadership was an attempt to solve some of these problems.

Styles

The traits approach to leadership attempts to distinguish leaders from non-leaders and to identify those personality traits which characterize persons who rise to leadership status. The styles approach proceeds from a different perspective. Leadership styles assume an a priori identification of the leader through either ascription or achievement and a general description of how the leader leads. This approach seeks to determine which style of leadership is best, or most effective, in a group by comparing one predetermined style with another.

The early research utilizing the styles perspective differentiated between three general styles of leadership. These three styles were generalized descriptions of the relationship between leader and followers based on the leader's general pattern of behavior—democratic, autocratic, or laissez-faire. The laissez-faire style of leadership was soon discarded because it was so difficult to define. Essentially, the hands-off policy indicated by the laissez-faire style implies that the leader leads through not leading at all. Even on a commonsense level a laissez-faire style of leadership is an anomaly. Nonleadership is viewed as leadership?

Numerous studies have compared the democratic and autocratic styles of group leadership. Those in business management commonly refer to the two styles as "participatory" and "supervisory" management styles. Unfortunately, because the two styles are considered diametrically opposed to each other, the comparisons between them are not always realistic. Typically, an extremely democratic style is compared with an extremely autocratic style. That is, the *democratic leader* is totally unselfish, seeks group participation at all times, and consistently functions in the best interest of the group as a whole; the democratic leader, then, tends to overemphasize the socioemotional dimension of the group. On the other hand, most comparisons require the *autocratic leader* to behave with an absolute minimum of group participation, give blatant orders, and work for highly selfish goals; the autocratic leader, then, overemphasizes the task dimension of the group. Realistically, of course, there are many leadership styles that exist between these two extremes. And a single leader may even be democratic at times and autocratic at other times.

Past comparisons, however, have discovered some differences between groups functioning under these two styles. For example, the group with a democratic leader typically experiences more satisfaction, and the group with an autocratic leader is more efficient and more productive—particularly when productivity is measured on the basis of efficiency (for example, fewer errors). But the differences between the groups tend to diminish over time as the group members accustom themselves to the style of their leader. Since the task and social dimensions are interdependent, the success experienced in one dimension affects success in the other. That is, because members experience greater satisfaction with a democratic leader, they tend to work harder and increase their productivity, and because groups are highly efficient and productive under an autocratic leader, the members experience greater pride in their achievements—hence, an increase in satisfaction.

The styles approach is not a fully satisfactory perspective from which to view leadership in a small decision-making group. It is intuitively obvious that no one style is more desirable or more effective for all groups and all situations. For example, a military leader in battle and an airplane pilot in a storm are autocratic leaders and undoubtedly should be. When the going is rough, neither of these two leaders can stop to take a vote. Rather, they give orders that must be followed immediately and without hesitation. Naturally, in less trying situations the pilot or the military leader often adopts a more democratic style.

It is possible for leaders to use a characteristic style, but this style cannot be entirely divorced from the requirements of the situation that the leader and followers are involved in. Leaders must utilize a range of behaviors, depending on the demands of the task and the nature of the followers with whom the leader must interact. Even leaders who have a consistent style are controlled by external factors. So a style might be a *typical* tendency, but it is still *relational* because the leader responds to the qualities of followers and situations.

PRESCRIPTIVE MODELS OF LEADERSHIP

Most early discussions of leadership tried to explain it by identifying the qualities of leaders. If you believe that leaders are born and not made then there is not much you can do about leadership; it cannot be taught or learned. Prescriptive approaches to leadership are based on theories about how individuals *should* lead in certain situations. These theories have attempted to combine individual traits with qualities of a task to prescribe how a leader should behave, and to better predict which leaders will be effective.

Situations

Because of the inability of the traits and styles approaches to provide robust explanations of group leadership, many investigators of group behavior have turned to other perspectives. A common perspective that is currently popular for studying group leadership is the situational approach. When people who rise to leadership positions are assessed from this perspective, the main consideration is given to what the leader does or needs to do for effective group functioning.

The situational approach to group leadership requires a thorough description of the group situation. Of the many situational variables that could be examined, perhaps the one more commonly studied is the group members' particular combination of personality traits—their level of interest in the task, their motivation, and so forth. A second variable often believed to have some bearing on the particular kind of leader required in a situation is the nature of the group's task. Other, less commonly studied situational variables include factors of the physical setting; for example, sitting at the head of a table has been associated with leadership in our culture (although seating arrangements have not proved to be highly successful indicators of leadership). The size of the group has also been thought to have some bearing on leadership. Obviously, as the group increases in size, the reduced availability of each member becomes more of a problem; on the other hand, charismatic leadership is closely associated with very large groups and with a corresponding increase in social distance between leaders and their followers.

At first glance, the situational approach to group leadership appears to solve most of the problems associated with the traits and styles approaches, but it has its problems too. First, it offers very few general principles to help prospective group leaders know what they should or can do in a given situation. Of course, there are many lists of do's and don't's to guide prospective leaders, but such lists have not proved very successful. Second, no comprehensive list of situational ingredients now exists; even compiling such a list may be quite impossible. Third, even for those variables which have been observed to exist within a situation, there is no way of determining which variables have the greatest impact on the situation. A fourth problem stems from the fact that what *functions* the leader should fulfill is the significant element in the situational approach. The head of a student group gathering information on campus activities needs to function differently and to draw on different skills than does the leader of a town council or a labor union; although each leader must direct followers and influence the group process, the situation and the content of the activity make for different behavioral needs. Overall, the fundamental problem with the situational approach is the generality of the term *situation;* thus, analyses of situations have failed to distinguish clearly between task demands, group size, resources, and so on (Hollander, 1985).

But the situational approach has drawn attention to how leaders are affected by the perceptions of their followers (as opposed to concentrating solely on the behaviors of individual leaders). Therefore, what began as a strong response to the traits and styles approaches has led to significant developments in understanding leader-follower relationships. One of the most important of these developments has been the contingency model of leadership.

The Contingency Model of Leader Effectiveness   One specific situational approach to group leadership is the contingency model, developed by Fiedler (1964, 1967). Central to his contingency model is the assessment of a particular leadership "trait" measured by a paper-and-pencil test. Originally Fiedler developed two such tests—one to measure the "assumed similarity of opposites" (ASo) and the other to evaluate the "least preferred coworker" (LPC). A score on the ASo test would be high if the individual perceived himself or herself to be quite similar to the group member who was perceived to be the most different. In the LPC test, the higher the leader rated the group member whom he or she liked least, the higher would be the leader's LPC score. Fiedler discovered that the scores on these two tests were highly correlated. Therefore, the contingency model is typically based on only the LPC test.

In regard to the behavior of leaders, leaders with high LPC scores have been found to be more socially oriented. That is, they generally concern themselves with the group's social dimension. Conversely, leaders scoring low in the LPC test tend to be more task-oriented and concerned with order and structure. The contingency model, however, does not attempt to determine how leaders behave in certain situations. Rather, the model tries to place a particular leader (that is, a high-LPC or a low-LPC leader) in a group situation in which that leader will be more effective. Thus, the contingency model provides something of a combination of the traits and situational approaches. That is, a leader with a particular trait (high LPC or low LPC) is thought to be most effective in a specific situation.

Fiedler determined that a leader's effectiveness would vary as a result of several characteristics of the situation. The most notable of these characteristics include the amount of structure or external demands that the task places on the group, how well the group members get along with one another (similar to cohesiveness), and the formal power given to the person occupying the leadership position (such as the power to reward and punish group members).

Numerous investigations of LPC leaders in different situations have resulted in conclusions concerning the favorability of various situations for the leader. For example, a situation is quite favorable for leadership when it contains a highly structured task with a low level of difficulty, high commitment of group members to the task, and high formal authority of the leadership position. The more "favorable" the situation, then, the more directive the leader (that is, the leader will have a low LPC score). The less favorable the situation, one might assume, the more likely it is that the socially oriented leader (one with a high LPC score) will be most effective.

Fiedler's contingency model is a combination of traits and styles approaches to leadership. That is, the LPC trait, measured by the paper-and-pencil test, is associated with a particular leadership style (directive or nondirective) that is very similar to authoritative and democratic leadership styles. Consequently, the approach to determining the potential effectiveness of the leader, contingent upon situational characteristics, is an attempt to match leadership traits and styles to a particular group situation. We therefore interpret the contingency model of leader effectiveness as a specific situational approach to leadership.

Fiedler's contingency model has been very influential in explaining leadership effectiveness. Proponents of the model report strong confirming support in a number of experiments (Strube and Garcia, 1981). Still others claim that since a leadership "style" is matched with a situation, the subordinates in those situations are more satisfied with the group experience. Chemers (1983) believes that the Fiedler model can predict and explain group member satisfaction as well as performance

There are other contingency models of leadership (e.g., Vroom and Yetton, 1973; House and Mitchell, 1974), but each is similar in that leadership tendencies are typically described along a continuum from highly directive, or autocratic, to participative and democratic and are then matched with situational contingencies, such as the nature of the task, member relationships, and environmental factors. These models then predict leader effectiveness and group member satisfaction. But the models are also incomplete in some significant ways. There is a tendency to assume that an LPC score, for example, is associated with particular behaviors. As we will see later in this chapter, leaders adapt their behaviors to a wide range of situations and are not often strictly "person-oriented" or "task-oriented." In fact, one study (Offermann, 1984) reported evidence that a leader's LPC score *changed after group interaction*. This study raises serious questions about the stability of the LPC score to measure leadership style. It is also true that many individuals can operate very effectively in both the task and social realms and cannot be easily categorized by the LPC measure. Nevertheless, contingency models, and Fiedler's LPC model in particular, have helped link individuals with situations and have provided the rudiments of an interactional approach to leadership.

Group Composition   Gilstein, Wright, and Stone (1977) also provided insight into group leadership from a situational perspective in their investigation of leaders in groups with differing compositional "mixes" of members. They attempted to determine the specific type of groups in which directive or nondirective leaders would be more effective. Among the conclusions, they state that, in their investigation, groups whose members had conservative sociopolitical orientations developed higher member satisfaction (that is, cohesiveness) with a directive leader. Conversely, liberal members preferred a nondirective leader. According to this and other studies cited by the authors, groups with nondirective leaders tend to generate more member-centered and task-responsive interaction; the members apparently perceive a greater degree of freedom to participate and thus have a feeling of greater responsibility to participate in the group interaction. Members of groups with directive leaders, on the other hand, often turn to the leader for guidance and succeed in shifting the responsibility for interaction to the leader rather than assuming the responsibility themselves.

   One should not be led to conclude that nondirective leaders will diffuse the responsibility for the group's interaction among the group members. Rather, members with particular personality traits and with specific sociopolitical orientations tend to respond differently to the perceived directiveness of their group leader. Thus, persons who are more assertive, more interpersonally sensitive, and more ideationally flexible tend to interact more and thus allow for greater group effectiveness when they are in groups led by a nondirective leader. But groups composed of less assertive, less sensitive members with more fixed ideas apparently prefer situations that are more structured. They therefore respond more favorably to a more authoritative, or directive, leader.

   The situational approach to leadership, although highly popular and traditionally the most accepted approach to group leadership, underscores the complexity of the group situation. The number of factors that can differentiate one group situation from another is extraordinarily large. Among such factors are the personality attributes of individual members, the nature of the task, the amount and kind of external constraints on the group, the degree of cohesiveness in the group, and so forth. Moreover, each of these situational factors is subject to change as the group continues to interact. To account for all the factors, let alone the variation of each factor over time, is an extraordinarily challenging and probably impossible task. Even though the situational approach to leadership is conceptually attractive, it is extremely difficult to implement.

The Leader-Follower Relationship   Later in this chapter, in the Functional Communicative Behaviors section, we will outline some specific behaviors that leaders typically perform and show that you can improve your effectiveness in groups by practicing these behaviors. While the odds are that such behaviors will serve you well, you must not forget that leaders exhibit communicative flexibility. They adjust their communicative behaviors and interpersonal relationships according to the favorableness of the situation and the nature of the people they must work with: that is, their followers. In some way this is counterintuitive, because we usually assume that leaders affect followers' behavior, but an important issue in the study of leadership and group processes is the reciprocal effects of leader-follower relationships.

In an early experiment, Farris and Lim (1969) tested whether or not leadership behaviors might be significantly influenced by the performance of subordinates. Leaders were assigned to work with groups. One group of leaders was told that the members of their groups were highly competent and among the best-performing group in the company. In a second situation the leaders were told that their groups were poor performers and among the worst-performing in the company. Later the behaviors of the leaders were described, and it was found that there were important differences between the two situations. The leaders were seen as more considerate and respectful of the high-performance group and as less considerate of the low. When leaders are working with competent and motivated followers, they tend to be more considerate, create less structure, and include their followers more in decision making. A number of other early studies in communication and psychology confirmed these findings. Followers can significantly influence the communicative behaviors of leaders.

Some recent research has suggested that the communicative functions performed by a group leader during the group process may vary considerably. That is, the group leader varies in his or her interactive behaviors, depending on the specific member of the group with whom he or she is interacting. Rather than perform consistent "leadership functions" throughout the interaction, the leader will function differently with different group members.

Ellis (1979) performed an analysis of the relational interaction (e.g., the symmetry and complementarity of the one-up, one-across, and one-down control modes) in decision-making groups. He discovered that the perceived leader of the group performed communicative functions quite distinct from other group members, not in terms of different behaviors that function to set the leader apart, but in terms of adapting specific functions to nearly every member of the group individually. That is, the leader, when interacting with each member, differed from the interaction patterns characteristic of the group as a whole. No other members of the group consistently demonstrated variable interactive patterns with other group members. They all tended to interact with every one else in much the same fashion.

Ellis's results suggest that the primary leadership function may not be in the form of specific communicative behaviors that differentiate a leader from nonleaders. Rather, the leadership function may be the adaptation of specific functions to specific group members. At the same time, nonleaders apparently interact with other members in the same way in which they interact throughout the entire group interaction. Ellis (p. 163) writes: "The leader does not 'do' one thing which sets him apart from other group members. Apparently, the leader takes stock of the individuals in the group and enacts behaviors which he considers appropriate for each individual."

We sometimes believe that the leader assumes the leadership role by structuring the interaction, by influencing the flow of the ideas and relationships in the interaction. Ellis's research implies that the leader may indeed attempt to structure the interaction with some members; but in interacting with other members, the leader may defer to their structuring and may not attempt to exert any relational authority over them.

One conclusion from Ellis's research may be that there is no such thing as leadership functions that a leader performs consistently throughout the group interaction. Rather, a leader functions as a leader in adapting different communicative functions to different group members. In one case, he or she may be an authority figure and initiate the direction of the interaction's flow. In another case, however, he or she may be a respondent to some other member's attempts to structure an interaction.

Thus, all group members perform important contributions to the group's interactions. Furthermore, these contributions may serve as "leadership functions" overall. But the leader, as an initiator, a respondent, and a reactor to these functions, is adept at knowing when to initiate and when to respond and with whom. The leader's interaction with each member is distinctive. The leader is able to adapt to every other member as a unique, contributing member of the group. Apparently nonleaders do not interact in such an adaptive manner.

The leadership function of adaptation is also the subject of an investigation performed by Wood (1977). She indicated in her report that leaders are able to adapt to situations and to past failures of the group. In terms of specific communicative behaviors, Wood indicated that leaders tend to promote what she called a collective identity—apparently similar to groupness. Perhaps the adaptation of specific functions to other members as unique individuals, such as Ellis depicted, is one way to weld individuals into a collective group identity.

One very interesting theory based on leader-follower relationships is proposed by Hersey and Blanchard (1982). They have been working with a *life-cycle theory of leadership,* which is a response to the difficulties of defining *situation* and to the importance of leader relationships with group members. The central tenet of Hersey and Blanchard's theory is that leaders should communicate and interact with followers based on the level of maturity of the followers. The emphasis is on followers. The followers determine the leadership style and the power of the leader. Hersey and Blanchard define effective leadership according to how well the leader operates within a particular situation. Rather than describing leadership as a single style or set of behaviors, they argue that a leader's style must be integrated with the behaviors of followers. A leader is *effective* when his or her style is appropriate to the situation and the other members of the group or organization. When leadership effectiveness is based on the interaction of leader behaviors and the environment (followers and other situational variables), it means that no single leadership style is always best. In a crisis-oriented organization, such as the military or the police, it is best for a leader to be highly directive and task-oriented because success depends on fast action and immediate responses; group members do not need as much socioemotional support.

The life-cycle theory of leadership is based on the life cycle of group development, and on the fact that groups develop toward levels of maturity. The primary element of effective leadership is the *maturity* of followers, and maturity is based on a number of components. First, mature group members are able to set obtainable goals and to accept feedback about how well they are progressing toward their goals. They are more interested in how well they are doing than in how well they are liked. Second, mature group members take responsibility and are both motivated and competent to handle responsibility. Third, mature group members are psychologically confident and able to perform their various tasks. They feel secure as individuals and are not easily threatened or shaken. And finally, mature group members realize that flexibility is important to goal accomplishment. They realize that many situational variables can influence a task and that they must diagnose and respond to these variables.

The life-cycle theory of leadership is displayed in Figure 7-1. The graph shows how task- or relationship-oriented a leader should be, depending on the maturity of the followers.

Quadrant I begins with followers who are low in maturity; that is, they are insecure, not very motivated, lack competence, and seek feedback that is irrelevant to the task. The theory predicts that an effective leader would concentrate on task behaviors. He or she would get the group organized, direct its activities, and oversee specific tasks. Relationship behavior would be kept to a minimum because the group requires much help in order to make progress on its tasks.

The bell-shaped curve in Figure 7-1 shows how the maturity level of a group or organization develops along a continuum from immature to mature. Quadrants II and III are medium levels of maturity where the leader would concentrate more on relationship behavior and alternate between being more or less task-oriented.

Groups and organizations in quadrant IV have developed into more mature organizations. Followers are now capable of performing their tasks

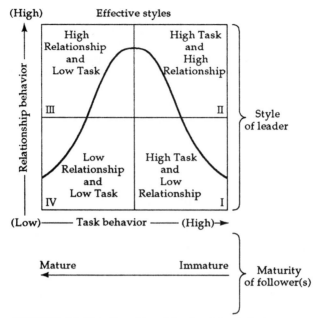

FIGURE 7-1 Relationship of leadership style to group maturity.

and are more self-confident. Individuals can provide their own rewards in quadrant IV and do not need the leader to provide their "strokes." The leader can reduce the level of his or her close supervision and include the followers more in decision making. The leader trusts the other members of the group and feels comfortable delegating responsibility.

Hersey and Blanchard also have a conception of leadership communication styles that are appropriate for each quadrant of Figure 7-1. Each style listed below is an attempt to establish a relationship between the task-level situation and the leader as the constituency moves through maturity. The bell-shaped curve is a prescriptive curve because it shows the appropriate leadership style associated with the level of maturity. It prescribes how a leader should communicate, given the conditions of that quadrant. The four leadership styles are "telling," "selling," "participating," and "delegating."

Quadrant I: "Telling" for Low Maturity   People who do not know their job, and who are perhaps unwilling, need to be told what to do. Since they are not competent or confident, it would make little sense for them to make decisions on their own. Sometimes group members or workers are simply unsure of what they are doing. Thus, a firm but direct "telling" style offers clear and specific communication. This style is task-oriented rather than relationship-oriented because friendly or supportive communication might be seen as permissive and rewarding of poor performance. Group members in this situation require direction and a focus on competent and effective task completion.

Quadrant II: "Selling for Low to Moderate Maturity   This style of communication is called "selling" because the leader must convince the followers to accept his or her way of doing things. Some constituencies lack skills but want to learn. The selling style is directive but includes interaction between leaders and followers so that followers can understand the reasons for decisions and come to accept them through understanding. The selling style is directive, because followers need to learn, but it is also supportive and reinforcing, because at this level of maturity the followers need to improve their work habits and enthusiasm.

Quadrant III: "Participating" for Moderate to High Maturity   According to Hersey and Blanchard (1982, p. 153) this level of maturity is for people who are *able* to perform for a leader but *unwilling*. This is typically a motivational problem for group members who might lack confidence or security, but are in any case reluctant to perform. The leader is essentially motivating the followers by having them "participate" in the decision making. The leader relies heavily on open communication and listening. This style of leadership communication is high on relationship issues, because the leader must facilitate a quality relationship with the others so they will feel actively involved in the group process and decision making.

Quadrant IV: "Delegating" for High Maturity   This fourth quadrant includes people who are highly mature. These workers are confident and they are ready, able, and willing to take on responsibility. Mature workers are competent professionals who are motivated. They respond well to a low-profile "delegating" type of relationship with their leader because these group members do not need much direction or support. Their leaders will certainly continue to define problems and assign them responsibilities for completing work. But these followers will require little communication or facilitation after that. Since they are psychologically and professionally mature, they do not need much direction.

A leader should also draw on the appropriate type of power base. Earlier in this chapter we defined power as the ability to exert control over others; the ability to get others to do what you want. The *power base* is the source that gives a leader his or her power. If a leader holds a position in an organization, his or her power derives from that position. The position gives him or her the power to fire people, raise their pay, and discipline them as necessary.

A person who is loved and respected also has power over others, which derives from that love and respect. Machiavelli, in his sixteenth-century treatise on power, posed the interesting question of whether it was better to have power based on love (personal power) or power based on fear (positional power). Machiavelli preferred power based on fear but warned that the skilled leader must not allow fear to turn into hatred. Hersey and Blanchard also warn that even if the leader's style is appropriate for the maturity level, the style will more likely be successful if it emanates from the appropriate

FIGURE 7-2 Appropriate power
base for level of maturity.

	Maturity level		
Low	Moderate		High

Q1	Q2	Q3	Q4
Coercive power	Reward power	Referent power	Expert power

power base. So the effective leader should vary both his or her style and the power base. Figure 7-2 shows the relationship between maturity level and the appropriate power base.

Q1: Coercive Power When a follower needs strong direction and a leader is utilizing a "telling" style, coercive power is necessary. People with low levels of maturity typically respond to the knowledge that negative consequences will result if they do not perform. Thus, a leader may have to resort to coercive threats such as firing, demoting, or punishing them in order to induce their compliance.

Q2: Reward Power This is the power base when a leader is in a position to reward or reinforce a follower. The "selling" style is clearly enhanced when the leader can offer financial or other types of rewards.

Q3: Referent Power An individual who has power over others because he or she is well liked, capable, friendly, and generally considered an appealing person has referent power. In other words, the leader is someone the followers identify with. A leader who is getting others to "participate" will be well served by a referent power base resulting from his or her good personal relations with the followers. This power base helps instill confidence and encouragement in others, which permits the leader to influence them because they like and admire him or her.

Q4: Expert Power Here the leader has power because she or he is a highly competent and credible expert. The followers will allow and expect the leader to "delegate" because they know she or he is probably the most competent person in their group and they recognize this expertise.

The Task and Social Dimensions of Leadership

With the exception of the functional approach that follows, all perspectives on leadership have considered it to be a role filled by one person. Bales and Slater (1955), however, began to consider the possibility that leadership duties might be divided among group members and that more than one person in the group could perform leadership duties. As we have seen, there is general agreement that there are two dimensions to any leadership situation—the task and social dimensions. The *task* dimension pertains to goals, production, structure, and the general accomplishment of tasks. The *social* dimension pertains to the quality of interpersonal relationships, consideration for others, socioemotional support, and individual feelings. Sometimes the task and social leadership functions in a group are handled by two different people. One person might be particularly adept at organizing the group and accomplishing goals, and another person might be skilled at forming and maintaining good personal relationships among group members. When both these qualities are present in one highly capable individual, you might have the "great man" model of leadership.

Some people are quite uncomfortable with the notion that there is a task and social leader in a group. And, in fact, it is possible to argue that most members of groups perceive task competence to be the primary determinant of leadership and expect a competent person to be a directive and assertive leader. The leader-follower relationship becomes important here, because of the following: When group members are highly involved in a task, they value a directive leader and expect the competent leader to guide the group toward its goals. But when group members are uninvolved, they resent directive leaders and look more for social support, which is to say that group members who, not satisfied with the situation, look to other people for agreeable social experiences; hence, uninvolved and unhappy group members perceive some people to be task leaders, whom they do not appreciate, and others to be social leaders, whom they do appreciate.

THE FUNCTIONAL PERSPECTIVE ON LEADERSHIP

All the perspectives on group leadership—traits, styles, situations—have one element in common. Each assumes that leadership is centered in the *person* who occupies the leadership position in the group's network of roles. The functional perspective shifts the point of emphasis from the person to the communicative *behaviors* performed. Although the functional approach is certainly not new, no consistent search for leadership functions has developed over the years. The function perspective has never achieved the significance or popularity enjoyed by each of the other perspectives at one time or another. One reason for this lack of popularity may be a confusion over what is meant by "functions." While some have considered group functions to be general principles essential to group operation, others discuss functions as specific behaviors capable of being performed by one person.

Most group functions are generalized "good advice"—principles with insufficient practicability. For example, some commonly listed group functions include: (1) advancing the purpose of the group, (2) inspiring greater activity among members, (3) administering procedural matters, and (4) building group cohesiveness. Essentially, these group functions imply some sort of influence that achieves desired results, such as greater cohesiveness, increased productivity, or greater group unity. Group functions, then, are little more than desired goals achieved rather than specific communicative behaviors that help achieve these goals.

Although there is no single acceptable list of individual functions—that is, communicative behaviors—several suggested lists indicate some individual behaviors that have been associated with leadership in the past. Cartwright and Zander (1968, P. 306), for example, distinguish between group functions and individual functions and provide such a list:

> It appears that most group objectives can be subsumed under one of two headings: (*a*) the achievement of some specific group goal and (*b*) the maintenance or strengthening of the group itself. Examples of member behaviors that serve functions of *goal achievement* are "initiates action," "keeps members' attention on the goal," "clarifies the issue," "develops a procedural plan," "evaluates the quality of work done," and "makes expert information available." Examples of behaviors that serve functions of *group maintenance* are "keeps interpersonal relations pleasant," "arbitrates disputes," "provides encouragement," "gives the minority a chance to be heard," "stimulates self-direction," and "increases the interdependence among members."

Mortensen (1966) devised five categories of individual behaviors that he labeled "attempted leadership." These five categories include "introducing and formulating goals, tasks, procedures," "eliciting communication from other group members," "delegating, directing action," "showing consideration for group activity," and "integrating and summarizing group activity." These five categories imply several characteristics of leadership behaviors. For example, Mortensen conceived of a leader as initiating proposals for action, asking focused questions, and summarizing group activity. These functions are also reflected in Cartwright and Zander's list.

Functional Communicative Behaviors

It is, of course, impossible to identify all the behaviors that leaders perform, and labeling any single message as functional and serving the needs of the group is probably an oversimplification. Nevertheless, we want to give you as workable a list as possible for learning and identifying leadership behaviors. Although you cannot learn to be a leader simply by reading a list of typical leadership behaviors, you can improve your effectiveness in groups by becoming familiar with common leadership behaviors and practicing them, always keeping in mind that an appropriate behavior depends on the situation and on your relationships with your followers. Deciding how to communicate in a group is a matter of making informed strategic choices about what communicative behaviors will be most effective. The following discussions are designed to help you make intelligent choices. The leader must function in three areas: groups procedures, task requirements, and social needs.

Group Procedures All groups must be guided through their tasks in an orderly manner. Every type of group establishes procedures for accomplishing goals. Putman (1979) explains how some groups prefer very rigid procedures while others are quite casual. The leader can perform the following functions to facilitate the procedural requirements of the group.

Plan an Agenda   Most people appreciate a sense of order. An agenda is a list of topics to be discussed during the group's meeting. The leader should either prepare an agenda before the group meets or direct the group before the meeting actually begins to agree on what it will talk about. The leader should also be prepared to stimulate discussion on each of the agenda items; the leader should not control the discussion, but should simply generate discussion and make sure that relevant issues emerge.

Handle Routine "Housekeeping" Matters   These are tasks that typically must be completed before the group begins considering the central issues of the meeting. The tasks could be such things as taking roll, calling the meeting to order, distributing handouts, or making any necessary announcements or modifications to the agenda. Handling all such tasks ensures that the group is prepared to complete its work.

Prepare for the Next Meeting   Group members need to be informed about such things as the meeting's location, date, and time. The leader should make sure that the physical conditions are appropriate; that is, the room is of sufficient size, there are enough chairs, and any equipment (e.g., projectors and slides) is available and operating. These may sound like small tasks to perform, but they are very important to the work of the group. The truly efficient leader gains the respect of the group by attending to small details.

Task Requirements   The leader plays an extremely important role in accomplishing the work of the group. Leadership behaviors that help the group achieve its goals are task-oriented behaviors. It is important to remember that leadership behaviors can be performed by any member of the group; as we will see later, research indicates that leadership communicative behavior is often shared by group members, or at least that no single person is the only one to communicate in a leaderlike manner. There are obviously many leadership functions that group members can perform, and it is sometimes difficult to separate task functions from procedural or social functions, but the following represent the most important task requirements.

Initiate a Structure   Effective leaders organize and direct things so that the group makes progress toward its goals. The leader suggests ways of doing things and proposes tasks and goals for the group. The "initiate a structure" function is general enough to include procedural matters as well as others. When a leader proposes an agenda, directs the group to proceed in a certain way, or suggests solutions to a problem, he or she is initiating a structure for the group. When group members withhold suggestions or wait for others to initiate ideas, they are not contributing to the orderly progression of the group.

Seek Information   We said earlier that groups can perform some tasks better than individuals because they have the advantage of collectivity. In order for groups to utilize all their resources and perform at their best, they must seek out all the relevant and pertinent information. Functional behaviors in this area include requesting facts, asking questions, and getting clarification on unclear points of information; the dysfunctional group member is neither aware of necessary facts nor takes the time to seek out information. Some leaders will prepare for group meetings by writing down questions to be asked.

Provide Information   Every member should be contributing valuable information to the group, but individuals who are leaders contribute more than others. They spend more time reading and preparing for the group than other members do. Very simply, leaders offer facts and information relevant to the group's concerns. Members who carry out fact-gathering assignments and report the results of their work to others gain an influential position, because access to information is always associated with power. Of course group members who exert leadership by providing information should do so in a manner that benefits the group rather than the individual leader.

Offer Informed Opinions   Perhaps you have heard the quip "Opinions are like rear ends; everyone has one." This may be true of general opinions, but it is not true of informed ones. Very few people have *informed* opinions. Whereas a general opinion is an unsupported belief about some issue or matter before the group, an informed opinion is a belief supported by data, evidence, and argument. Leaders seek information so that they can offer informed opinions; it is counterproductive to confuse the members with ambiguous or indefensible opinions. Leaders also offer their informed opinions at the right time, neither stating them too soon nor remaining silent too long. For instance, a member who knows that his or her opinion is likely to sway the group might let other members express themselves first so as not to influence them unduly.

Clarify and Elaborate   Reducing ambiguity and clarifying ideas by asking questions and making statements are important leadership functions. A good leader can recognize when the members are confused or unclear about an idea because it has been expressed in abstract language. Technical or socially inappropriate language can sometimes be a problem too; if the group is preparing a public document, the leader should make sure that it is appropriate for the external audience, free from jargon or specialized language that might not be very communicative. The leader should also be capable of relating one idea to another and of seeing the big picture. Because group members are often preoccupied with their own ideas, it is up to the leader to clarify the connections between ideas so that the members understand the ideas' implications.

Summarize the Group's Main Points and State Its Consensus Group members usually express many opinions and ideas during the course of a discussion. Some of these are carefully thought out, but others are rather haphazard and superficial, and in either case it is important that they be summarized. A leadership function has been performed when someone restates the main points in clear language and summarizes the member's various arguments. A truly skillful and balanced summary will include all the main points and arguments, and it is dysfunctional for a leader to favor one position over another. At some point in the group's deliberations the leader will say, "I think we have agreed on the following points," then state what he or she believes to be the group's consensus, and engage the group in additional discussion about those points on which there is no consensus.

Social Needs Groups also have social needs. A leader who attends to social needs is concerned with promoting a harmonious and pleasant social environment in the group; this requires the leader to be sensitive to the group's individual members and their interpersonal relationships. But it is impossible to separate a group's task requirements from its social needs completely, because each influences the other, so the task and social dimensions should really be considered together. The group's success depends on both, and conflict between the two can be disruptive to the group. If a group's leader and members are concerned only with achieving their task goal, their interpersonal relationships and sense of personal well-being will suffer; on the other hand, if the leader and members spend all their time socializing and "liking" each other, the task will suffer.

It does not take much imagination to see how a member's performance on the group task can be hindered by a poor social environment. If the member feels unappreciated and has tense social relationships with other group members, he or she is not going to perform well. The following example shows how the task and social dimensions are related in a significant way. Jim states an opinion and Bill disagrees with it.

JIM: Since so many minority students are concentrated in a few schools, the only way to achieve racial balance is by busing.
BILL: Well that's a pretty dumb idea. It's been tried before and always causes all sorts of problems. Forget it.

Although Bill is responding to a particular idea that pertains to the task, he is doing it in such a way that Jim is likely to feel personally inadequate. Bill's comment is a clear enough statement of his opinion about a task-related matter, but it also says something about how he views Jim. Because Jim is surely going to interpret Bill's statement as an expression of a negative attitude toward himself, Bill's message about a task matter will have a deleterious effect on his social relationship with Jim.

A leader must analyze the group at any moment and decide which behaviors are best to meet the group's needs. Should a leader decide that the group members would benefit by some dialogue in an attempt to understand one another and get along better, the following types of communicative behaviors might prove useful.

Express Feelings This is very difficult in most work groups. People simply feel vulnerable and weak if they express feelings that are highly personal. Nevertheless, there are times when it is important. A leader should not force group members into a soul-searching session but can call attention to feelings that are bothering people. A leader can provide support for a group member who has been personally attacked and can reinforce a less confident member. A leader who freely expresses feelings and shows concern for the feelings of others will establish a friendly and productive work environment. And the best way to stimulate others to talk about their feelings is to do it yourself. So if as a leader you say what is on your mind, others will likely follow.

Facilitate Involvement and Communication Almost all groups have members who do not participate or are not very involved in group life. Some people are simply apathetic, and others are shy or feel overwhelmed by the group. Leaders must work to keep everyone participating; otherwise, the group loses valuable input. And if members are not stimulated enough to participate, they withdraw emotionally from the group and become part of the problem rather than part of the solution. There are a number of ways to stimulate communication and involvement, but the following three are the most common and effective:

1. *Make sure you reinforce any attempts to participate by shy or reluctant members* Verbal reinforcements are simple and effective, such as saying, "Good idea, I hadn't thought of that." Everyone likes to think that his or her ideas are being treated seriously and appreciated. Studies show that verbal reinforcement is very likely to increase the frequency with which a group member participates. Even if you do not agree with what a member says, you can communicate disagreement in a socially acceptable manner. In the example above, Bill could have said something like "That's one solution that has worked, but there are a few others we haven't considered."
2. *Directly engage people in communication* A leader might find it necessary simply to remind group members that they have an obligation to participate, telling them directly that the quality of the discussion depends on their participation. It is always easier to sit back and listen, so some members need a little prodding. Also, a leader can address questions directly to individuals. This will pull a person into the interaction, and if the person's contributions can then be reinforced, there will be even stronger incentive for him or her to continue participation. It takes practice and skill, however, to do these things tactfully; if the leader is perceived as being condescending, then his or her efforts will not only fail but will do more harm than good. Giving assignments is another way to encourage involvement in the group. At the close of a meeting or work

session, a leader should give directions for the next time, and group members who are responsible for some type of work and must come prepared to report will naturally be involved in the interaction. When such an assignment makes use of an individual's experience and expertise, the individual is even more likely to succeed.

3. *Increase the chances for participation* Sometimes groups are so large that people find it difficult to "jump in." The leader might consider dividing the group into small clusters to give everyone an equal chance to participate. There is also the problem of the overpowering member or subset of members who dominate the discussion. Just as there are shy people who hesitate to be involved, there are extroverts who are ambitious and have an opinion about everything; a leader should not allow one member to dominate the discussion. Finally, the leader can use the structural arrangement of the group to advantage. Recall that Chapter 3 discussed the concept of structural centrality; that is, a person who is in a more central position sends and receives more messages. Place a group member in a central position (such as in the middle of a network or at the head of a table), and this will increase the frequency of the member's participation.

Harmonize   A leader should attempt to reconcile disagreements and reduce tension. This can be achieved either through humor and relaxing comments or through more direct attempts at conflict resolution. (Conflict resolution will be discussed in the next chapter, but here it is important to identify it as a social skill that a leader should possess.) *Harmonizing* is getting the members to cooperate and creating a supportive climate in the group. The skilled harmonizer knows the difference between (1) a healthy and valuable exchange of ideas, which may include honest disagreement, and (2) nasty arguments that interfere with the group's productivity and are based on individual egos and ambitions. All the theories and techniques of conflict resolution notwithstanding, a leader can always simply restate opposing positions, ask the members to clarify their views, and then try to find compromises.

The Leader as Medium

It is increasingly apparent that leadership is a complex process. It is a mistake to try and make leadership something that is reduced to a few simple concepts. Leadership is not simply a personality trait or a style; it is much more complex than that, and current theories try to take this complexity into account. Some theories (e.g., Ellis, 1979) have found that leaders adapt so much and alter their behaviors so often that it is impossible to identify stable leadership behaviors. Leaders are less likely to perform specific functions than they are to be complex themselves and communicate in ways that exhibit complexity. Leaders behave differently with different people at different times in different situations.

Karl Weick (1978) has suggested that a leader is a *medium* who manages complexity. When a group begins the decision-making process it makes a whole series of decisions about information and what to do with it. Those decisions must be processed "through" the leader. If the information and group decisions are complex, the leader must be complex in order to process and manage the information. A good leader-as-medium will communicate in a diverse and flexible manner. Moreover, complex leaders will not simplify information just for the sake of simplicity or ease. The leader acts as a medium when she or he considers a number of alternatives and interpretations, integrates them, and reaches a conclusion—all without becoming confused. The leader will continually assess the maturity level of his followers and adapt accordingly. In short, the successful leader is a medium through which information flows, and is more complex than nonleaders.

Functionalism and Leadership: Conclusion

In sum, the list of leadership functions given above does note some specific behaviors associated with leadership. Moreover, the functions emphasize those behaviors which facilitate group task accomplishment. A more specific list of behaviors comprising all the functions performed by a leader is probably unrealistic, but the partial list given above may be used as a springboard for further consideration. Certainly the performance of appropriate leadership functions requires a social awareness of what function needs to be performed, when it needs performing, and the ability to perform it.

The functional perspective on leadership is not without its shortcomings, however. While the approach itself has potential, the state of knowledge about leadership functions is small. First, the leadership functions that researchers now recognize and use are still too global and not easily applied. Second, most past efforts to discover leadership functions attempted to describe communicative behaviors or their consequences in isolation, without viewing leadership acts within the interstructured sequence of group interaction. What type of act precedes and follows a leadership act? Perhaps the leadership act can be defined as a leadership function only in terms of the act that precedes and follows it. If leadership involves a reciprocal relationship of leader and follower, the behavior of the leader is probably meaningless when isolated from the behaviors of the followers. Thus, leadership functions should reflect the interdependence of communicative behaviors performed by both leader and followers during the process of group interaction.

The problem of identifying leadership acts is real. Functionalism suffers from the uniqueness of the situational perspective. Although the explanations of leadership behavior are more explicit in the description of leadership emergence given later in this chapter, the basic axiom identifying a leadership act is appropriateness within a given interaction sequence. That is, what may be a leadership act at one time during the group's interaction may be quite inappropriate at another time.

Shifting the focus of leadership from the person to his or her communicative behaviors, the functional approach no longer implies that leadership acts are necessarily performed by only one person. Typically, members of a decision-making group have a single member as their leader in that the bulk of the leadership acts is generally performed by just one person. But it would not be extraordinary if several persons performed the leadership functions and hence provided the group with shared leadership. But shared leadership in no way implies that one person is a task specialist while the other is a socioemotional specialist. Rather, inherently implying the interdependence of the two dimensions, group leadership functions are shared, in that several members perform these functions without partitioning their leadership responsibilities into neat pigeonholes.

The functional approach also allows for, and serves to explain how, leadership changes from one person to another within the same group or in different situations. Mortensen (1966) discovered that some leaders consistently performed leadership behaviors throughout all periods of the group's interaction and hence maintained their leadership positions. Other leaders, however, noticeably declined in their attempted leadership acts, thereby indicating their fall from leadership status. As the deposed leader decreased his or her performance of attempted leadership acts, another member or members apparently performed those acts and took over as leader.

Finally, the functional approach makes it possible to define which functions characterize good, effective leadership and, conversely, which functions characterize poor, ineffective leadership. Other perspectives are less capable of defining qualities of effective leadership, for to do so requires evaluating what the leader actually does. Hence, the functional perspective is necessary in order to be able to evaluate leadership behaviors.

THE DESCRIPTIVE MODEL OF LEADERSHIP EMERGENCE

In the event that a leader is appointed by some authority outside the group, the process of leadership emergence applies to the emergence of the informal leader. Most groups have a leader who emerges gradually over time, in which case the process is important. When people achieve leadership status gradually, the process is termed *leadership emergence*. This process is especially apparent in juries where no leader is appointed, in battlefield promotions, and in the development of political and organizational leadership.

Most religious and political emergent leaders, as well as small group leaders, inspire allegiances and positive associations in their followers. When leaders are popular and successful, it is usually because they are not autocratic. Most emergent leaders have a large and impressive following who identify with the leader, and sometimes the identification is so strong that the followers fail to examine their reasons for feeling so strongly about the leader. This is not a typical problem in small groups, but there are ample examples of political and religious leaders who fit this model. Leaders emerge with a dedicated following because they treat people well and tell them what they want to hear. Actually, the notion that leaders emerge from a consensual base is exaggerated, because most leaders spend considerable time encouraging and cultivating followers.

People want to lead for numerous reasons, but most of them fall into one of the following five categories:

1. *Information* The leader is often a person who has special information that cannot be communicated easily to others.
2. *Rewards* The individual seeks the rewards associated with leading.
3. *Expectations* The individual believes that the task can be accomplished and that he or she can do it.
4. *Acceptance by other group members* Individuals who are reinforced and affirmatively evaluated by group members are likely to attempt leadership.
5. *Status* People who bring status to the group often attempt to lead. This status can be in the form of a previous leadership role or of some other valued activity or resource.

Who emerges as a leader has been an important subject of study, and research shows that communication is the major determinant (Hollander, 1985). In fact, the amount of talking, as opposed to its quality, is the most important determinant. The person who makes many contributions to the group is perceived to be motivated and therefore to be an attractive leader for the group. The *quality* of what is said becomes more important later in the group process, when the members can be impressed with content. Who speaks first is another indicator of who will emerge as a leader, for people who speak up immediately are perceived to be motivated and self-assured, characteristics that group members find appealing in a leader. Moreover, group members who speak up first have the attention of the remainder of the group and can exercise influence.

Schneier and Bartol (1980) found that women are less likely than men to emerge as leaders, but one interesting difference is that women are often rated the same as men on certain leadership behaviors. In other words, women are perceived to be the same as men when it comes to communicating in a leaderlike manner; however, when leaders are actually identified, there are fewer women than men. We will take a closer look at sex differences and leadership later in this chapter.

Fisher's Model

Fisher (1980) created what he called a hypothetical model of leadership emergence. Based on his observations of classroom groups, he proposed a model in which members of groups contend for leadership and then go through a process of elimination. The model can be understood as an explanation of how the leadership *process* works after some members make leadership attempts (perhaps seeking leadership for some of the five reasons listed above). Figure 7-3 is a pictorial representation of this hypothetical model; it shows that there are three stages in the process.

At least theoretically, all members of the group are candidates for leadership. Some members, through the quantity and quality of their communication, will make their interests known immediately. During stage 1, some members (e.g., member E in Figure 7-3) will fall from contention immediately for any number of reasons. They simply feel uninterested or are incapable of emerging as a leader because of their personality (such as being overly shy), their lack of expertise, or their general failure to communicate as a leader. Stage 1 is usually pretty brief. Noncontenders are quickly recognized by other group members and just as quickly eliminated as leader contenders.

During stage 2, several members are strengthened in their bids for leadership by gaining the assistance of other members to support their candidacies. Thus, members A and C remain contenders for group leadership while members B and D drop out of personal contention and serve as lieutenants of A and C, respectively. As a lieutenant, each becomes less an initiator of action and more a supporter of proposals initiated by one of the contenders. In stage 2, two opposing factions (or coalitions) develop around each of the remaining contenders. Stage 2 is typically a lengthy phase and often involves some verbal sparring. But as this stage comes to an end, one of the contenders loses the bid for leadership and leaves the remaining contender alone at the top. The member who characteristically drops from contention during stage 2 tends to be overly directive and uses offensive verbalization, such as stilted language or incessant talking.

Stage 3 concludes the process of leader emergence as member A remains the sole contender after the demise of member C. Member E may reenter the emergence process by supporting member A, thereby swinging the balance of power to the A-B coalition. Realistically, however, member E's support is probably not particularly significant, especially if E has continued to be a low-participating member during stage 2. If, on the other hand, member E takes a more active role in group interaction, E's support is sought by members A and C during stage 2. Then E's decision to side with one or the other is a crucial factor in the final emergence of member A. Of course, member C could also drop out of contention if the support of member D as a lieutenant is lost, particularly if member C is overly directive and verbally offensive as perceived by D. Member D could easily shift the balance of power by transferring his allegiance and support to member A.

Figure 7-3 represents a basic model on which many variations might occur. For example, successful leader emergence may involve only two stages, in which just one contender picks up a lieutenant and all other members jump on the bandwagon. This variation is not at all uncommon and signifies a socially painless process of leader emergence. It evolves very quickly and allows time for the group members to develop their status hierarchy and level of cohesiveness quickly and generally satisfactorily.

Another variation involves the early emergence of a group leader who is then deposed as group leader, leaving the group once again in a leaderless

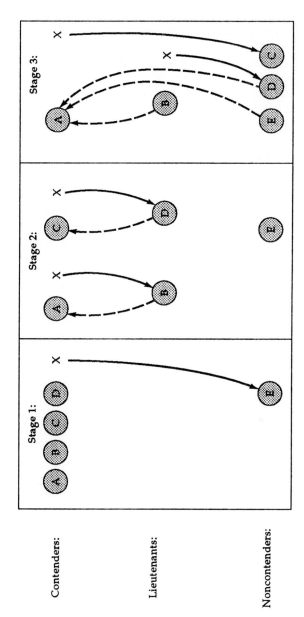

FIGURE 7-3 A hypothetical model of leader emergence.

situation. The process of leader emergence would then recycle back to the beginning of stage 2 and begin all over again. Unless the nonparticipating member's level of participation and involvement has abruptly increased, he or she remains out of leadership contention. The deposed group leader could even regain leadership status but would undoubtedly have more difficulty the second time around.

A third variation of successful leader emergence involves the absence of stage 3. In this case, two or more members share the leadership functions and are recognized equally as leaders. While shared leadership is not extraordinary, neither is it the typical case. One can generally expect a single person to emerge eventually as the leader of a small decision-making group.

Legitimacy and Leader Behavior

The principle of legitimacy is generally defined as prescribed or ascribed approval of norms, values, roles, or other behavioral standards. Typically, an organization endows certain roles with legitimate status by prescribing a formal status hierarchy independent of the persons occupying positions in that status hierarchy. For example, a colonel in the armed forces has legitimate authority of leadership over all those of lower rank by virtue of the rank given by the organization itself and not necessarily because of any achieved informal status. A familiar theme of war movies is a story of veteran soldiers who resent the leadership of a young "90-day-wonder" second lieutenant who does not have the experience or achievements of some of the soldiers of lesser rank. But, nevertheless, the veterans formally recognize his authority because it derives from the legitimate rank of commissioned officer. All leaders depend on followers for legitimacy.

Normally, legitimacy refers to formal recognition or approval by some external agency that has authority over the group. In some groups no such agency exists outside the group. In a university classroom the instructor and the values of the student culture both exert an impact on the classroom group. Some members may have legitimate approval of their roles by virtue of the instructor's designation or campuswide status as a "mover and shaker." Such quasi-legitimate recognition may endow a member with some vestige of formal leadership. But the member then must earn informal recognition of leadership status during the process of leader emergence.

Legitimacy exerts little direct influence on an emergent leader, but the group itself manufactures its own symbols of legitimate recognition. Certain symbols of authority are endorsed with a kind of legitimate approval, and the member who possesses one or more of these symbols takes on the aura of legitimate recognition of authority. Numerous examples of such symbols may be found in a classroom group. Some instructors ask classroom groups to record their interaction during each meeting on audiotape. The member who takes possession of the tape recorder, adjusts the microphone, and controls its operation possesses a symbol of authority. It is not uncommon for members who are contending for leadership to fight over the right to possess this authority symbol.

One classroom group using transistor cassette recorders encountered a problem in operating the machinery. For some reason it did not work properly, and the member who had habitually taken charge of it was unable to get the recorder working. Another member who conveniently owned a similar recorder easily spotted the trouble and fixed it. His leadership status received a big impetus with this seemingly unrelated act. His fellow members insisted that he take charge of the group's cassette recorder in subsequent meetings. He did—and later emerged as the group's recognized leader.

Often a group sits around a rectangular table and leader contenders race to the meeting room in order to be able to sit in the chair at the head of the table. One classroom group held meetings in an instructor's office with the alleged seat of authority the instructor's swivel chair behind the desk. Perhaps not coincidentally, the group's emergent leader turned out to be the member who consistently occupied the swivel chair during group meetings. He admitted afterward that he initially wanted to sit in that chair because it was the most comfortable one in the room. He also expressed his surprise on several occasions when he had arrived late for a group meeting to discover that the other members had left the swivel chair vacant for him. He believed that seat was a symbol of his leadership authority, apparently recognized, perhaps at a low level of awareness, by his fellow group members.

Another classroom group's emergent leader was the sole member who took notes during group discussions. As a result of his trusty legal pad, he was always an expert on what the group had decided and accomplished during past meetings and was able to organize its future activity. He often referred to his legal pad, and he was consistently asked by other members what was written on it. For him and his group, that legal pad became a legitimate symbol of authority.

But a legitimate symbol of authority need not be a physical object. Often an activity by a group member receives formal recognition by the group and takes on a legitimacy by itself. One group frequently met outside class hours at the apartment of one of the members. She became the hostess of the group meetings, served coffee and pop, potato chips and snacks, and enveloped herself in the legitimacy of being the authority in her own apartment. She was recognized as the emergent leader—quickly and painlessly.

Although there are many more examples of manufactured legitimacy in groups, all cases have one ingredient in common. Whether it be a physical object or an activity, the legitimate symbol of authority is associated with (1) a single person who has assisted the group in making progress toward its goal and (2) this person's relationship with other group members. The symbol is not prescribed by some outside authority, but receives formal and relatively permanent recognition by the group members themselves. Instances and symbols of manufactured legitimacy do influence the process and highlight a person who is contending for leadership. The combination of leader-member relationships and symbols of manufactured legitimacy allows the group or an outside observer the opportunity to perceive the process of leader emergence in operation.

MALES AND FEMALES IN LEADERSHIP ROLES

What effect does the sex of the leader have on the group? Do males and females differ in their contributions to group interaction when they are in the leadership roles? Are leaders more likely to be male or female? Questions such as these are significant elements in group phenomena in light of the increased emphasis on the role of women in our society. Unfortunately, the answers to these questions are impossible to determine definitely. Sex-role stereotypes, although still prominent in our society, are currently in a state of flux given the increased appearance of women in nontraditional societal roles. Any attempt to answer such questions, then, is destined to be incomplete and outdated within a very few years. The following discussion is not intended to be definitive but to suggest the flavor of the transition of changing stereotypes and human perceptions in the American culture.

One of the most persistent findings of research on gender and leadership is that the same messages are evaluated differently depending on the source of the message (Butler and Geis, 1990). In other words, men and women can behave and communicate in exactly the same way, but those behaviors will be interpreted differently. There is typically a male bias. For the same behaviors, females will be rated as bossier, more dominating, and emotional. In one study men and women scrutinized other group members who were delivering exactly the same message. But the males were judged to be (1) more responsible, (2) showing more leadership, (3) more likely to be hired, and (4) offering higher-quality contributions. In a study by Seifert and Miller (1988) the very same message was described as clearer when attributed to a male rather than a female leader. The issue of different interpretations of the same communicative behaviors is important because leadership depends on others' *recognition*. The complexity of leadership, as discussed earlier in this chapter, is apparent when group members judge the exact same behaviors differently depending on the gender of the person under scrutiny.

Male and Female Patterns of Communication

The question of whether there are real differences between male and female leaders remains. Some studies and books have argued that women do have different "ways of knowing" (Gilligan, 1982) and patterns of communication. Research on all female groups claims that women have a more egalitarian orientation. The stereotype is that women are more cooperative and relationally oriented; that is, that they are more cooperative than competitive, growth-oriented than rigid, supportive than aggressive. Nelson (1988) suggests that women are the "real team players."

If women do interact differently, they should lead differently. This is a very complex matter that involves numerous variables, and there is evidence supporting both differences and similarities between males and females. Helgesen (1990) explains that men are more likely to prefer hierarchical leadership, and that women are more likely to rotate leadership. Moreover, women do seem to gravitate more easily to cooperative, supportive, and democratic styles. Men, on the other hand, are more likely to be rational, decision-oriented, and demanding. Helgesen reported on some interesting case studies of successful female leaders and argued that these women were successful because they

1. Created and developed a web of relationships throughout all levels of an organization
2. Responded to people and problems with flexibility and adaptiveness rather than rigidity
3. Broke down barriers between employees and people at all levels of the organization
4. Disseminated ideas and information quickly, efficiently, and accurately throughout the organization

In short, they practiced the "leader-as-medium" style, in which complexity is important.

Simple verbosity and participation is consistently associated with leadership. People who participate more in groups are frequently named as leaders more often than less talkative members. The overall greater verbosity of men in task-oriented groups often negatively influences female leadership emergence. In a study by Butler and Geis (1990) it was found that even when presenting the same arguments women receive more negative feedback. They are more easily questioned and doubted. This negative reinforcement surely discourages the participation of women.

One study suggests little discernable difference between male and female group members in some respects. DeStephen (1977) discovered that, overall, male and female group members did not differ significantly in terms of the communicative behaviors they contributed to the group's interaction process. On the other hand, leaders differed considerably from nonleaders in that they showed a greater tendency to clarify task issues and seek evaluations of task issues than nonleaders did. But in attempting to distinguish between the communicative functions of males and females in the leadership role, De-Stephen found little difference. In fact, female leaders performed the same "leadership functions" as male leaders, only perhaps more so. For example, females tended to clarify even more than male leaders did. But leaders, regardless of their sex, appeared to perform more clarifying functions than nonleaders did. One may conclude, then, that the distinction is greater between leaders and nonleaders than between males and females in the leadership role.

Even though it is clearly difficult to draw firm conclusions about male and female leaders, one might speculate as to the reasons why people perceive differences between male and female leaders, even though those differences may not be apparent in the actual behaviors. In other words, we might speculate that people tend to behave in a manner consistent with the way we think they should respond. That is, we have certain expectations about how males and females, leaders and nonleaders, are supposed to act. When our expectations are thwarted (for example, when males or females do not behave as we expect them to), we tend to perceive differences, but our perceptions may not be based on our actual observations.

On balance, there is considerable evidence that male and female leaders are likely to be perceived and treated differently. Studies continue to report that people prefer men to women as bosses and as professional colleagues. Many men mistrust the competence of women and assume that they are less capable of successful task completion than men are. One study (Rice, Bender, and Vitters, 1980) at the U.S. Military Academy compared male and female cadets as leaders. In this study, the gender of the leader did not appear to influence the cadets' performance and morale, but it did influence their perceptions of their leaders. The cadets attributed the success of female leaders to luck, but they attributed the success of male leaders to ability. Another study (Rice, Instone, and Adams, 1984) confirmed the finding that male leaders were more likely to be thought of as have succeeded through hard work and ability than female leaders were. This same study also reported that women were harsher judges of other women than men were.

Many of the perceived differences between male and female leaders are little more than bias, confusion, and snapshots in time. The stereotype that men are confident, dominant, and task-oriented and women are democratic, accommodating, and relationship-oriented is just too simplistic and fails to account for many situations and influences. True, males and females are socialized differently and bombarded with different media images of sex roles. But these influences are very fluid and change over time. Many of the findings about men and women reflect the current state of our culture. We should add that most of the studies on gender and leadership are limited to people who are white and middle class. The notion of "effective" leadership will surely change when research includes more diverse groups. Nevertheless, women leaders will still encounter more disadvantages, but these should dissipate as leadership becomes more a matter of managing complexity than of behaving in a prescribed manner.

HOW TO AVOID EMERGING AS LEADER

In many ways it is difficult to know how and why certain members emerge as group leaders. The process of eliminating leader contenders, however, suggests that it may be less difficult to determine how and why certain members do *not* become group leaders. If certain people truly wish not to become leaders (as some people are quick to assert), the following list of "rules" should allow them to fulfill their goal. These principles are guidelines for assuring yourself of a low-status position in your group. Follow them faithfully, and we guarantee that you will not emerge as your group's leader.

Rule 1. Be Absent from as Many Group Meetings as Possible. You will be even better at avoiding leadership responsibilities if you provide no reasons for your absences. But with or without reasons, absence from group interaction is an effective tactic.

Rule 2. *Contribute to the Interaction as Little as Possible.* You might also consider contributing incompetently to the group's interaction; such a strategy, however, is more dangerous, for other members may perceive competence in what you consider to be incompetent. The safer practice is to avoid contributing and thus let other members think you are incompetent or disinterested rather than to interact too much and thus remove their doubts.

Rule 3. *Volunteer to Be the Secretary or the Record Keeper of Your Group's Discussions.* The role of recorder or secretary in a group is rarely associated with the role of leader. You do risk the problem of demonstrating interest and commitment to the group by volunteering for what is indeed a valuable role. You will probably be assigned a rather high status. You should probably consider this strategy a compromise. By avoiding leadership, you may be substituting a high-status role. But if you truly wish to avoid becoming a leader, you should be willing to compromise.

Rule 4. *Indicate That You Are Willing to Do What You Are Told.* This strategy is sometimes as risky as becoming a secretary. By showing your commitment to the group in your willingness to perform activities beneficial to the group's task efforts, you may be indicating too much commitment to the group. Lack of interest in the group is more effective in avoiding leadership responsibilities, but a subservient or acquiescent commitment is the next best thing.

Rule 5. *Come on Strong Early in the Group Discussions.* The timing of your verbally aggressive and directive behavior is extremely important when following this principle. If you advocate something strongly later in the group interaction, your activity may be misinterpreted as an attempt to assist the group in solving its decision-making task. It is vitally important that your advocacy be extreme and that it demonstrate an unwillingness to compromise your position, especially if another member should resist your ideas. Attempt to be unsuccessful in your early advocacy of your positions. Failure in these early stages of the group process is important. Too much success, particularly in the early stages of group decision making, is likely to lead to the undesirable effect of having other group members think you are contending for leadership. Later stages in group decision making, during which members are advocating ideational positions, are the times to show your apathy regarding which decision proposals will achieve consensus.

Rule 6. *Try to Assume the Role of Joker.* By telling lots of jokes early in the discussion, you will get people to like you while you are in the process of avoiding leadership. Sometimes contenders for low-status roles tend to be uncomfortable when other members show dislike of them. If you become a joker, however, you will probably avoid such negative reactions. On the other hand, they will probably not take you very seriously. Make sure, however, that your jokes are consistently off the topic and are not combined with any opinion or information concerning it. Your funny-person role should also be consistent. Don't do anything that would indicate that you are anything but a joker.

Rule 7. *Demonstrate Your Knowledge of Everything, Including Your Extensive Vocabulary of Big Words and Technical Jargon.* This strategy is also a bit risky in that members may misinterpret your know-it-all attitude and command of esoteric words as signs of intelligence and breadth of background. You can't afford to be timid when using this tactic. Express a comprehensive knowledge of every topic and a continuous use of words that other people probably don't understand. Consistency is the key to successful employment of this strategy.

Rule 8. *Demonstrate a Contempt for Leadership.* This method is rarely used, but it is always successful in avoiding the leadership role. One classroom group member, whom we shall call Sean, was quite successful and adept in utilizing this strategy. He verbalized frequently and vehemently his distaste for all leaders and the concept of leadership itself. He consistently expressed his strong belief that all leaders are corrupt. One of his reactions to an early group meeting was most explicit in revealing his attitude: "I do not want to hear any fascinating facts about leadership. Leadership is for whoever wants it. If you have an average IQ and a corrupt tendency to dominate people, you can become a leader. Those who manipulate leaders are those who dominate very furtively." Sean succeeded beyond the highest expectations of all leadership avoiders. In his six-member group, he was unanimously voted the least liked member in both social and task areas. But one must be aggressive in using this strategy and must consistently resist and label every attempt at leadership contention by other members.

Of course, these "principles" for avoiding the leadership role are presented in a tongue-in-cheek manner. They are characteristic of those behaviors of persons who are eliminated from leadership contention. Rarely, if ever, does any person intend to avoid becoming a leader. Although individual group members may not intentionally attempt to be the group leader, they also do not intend to avoid leadership, at least at a very high level of awareness. During the normal functioning of the group process and group interaction, the group works out the role of each member, including the role of leader. Such functioning of the group process in quite normal and typical. Moreover, the process is functioning even though the members may not be aware of it until the process has been completed.

SUMMARY

Perhaps the most pervasive element of social systems is the existence of leadership and a status hierarchy. In groups, roles fall into several hierarchical levels, typically two or three, proportional to the contribution of each member in helping the group achieve its goals. In some groups, each member achieves a status level through communicative behaviors rather than through being given status by some authority outside the group. The leader's status is based on the reciprocal influence of leader and followers—an interdependence among the communicating members in the group.

Several perspectives of viewing leadership have been popularly employed in the past. They include the trait, style, situational, and functional approaches to group leadership. The functional perspective focuses on the communicative behaviors of individual members and their relative contributions to the group's progress. This perspective deemphasizes leadership as defined by the person who occupies a given position in a network of roles. Because there have been so few studies of leadership utilizing the functional perspective, no comprehensive list of communicative behaviors associated with leadership yet exists. But a partial list of behaviors is available.

Employing the functional perspective, leadership is viewed as a process whereby a group leader achieves status gradually over time as a direct result of group interaction patterns. This process, termed *leader emergence*, may generally be described as a process of elimination in which each member is a contender for leadership, but each is eliminated, one by one, until a single person remains and is recognized as the group's leader.

A basic model of leader emergence hypothesizes three stages of elimination. In stage 1, uninformed, low-participating members are eliminated. In stage 2, two or more contenders emerge by gaining lieutenants who support their leadership contention. Those contenders eliminated in stage 2 are typically overly directive and use offensive verbalization. In stage 3 there is only one remaining contender, who achieves recognition as leader. Several variations on this basic model are possible in a particular small group.

The leader-follower relationship is very important. Behaviors associated with leaders include being verbally active, demonstrating communication skills, consistently initiating themes, seeking opinions and information in the early and intermediate stages of group development, stating opinions and attempting to persuade other members in the intermediate and later stages of group development, and adopting an informed and objective argumentative stance. The life-cycle theory of leadership relates a leader's style and power base to the group members' maturity.

Groups manufacture formal symbols of legitimacy in group interaction. Such symbols, which may be physical objects or member activity, are associated with a particular member and with the formal authority of leadership, although they may vary from group to group.

Stereotyped attitudes of sex roles remain prominent. Consequently, men and women who function as group leaders probably do not differ significantly from one another in terms of the communicative actions they use in leading. However, the group members or followers may perceive differences because of their previously held attitudes regarding sex-role stereotypes.

CHAPTER OUTLINE

MUCH CONFLICT ABOUT SOCIAL
CONFLICT

Intergroup, Cognitive, and
Interpersonal Conflict
Affective and Substantive Conflict
Destructive and Constructive Conflict
Reactions to Social Conflict

INFLUENTIAL FUNCTIONS OF
CONFLICT AND DEVIANCE

Influence on Cohesiveness
Influence on Productivity
Influence on Consensus
Influence on Social Growth and
Change

THE NORM OF CONFLICT AND
DEVIANCE

Idea Testing in Decision Making
Formation of Coalitions
The Leadership Paradox—Conformity
and Deviance

THE PROCESS OF SOCIAL CONFLICT
AND DEVIANCE

Flight Patterns
Innovative Deviance
Phases of Conflict

MANAGING CONFLICT

Standard Conflict-Avoidance
Techniques
Solutions Based on Gains and Losses
Styles of Conflict Management
Conflict Style and the Leader as
Medium
Regulating Conflict
In Conclusion

SUMMARY

KEY TERMS

COGNITIVE CONFLICT

INTERPERSONAL CONFLICT

AFFECTIVE CONFLICT

SUBSTANTIVE CONFLICT

ROLE DEVIATION

OPINION DEVIATION

DESTRUCTIVE CONFLICT

CONSTRUCTIVE CONFLICT

ENCAPSULATION

CONFLICT

CONFLICT MANAGEMENT

ASSEMBLY EFFECT

COALITION

IDIOSYNCRASY CREDITS

INNOVATIVE DEVIANCE

CONFLICT PHASES

CONFLICT AVOIDANCE
TECHNIQUES

Majority Vote
Authoritative Rule
Third-Party Arbitration

LOSE-LOSE APPROACHES

Compromising

WIN-LOSE APPROACHES

WIN-WIN APPROACHES

STYLES OF CONFLICT
MANAGEMENT

Avoiding
Compromising
Competing
Accommodating
Collaborating

INTEGRATIVE COMMUNICATION

DIVISIVE COMMUNICATION

CHAPTER 8

Conflict and Deviance

The past four decades have witnessed numerous instances of social conflict and deviant behavior within our society. Many people believe that this upsurge of dissent is unparalleled in our history, but dissent has been present since our system was founded. Many eligible young men resisted the draft during the Vietnamese war, but draft resistance has been prevalent since the first Selective Service during the Spanish-American War. Hundreds of thousands of protesters marched on Washington, D.C., several times during the decade of the 1960s, but so did veterans of World War I some forty years before. The civil disobedience of Martin Luther King, Jr., led to his imprisonment, just as civil disobedience led to the same for Henry David Thoreau, Eugene Debs, and countless labor organizers during the early struggles of the labor movement in the United States.

Dissent is not unique to the present. Many people believe that such social conflict is detrimental and reflects some failure within our culture. Others believe that social conflict is symptomatic of a healthy society. The truth, as in most cases, undoubtedly lies somewhere between the two extreme positions. Obviously some conflict within a social system is detrimental, just as some conflict is beneficial. The point to be emphasized is that social conflict, both good and bad, is normal and a recurring phenomenon of our social system throughout its history. Moreover, social conflict has been normal in the functioning of every social system throughout the history of human civilizations.

MUCH CONFLICT ABOUT SOCIAL CONFLICT

Many sociologists view a social system as a delicate balance of opposing forces—forces that threaten to disrupt the system and forces that maintain the system. According to this view, a social system is perpetually in a state of conflict that may at any time tip toward the disruptive forces and destroy the system.

215

The perspective of this book—communication and the group process, with emphasis on their interdependence—is not consistent with viewing the system as a balance of opposing forces. The process viewpoint assumes that such forces are natural, so they cannot be separated or be in opposition to each other. For example, "temperature" is hardly an arithmetic difference between forces of heat and forces of cold. If it were, one would be comfortable if one held a block of ice in one hand and a burning coal in the order. Temperature is a single reading, not a balance of two readings, one high and one low. In the same sense, conflict is also a single force.

Intergroup, Cognitive, and Interpersonal Conflict

To understand the nature of social conflict, one must first identify who or what is in conflict. Probably the most common view of social conflict is *intergroup conflict*—that is, conflict between opposing social systems. Intergroup conflict involves conflict between groups or societies rather than between single individuals. It embraces labor-management relations, particularly during periods of contract negotiations, as well as conflicts between nations. An individual human being, when involved in intergroup conflict, participates not as an individual entity, but as a representative of an entire social system.

Although intergroup conflict is a fascinating area of concern and some examples will be drawn from it, a study of this type of social conflict does not suit the purposes of this book. Since our purpose is to understand the communicative process that characterizes group decision making, intergroup conflict is not highly pertinent.

Cognitive conflict, as the term implies, involves the psychological conflict that rages within the individual (Roloff, 1987, pp. 486–489). The cognitive view alleges the existence of opposing forces within a person's mind that determine actions, beliefs, and values. Numerous balance theories attempt to explain individual behavior through cognitive conflict. They include cognitive dissonance theory, congruity theory, equity theory, exchange theory, and consistency theory, among others. Roloff (1987) has also explained conflict through the concept of ambivalence—a balance of internal forces that attract or repel.

But cognitive conflict is not our main concern here either. In the first place, internalized conflict cannot be directly observed through communicative behaviors and may or may not be indirectly reflected in group interaction. Then, too, cognitive conflict relies more on the psychological makeup of the individual person as the basis for understanding the small group than on the process of interaction based on the interstructured communicative behaviors of all members.

Interpersonal conflict is most pertinent to the perspective of communication and the group process. But interpersonal conflict, for our purposes, does not necessarily imply a personality conflict between individuals. Quite the contrary, it is defined solely in terms of interact patterns. Thus, interpersonal conflict is observable through sequences of communicative behaviors performed by members of the group. The personalities of individual members are not considered to be in conflict; rather, it is the behaviors engaged in by two or more members that conflict with one another.

Affective and Substantive Conflict

A second view of social conflict considers the basis of that conflict—whether conflicting issues are affective or substantive. Typically, in reference to interpersonal conflict, *affective conflict* implies emotional clashes between individuals within a social system, generally over procedural or how-to-do-it problems. Such conflict does not ordinarily stem from a disagreement on opinions or beliefs, but from a struggle based on selfish or personal issues. *Substantive conflict*, on the other hand, involves an intellectual opposition of group members to the content of ideas or issues pertinent to the group task.

Since social conflict and deviance are considered a single phenomenon in group interaction, the affective-substantive differentiation of conflict may also be called *role deviation* and *opinion deviation*. While an opinion deviate disagrees with other group members about the content of ideas, a role deviate is a type of person who is not desired by other group members. One member of a student group found herself to be a role deviate in her group. She received low sociometric rankings from nearly all her fellow group members. Concerned, she asked them why. Her diary immediately following that group meeting describes their reactions:

> They also said that they had projected me as being the type of person I played in class; they projected that role as being my true personality. . . . Now that they know me a little better, they could see I wasn't "Susie," a dominating woman, but "Susan"—a different individual altogether.

Role deviation and opinion deviation differ significantly in their impact on group interaction (Putnam, 1986). Other group members increase their interaction with an opinion deviate and exert pressure on him or her to conform to their majority opinion. But the group ignores the role deviate, apparently perceiving this type of person as a hopeless case not worthy of pressure. A social system tends to view deviance either as a behavior apart from the individual personality of the deviate or as a personality trait of the individual. As behavior, deviance affects the group process of interaction and is therefore central to the perspective of this book.

The opinion deviate is tolerated and perhaps even admired by fellow members. After all, we have been taught from childhood that rationality and independence are virtues in our society. We are urged to be masters of our own fate, to make up our own minds. "Know thyself" was the advice of Socrates. Advertising campaigns appeal to our rational independence by urging us to buy the product that gets us away from the crowd. The virtues of rationality and independence are often reflected in adolescents' rejection of their parents' ideas and beliefs. Their parents, often to their chagrin, have experienced the ultimate success in teaching two of our society's cardinal virtues.

Lewis Coser (1956, pp. 48–55), the eminent sociologist, distinguishes between realistic and nonrealistic conflict, which appears to be another dimension of substantive and affective conflict. According to Coser, *realistic conflict* is a means to an end; it is a deviant behavior intended to further the group's progress toward its goal. But *nonrealistic conflict* is an end in itself not directly associated with any goal. For example, one worker may go out on strike to gain higher wages and better working conditions, but another worker may engage even in the same strike because of some oedipal hatred of the employer, and this displaced hatred could as easily be directed against any authority figure. The point is that the first worker, the person who engages in deviant behavior as a means to achieve some goal, is said to be engaged in realistic conflict.

The view of conflict that best serves the purposes of this book is, of course, substantive conflict—that conflict expressed as a deviant behavior in intellectual opposition to ideas or issues associated with the group's task or goals. Substantive conflict is realistic to the extent that it serves as a means toward accomplishing some goal.

Destructive and Constructive Conflict

There is enormous disagreement over the effects of conflict on the social system (Folger and Poole, 1984, pp. 5–7). One school of thought seems to view conflict as inherently undesirable since it inevitably leads to disruption of the social system. An opposing view considers social conflict essential to the effective functioning of every social system. It is intuitively obvious that neither view is absolutely accurate. Some conflict and deviance disrupts the system, and other instances of conflict and deviance are beneficial to the system. Discriminating between the two kinds, however, is no simple task.

Many functions of the social system of the United States are predicated on the existence of conflict. Our economic subsystem of free enterprise assumes conflict and free competition among producers and retailers for the consumer dollar. The basis of our political system is the free and open marketplace of ideas in which societal values gain social consensus. Candidates for political office air conflicting views on the issues during the course of a political campaign. Our judicial system is based on the adversary system in which the accuser confronts the accused. Many of our recreational activities include games based on conflict—football, tennis, handball, chess, Monopoly, among others. Conflict is undoubtedly an integral part of our nation-society.

But despite the pervasive influence of social conflict in our society, most Americans are ambivalent about many of its forms. Probably the best example is the right of minority dissent, constitutionally assured in the Bill of Rights. Freedom of speech is one of our most cherished national values, epitomized in such statements as Voltaire's "I disapprove of what you say, but I will defend to the death your right to say it." National opinion polls have reaffirmed that nearly all Americans steadfastly uphold the freedom of speech of all Americans—majority and minority. But many of those same Americans, the polls tell us, would refuse to allow a professed Communist give a public lecture. Battles over censorship laws are common in our social system. Apparently not all members of our society consider all realistic and substantive conflict (or opinion deviation) to be constructive. Indeed, many people consider much substantive conflict highly destructive.

A social system is too often viewed as an abstract ideal—a system of pure cooperation—so that any deviance must be unnatural. If a social system is idealized, members of the system strive for the perfection of pure cooperation. Any deviant behavior, then is considered a failure of the social system and must therefore be eradicated. The typically shortsighted view of common sense would have us believe that a "perfect" social system is worth striving for. But as we will illustrate, the "perfect" social system free from conflict and deviance is doomed to failure because of its inherent inflexibility, its inability to cope with environmental stresses, and its lack of capacity for growth and progress.

The Advantages of Conflict   The positive side of social conflict is represented by the functionalists—George Simmel (1955), Lewis Coser (1956), and Talcott Parsons (1951), among others. The functionalists do not deny that some social conflict disrupts the functioning of a social system and is therefore destructive. But the functionalists do emphasize the socially constructive functions of conflict and advocate an understanding of social conflict so that the social system will be able to take advantage of its positive aspects (see also Putnam, 1986, pp. 177–178). Some of the positive functions performed by social conflict are listed below.

Increased Understanding of Issues   It is easy to assume that others understand things the same way we do. This is frustrating and we can spend our time cursing the ignorance of others. Or we can do something about it. Conflict forces group members to see that others hold strong and defensible positions on an issue. This causes people to question their own positions and seek out information and clarification. Conflict sees that both sides of an issue are presented and that there may be flaws in one side or the other. It helps us understand all the issues in a discussion.

Increased Cohesiveness   Groups that experience tension, frustration, and conflict and then work through these problems feel closer to one another. Countries, athletic teams, corporations, families, and groups that struggle with one another to work out problems feel much closer and stronger for the experience. Moreover, since conflict increases the quality of decisions, cohesiveness is enhanced because groups have succeeded in both the task and social dimensions.

Improved Decision Quality   Solving a problem and making a good decision is the essential function of groups. Experiencing substantive conflict simply increases the likelihood of good decisions. When groups disagree and then explore why they disagree, they expose the key issues and points of misunderstanding. Conflict brings out all the issues and forces group members to test ideas and information. If one member challenges the opinions of another, that person is forced to defend himself and justify his ideas. Groups that experience substantive conflict expose more issues and discuss implications.

Increased Interest and Motivation   Even though some people fear and avoid conflict, many others are energized by the experience. Lively, active, and involving discussion arouses group member interest and attention. Groups that are composed of people who do not care and who "give in" easily are probably the most likely to perform poorly. Conflict is a sign of interest and motivation, and it is self-fulfilling. In other words, as groups experience conflict they are stimulated to learn more about an issue and explore options further. Many people are simply competitive. When they are challenged and forced to defend themselves, they increase their motivation to perform well.

The Disadvantages of Conflict   If conflict were always beneficial, groups would not spend so much time fretting about it. It is important for groups to experience constructive and substantive conflict. There is no doubt that a healthy dose of conflict is good for a group. But conflict must be managed because it can be harmful to the group if left unchecked. Some of the negative effects of conflict are listed below.

Decreased Group Cohesiveness   If conflict goes too long and does not get resolved effectively it will decrease cohesiveness in the group. This is why a leader's skill in conflict resolution is particularly important. Although conflict can increase member commitment to the group, it will have the opposite effect if not resolved. Sometimes group members simply do not want to communicate with members who do not share their opinions. At the same time, members who feel that their attitudes and values are not being confirmed may begin to withdraw from the group.

Ill Will among Group Members   Conflict among people is often distasteful to group members. It causes anger, frustration, and bad feelings, especially among immature group members who cannot separate their ideas from their personal feelings. Substantive conflict over ideas and issues can lead to benefits for the group. But conflict that becomes personalized can have negative effects on the group as well as on the individuals involved.

Destruction of the Group   Groups that do not successfully work through conflict will simply come apart. When intense conflict continues, it causes group members to seek other alternatives. It no longer becomes rewarding to keep the group together.

Reactions to Social Conflict

The typical reaction to social conflict is to search for ways to resolve it—that is, to get rid of it. At the very least, according to this view, conflict must be controlled so that it doesn't get out of hand. Naturally, some conflict must be resolved or controlled because it is potentially destructive. Destructive conflict, unchecked, would lead ultimately to dissolution of the system itself. Hence, methods of conflict resolution are essential for instances of destructive conflict. Modes of conflict resolution include such devices as compromise, bargaining, appeasement, negotiation, and mediation.

Occasionally, cure-all "formula" solutions are offered as substitutes for genuine methods of conflict resolution. Such formulas are usually not realistic and stem from a oversimplified view of social conflict. One such formula answer is "more cooperation." If cooperation were so simple, the conflict would not have to be resolved in the first place. A more commonly suggested formula, offered to solve virtually any social conflict, is "more communication" or "opening channels of communication." If there is no communication at all between conflicting parties, which is rarely the case, some communication is obviously called for. But communication inherently assumes specific forms, such as negotiation. "More communication" is meaningless. If present communication is ineffective, increasing the amount of communication does not render it suddenly more effective. More often, "more communication" is suggested as a substitute for any real effort to resolve conflicts. Such a formula stems from an overly naive and grossly inadequate understanding of the nature of the communicative process.

When parties in conflict cannot satisfactorily resolve their disagreement, they search for modes of controlling that conflict. One common and often effective means of controlling conflict, particularly intergroup conflict, is *encapsulation*. Conflict that is encapsulated does not cease to exist; rather, it continues under the governance of an agreed-upon set of rules. The "Cold War" (which is now supposedly over) was a euphemism for international conflict that had been encapsulated within the rules of international diplomacy—embassies in each country, exchanges of diplomatic notes, treaties limiting nuclear testing, talks and treaties on arms limitations, trade agreements involving nonstrategic materials, reciprocal visits by high-ranking dignitaries, etc. All conflicting nations agreed to the rules and thereby controlled the conflict between their countries without attempting to resolve it.

Even wars are encapsulated, in part, by certain international "rules" of warfare, such as those of the Geneva Convention and the Geneva Accords. Thus, even armed conflict with the avowed purpose of annihilating the enemy nation is governed by rules and therefore encapsulated. Encapsulation of conflict is a common ingredient of international relations.

The belief that conflict must be immediately resolved or controlled is consistent with the view that conflict is inherently destructive. But resolution and control are inappropriate reactions to numerous instances of social conflict—particularly the kind that serve positive functions. In fact, such conflict should even be encouraged and utilized to further the system's progress toward its desired goals. Utilizing social conflict in the best interests of the system requires a thorough understanding of conflict itself and the ability to manage it in order to benefit from its positive aspects.

For the purpose of understanding the process of small group decision making, our primary interest is social conflict that is interpersonal, substantive, and constructive. Our goal is to understand social conflict and deviance as a process and to manage it constructively to the benefit of the group. This view does not deny the existence of destructive forms of conflict, but it does emphasize a view of conflict too often overlooked.

INFLUENTIAL FUNCTIONS OF SOCIAL CONFLICT AND DEVIANCE

According to one of the foremost functionalists, Georg Simmel (1955, p. 13), conflict is inevitably a "form of sociation." It is impossible to have social conflict without interaction among the parties in conflict, and interaction is certainly a form of sociation. Simmel says of social conflict, "it is a way of achieving some kind of unity, even if it be through the annihilation of one of the conflicting parties." Although the reference to annihilation may be tongue-in-cheek, it is indisputable that social conflict cannot exist with an individual person in social isolation. Certainly conflict is a distinct type of interaction between at least two persons. And interaction is one of the basic requisites of a social system (Folger and Poole, 1984, pp. 8–9). One can only conclude that anything that encourages interaction must be a potentially positive force in the development of a social system. It is on this deceptively simple assumption that the positive social functions of conflict are based.

While we might think of conflict as some disruption in the interaction process, quite the opposite is more the case. In fact, social conflict inevitably requires social interaction. Likert and Bowers (1972, p. 117) are quite emphatic on this point: "Every conflict, other than those internal to a particular individual, involves an interaction among persons, groups, organizations, or larger entities and occurs through an interaction-influence network." When people engage in conflict, they inevitably engage in interaction, and we should not be overly concerned that conflict is present in the interaction. We should be more concerned if and when conflict functions to disrupt or discontinue the group's efforts. The important point to remember is that conflict requires interaction among parties to the conflict. Conflict is thus an ingredient of the group process.

Furthermore, the distinction between conflict interaction and nonconflict interaction is the nature of how the actions relate to each other. According to Deutsch (1973, p. 10), "*Conflict* exists whenever *incompatible* activities occur." A conflict thus involves a sequence of activities that are incompatible with each other. For example, a statement favoring a decision proposal followed by a statement opposed to the decision proposal is an instance of a conflict interact. A one-up comment (see Chapter 4 and Appendix 1) followed by another one-up comment is a symmetrical and incompatible interact, thus reflecting a relational conflict. Conflict would also be present in a one-down comment followed by another one-down comment. A statement followed by a disagreement is a very common form of conflict in group decision making. In any case, conflict requires interaction for it to take place. Furthermore, conflict is characterized by a sequence of incompatible activities performed by the parties to the conflict. Being able to distinguish social conflict is one thing, but understanding its influences in group decision making is another. And those influences are the subject of the discussions that follow.

Influence on Cohesiveness

Conflict breeds not only social interaction but also increased involvement (Tjosvold, 1982). The member who is apathetic toward the group and toward the worth of the group task has little reason to engage in the painful process of social conflict. Moreover, the virtual absence of social conflict in group interaction is a trustworthy indication of the low involvement or commitment of group members. If the group develops even a moderate level of cohesiveness, its members will engage in rather frequent, though not extended, periods of social conflict. Thus, the natural development of group cohesiveness presupposes social conflict. In this sense, social conflict is not only desirable for the development of groupness; it is quite inevitable and should be expected as part of the *normal* sequence of group interaction.

Of course, social conflict, if it is to be benefical to group cohesiveness, must not be perceived as threatening the group's social fabric. Substantive conflict serves to precipitate secondary tension. Therefore, the successful group develops mechanisms for managing social conflict as it arises. And a history of successful conflict management builds group cohesiveness.

Lest the term *conflict management* be misinterpreted, it is important to note that the group does not necessarily resolve the conflict or even control it through limiting its boundaries. Conflict management refers to the interaction sequences developed by a group to deal with social conflict and consistently used by the group when social conflict occurs. Generally, conflict management implies that social conflict will definitely occur again, although probably in slightly different form. The normal process of conflict management is part of the process of decision modification.

Social conflict also aids group cohesiveness by providing an outlet for hostility. According to Napier and Gershenfeld (1985), a group must discover methods for venting hostility in order to gain and maintain even a moderate degree of cohesiveness. If the group develops norms that do not permit the expression of hostility, the group members either become apathetic or drop out as their deep-rooted negative feelings become ingrained. As group members shed their inhibitions about expressing negative feelings, they develop stronger ties to their group membership. One student group member, after a particularly fruitful meeting, experienced just such a reaction. Her diary contains her sentiments about what occurred during that meeting:

> We began to function as a group. Each of the individuals in the group expressed feelings. Before really talking about our topic, we only had some "small" talk. . . . There were real differences of opinion. . . . The group became more cohesive.

> I began to think of myself as a member of the group. I felt more at ease with the members in my group to the extent that I felt free to disagree.

The more inhibited the group members are in expressing their feelings, the greater the frustration they experience because of their suppressed conflict. And frustration leads directly to secondary tension. Thus, social conflict may in fact serve as a form of releasing social tension.

Conflict performs a catalytic function in developing the social organization of the group. Putnam (1986, p. 186) emphasizes the role of conflict in increasing a group's social organization, particularly the interdependence of group members. Roloff (1987) takes this further, stating that groups go so far as to induce, permit, and sustain deviant behaviors of members in order to develop a social organization. Deviant behaviors allow the group members to identify and strengthen their norms and other behavioral standards. As an analogy, a law on the books that is never violated and hence never enforced soon loses its strength and visibility as a law. It becomes a "blue law" without any impact on governing the behavior of the society's members.

The deviate also allows the group to focus on a concern common to all members—the deviate himself or herself—about whom something must be done. Since the deviate is of concern to the group as a whole and not to each member individually, the group's visibility becomes greater than any individual self.

For these reasons, then, a group induces deviant behavior by one of its members when deviance does not occur through the initiative of one of the members. In order to maintain group solidarity and organization, the successful group not only permits deviant behavior, but ensures that it is evident in the group interaction. The group is in trouble when members avoid or ignore deviant behavior. Recall that the socially successful group learns to confront problems head-on by recognizing deviant behavior and doing something about it. It may be said now with some confidence that the cohesive group thrives on social conflict—or, in more memorable words, "The group that fights together stays together!"

Influence on Productivity

Since this book deals with group decision making, its major concern is substantive conflict—intellectual opposition over ideas and issues. It seems paradoxical that a group whose members continually argue over ideas and issues can be very productive. But group productivity is measured in terms of the quality of its decisions and not in terms of its use of time. Obviously a group with substantive social conflict will take more time to arrive at decisions than will a group without any conflict. But efficient utilization of time is not a characteristic of the group process anyway.

Substantive conflict leads directly to consensus, owing to the increased involvement of group members in their task performance. As conflict over issues increases, group members tend to concentrate greater effort on those issues in order to bring about solutions. Donohue (1981) discovered that conflict over ideas causes groups to search for more alternatives and thereby to improve the quality of their group decisions. Conflict, then, serves as a prod to critical thinking and stimulates members to test their ideas. It logically follows that the issues that precipitate social conflict exert the greatest influence on those decisions that eventually achieve group consensus. And since those issues have survived the critical tests of ideational conflict, the decisions are probably of higher quality.

All members of the group benefit from the critical exchange of ideas. Committed members who engage in substantive conflict quite obviously receive the rewards of stimulated critical faculties. The undecided members, the low participants, also gain information necessary to commitment through observing the committed members "fighting it out."

One student member of a classroom group maintained that she played the role of a deviate in her group for just this reason—to stimulate the uninvolved members of her group. She analyzed her own role in the following excerpt from one of her diaries:

> I am the negative force in the group, i.e., I *can't* agree with everything that is being said. Other members in the group don't agree with decisions but are *too polite to say anything!* I voiced my opinion both for the silent majority and for myself. Also, it was a means of manipulation to get things rolling. It worked! Without this, nothing would have been accomplished. The group members agreed with me after some discussion.

One of the problems that haunts every decision-making group is the possibility of superficial or false consensus. That is, members agree on the final decisions but remain uncommitted to them. Hence, the decisions are never put into effect or are implemented only halfheartedly and consequently fail. An early study by Riecken (1952) found that quite the opposite was true of decisions reached after uninhibited social conflict. Phillips and Erickson (1970, p. 77) also asserted, "Once the public conflict has been played out in a democratic group and a consensus of policy and action has been derived, there is a strong personal commitment on the part of the members that motivates them to act legitimately to implement group decisions rather than to subvert them." If members are committed enough to sustain social conflict over issues, they should remain committed once consensus is achieved. Superficial or false consensus is more likely to result from suppressed conflict than from expressed conflict.

Influence on Consensus

If consensus is the goal of group decision making, it is important to note the influence of social conflict on consensus if we are to understand fully the influence of conflict on productivity. The most commonsensical response to the relationship between conflict and consensus is probably to think of conflict as the opposite of consensus. After all, conflict indicates incompatibility of actions, and consensus should reflect compatibility. When we think of consensus as the result (or outcome) of group decision making, conflict is probably opposed to consensus. On the other hand, if consensus is a process, conflict interaction may perform a valuable function during that process and lead to the successful outcome of group decision making.

Torrance (1957), investigating the relationship between group decision making and disagreement, provides evidence to suggest that conflict (in the sense of interaction sequences involving disagreement) is highly valuable in achieving consensus. Among other characteristics he discovered, he found that effective decision-making groups tend to exhibit a wide divergence of judgments expressed by their members. Certain members of these groups are apparently quite willing to oppose the opinions of others and to disagree whenever they feel that the situation requires it. The conclusion of Torrance's investigations provides a strong link between consensus and conflict. In fact, greater consensus is obtained when a group experiences a greater amount of disagreement during decision-making interaction.

The four-phase model of decision emergence discussed in Chapter 6, supports Torrance's conclusions. You will recall that the conflict phase (the second) is one element in the process of successful group decision making. This phase contains significant amounts of disagreement and the formation of coalitions of members opposed to one another on the substantive issues of the task. The evidence appears sufficient to warrant the belief that social conflict (at least substantive conflict) is an integral part of the process of achieving consensus in group decision making.

One problem in viewing the relationship between consensus and conflict may be a mistaken belief in the notion that consensus is somehow similar to cooperation. If that were true, conflict would be quite different from either consensus or cooperation. A greater similarity exists between conflict and cooperation than between cooperation and consensus. There are three basic differences between consensus and cooperation. Consensus indicates internal agreement, but cooperation does not include such an assumption. Consensus specifies agreement on the content of behavior (the substantive ideas), but cooperation means agreement only on the form of behavior. For example, we agree to disagree and thereby cooperate. Finally, cooperation requires that cooperating persons tolerate one another's differences, but consensus requires that any substantive differences should be abolished.

Whether this analysis of consensus, conflict, and cooperation is accurate is not really the important issue. More significant is the fact that conflict interaction requires considerable cooperation. Of course, conflict may exist as a struggle within one specific group member. That is, a member may have ambivalent feelings toward an object or idea and simply not have formed a firm opinion. Or conflict may be bound to the situation in the sense of a struggle over scarce resources. For example, whole nations engage in conflict in order to ensure a supply of strategic products, such as petroleum or uranium. But conflict, in terms of interaction sequences, requires a certain amount of cooperation in order for it even to occur. When people are engaged in substantive conflict over ideas, they are engaged in communication with one another. In the process of communication, they are essentially cooperating with one another.

In group decision making, the parties to the conflict are united in their quest for a common goal. Typically that goal is consensus. When the United Auto Workers and General Motors engage in collective bargaining, they are involved in conflict interaction. At the same time, they are cooperating in order to realize their common goal: agreement on a new contract. Without that common goal, the United Auto Workers and General Motors would find little reason for interacting with each other. Nor would there be any reason for their conflict. Social conflict provides a strong influence on group productivity. Not only does it influence consensus, but it also reflects cooperative interaction among persons or groups that are oriented toward a common interest.

One final note on the influence of social conflict and deviance on productivity concerns the *assembly effect*—the nonsummativity of group members that distinguishes group decision making from the decision making of its individual members working alone. Social conflict is one of those group elements which a decision-making individual is inherently incapable of replicating. Quite assuredly, social conflict—particularly realistic substantive conflict—contributes to the assembly effect. Without it, the group decision-making effort adds nothing to a lone individual performing the same decision-making task.

Influence on Social Growth and Change

Viewing a group from a process focus highlights the perpetual change that every social system undergoes through time. Our nation, for example, has experienced phenomenal growth and change within the brief two centuries of its existence. As conditions within and without the system change over the years, the social system adapts to those changes if it is to continue to exist. If any system is to keep up with the times, it cannot stagnate. Progress is essential. And progress can occur only through innovation. And innovation is, by definition, deviant from the traditional norms of the past.

Social growth and change are usually explained through the principle of feedback—a concept borrowed from the field of cybernetics. Feedback, as it functions in the form of interaction sequences, has been explained and illustrated in previous chapters—especially in Chapter 1. Social growth and change in a social system occur through the amplification of deviant behavior; that is, through feedback cycles. Negative feedback loops serve to counteract deviant behavior. The conflict phase of group decision making (discussed in Chapter 6) exemplifies the existence of negative feedback cycles, and these cycles begin to show their strength and effects during the emergence phase. The reinforcement phase includes many positive feedback cycles as they occur to further the commitment of group members toward the decision already made.

The normal process of managing conflict and deviance in group decision making undoubtedly involves the functioning of positive and negative feedback cycles. Perhaps the most critical factor in conflict management is the element of time. Attempts by group members to resolve conflict too quickly or to control deviant behavior prematurely are unfortunately shortsighted. As Tolar (1970) states, "No matter how conducive to conflict resolution circumstances are, after a certain critical phase in the dispute has been attained [perhaps the conflict phase of group decision making], further progress must await the passage of a 'respectable' amount of time." Patience is a virtue of members in effective decision-making groups.

THE "NORM" OF CONFLICT AND DEVIANCE

To call conflict and deviance a "norm" appears to be a contradiction in terms. Deviant behavior is by definition contrary to group norms. But the perspective of communication and the group process must not be ignored. To view conflict and deviance as either constructive or destructive is to consider only their effects and to deny the *process* of conflict. When viewed from the perspective of communication and the group process, realistic substantive conflict and deviance can readily be seen to serve positive functions in the group, which leads to the startling observation that conflict and deviance are normal in group interaction patterns. That is, since realistic substantive conflict and deviance exist in nearly all groups, occur in many phases of group interaction, and constitute a significant part of this interaction, they must be considered normal.

Idea Testing in Decision Making

Some conventional wisdom maintains that since group decision making is a cooperative venture (which it certainly is), arguments, disagreements, and conflicts over ideas should be avoided. But even if it were possible to avoid interpersonal disagreements (a highly unlikely event), such conventional wisdom is simply bad advice. Interaction during group decision making is a curious blend of persuasion, compromise, negotiation, argumentation, flexibility, and firmness of opinions. Issues are thrown into the hopper of group interaction and provide the raw materials for the group's final consensus decisions.

During group interaction, every idea, opinion, proposal, or suggestion contributed to the group is tested under fire. Involved members focus their critical abilities on these ideas and submit them to rigorous examination. During this process of critical discussion, some ideas are accepted, others are rejected, and many are modified and combined with others. The eventual outcome of idea testing includes those decisions that achieve consensus. Because the group task is to achieve consensus on decision, the critical exchange of opinions, ideas, and information is quite normal in the process of group interaction during decision making. A more detailed description of this process is included in Chapters 6 and 9.

Formation of Coalitions

Within every social system of any size, subgroups form around some issue or idea. Subgroups typically form and maintain themselves because of some social conflict within the larger system. These groups within groups often command greater loyalty from their members than does the larger social system of which the subgroup is a part. Criminals in our society, for example, have a legendary code of conduct that the larger society has apparently been unable to break. "Honor among thieves" and the "code of silence" are familiar terms to describe this particular subgroup's norms. A small work group in a large organization also has a greater influence on its members than the large organization does. In a university, for example, students and faculty alike often identify most closely with their affiliated departments. The students generally consider themselves communication majors, education majors, physics majors, or engineering majors first and members of the larger university community second.

The formation of subgroups is neither desirable nor undesirable to the larger social system. It is inevitable and should be fully expected as a normal occurrence. Too often subgroups, particularly those representing a minority, are ignored. The larger social system would do well to recognize their existence and take advantage of their apparent group strength.

Even a small group typically contains subgroups during the normal process of group decision making. Since the subgroup is usually temporary, a more appropriate term is *coalition*. This type of coalition is a *temporary alliance, among two or more members of the group, oriented toward a difference of opinion regarding the means to achieve the group's goal*. Specifically, a coalition unites certain group members who agree with noncoalition members on the nature and value of the group goal but who disagree on how that goal can best be achieved. Such a coalition, then, involves social conflict and deviance over means but, typically, agreement on the goal itself.

Coalition formation requires a minimum of three members in the group. With only two members, social conflict is either destructive or unmanageable. Social conflict in a dyad (a two-member group) exists without deviance. There is no minority, no prevailing opinion upon which to base a norm. Thus, dyadic conflict is resolved typically by one member dominating the other. And dominance-submission relationships thwart the group process of idea testing during decision making. Any consensus following conflict in a dyad is destined to be false or superficial consensus.

With at least three members, two-one coalitions are possible. In a four-member group, several three-one and two-two combinations are possible coalitions. The five-member group is often viewed as the optimum size for small group decision making because of the numerous possibilities for coalition formation and management. But there is no hard-and-fast rule governing the number of members required in a small group as long as the minimum membership is three. As long as groupness can be achieved, no maximum limit is placed on the size of a small group.

The Leadership Paradox—Conformity and Deviance

Leadership is a most interesting role in a small decision-making group. As a high-status member who is committed to the group, the leader is a strong conformist. Numerous research studies have illustrated the tendency of a leader to conform closely to group norms. The conformity of a leader has even found its way into the conventional wisdom of corny jokes. You may be familiar with the story of the rotund little gentleman during the French Revolution who was observed huffing and puffing in the wake of a riotous mob. When asked why he was chasing after the mob, he replied innocently, "I have to follow them. I am their leader."

The humor of this little story stems from the paradoxical nature of the leader's role as both conformist and deviate. A leader functions as an innovator who aids the group's progress toward goal achievement. In times of crisis, the leader must find new directions contrary to traditional norms in order to maintain the group and save it from impending disaster. A leader who doesn't innovate is soon deposed in favor of someone who can. Thus, the leader gains and maintains that role by functioning both as a conformist and as a deviate.

Several explanations account for the self-contradictory behavior of the group leader. Hollander (1985) has suggested perhaps the most plausible explanation. He describes gaining and maintaining leadership as an economic model whose central concept is "idiosyncrasy credits." In early stages of leader emergence, the leader conforms to the group norms and accumulates credits, much as one deposits money in a bank account. Later, the leader who successfully exerts influence through innovative behavior is not regarded as a deviate; having accumulated sufficient credits from the bank account, he or she cashes them in in order to innovate. According to Hollander, strict adherence to traditional group norms during periods of crisis is fatal to the leader's position and damaging to the group. Members perceive a leader who continues to conform in a stress situation as not knowing what to do and not helping the group achieve its goals.

Hollander's economic model of idiosyncrasy credits is a credible explanation for how a leader is able to deviate as well as conform. But the model should not be construed to imply that a leader innovates only during group crises. Indeed, a leader innovates through initiating themes and performing other leadership functions throughout group interaction. In fact, the leader must be recognized as an innovator *before* the crisis period so that the members expect innovative behavior and look to the leader for assistance.

If there were any doubts that deviant behavior is beneficial to a group, those doubts should now be dispelled. Maintaining the social organization of a group virtually demands deviant behavior. And the group demands deviant behavior not just from low-status members, but from the highest-status member of all—the leader. Moreover, the leader's deviant behavior is not only beneficial; it is normal and to be expected.

THE PROCESS OF SOCIAL CONFLICT AND DEVIANCE

It is important to keep in mind that the process perspective inherently defines the deviance and conflict instrumental to the group process as *behaviors* performed by members and not as roles occupied by one or more of the members. While role deviation may be present in a group, it has no significant impact on the pattern of group interaction. The process view, emphasizing the principle of interdependence, also stresses the interdependence both of conformity and deviance and of cooperation and conflict in forming and maintaining groupness. As interdependent elements, they are viewed not as different processes, but as different dimensions of a single process. And this process embodies all the communicative behaviors of all the group members.

Flight Patterns

Several independent studies of small group interaction have discovered what appears to be a phenomenon common to many groups. When confronted with social conflict within group interaction, members typically run away from it; that is, they take flight in their interaction patterns. Some observers, for example, find that a period of social conflict will typically be followed by a period of interaction in which members avoid discussing the task. Gouran and Baird (1972) found that group members tend to change the topic under discussion soon after a period of social disagreement.

Why a group's interaction pattern exhibits flight from social conflict can be explained in several ways. One explanation assumes that conflict and deviance are unpleasant stimuli that group members wish to avoid. But this explanation is not very plausible in that it smacks of ignoring a problem and hoping it will go away. Sooner or later the group members must face the problem and resolve, manage, or control the conflict. Such a view also alleges that members invariably view social conflict as destructive.

A second explanation is that flight patterns are not an avoidance of anything, but merely a reflection of the short attention span of groups. A third explanation is that flight patterns reflect the normal process by which groups progressively modify decisions on their way to achieving consensus.

Neither of these views assumes that conflict is inherently destructive or constructive.

Whatever the explanation for the apparent flight patterns in group inter-action, it is obvious that disagreement spawns more disagreement, at least temporarily, in brief flurries of social conflict. It is also apparent that groups do not overtly attempt compromise as their initial response to social conflict; groups often perceive compromise to be an unsatisfactory solution to group conflict. A group's first response to conflict between its members is appar-ently to fight it out in frequent, albeit brief, periods of interaction and to then abruptly cease consideration of the issue.

Innovative Deviance

Robert K. Merton (1957, p. 140) a noted sociologist, has discussed several varieties of deviant behavior in social systems. His classic discussion of deviance suggests four different varieties, not all of which are beneficial to the successful functioning of the social system. In fact, three of his classifications of deviance are probably disruptive and harmful to effective functioning.

One form of deviance in Merton's classifications is *ritualism* (which we have tended to call blind conformity). A ritualist is a person who conforms blindly to social norms solely for the sake of conformity, merely going through the motions of conformity without any real understanding or realiza-tion of why the norms are being followed. Another form of deviance is *retreatism*, a withdrawal from society (as a hermit or dropout does). And a third is *rebellion*, a disruptive form of deviance that involves rejecting the social system's values. Rebels seek to overthrow the existing social system and replace it with a new and presumably better one.

The lone form of deviance that appears to be most conducive to providing benefits to the social system is what Merton calls *innovation*. Innovators in a social system are members who are quite committed to the goals of the system or group but who believe that the socially approved means to achieve these goals need to be revised. Innovative deviance is perhaps the most common type of deviant behavior in the interaction patterns of group decision making. The silent or uncommitted member might be a retreatist, the member of a classroom group who wants to get an A but is concerned only with satisfying the instructor might represent a ritualist, and the person who hates leaders would probably represent a rebel. But innovative deviance, according to Merton, involves behavior that reflects a rather strong commitment to the group in the form of an agreement with the goals of the group; the innovator simply disagrees with the prevailing (or majority) view of the acceptable means for achieving these goals.

Valentine and Fisher (1974) utilized Merton's concept of innovative devi-ance as the basis for analyzing communication. They attempted to observe group interaction more closely in order to determine how deviant behavior functions during the process of group decision making. The results from their analysis, although not conclusive, provide some interesting speculation about how innovative deviance functions to benefit the natural process of group decision making.

Oddly enough, Valentine and Fisher discovered that innovative deviance is not associated with any particular member or members. That is, nearly all members of the group contribute some innovation to the interaction. Moreover, no one or two members appear to contribute significantly more innovatively deviant behaviors than other members. This phenomenon may not be true of all forms of deviance, but innovatively deviant behavior is apparently a phenomenon of group decision making that is not necessarily associated with one or two particular members who would then be labeled "deviants."

Valentine and Fisher also discovered that innovatively deviant behavior accounts for a rather significant proportion of the entire group interaction. An average of 27 percent of all the communicative actions performed by the group members they observed was characterized as deviant behavior. Furthermore, all but a small percent of deviant behavior was innovative deviance. Innovative deviance during group interaction appears to be most acceptable during the conflict phase and, to a lesser extent, during the emergence phase of group decision making. On the other hand, such deviant behavior is probably detrimental to the group process during the formative phase of group development (the orientation phase) and during the final phase of reinforcement as the group nears consensus (see Chapter 6).

What does innovative deviance look like during group decision making? According to the interaction categories utilized by Valentine and Fisher, innovative deviance occurs in the form of a contradiction or rejection of an assertion. Continuing a disagreement initiated by others is also classified as an innovatively deviant act, as is advocating a previously attacked assertion or negatively modifying another member's assertion. A statement that supports a previous innovatively deviant statement is also classified as innovative deviance.

Another result consistent with the analysis reveals that most innovatively deviant behaviors appear in the interaction before the majority position of the group is clearly established. That is, most innovative behavior occurs before consensus and is apparently instrumental in formulating that consensus. This discovery seems to confirm the belief, stated earlier, that conflict leads to consensus.

While innovative deviance may generate further deviant behavior, these spurts of deviant interaction are not sustained indefinitely. That is, decision-making groups interact in bursts of deviant behavior followed by periods of interaction in which little deviant behavior is present. After a period of nondeviant interaction, the members then engage in another spurt of deviant interaction patterns. These peaks and valleys of deviant interaction suggest patterns of "flight" behavior in which members appear to avoid deviance and social conflict after brief periods of deviant interaction. But the suggestion of the fight-flight pattern in group interaction does not necessarily indicate that group members typically avoid conflict and deviance. Rather, group members may be able to withstand only so much social conflict and deviance before they abruptly change the topic under discussion. The fact that group members are apparently not avoiding conflict is even more evident when one realizes that the group members invariably return to those topics which had earlier precipitated deviant behavior and social conflict.

The conclusion from Valentine and Fisher's study regarding the identification of members as deviants is worthy of further discussion. You will recall that the results of their interaction analysis indicated that nearly all members of the decision-making groups they observed performed innovatively deviant behaviors. This conclusion emphasizes the fact that deviance, at least innovative deviance, is probably best defined in terms of behaviors. That is, innovative deviance constitutes a normal and rather substantial proportion of group interaction. Furthermore, it is apparently not a role position occupied by one or two members within a group's network of roles.

Phases of Conflict

In an additional study, Ellis and Fisher (1975) attempted to observe conflict interaction during group decision making. The purpose of this study was to provide some insight into the potential of conflict for social integration, that is, for developing groupness. This particular investigation, utilizing interaction analysis, suggests the possibility that group decision making can be classified into three phases of conflict integration. The first third of the group interaction involves *interpersonal* conflict, the middle third of the interaction can be characterized as *confrontation*, and the final phase involves *substantive* conflict.

Ellis and Fisher described the interpersonal-conflict phase as resulting from the individual differences between the personalities of the group members. During the early stages of group decision making, the members have not had sufficient time to generate group-centered issues; therefore, they involve themselves in conflict that is based more on their identities as unique human beings than as group members.

The second phase of conflict, confrontation, includes interaction that tests ideas. Present in such interaction patterns are agreement and disagreement with specific decision proposals. In the sense that confrontation involves choosing up sides and fighting out the issues, it appears to pit one coalition of members against another. The second phase of conflict interaction probably includes both the conflict and emergence phases of group decision making.

The final phase of conflict interaction is characterized by the positive functioning of information in group interaction. Nearly all contributions by the members involve statements directly addressing those issues and proposals that achieve group consensus. Substantive conflict clearly indicates effective management of social conflict, or, at least, the outcome or result of effective conflict management during earlier phases of group interaction.

Ellis and Fisher pointed out that for effective decision making, groups need to devise conflict management techniques that are adapted to the specific type of conflict occurring in the interaction. For example, the techniques for managing interpersonal conflict differ significantly from those used for managing confrontation (or substantive conflict). Interpersonal conflict results from a lack of information about task issues; therefore, having all group members generate more information directed at the group's task is an effective way to help manage the interpersonal conflict that arises during the early phase of group decision making. On the other hand, confrontation results from the problem of integrating voluminous amounts of information; that is, the members have generated so much information that they are having difficulty determining which information is the most and the least valuable. Thus, whereas managing interpersonal conflict involves *generating* additional group-related information, managing confrontation involves *integrating* existing information. By being able to make such distinctions between specific types of social conflict, effective decision-making groups become able to develop techniques for managing each particular type.

Folger and Poole (1984, pp. 20–23) concluded from a comparison of phase theories that groups go through a *differentiation-integration* cycle. Every group experiences a differentiation phase—it experiences conflicts that draw out sharp differences between its members. At some peak point, when the group cannot tolerate the conflict any longer, integration begins—the group moves toward a solution that is at least acceptable to its members. If attempts at integration are not successful, then the group returns to differentiation and begins the cycle again.

Understanding the phases of conflict development in groups is important, because they put each type of conflict in a meaningful context and thereby teach group members what they must deal with in order to move through conflict. Phase theories suggest that there are patterns of conflict that help shape the expectations of group members. The study by Ellis and Fisher, for example, showed that ambiguous comments occur in both the early and late phases but are interpreted differently in each. Ambiguity in the early phase represents indecision; ambiguity in later phases represents movement from one idea to another to help the group reach a decision. Therefore, an understanding of the general phase the group is experiencing provides a way to interpret specific communicative utterances.

MANAGING CONFLICT

Up to now we have been talking mostly about conflict as a normal characteristic of group decision making, and we have noted that conflict needs to be controlled. We have also discussed the control of conflict as a problem of management, not as a problem of getting rid of conflict. Since conflict is inevitable and can be a positive characteristic of the group process, it is important to *manage* conflict rather than eliminate it. Group members should thus be careful to avoid the tendency to think of conflict and deviance as harmful, disruptive, or simply "bad"; they must think about conflict both as potentially disruptive *and* as beneficial. The problem of management thus becomes one of how to maximize the benefits of conflict and avoid the consequences of destructive conflict.

Standard Conflict-Avoidance Techniques

The following are some ways that groups can make decisions by avoiding substantive conflict. These techniques are sometimes counterproductive because they force decisions the group is not ready to make. None of the techniques is based on the group's working through conflict and arriving at a decision that reflects consensus, but each is used quite often to force decisions and bring conflict (and communication) to a close.

Majority Vote   Our democratic traditions have conditioned us to take majority-rule votes. After a little discussion in a group, there is always someone who says, "Well, let's take a vote." Majority votes make for quick decisions and certainly save time. But have you ever heard the phrase "the tyranny of the majority"? Majority votes satisfy only one portion of the group. And if a coalition consistently votes together and constitutes a majority, it can certainly become tyrannical. Groups that solve all problems by taking majority-rule votes are thwarting the benefits of the group process and placing too much value on closure at the expense of consensus. Majority votes also divide the group; after the vote there are "winners" and "losers," with all the accompanying hurt feelings and animosity. Majority-rule votes are not very effective for small group decision making.

Authoritative Rule   A group member who has power, authority, and status can always force a decision. Say that an executive vice president who has been leading a problem-solving group for the past few months says: "We have been working on this for some time and are unable to come up with a decision. Rather than continuing this any further, I am going to make the decision for us." This will force closure and avoid additional conflict, but it can also lead to anger, anxiety, and other adverse effects on the group. If group members are not committed to the decision, they will not work to make it succeed.

Third-Party Arbitration   This occurs when a disinterested third party is brought into the group to make the decision. Arbitrators are not common in small discussion groups. They are, however, used extensively to solve disputes among large competing groups, such as labor versus management, government versus citizens, and situations with many competing interests, such as environmental disputes (Goldmann, 1980). Arbitrators can have special respect and credibility in the eyes of the group because they are supposed to (1) be disinterested, (2) be requested by each side of the issue, (3) have special skills in conflict management techniques, and (4) bring fresh ideas to the process. In practice, third-party arbitrators are often imposed on groups and force decisions that have the same problems as compromises. Sometimes groups are neither committed to the process of arbitration nor respectful of the intervenors. This is very harmful because it encourages the parties to avoid responsibility for the decision.

Solutions Based on Gains and Losses

High-quality decisions that meet everyone's needs are an ideal of group decision making. Naturally, groups do not always achieve this ideal but they do strive for it. Nevertheless, many conflict-resolution techniques are characterized by losses or gains for group members or other groups. These losses or gains are usually described as lose-lose, win-win, or win-lose situations, depending on who gains and who loses after conflict is resolved."

Lose-Lose Approaches   Approaches to conflict that can be described as lose-lose are those in which the conflict results in some loss for everyone concerned. A husband and wife arguing viciously in divorce court will probably end up in a lose-lose situation. Neither party will get what it wants and both will end up being hurt emotionally and financially. The same can be true for labor-management negotiations. If the parties involved both take extreme and hard-line positions, there will be nothing but loss—in terms of time and money—for everyone.

Interestingly, *compromise* can sometimes be considered a lose-lose technique. If both sides give a little, then both sides lose a little. Compromising may satisfy the pressure to resolve conflict, but everybody loses something nevertheless.

An attitude of *denial* toward a conflict is the fastest way to establish a lose-lose situation. This occurs when two parties or group members ignore an existing conflict by disguising their feelings and refusing to acknowledge the problem. Left unresolved, the problem persists and its negative effects continue. True, ignoring conflict can have the benefit of avoiding unpleasant interactions and difficult disputes, but the potential for the original problem to escalate is a mjaor disadvantage. Ignoring conflict is a classic tactic between married couples or intimates. Although such interpersonal conflict is not the subject of this book, it is a good example of how problems can build when conflict is ignored.

Win-Lose Approaches   These techniques of resolution are the ones most people associate with conflict. A win-lose situation exists when one party gains and the other loses. A baseball game is a good example of a win-lose situation. One team must win and the other must lose. These are conflict techniques that pit one group or coalition against another. Both groups try to use their power, resources, and skill to beat the other.

The simple *imposition* of a decision or solution on an individual or group without trying to establish consensus, is a win-lose technique. Sometimes a person or group in power will simply force a decision on others and expect them to willingly agree. Again, we do not want to be completely negative about any conflict management method because they all have some advantages. Even using legitimate power to force a decision has the advantage of a quick and final settlement of a problem. But for the most part, win-lose techniques end up disenfranchising the losing group, resulting in sabotage and resistance to the solution. Moreover, the losing party will more than likely withdraw its commitment to the objectives of the group.

Win-Win Approaches   These are the ideal methods of conflict resolution. As the name implies, both parties gain from the resolution of the conflict. Win-win approaches rely on two techniques. The first of these is to require participation by everyone involved. This ensures a commitment to the solution and allows everyone to feel invested in any final decisions. The second technique of a win-win approach is to emphasize stable, long-term decisions rather than solutions that may offer immediate gratification only. Decision making as we have been discussing it throughout this book is a win-win approach to conflict. When both parties work to satisfy their goals and settle only on solutions that are acceptable to everyone, they are using win-win approaches to conflict resolution. The section below on conflict management will discuss a win-win problem-solving approach in more detail.

Styles of Conflict Management

Some specialists in conflict (e.g., Thomas, 1976; Canary and Spitzberg, 1987) suggest that your individual orientation toward conflict will determine how you deal with it. More specifically, individual attitudes toward conflict can be reduced to two fundamental orientations: the extent of your desire to meet your own needs, and the extent to which you want to meet the needs of others. These two basic orientations result in five different styles of handling conflict, as illustrated in Figure 8-1. These five styles can be described in terms of the following behaviors and approaches toward communication:

Avoidance	People in this category do whatever they can to ignore conflict and hope it will go away. They behave with indifference toward other people and are neither assertive nor cooperative. The avoidance style says "don't involve me." Avoiders often seek to solve conflict by resorting to bureaucratic rules or appealing to historical precedent.
Compromise	Compromisers occupy a sort of midpoint between the assertive and cooperative categories. They are willing to give up something and find a middle ground for the sake of "keeping the peace." Compromisers like negotiation, trade-offs, deals, and comfortable solutions.
Competition	This is the style of dominant, aggressive, "high-achievers." Competitive people often fail to acknowledge the desires of others and generally seek win-lose outcomes. The competitive style relies on rivalry, power, and imposed solutions. Individuals with competitive styles are typically assertive and energetic in pursuit of their own victory.
Accommodation	People who use this style are friendly and unassertive. They give things away and comply easily. They say things like, "Sure, whatever you

FIGURE 8-1 Conflict management styles.

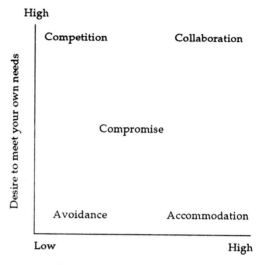

want," and "Yeah, I'd be happy to do that." Accommodators appease others because they have a greater desire to meet others' needs than their own.

Collaboration   The collaborating style is very close to the negotiating and problem-solving orientation we have been advocating. Collaborators are motivated to meet both their own needs and others'. They are not afraid to share information and feelings and to think and act critically. Collaborators look for integrative solutions that enable everyone to win. Collaborators are not afraid of hard work, and they define problems and conflict as challenging.

Conflict Style and the Leader as Medium

In the last chapter we mentioned the work of Karl Weick, who has described the leader of a group as a medium who manages complexity. One of the main tasks of these leaders is to manage conflict in a healthy and productive manner. A good leader will recognize and accept the inevitability of group politics (see Chapter 5). That is, a good leader realizes that individuals have different interests, aims, and objectives and will likely use their membership in a group to advance their own ends. The complex leader further understands the positive and negative functions of conflict. Hence, the fundamental concern of the complex leader is to manage conflict in ways that benefit the group and, of course, his or her own interests.

The leader might use conflict as a way of achieving some desired end. For example, conflict can energize the group. It can help combat lethargy and compliance by keeping everyone involved. Conflict can also do much to stimulate learning and change, helping to keep the group in touch with necessary information. But given that conflict can also cause pain and have negative effects, one of the main tasks of the complex leader is to maintain the right type and level of conflict. The various styles discussed above are available to the leader who takes on the task of managing conflict. A leader certainly has a preferred style, but all the styles disccussed in Figure 8-1 may be necessary and appropriate at one time or another.

Sometimes a leader needs to delay things and "buy time" and may therefore engage in *avoidance* behaviors. A leader may decide that an issue is unimportant or not solvable at the moment and choose not to take action. Or, understanding that some problems require decisive action and the implementation of an unpopular solution (like cost cutting) with no room for compromise, a leader might decide to employ a *competitive* style. At another time the leader might foster *compromise* because she or he has concluded that a temporary settlement to a complex issue is in the best interest of the group. A compromising style would also be appropriate when the immediate goals are less important than maintaining good relationships within the group. The successful leader should be strong enough to know when he or she is wrong and needs to be accommodating. Sometimes the issue at hand is simply not important to the leader so accommodation is simple and satisfies everyone. Finally, some problems require skilled *collaborative* styles. In these cases, the leader must find high-quality integrative solutions and work with others to achieve these goals.

Of all the conflict management styles and techniques, collaborative problem solving is the most important and difficult to learn. It requires skill and a commitment to working with others. The final section of this chapter is devoted to the most time-honored principles of regulating conflict.

Regulating Conflict

In this section we will give you some help in putting collaborative conflict management style into *practice*. We will suggest ways to improve a group's chances of working with conflict constructively. As usual, we provide no pat answers or tried-and-true rules. Rather, we offer intelligent strategies distilled from much of the best thinking about conflict management (see Folger and Poole, 1984, especially Chapter 6; Filley, 1975).

Clarify the Issues A group's first task is to clarify the conflicting issues about the problem it is addressing. This clarification is one of the group's most important tasks, and it is accomplished during the differentiation phase—in which the group identifies, defines, and sharpens the issues. Once the group has successfully differentiated the issues, it has a clear and accurate picture of the areas of conflict, understands the consequences of the conflict, and has some idea about what kinds of action are necessary. During this phase, the group must strive for communication that defines the problem's issues clearly and that encourages flexibility and creativity.

Folger and Poole (1984, pp. 192–194) suggest four ways to help clarify a problem's conflicting issues. These four strategies have been used effectively by group members as well as by third-party intervenors.

1. *Discuss the historical roots of the problem* The issues become more distinct when the group has a thorough understanding of the factors that created the problem. Sometimes the issues become clearer as the group argues about the problem's historical development. Groups often gain new insights as they discuss the problem's chronological development.

2. *Create a positive discussion atmosphere* One of the most basic reasons why a group does not define a problem's issues clearly is that its members feel insecure about stating their opinions. They often believe that being honest will result in argument and personal animosity; moreover, they sometimes feel vulnerable and subject to retribution if they express their opinions openly. The group should work to ensure that the general communication climate is sufficiently open and free that all members will express their opinions. The leader can play an important role here, because he or she is in a position to encourage good, hard-hitting discussion and to discourage any of its negative consequences. The leader can control the agenda, govern who talks to whom, and direct the general flow of communication. Dealing with people individually, the leader can also work to redirect destructive emotions and bad feelings.

3. *Discuss needs rather than solutions* When a group finds itself in conflict over unsatisfactory solution proposals, the cause of this conflict is that the members have diverse and incompatible needs that the proposed solutions do not satisfy. When such conflict occurs, posing further solutions does not help. Rather, the causes of the conflict need to be addressed. The group should (1) stop discussing solutions until the members' needs have been clarified, (2) insist that the members discuss their needs, and (3) work to avoid interpersonal conflict. In managing this aspect of conflict, a group leader can ask the members to deal with the following questions: What are the members' needs? How does solution X meet these needs? How does the member view the needs of other members?

4. *Categorize the issues* When the conflicting issues are complex and multi-layered, trying to clarify them can be very frustrating. As a result, certain members may launch into personal attacks against other members or express frustration about something outside the group's control, and such behavior can disrupt the group's work. Loud, belligerent discussions are usually a sign of aggression and displaced personal antagonisms, and a perceptive leader (especially if he or she knows the members individually) can often recognize such sources of conflict. When such behavior occurs, it is useful to divide the problem into small categories and deal with each one individually. Furthermore, the group will be able to manage each category's issues more carefully if it can separate out extraneous matters and concentrate on one issue at a time.

Promote a Positive Climate   Folger and Poole (1984, p. 84) define *climate* as "the relatively enduring quality of the group situation that (a) is experienced in common by group members, and (b) arises from and influences their interaction and behavior." The climate is the general environment of the group; it is the mood, feeling, or "air" that pervades the group situation. Changing a poor climate is difficult but necessary. Group climates arise from communication and the relationships between group members. The climate can be positive or negative, flexible or rigid, enabling or thwarting, friendly or hostile, supportive or threatening, authoritative or participatory, and so forth. It takes time to make the group climate conducive to good conflict management, and it is certainly not something that can be changed easily. The best ways to analyze a group climate are to (1) observe the group over a period of time, (2) interview people, and (3) listen to the language of the members and how they talk about themselves. Here are two suggestions for promoting a more positive group climate:

1. *Encourage open discussion* The group simply must feel free to communicate without negative consequences. This is easier said than done, but it is something the group must strive for. Discussion should be focused on issues and kept away from personalized argument; the members should be free to communicate their feelings, but these should always be related to the central issue. The most useful technique for promoting open discussion is to reinforce it. A group member, perhaps the leader, should begin by honestly expressing feelings and disagreements. This will stimulate others to communicate in the same manner. The leader or group member then reinforces these others either by giving them direct feedback ("I'm glad you said that. Now I understand.") or by extending the discussion with contributions of his or her own.

2. *Change the talk* One way to alter the group climate is to begin talking about it differently. For example, all group members like the feeling of cohesion and unity that comes with group membership, and sometimes what makes it difficult to work through conflict is that the climate is not one of cohesion—so a simple way to correct this is to change the language to "we" when talking about the group. This gives the members the feeling of belonging to a social unit; it creates a comfortable evniroment in which members feel they have something in common. There is the story of the fraternity pledge class that was asked by members how many pledges were in the group; each pledge would answer, "One, sir; we are a unit." This sort of dramatized example shows how changing the language can alter the perception of the group climate. Groups that give themselves special names and codes show that they have a climate of strong solidarity.

Allow Group Members to Save Face   When people engage in face-saving communication, they are attempting to protect their image and personal identity (Folger and Poole, 1984, pp. 149–167). Face-saving is a very emotional group activity, responsible for numerous difficulties in conflict interactions, for group members want to be perceived as capable and competent and thus do their best to make sure that others have this image of them. A strong concern for self-image can surface when members are involved in conflict interaction, because in conflict situations they are exposing their opinions and attitudes and thus feel vulnerable, not only open to personal criticism but also risking the loss of other members' esteem; that is, conflict is a situation in which one's identity is threatened. (Consider, for example, that corporations often save face by making out-of-court settlements with injured customers, thereby making reparations and satisfying the injured parties without admitting to wrongdoing or criminal negligence.) Thus, conflict has to be conducted in a manner that allows group members to preserve their personal and relational identities.

The following are some useful techniques for promoting face-saving communication:

1. *Establish a proper climate* The climate established in the group is perhaps the most important means of preventing face-saving problems. If members agree that it is acceptable to state opinions and feelings openly without being threatened, they will have little concern for face-threatening communication. Such a climate develops from the previous behavior of the group. Reinforcing individual acts with support and tactful behavior is the best way to ensure a climate conducive to face-saving.
2. *Reduce defensiveness* Folger and Poole (1984, p. 182) show that people who are threatened become defensive. They feel "backed against a wall" and must do whatever is necessary to save face and regain their image. Defensiveness can be reduced by having each party to a conflict state that he or she understands the other side of the issue and recognize its validity; for example, group members can explain that they understand how another member can feel threatened. Tying the current instance of defensiveness to a previous one is another way to show support and sympathetic understanding of the problem. Recognizing the other party's feelings will not necessarily make these feelings go away, but it is a step toward establishing a climate receptive to open discussion.
3. *Avoid accusatory and intimidating messages* Messages that accuse, intimidate, or generally threaten challenge the self-image of the other party. Some particularly manipulative individuals feel that such a message can be a show of strength and that it helps their position because it weakens the other party. But this strategy rarely works, for such a message requires a reaction, which is usually defensive or counteraccusatory. The group has then created a new problem that necessitates another response and redirects the communication away from productive conflict management. If the group ignores these messages, it is allowing this behavior to influence future interaction. Members who feel intimated must be encouraged to make their feelings known. They must describe why they feel as they do, addressing *specific* behaviors, and must encourage the intimidating members to explain their behavior. Escalation and increasing tension are the consequences of a failure to address acts of intimidation.

Some groups set aside some time to evaluate the group's progress and discuss problems and directions. This is an excellent time to address issues related to face-saving and intimidation, for the time period legitimizes such discussions and, moreover, does not interfere with the group's normal work.

Develop Integration Skills People generally spend more time learning about competition (e.g., sports, games, grades, business) than about coopera-tion. Our market economy and our society's traditions of individuality and success foster competitive attitudes. These attitudes have served us well in many arenas, but more occasions call for cooperation than for competition.

Some people think group communication and decision making are pri-marily competitive, win-lose situations. But solving group conflict should *not* be a win-lose situation only. The best decisions and approaches to conflict are *integrative* and *collaborative*, which means that the members of the group integrate their resources to work toward a common goal.

Group members must learn how to communicate and behave in an integrative manner. After they have clarified a problem's issues and clearly stated their differences, they must move to an integrative approach. The emergence phase of the decision-making process utilizes integrative behav-ior. To help groups become more specific and directive in approaching a problem from an integrative perspective, here is a description of divisive versus integrative communicative behavior from Patton and Giffin (1988, pp. 432–433):

Divisive Behavior	Integrative Behavior
1. Use purposive behavior in pursuing your *individual* goals.	Use purposive behavior in pursuing *common* goals.
2. Be secretive.	Be open.
3. Publicly disguise your own needs, keeping private what you really want.	Accurately and openly express your own needs.
4. Use threats and bluffs.	Use no threats or bluffs.
5. Be unpredictable, and use an ele-ment of surprise.	Be predictable; your behavior is flexible, but it is not designed for surprise.
6. Use nonrational and irrational argu-ments.	Use rational and innovative arguments.
7. Attempt success by stereotyping the other side and increasing hostility; demand ingroup loyalty.	Instead of stereotyping the other side, consider its merits; work to reduce hos-tility and to promote positive feelings.
8. Use a zero-sum approach; assume that preventing the other side from reaching its goals will facilitate your own goals.	Use a non-zero sum approach; assume that the goals and solutions will benefit both parties.

Groups must avoid an us-versus-them or a superiority-inferiority approach to conflict. Both are divisive and just splinter the conflicting parties. There is a tendency during conflict, especially when issues are difficult to resolve, to stereotype the other side; statements such as "typical management" reflect the fact that group members see the other side as inflexible and of one mind.

Folger and Poole (1984, pp. 194–197) describe two other ways to induce integration:

1. *Develop common goals* There is usually more room for agreement in a conflict situation than most people think. It is likely that the parties in conflict will begin by accentuating the differences between them rather than discussing their commonalities. Have someone try to keep track of the points of agreement. If both parties can agree on goals, then they can focus the discussion on the means of reaching the goals. This is usually an easier problem than working out differences in goals. Communication that emphasizes common goals is also encouraging for group members, prompting them to adopt a more integrative approach to the conflict.
2. *Clarify the integrative process* The conflicting parties should state emphatically that they want to move toward integrative solutions, and attempt to control the process. This helps establish the proper attitudes and emotional conditions for integration.

Filley (1975, pp. 92–106) describes some ways to promote an integrative solution:

1. *Adjust relational conditions* This is similar to establishing a cooperative climate.
2. *Adjust perceptions* The group uses the procedures outlined by Filley to clarify the nature of the conflict.
3. *Adjust attitudes* The parties clarify the emotional issues, including how they feel about the conflict.
4. *Problem definition* Depersonalize the problem and define it in a manner separate from individuals.
5. *Search for solutions* Generate solutions in a nonjudgmental way.
6. *Consensus decision* Evaluate the alternative solutions and choose a single solution.

In Conclusion

Managing conflict is not easy and is always risky. Even though we have offered a number of steps and strategies, there is no guarantee that all conflict can be regulated in a successful manner. Moreover, it is foolish and naive to think that all groups are trustworthy and will work for cooperative solutions. But this is a goal worth striving for, because even with the strong pressures in our culture to succeed and gain, often at the expense of others, it remains true that decisions of real quality and permanence are based on integrative communication that leads to mutually beneficial decisions.

SUMMARY

The right of dissent in our society is one of our most cherished privileges, although conformity, inescapable and inevitable, is more often the rule. Conformity to the behavioral standards of a social system implies not only uniformity of behavior, but uniformity based on conflict between alternatives and on avoidance of unpleasant social pressures. Pressures toward conformity in the small group are extraordinarily severe, although a deviating member gains strength to resist such pressures by having publicly committed himself or herself to a deviant position or by receiving the support of another member who agrees with the deviant position.

Many people in our society are ambivalent about social conflict and deviance and often view the social system as functioning in a delicate balance of supportive and disruptive forces. Thus, conflict may be seen as existing within one person, between two or more persons, within a social system, or between two or more social systems. Social conflict is also classified as affective or substantive—emotional or intellectual.

When a perfect (or ideal) social system is assumed, social conflict appears to be a failure of the social system and inherently destructive. However, those who adopt a functionalist approach perceive social conflict and deviance as often performing desirable, constructive, and even essential functions instrumental to the effective operation of the social system. If conflict is destructive, it must be resolved or controlled. On the other hand, constructive conflict must be understood and managed in order to achieve its social benefits. The multifaceted nature of social conflict and deviance dictates the emphasis on interpersonal substantive conflict serving constructive functions for the small group.

Social conflict and deviance perform many functions beneficial to the group process. Conflict furthers group cohesiveness and increases productivity. Innovative deviant behavior is essential for progress as the group grows and changes through time. Groups manage deviant behavior through feedback loops and cycles.

Realistically, social conflict and deviance are so common in the process of group development that they are considered normal within the group process. A decision-making group invokes social conflict as members test ideas in a critical exchange of information and opinions. Coalitions form temporarily over conflicting ideas before typically merging as the group achieves consensus. And the leader, paradoxically enough, normally conforms to and deviates from group norms in the process of gaining and maintaining leadership status.

Verbal innovative deviance, an agreement on group goals but a disagreement on the means to achieve them, is suggested as an insight into the ongoing process of social conflict in group interaction patterns. Verbal innovative deviance seems to account for a significant proportion of group interaction and appears in clusters or spurts of deviant behavior that alternate with normal periods of group flight behavior.

Different types of conflict occur during the process of group decision making. Social conflict may be interpersonal, confrontational, or substantive, depending on the phase of group decision making in which it appears. Consequently, strategies for managing conflict and conflict styles vary considerably. Nevertheless, some general tactics for conflict management are possible. These strategies include clarifying issues, saving face, promoting a positive climate, and developing integration skills.

CHAPTER OUTLINE

COMMUNICATION DURING
   DECISION MAKING

IMPROVING EFFECTIVENESS
   IN GROUPS

PRINCIPLES OF EFFECTIVENESS

IMPROVING EFFECTIVENESS:
   ATTITUDINAL FACTORS

Attitudes toward the Group
Attitudes toward Interaction
Creativity
Criticism

IMPROVING EFFECTIVENESS:
   INTERPERSONAL FACTORS

Active Verbal Participation
Communication Skills
Supportive Communication
Responding to Others

IMPROVING EFFECTIVENESS:
   GROUP IDENTITY FACTORS

Sensitivity to Group Process
Commitment to the Group
Attitude toward Group Slowness
Formula Answers
Analyzing Group Episodes
Communication-Based Qualities
   of Effective Groups

SUMMARY

KEY TERMS

ORIENTATION PHASE

CONFLICT PHASE

EMERGENCE PHASE

REINFORCEMENT PHASE

JARGON

ABSTRACTION

MESSAGE FUNCTION

DEFENSIVE COMMUNICATION

SUPPORTIVE COMMUNICATION

Anatomy of Communication in Decision-Making Groups: Improving Effectiveness

COMMUNICATION DURING DECISION MAKING

The purpose of this final chapter is to take a closer look at how communication works during the process of decision development. In Chapter 6, we described four phases involved in the process of decision making. These phases—orientation, conflict, emergence, and reinforcement—are characteristic of the normal process of many groups. Groups certainly experience these phases in many ways. Some go through the phases quickly, and others more slowly; some groups spend a different amount of time in each phase; and, as Poole's (1983b) work indicates, some groups are very idiosyncratic and undergo different sequences of interaction. But the four phases, in addition to other research on group cycles and the group process, capture the essence of group development regardless of their variations. Almost all groups get organized (orientation), experience some sort of conflict (conflict), develop decisions (emergence), and justify what they have done (reinforcement).

This first part of this chapter focuses on the specific communicative utterances made by specific members during actual group interaction, reflecting the "flavor" of the group discussion. It describes the communicative exchanges of specific group members as the group progresses through the four phases of decision making. The second part of the chapter identifies the principles that contribute most to effective group decision making.

The interaction described below was taken from audiotaped transcripts of group meetings and illustrates the four phases of group decision making. It might be useful to review the model discussed in Chapter 6 during and after your reading of this interaction.

The Situation A six-member jury (all men) is deliberating over a verdict after observing a mock trial. The dramatized trial involved a civil suit seeking damages for alleged injuries suffered in an automobile-pedestrian accident.

The plaintiff, Alfred Derby, was the pedestrian who brought the suit. The defendant, Roger Adams, was the driver of the automobile that struck Derby. The jury group ultimately decided in favor of the defendant, Adams, and did not award damages in any amount to the plaintiff, Derby. Instrumental to this final verdict, the jury achieved consensus on a key decision that the plaintiff was negligent and therefore contributed to the accident.

Orientation   The opening excerpt of group interaction occurs during the first five minutes of the jury's deliberations. The six group participants are designated by the letters *A* through *F*. The ellipsis (. . .) signifies a pause in the interaction, not omitted materials.

A: First of all, we decide whether it's a case of liability or negligence.
D: Yeah . . . negligence.
A: It's the same thing. In other words, you all feel that Roger Adams alone was negligent without the contributory negligence of Derby—or was it Derby's fault as much as Adams's fault—or was it either's fault—or was it just plain accident?
C: Guilty or not guilty.
A: It's not just those two choices, though. We've got three choices.
D: What else can there be, though? I mean . . .
A: It's not a criminal action like whether he robbed a store. It's just whether he is negligent, both of them are negligent, or whether . . .
D: Yeah, I see. But there are still only two verdicts. Do we give the plaintiff any money or not?
A: First of all, how many people here feel that just Roger Adams alone was negligent and that Alfred Derby, the person who was hit, in no way contributed to this negligence and therefore should receive compensation?

In the orientation phase members attempt to accustom themselves to the topic and to the procedure. In this case they must accustom themselves to the procedure of the law and the legal directions they received from the judge.

In the excerpt above, the members proceed to discover what choices of final decisions are available to them. Essentially they are asking themselves, "What precisely is the task we are expected to accomplish?" With this fundamental step out of the way, the members proceed to probe one another's attitudes. Member *A*'s final comment requests a preliminary survey of the first impressions of group members. How difficult will it be to achieve agreement? This first excerpt, then, typifies the early efforts of members to acclimatize themselves—first to the procedures, and then to one another.

Later, member *B* responds to member *A*'s request for his initial opinion and stimulates responses that are typical of the orientation phase. A and D respond by invoking procedural rules formulated on the spur of the moment. In essence, they are telling the others to withhold his evidence and reasons until later, at which time the group will thrash things out. For the present, *A* and *C* don't want to "rock the boat." A more typical manner of expressing a member's initial attitude during the orientation phase is the following comment of *A*:

A: I feel that . . . I don't know about you guys, but it could have been me. I'm a reckless driver, and I can picture myself in a hurry to school. And there were a lot of mistakes brought out in the testimony . . . on both sides. First of all, I have always thought that the Banker's [parking] lot is the one next to Administration.

A is attempting to advance his opinion and includes supporting reasons. But his specific opinion is not clear from this comment. His manner of presenting his attitude is tentative and ambiguous. He even seems to apologize for attempting to express an opinion. He includes self-depreciation lest his attitude appear too forceful to the other members. He tempers his attitude by condemning "both sides" for having made mistakes in their testimony. He concludes by citing an innocuous error of fact—the location of a parking lot; he calculates that his remark will offend no one and even attributes it to his own misunderstanding. He delivers this comment with considerable hesitancy, with numerous pauses, and with trepidation. Such ambiguity is characteristic of nearly all substantive comments during orientation.

Another excerpt of the group's interaction demonstrates a series of ambiguous responses following the initiation of a decision proposal of questionable relevance to the forthcoming decision:

A: I'm a little bit confused about this whole thing. I don't know if we can assume that what the attorneys said is true or not.

C: Not in summation you can't—unless it was brought out in testimony.

D: That one in the gray suit based his mostly on emotion, and if we were to go by that alone without regarding anything . . . I mean emotion is fine, but . . .

A: You're right. A lot of it was based on emotion. I realize that, but still I don't know whether we should accept it or . . .

C: That was his job. We can't blame him for . . .

A: I guess not, but . . .

A originates this decision proposal by claiming that he is confused and is seeking clarification. He does not appear to be looking for any argument. Only *C* expresses a definite attitude toward this proposal concerning the credibility of the attorneys. *A* and *D* respond to the proposal with ambiguous reluctance. The members continue to participate hesitantly. Note the number of unfinished sentences and phrases left dangling. Two members, *A* and *D*, appear to favor the decision proposal, but they are carefully tolerant of other members' opinions. *A* twice agrees with the attitude that he apparently disfavors, but he qualifies his agreement with a hint of disagreement—for example, "you're right . . . I realize that, but" . . . and "I guess not, but . . ." Including the qualifier "but" and implying both a favorable and an unfavorable opinion toward the proposal typify ambiguous attitudes toward nearly all decision proposals during the orientation phase.

Conflict   Following the transition to the conflict phase, the members have completed developing their opinions. The period of testing the group atmosphere is over, and the general trend of idea development seems to be clear. Opinions and ideas in the orientation phase existed in their formative states. During the conflict phase, the process of formulation is complete. At this point, the group members proceed to choose up sides and engage in verbal battle over substantive issues. The following excerpt is typical of the interaction during the second phase of group decision making—the conflict phase:

A: The thing to decide is, was Roger Adams in a hurry? And did he act in such a manner that a reasonable, adult, mature person would?

C: You have to consider him a reasonable, prudent person. He was waved on by another person who was going to make the turn, irregardless [sic] of whether he was in a hurry or not.

A: I would say that if he is reasonable, he wouldn't take another person's word for it.

C: Oh, come on now! There is only one car on the street.

A: I certainly wouldn't do it.

C: Do you consider yourself reasonable?

A: I'm not reasonable. I'll admit it, too. But what does that have to do with it? I wouldn't want to use myself as an example. That doesn't say that he wasn't reasonable.

B: Then we're not going to get anyplace. You have to give some criteria. You can't just say he wasn't reasonable and let it go at that.

The tentativeness of expressed opinions, characteristic of interaction during the orientation phase, is certainly absent during interaction of the conflict phase. Member A's comment, which initiates the decision proposal concerning the possible negligence of the defendant, does not indicate his opinion toward the decision proposal. It is a comment expressing an ambiguous opinion toward the proposal. But the tone of this ambiguous comment is certainly different from the tone of the typical ambiguous comment of the orientation phase. At this point, A does not hesitate, verbally or ideationally. He self-assuredly asserts, "The thing to decide is. . . ."

Tolerance for any dissenting opinion is not apparent in the language choices of any of these commitments. The comment implying "This is my opinion but I could be wrong," which was characteristic of the orientation phase, becomes, in the conflict phase, the comment indicating "This is my opinion and it is correct." C also asserts, "You have to consider him . . ." and B asserts, "You have to give some criteria. You can't just say . . ." These stylistic characteristics of the communicative acts implicitly *compel* the responding group members into a for-or-against choice. Neutral opinions are no longer acceptable. The language used during the interaction of the conflict phase forces the members to express definite opinions. Essentially stylistic features of the interaction itself force members into conflict or ideas.

Member A is now clearly identified as a spokesman for the plaintiff, and B and C appear to be spokesmen for the defendant. The next excerpt from group interaction involves a discussion of the same decision proposal and illustrates more vividly the ideational division of the group members:

C: Most people, I think, would make sure that the other side was clear for him to go. I think it would be reasonably prudent to take a glance over there to make sure that the guy was still signaling you on.

A: I don't think you can trust another person. It's a fact that . . . I don't know if you've ever traveled on the highway behind a semitrailer . . . You're following, and semitrailers don't usually go as fast as you would like or necessarily the speed limit. You're back of the semitrailer. You keep swinging out to see if you can pass. You see the driver wave his arm out like this. That's illegal. You can't use this as evidence in court that it was safe to pass the truck.

C: We can't consider that. We judge on the testimony we heard in court today and yesterday.

D: That's kind of irrelevant.

A: But the truck driver said it was safe to pass just like this guy in court said.

D: It is the custom on the highway, illegal or not, for big trucks to be courteous enough to flick on and off their lights when it's safe for the guy behind him to pass.

A: How long has it been since you have traveled on the highway?

D: Last fall.

A: Well, most of them don't do it anymore. Besides, if this guy was a reasonable man, he would have wanted to find out for himself. Not just take another guy's word for it.

C: We shouldn't take in anything that we didn't hear in court.

A: But this pertains to what we heard in the courtroom. If he was a reasonable man, he wouldn't have taken this driver's word for it that he should go.

C: How many people agree with you on that statement? I don't, for one.

D: I don't.

B: I would take the driver's word for it.

A: No, you wouldn't.

C: A reasonable person would.

The dissident *A* is fighting a losing battle to have the group consider his analogy regarding highway driving. His antagonists continue to be *B* and *C*. These three members engage in a heated verbal exchange over this issue.

During the conflict phase, group members know which members are on which side in the conflict over ideas and feel fewer inhibitions regarding the necessity for social facilitation. Disagreement is not only definite; it is vehement. Comments such as "Oh, come on now!" and "No, you wouldn't!" are quite common during the conflict phase. In fact, some comments are virtual insults and certainly not intended to win close friends. The question, "Do you consider yourself reasonable?" may be insulting; but *C*'s final comment in the excerpt above, "A reasonable person would," is more than insulting. In the context of this interaction, that comment is tantamount to character assassination.

At this point, *A* appears to be the only member of the group who favors the plaintiff's side in the civil case. Member *D*, not very active in earlier interaction during orientation, sides against *A* on this issue. But *D*'s comments don't appear to be as vehement as *B*'s and *C*'s opposition. Note that *D* tones down his charge of irrelevance by saying, "That's kind of irrelevant," while *C* flatly assets, "We can't consider that." Later *D* dispassionately appeals to *A*'s reason about "custom" and disregards the issue of its legality. In fact, *D* continues to discuss the issue as though it were relevant.

Eventually *D* disagrees with *A* on this issue, but his disagreement is clearly not equivalent in tone, language, or manner to the disagreement of *B* and *C*. The next excerpt from the conflict phase casts more light on the role *D* plays in this second phase of decision emergence.

A: Do you think our Roger Adams testified truthfully on the stand?
D: I think he fudged a bit.
A: I do, too. That was my opinion. I realize that these are fixed situations, but let's pretend that it isn't. I mean, I think that he was trying to get himself out of a bad situation . . . as any normal person would, I suppose.
C: But the three witnesses for the defense—they all collaborated [sic] his testimony perfectly.
A: Which ones?
C: All three for the defense.
B: The guy that waved him on, the girl . . .
D: That is not strictly true, because the girl was a little off.
A: One person said that he stopped for one or two seconds and then shot out. Another one said he was there for half a minute. They didn't collaborate [sic] on that.
E: But one of them was watching him, and the other one was driving his own car and getting ready to go. They collaborate [sic] on the things that were important, though.
A: I can't see how you can say that. They didn't collaborate [sic] at all. Time was just one of the factors they didn't agree on.

Member *A* seems to have procured a lieutenant in *D*. Both are now identified with the plaintiff, while *B* and *C* continue to favor the defendant. One of the two most infrequent contributors to the group interaction, member *E*, identifies himself with the defendant in the excerpt above. Hence, two coalitions appear to be developing in this second phase of the group decision-making process. *A* and *D* form one coalition, which favors the plaintiff. *B*, *C*, and probably *E* are members of the other coalition, which favors the defendant. Only member *F* remains clearly outside either coalition.

This jury is composed of six members. The sixth member, *F*, is still to be heard from in the excerpts taken from the group interaction. He has contributed to the group interaction sparingly, and his participation during the conflict phase is virtually nonexistent.

One can probably speculate that *F*'s withdrawal from group participation results from a feeling of discomfort brought on by the vehement substantive conflict over ideas during this phase. He is aware of his low status in the group, which may or may not be of his own volition. Whether from apathy toward the group's purpose or from a fear of social conflict, *F* has chosen to withdraw from group interaction rather than take a stand and join one of the coalitions involved in social conflict over ideas.

In terms of the developing status hierarchy in the emergent group setting, leader-contenders are clearly emerging during this conflict phase (see Chapter 7). Member *A* is the most vehement spokesman for the "plaintiff's coalition." Member *C*, or possibly member *B*, seems to represent the strongest leader-contender for the "defendant's coalition." The conflict over substantive issues is undoubtedly relevant to the contention over the leadership roles too. But member *A*, the leader-contender for the coalition opposed to the decision that will ultimately achieve group consensus, will not remain in active contention for leadership much longer. As a member who has committed himself to a position opposing the consensus decision, his bid for leadership is doomed.

Emergence   Following the transition to the emergence phase, the substantive conflict between the members begins to dissipate, as illustrated in a later excerpt taken from the group's interaction:

A: Let me ask one more question. Do you think Derby the plaintiff was in the crosswalk?

D: I don't think so.

C: No, I don't. I don't think that has too much to do with it, though.

D: I agree.

C: I know there are some statutes about the crosswalk, but I mean the fact that he was in . . . I don't know. That might be kind of important.

D: He was on the roadway is really the issue.

C: I don't think it really happened exactly the way the defendant described it. I think he embellished it a little toward his side. I think it happened close enough to it, though.

F: As far as that goes, Derby may have his own story too. I mean each would be looking out for himself. That's only natural.

D: Of course you are going to get this in any situation.

F: That's just it. Both of them. You can't use the two prime subjects. You have to try and go on the witnesses. Of course they are witnesses, too, and you have to consider them. And they are important, too, but . . .

Member *A* has initiated another proposal for consideration, but his initiating statement expresses an ambiguous opinion toward it. He uses simple and straight-forward language without argument. The communicative acts in response to his proposal emphasize the irrelevance of his proposal rather than attempt to deny its factual nature. During the conflict phase, the responses to such a proposal would probably have been an intense denial and consequently an additional substantive conflict. In the emergence phase, though, the conflict over issues is muted.

In the second phase, the members hammered out the issues and proposals they felt were important to getting their task accomplished. But their
response to a new issue in the emergence phase is to dismiss it as irrelevant
rather than to engage in additional conflict.

The level of social tension (see Chapter 2) seems to be appreciably lower
during the emergence phase. Member C is now much more tolerant of A's
opinions and feelings, as illustrated in the last excerpt. He admits to the
possibility that the issue raised by member A "might be kind of important."
He even goes so far as to concede that the defendant "embellished" his
testimony, an admission he would never have made in the conflict phase.

The emerging decision becomes progressively clearer during the emergence phase, and all members seem to sense the direction the group has
taken. Even F joins the interaction, jumping on the bandwagon to offer his
opinion in support of the defendant. When the other members don't whole-
heartedly welcome his offer to join their side, F begins to flounder in his
comments and becomes extremely ambiguous and vague in his comments.
His final remark is a classic example of ambiguity. At any rate, the decision
becomes increasingly evident, and even F knows it.

The conflict over substantive issues characterizing the conflict phase
moderates during the emergence phase. Both A and D ameliorate their
dissent from the decision proposals favoring the defendant. For example,
while A vehemently and tenaciously expressed his dissenting view during the
conflict phase, he expresses only ambiguous opinions without much tenacity
during the emergence phase. The following excerpt clearly illustrates this
change in A's verbal behavior.

A: I just wondered. Maybe this isn't really relevant, but I never really understood exactly where the point of impact was. Not in relation to the car, but
in relation to the street. How far out from the curb he was. It appeared
from the drawing and three or four witnesses that it was in the lane
closest to the curb that Derby stepped off of. If this is the case, Adams
made an illegal left turn. Of course, I might be mistaken.

C: Yeah, Right.

B: I think it was right in the middle.

C: Was it in the middle?

D: It was probably about twenty feet off. That might be closest to this curb.

E: He said he was about eleven feet off the curb, but he also put him closer to
the middle.

A: If it was closer to the curb than it was to the intersection, it wasn't an illegal
left turn. But it might have been eleven feet this way, and that would
have been an illegal turn.

D: Eleven feet puts it right about in the middle. No illegal left turn.

C: Remember he's turning, so he's got to come a little bit into the other lane
on the turn.

D: Well, not necessarily.

C: It's pretty hard not to, with at least his front bumper.

B: It's pretty close, but he was probably all right on his turn. If he was out eleven feet, he was right there in the middle.

D: In that case he was only . . . He's not negligent.

A: This is irrelevant, then.

C: I don't think it's possible to hit him in the middle. I don't think that it is physically possible.

A: No. He did make a wrong turn, but he wasn't completely out of his lane from where he should have been.

C: He was probably wrong in not watching exactly as he was turning. But I don't think it was too far away to be reasonable.

Another last-ditch effort by *A* to advocate the plaintiff's side in the discussion: Did the defendant make an illegal left turn? But *A* fails to raise many doubts concerning what is becoming increasingly apparent as the consensus decision. But the strength and tenacity of *A*'s argumentativeness have dissipated. He initiates his proposal with reluctant ambiguity. Note his apologetic phrases, which appear throughout his contributions—"I just wondered. Maybe this isn't really relevant," "It appeared . . ." "If this is the case . . ." and the final "Of course, I might be mistaken."

During the ensuing discussion, *A* contributes another ambiguous argument indicating only the possibility—not even the probability—that the defendant was negligent in making an illegal left turn. Compared with his self-assured stance in the conflict phase, *A* has moderated his attitude considerably. He does not express certainty about any opinion he expresses in the emergence phase. He qualifies nearly everything with ambiguous language, such as "if" and "might." He resigns himself to losing the fight over this issue. In fact, he doesn't even try very hard to win it. He offers his resigned statement of capitulation, "This is irrelevant, then," even before the other members have completely rejected it. In fact, *C* again expresses amazing tolerance for *A*'s proposal and once more appears to give it serious consideration before he rejects it. *A* has evidently succumbed to the apparent consensus decision. *C* apparently knows it and is softening the blow somewhat. *C* is definitely the leading contender for group leader, and he is willing to accept *A* as a high-status member whose opinions are worthy of consideration.

The two coalitions of the conflict phase also appear to dissipate during the emergence phase. Members of opposing coalitions responded to their "opponents" with open hostility and even contempt in the conflict phase, but they now respond with active rational consideration. The prime example of this change is illustrated by *C*'s comments. He preferred to insult *A* during the conflict phase as a response to *A*'s position favoring the plaintiff. But, during the emergence phase, *C* considers *A*'s proposal, admits to its potential significance and credibility, and then rejects it.

Again, the basis for rejecting proposals favoring the plaintiff's case is irrelevance. Members argued against proposals during the conflict phase on the basis of their truth or falsity, but the basic issue on which members typically evaluate proposals in the emergence phase seems to be relevance.

Reinforcement   In the reinforcement phase, decisions have completed the process of emergence. Interaction during this final phase of the group process confirms decisions already made and develops the members' commitment, or consensus, toward those decisions. The following excerpt appears very early in the reinforcement phase:

E: Everybody saw the car coming.

B: Besides that, he said his lights were on.

C: His turn signal was on. It was obvious that he was coming. That would make it all the more easier [sic] to see the car coming.

D: Practically everybody saw that car coming. His lights turning.

E: That guy that was on the sidewalk . . . He saw all this traffic, and he also saw Adams coming. That's why he didn't go. Why did Derby go? He has to be at some fault.

C: I feel sorry for him, and I'd like to help him out, but I just don't think I can.

D: I agree.

B: You can't base it on an emotion . . .

D: Of course not.

C: I don't think we should take into any account what they told us at the beginning, either—about Adams being a drunkard and that.

B: No. Don't even mention that.

F: No. Don't worry about it.

C: No.

Members *B, C, D,* and *E* all express agreement with the decision proposal that Derby, the defendant, was guilty of contributory negligence. They not only agree with one another, but they provide superfluous evidence to support their agreement. Interaction consistently includes statement after statement expressing agreement with the one before it.

The major dissenter, *A,* is conspicuously absent from the previous interaction. But his former lieutenant, *D,* has certainly joined the other coalition. Even *F* is growing bolder and bolder with his comments, now that absolutely no doubt remains regarding the decision made by the group. As the group's interaction draws to a close, *A* leaves no doubt as to his completely modified position:

A: I guess I'd have to say that it was both their faults.

C: I say it is both their faults.

A: Evidently it probably is.

B: Derby really never should have stepped off the curb.

D: Right.

E: And there he was out eleven feet already, and he was trying to avoid another oncoming car. That's just plain stupid.

F: When you step off the curb, you know you are taking chances. You have to stay on your toes.

A: Well, he obviously didn't see him turn. But he should have.

F: He was right in front of him. He should have seen him turn.

D: Right. He must have been looking someplace else.

A: I think Derby stepped off the curb, started walking, and was halfway through the first lane when this guy started to make his turn. It doesn't take long for all this to happen. Only a few seconds.

C: The plaintiff was making some kind of inference that Adams was going excessively fast across the turn. I don't think that's really possible.

D: No.

B: How fast can you take a turn without crashing into the corner or something?

D: Yeah. When you're accelerating, you still aren't going more than nine or ten miles per hour.

C: The average turn is about six miles per hour, maybe a little faster, but that isn't excessively fast.

B: It varies if he was trying to beat this other car.

C: But he couldn't have been going even fifteen miles around a turn.

D: If you do, you're pulling out like a sports car.

C: If you have good cornering, you'll probably make it. If you don't, you might not.

A: We agree unanimously right now that is both their faults.
   (A chorus of "Yeah!")

A: It was both their faults. There is nothing more to do, then.

E: I would say that it was mutual negligence—more Derby's fault.

F: I say it is all Derby's fault.

A: You say all Derby's fault?

F: Yes.

A: I think it is more Adams's fault. But both are still negligent.

C: Okay. Then it's unanimous.

F: I say that Derby was completely at fault. He shouldn't even be suing.

C: You mean that Adams should be suing?

F: Right.

A: There are two possibilities on this sheet. Let me read them both. "Number 1: We, the jury, find in favor of the plaintiff and against the defendant and assess damages to the sum of . . ." In other words, we think it was Adams's fault, and Derby should pay.

C: Throw that one out.

A: Okay. We'll throw that one out. "Number 2: We, the jury, find in favor of the defendant and against . . ." In other words, if they think it is more Derby's fault.

D: No. Just the plaintiff.

C: In favor of the defendant legally means it isn't the plaintiff. It doesn't mean that the defendant can claim damages. It just means that the suit has been dropped.

B: We find in favor of the defendant.

C: Yes.

A: That's how we do it, then.

B: Write "Contributory negligence."

D: We are all decided.

C: Unanimous decision. No dissenters.

Throughout these final moments of group interaction, there is a pervading spirit of harmony and unity. All members agree, and everyone knows that all members agree. But they continue to discuss the decision while verbally slapping each other on the back, even to the point of initiating another straw-man decision proposal. Three of the members join in verbally demolishing the plaintiff's agrument concerning Adams's excessive speed.

Meanwhile, A firmly commits himself to the position that Derby is also at fault. His language still includes traces of reluctance. But his expression of agreement is completely understandable, given his earlier attitude of vehement opposition during the conflict phase. He closes his comments in the language of willing reluctance with such statements as "I guess I'd have to say . . ." and "Evidently it probably is." Nevertheless, he is firmly committed to the consensus decision.

The nonparticipant in the conflict phase, F, is caught up in the spirit of consensus, and he overreacts to the obvious consensus decision. He goes so far as to assess 100 percent negligence to the plaintiff. Not even members B and C want to go this far. They don't pay too much attention to F's Johnny-come-lately enthusiasm. They have made their decision, and they have reinforced it.

To avoid any doubts, and probably in deference to A's rationale for making the decision unanimous, B suggests that the group explain to the court that the basis for its decision was "contributory negligence." The addition of the members' rationale is superfluous, but they do it anyway. The final comments allude to the written record, which they return to officials of the mock court, confirming their consensus decision.

Summary The process of group decision making thus progresses through four phases of interaction—orientation, conflict, emergence, and reinforcement. The decisional process, closely allied with characteristics of the social dimension reflecting the interdependent relationship of the two dimensions, is a cumulative and cyclic process. Group members anchor their interaction to tentative decision proposals that lead to and culminate in consensus, or final group decisions.

Excerpts from an actual group's interaction reflect the "flavor" of the discussion and the importance of stylistic features of the language and changes in individual members' attitudes as their group progresses toward consensus. Although the four phases seem to be clearly separate in the excerpted interaction from each of the four phases, the transitions between phases are in reality quite gradual and not nearly as dramatic as they appear in selected excerpts. This, then, is the process of group decision making in action.

IMPROVING EFFECTIVENESS IN GROUPS

Perhaps our most important goal in this book is to help you improve your performance in groups. By now you have read Chapter 6 and the first part of this chapter and should have a good understanding of communication and the group process. At least you should understand that groups and communication are complex processes. This is a first step toward improving effectiveness. But becoming really effective in groups takes time, and there are no easy answers. We will present many issues and recommendations for improving communication in groups, but there is still no simple formula for success. You might think that because you communicate every day, all this practice would make you an effective communicator. Such an expectation is quite false. On the contrary, most people are not very effective communicators and do little more than practice bad habits.

But you can improve your communication with understanding, knowledge, and practice. Compare your communicative health to your personal health. You certainly do not think of health in taking medicines when you get sick. Health is living normally from day to day. And if you know and understand your biological processes, you will know what to eat, what to wear, what activities to perform, what to avoid, and so forth. So it is with communication. The healthy communicator does not rush around seeking miracle cures. Rather, he or she learns about communication and what behaviors are most appropriate. Beware of books and people who sell "cures" for ailing groups and "vitamin supplements" for successful communication. Our position here is very clear: It is possible to improve your communication and group behavior, but not by slavishly and uncritically applying all sorts of tricks and techniques.

PRINCIPLES OF EFFECTIVENESS

Effectiveness comes with knowledge and practice. It is true that "practice makes perfect," but only when the practice is based on understanding. More experiences and a greater variety of group experiences will lead to more effective group participation. You must have knowledge and experience. Reading a book about how to shoot a basketball will not do much for your shooting. You must practice. A book will provide you with indispensable knowledge about chess, but it will not make you an expert. The same is true of communication. Reading a book and never participating in groups will not do much for your skill in groups; and, conversely, participating in groups without the requisite knowledge and understanding will also place you at a disadvantage.

The principles of effectiveness that follow are designed to capitalize on the interdependence between knowledge and experience. We present these principles in three areas—individual attitudinal factors, interpersonal factors, and group factors.

IMPROVING EFFECTIVENESS: ATTITUDINAL FACTORS

Probably the first place to begin the search for improvement of effectiveness is with oneself—the individual group member. Because every person is, in some respects, a unique human being, it is difficult to discuss the idiosyncracies of the members of any decision-making group. On the other hand, some general principles related to the attitudes and values that are typical of members of effective groups can be isolated.

Attitudes toward the Group

Your psychological orientation to the group and to other group members is very important to the success and effectiveness of group decision making. Rarely do such attitudes exist before the formation of the group, however. Rather, members develop a certain orientation to the group and to other members during the process of group development. If a member does possess an attitude before the group is formed, an attitude conducive to effective group process, this orientation is probably one of open-mindedness. That is, the member enters the initial group meetings without prematurely having decided whether the group experience will be undesirable. This state of open-mindedness will also involve a considerable amount of interpersonal sensitivity in which the member is open to the beliefs and feelings of others. Such an interpersonal sensitivity persists even though the beliefs and ideas of the others are quite dissimilar to those of the interpersonally sensitive member.

We have consistently stressed the principle of commitment in the sense of group consensus and cohesiveness. Individual members who are committed to the group experience a strong feeling of loyalty to it. That is, members believe in the potential effectiveness of the group process to the extent that they will sublimate their own goals in favor of those of the group. Commitment requires a belief that the group process will fulfill the goals of the individual and that group membership will provide benefits important to the individual.

With the attitude of commitment toward the group comes a feeling of responsibility. The committed group member is willing to expend time and energy for the benefit of the group. Often members of classroom groups will excuse themselves from contributing very much to the group effort by citing other considerations (for example, the student has a part-time job, time is required for other classes, the class is not the student's major, or only three credits will be earned in the class). But the group member, if committed, feels a sense of responsibility and will find the time and expend the effort for the group.

Attitudes toward Interaction

A member who is committed to the group is never a silent member. Regardless of any personality traits (such as shyness or apprehension), the committed group member simply cannot remain a low participant. Indeed, such members find that they cannot remain silent on issues that confront the group, even though outside the group the person may remain silent even when being negatively evaluated as an individual. Group loyalty is typically stronger in affecting the amount of interaction of individual members than other aspects of the individual's own self.

A classroom group of a few years ago exemplifies the problem of the uncommitted member whose attitude toward the group carries over into his or her participation in the group interaction. This particular group was engaged in discussing the current practice of evaluating the courses and instructors in the university. The group suffered from a woefully inadequate amount of information concerning the topic, and this inadequacy was reflected in its report of its task accomplishments. Knowing that the student association of the university was performing a lengthy and comprehensive analysis of the evaluation forms and recognizing that one of the group members was involved in the department's student advisory committee, we asked him whether he was aware of the universitywide study of course-evaluation techniques. His reply went something like this: "Of course I know about it. But this bunch of turkeys in this group wouldn't know what to do with the information, anyway. They already had their minds made up. I thought I would just let them hang themselves." Only a member with a very low level of commitment to the group would have expressed an attitude of so little responsibility and remained so inactive in the group's interaction.

Chapter 6 discussed the tendency of successful groups to engage in considerable disagreement and social conflict over task-oriented issues. Although conflict can be considered an effective format for the critical testing of ideas, the willingness of the individual members to engage in conflict may be more important to the effectiveness of group decision making. Why would anyone engage in conflict interaction and run the risk of being wrong unless one is concerned about the group and its successful outcome? For most people, argument with friends or peers is painful and socially uncomfortable. But for conflict to exist and to result in successful task performance, group members must be willing to participate in conflict. For this reason we normally think of the cohesive group as a group that is not afraid to experience conflict, to overcome conflict, and to remain cohesive despite the potentially disruptive influence of conflict.

With a social climate that is less conducive to expressing conflict, members feel inhibited. Consequently, the level of cohesiveness in that group and its ultimate effectiveness in performing its decision-making task suffer. The committed member is thus willing not only to express his or her own point of view but also to encourage the expression of other viewpoints. The result is a free and open attitude toward group interaction. Unruly? Yes. Disruptive? Potentially. But more important, such attitudes toward interaction lead to more effective communication and group decision making.

Creativity

Although there is obviously a point of diminishing returns, the greater the volume of ideas and decision proposals that members contribute during group interaction, the higher the quality of consensus decisions. Also, leaders initiate a large number of themes during group interaction, as we saw in Chapter 7. Each of these two findings implies that one ingredient of communicative effectiveness is creativity. As a participant in group decision making, then, you would be well advised to increase your creative capacity. Let your mind go. Give your imagination a free rein. No relevant idea should be considered too irrational or too farfetched. The best advice for developing creativity is not to stifle the formation of ideas. Be a divergent thinker (see Chapter 6).

Certainly groups do not accept all ideas that members contribute during group interaction. In fact, the more ideas the members contribute, the more ideas the group will reject. Indeed, the period of idea testing during group interaction, particularly during the conflict phase, involves the rejection of many decision proposals. But this is the period during which members should be encouraged to contribute new ideas too.

Members who do not fully comprehend the nature of the group process will probably consider the group's rejection of their ideas a rejection of their selves, a rejection of their value as group members. Consequently, such members tend to inhibit their creative impulses, and this restraint leads to their contributing fewer ideas. Brainstorming techniques, which have been devised to account for this human tendency, do not allow brainstorming members to respond critically to any contributed idea despite its apparent irrelevance. Effective group members, on the other hand, know in advance that the other group members will reject many of their ideas, but this knowledge does not inhibit their creativity. They continue to introduce new and different proposals for group consideration. These members probably suffer psychologically from the group's rejection of their ideas, too, but their creativity does not suffer as a result.

Actually, the slowness of the group process and the inherent start-and-stop process of modifying decisions encourage creativity from group members. Each member has the time and the opportunity to mull over his or her own ideas and the ideas of others and to develop new insights. Experts in creativity consider the incubation period essential to the creative process.

The phases of group decision making suggest the importance of timing. New and different proposals benefit the group efforts most during the orientation and conflict phases. During these early stages of group interaction, the creativity of members in devising new and different ideas should be at a maximum. During the emergence phase, members should confine their creativity to reformulating and combining previously discussed proposals. During the reinforcement phase, creativity in any form is definitely not an asset to the group process, but a liability.

Criticism

A very normal and understandable human tendency of inexperienced group members is to avoid criticism of, and conflict with, other members. Normally, no one wants to run the risk of hurting another person's feelings. Inexperienced group members tend to avoid criticism for fear of harming the developing feeling of groupness. All of us have been taught from childhood that courtesy and tact are infinitely superior to rudeness and boorishness. So we examine an atrocious painting on our neighbor's wall and call it "interesting." We may suffer through a boring party, but we will invariably tell the host and hostess as we leave that we had a great time. Certainly, effective group decision making does not require that we rid ourselves of good manners and respect for others during group decision making.

Group decision making is in some respects a unique social situation. What we would consider courtesy and tact in one situation is tantamount to ineffectiveness and avoidance of social problems during group decision making. The fear of hurting the feelings of others and suppressing realistic opinions characterize members of a group with rather low cohesiveness. Criticism and conflict are typical norms of a highly cohesive group. In fact, group decision making may not be so unique after all. For instance, we rarely if ever have arguments with acquaintances, but we argue vehemently and say whatever we feel with our very close friends. Knowing that you can be honest with one another is knowing you are in the company of good friends.

The amount of criticism is irrelevant to the group process, but the timing of criticism is again all-important. Criticism in the wrong place at the wrong time is as harmful to the group process as no criticism at all. Let yourself go in exercising all your critical faculties during the conflict phase. At other times, you should probably control your critical impulses and use them sparingly.

Basic to the principle of criticism during group decision making is the avoidance of neutrality. It is absolutely impossible to remain neutral and be an effective participant during group interaction. High-status members are invariably dynamic contributors who take stands and defend them. Other members consider these stands helpful to the group's performance of its task. A "mugwump" is destined to be a low contributor and an ineffective group member. Group interaction usually compels members to speak out on issues and assume an argumentative stance. (The opening section of this chapter illustrated how the very language used in a comment by one or another member often forces the other members into taking a stand during the conflict phase of group decision making.) A neutral member is usually perceived to be wishy-washy and is generally peripheral to the action of group decision making.

One important ingredient of group decision making and one of its principal advantages over individual decision making is the process of testing ideas. Such idea testing among multiple sources of criticism results in higher-quality decisions when high social acceptance is a key criterion of decisional quality. This process of socially testing ideas is the principle behind the "free and open marketplace of ideas," in which criticism is absolutely essential. During idea testing, the group norm should encourage as much criticism as possible, both in the amount and the diversity of that criticism. Effective group members are not necessarily tactless but are highly critical of others' ideas as well as of their own.

The following are some tips for improving your critical effectiveness in groups; these are questions you can ask yourself or the group to ensure that the group exercises the best judgment possible:

1. How well are the members using communication skills to discuss issues? Do they focus on information? What is their vocabulary, word selection, and phrasing like?
2. What is the quality of the information? Are there ample data, evidence, and facts? Has this information been tested and discussed?
3. What is the social climate like? Is the group cohesive, and why or why not? Can the group disagree without serious tension? Do the members reward one another? Are the interpersonal relations good? Do the members share an identity?
4. How good are the group's work norms? Are the members committed to the task? Do they complete assignments? Do they work to think creatively about problems? Do they follow procedures outlined by the group?
5. How effective is the leadership? Is the leader skillful in procedural matters, such as agendas, meeting schedules, and resources? Does the leader keep things on track? Does he or she manage conflict skillfully? Does the leader summarize, provide useful information, and generally structure the group?

IMPROVING EFFECTIVENESS: INTERPERSONAL FACTORS

By first discussing attitudinal factors and now interpersonal factors of communicative effectiveness, we do not imply that these factors are clearly separable. Just as a person's attitudes or psychological orientations will affect that person's participation in decision-making interaction, so also will one's interaction with others affect one's orientations and attitudes. Improving one's effectiveness in communication is plainly an attitudinal, as well as an interpersonal, phenomenon.

Active Verbal Participation

It should be obvious that effective group decision making is correlated with the active verbal participation of the members. In other words, the effective participant actively participates verbally during group interaction.

The silent member does little to benefit the process of group decision making. Moreover, contributing only infrequently to the group's interaction does not significantly benefit the individual member. Bench warmers on a football team do not contribute much to the team's success or to the development of their own abilities. Spectating is not playing. One learns to play the game by playing it. The bench warmer may have little choice about getting to play, but the group member is silent solely of his or her own volition.

Active verbal participation does not imply equal participation by all members. Obviously, equal participation is not only abnormal and impossible, but also not desirable. The contributions of some members are more valuable than those of others. The more capable members should participate more. Abilities and expertise vary among the members. Each member should seek during group interaction to participate actively, but not necessarily equally, with every other member.

Also, active verbal participation does not imply that any member should attempt to monopolize the discussion or control the group interaction. Active participation implies frequent contributions, but not necessarily lengthy ones. The knowledgeable and verbally active member contributes brief comments but does so without inhibition. The first general principle for increasing one's communicative effectiveness in group decision making may seem overly obvious but is nevertheless essential: The effective communicator has something to say and says it.

Communication Skills

There exists an old and hackneyed controversy among authorities in communication. The controversy dates back to ancient Greece, centuries before Christ, and is heard even today. It concerns the relative importance of *content* and *delivery* in the effectiveness of communication. Which is more important for effective communication: what is said or how it is said? Most authorities today consider the controversy naive and largely incomplete. Not only is the content of a message inseparable from its delivery, but the communicative process includes additional and highly significant elements that the controversy ignores.

First of all, the value of an expressed idea is determined in part by the manner in which it is presented. A skillful presentation affects the perceived importance of the message. Only the most naive student of human communication would argue that an idea has intrinsic worth apart from its use in the communicative situation and its expression within the sequence of communicative acts. The evidence that communication skills do affect the message content is virtually indisputable.

Specific characteristics of communication skills are rather unclear. Certainly the skillful communicator is fluent, articulate, and dynamic in the conversational situation. Communication skills also involve a knowledge and understanding of the communicative process and the ability to be flexible, adapting to the demands of the social system and the situation. Without such knowledge and adaptive ability, the communicator is perceived to be not so much fluent and articulate as merely glib. The stereotyped used-car salesperson, for example, is considered glib and smooth, but these are negative characteristics, while skill is generally considered a positive attribute.

Learning communication skills is not at all similar to learning the skill of hitting a baseball or playing a trumpet. These kinds of motor skills are based on mastering techniques and performing those techniques as an individual. Communication, however, never occurs in isolation, but always in a social system with the interconnected communicative behaviors of other persons. The ability to analyze the other person and the situation and to be perceived as articulate and dynamic requires a thorough knowledge of the communicative process and a great deal of hard work. Certainly, experience and practice in many and varied communicative situations are essential for developing communication skills. And that experience always occurs in the presence of other people—the complex social system.

It would be pretty silly, and impossible, to attempt a very complete list or survey of all the communication skills useful to group members. In fact, this entire book is devoted to communication skills in groups. But in the spirit of working with a small and manageable set of principles that can help you most efficiently, we present the following as fundamental communication skills you can develop.

Language Strengthening   Most of the meaning in messages is carried by language—words and their use. People use language to communicate clearly, but they also use it to hide, deceive, and manipulate others. Some in the group will use technical or formal language to impress others by sounding as if they are knowledgeable. In the opening section of this chapter we saw how language varied with the stages of group development; some language was nice and polite, and at other times the language became intense and strident. Group members who do not have sufficiently developed language skills usually have trouble expressing ideas. For instance, listen to the following group member try to explain the distinction between two ideas:

SCOTT: Ah, you know, they just aren't the same thing. I mean one is not the same as the other. They don't really go together because they do different things.

Scott "feels" that two ideas are different, but he cannot find the words to express the differences.

The best way to improve is to pay attention to language. Read widely and listen to how people use words. Develop good habits, such as always using a dictionary, thinking about words, and taking the time to learn the meaning and use for new words. This all sounds simple, but it is fundamental to good communication. Your experiences in groups and with other people rely on meaning. And the only way to express specific and finer shades of meaning is to have the proper vocabulary. You must also think about the relationship between words and context. It might be appropriate to use slang or a vulgar word with your best friends, but not at work or in your group meetings. Try to use language that "fits" with the people around you.

Special Language   As a communicator you are most concerned with conveying an idea. To do this well, you need many types of words at your disposal. Most words have a straightforward dictionary meaning, the meaning that any native language user would associate with the word, but these words can also have special meanings that are highly personal or individualistic. Say that you were irritated at a group member and called the person "handicapped." There is a simple dictionary definition of this word, but it also carries extra meaning. It might be highly offensive to someone. How would you like to find out that the person had a handicapped family member!

In addition to the special meanings carried by words, there is an entire class of words called jargon. *Jargon* is the specialized language of a particular group of people who have training or experience in common. A group of doctors would use jargon to discuss a medical problem among themselves. But it would not be very good communication to use jargon with a patient who did not understand the language. There is nothing wrong with jargon if the others involved in the communication understand the terms; indeed, learning the language, or the jargon, is part of becoming a specialist or an expert in some area. Jargon can be quite useful when everyone understands it because jargon has specific meaning that helps avoid confusion.

The Ladder of Abstraction   All language moves from concrete to abstract. Jane might refer to her "1989 Honda Accord" and we would know that she was talking about a very specific car. If she talked about "Honda Accords," that would be a little more abstract, because it could refer to any Honda Accord. The word "car" would be even more abstract. Group members should try to communicate as concretely as possible, for abstraction usually leads to confusion. If the group wanted to talk about "fuel economy," there would be a considerable difference between talking about fuel economy in all cars and talking about fuel economy in the 1989 Honda Accord. The latter is much more concrete and manageable.

Again, there is nothing "wrong" with abstract language. Sometimes it is perfectly communicative. In Chapter 3 we referred to Eisenberg's (1984) claim that some ambiguity and abstraction can be good for the group. Abstract language does not always lead to confusion. But generally it is best to start with concrete language. As the group develops and people adjust to one another and their language, it becomes easier to use abstract language effectively.

Message Functions   The messages uttered by individuals perform various functions. A *message function* is the action that the message performs. In

Chapter 6 and Appendix 1 you will find a discussion of various interaction-analysis schemes, such as Ellis's relational coding schemes and Fisher's system for tracking decision development. These are attempts to capture the functions of messages. For example, a group member might say, "Sixty-five percent of property taxes are used to fund public schools." This utterance would function as a statement that *gives information*. Other statements might be composed of completely different content and subject matter but still function to give information.

You must learn to recognize what people are *doing* with their language. Are they giving information, stating opinions, disagreeing, acting friendly, or what? The function of a message is not always apparent. If a father sees a son's shirt on the floor and asks, "Is that your shirt on the floor?" he may not be asking a genuine question. The utterance may function to mean "Pick up that shirt and put it on a hanger!" Group members often say things indirectly. The ability to recognize message functions improves as groups and relationships develop.

Supportive Communication

Gibb (1961) has discussed two different "climates" of communication that develop because of communicative actions performed by interactants. These communication climates include *defensive* communication and *supportive* communication. While a defensive climate results from defensive communicative behaviors, a characteristic of such a climate is a reduction of effectiveness due to an erosion of interpersonal trust and groupness. Gibb strongly suggests that the most effective communication is that occurring in a supportive climate and resulting from supportive communicative actions.

Characteristic of defensive communication are behaviors that both threaten the other person and originate from a perceived threat from the other person. Such defensive behaviors include personal evaluation, attempts to control, and behaviors that appear to convey an attitude of superiority or extreme certainty of belief. Generally speaking, defensive communication tends to be perceived as judgmental, manipulative, insincere, or deceptive. Being defensive oneself tends to arouse defensiveness in the other person (reciprocity at work) and results in lowered effectiveness of group interaction.

Supportive communication generally proceeds from one person's feeling of empathy with another. Supportive communication is other-directed or problem-oriented to the extent that someone who communicates supportively is genuine, sincere, honest, and spontaneous. Supportive communication is characterized by actions that do not seek to evaluate others, although supportive communication could evaluate a problem or issue. Defensive communication results when evaluative comments appear to be directed toward the person rather than the issue.

Defensive communication typically involves little social risk, but supportive communication involves high risk. Individuals create a climate of mutual trust and respect. Although status differences will occur in the group (based on power, ability, etc.), individual members supportively communicating with one another appear to attach little importance to these differences. Group members thus generate considerable cohesiveness and consider themselves unified as a group even with the presence of a status hierarchy. To recognize leadership and status in an informal group with a supportive climate is not to disrupt the sense of groupness that members feel.

Attempting to maintain a clear distinction between attitudinal and interpersonal factors of communicative effectiveness becomes virtually impossible when discussing defensive and supportive communicative actions. Supportive acts create a climate of mutual trust and are tantamount to each person's trusting the other and perceiving that this trust is reciprocated by the other. Supportive communication is consistent with a feeling or attitude of mutual support on the part of each member. Conversely, this feeling of mutual trust develops as a result of the members' supportive communicative behaviors. We are again faced with the dilemma of the chicken or the egg. Which came first—the *feeling* of trust or the trusting *behavior*? The supportive communicative *climate* or the supportive communicative *behavior*? The answer, of course, is that they develop together. One is as much a result of the other as it is the cause.

Responding to Others

The tendency to emphasize the pragmatic perspective of human communication in previous chapters may have led to an implication that the actions performed by individual members are the key elements in the group decision-making process. Actually, the actions of each individual person are less significant than the *inter*actions among individuals. That is, one person's action may always be characterized as a response to the action of another person. Treating each action as a response to a previous action allows for the development of some general principles on how to respond to others. These principles may be used as guidelines in determining how one should respond to others in the interactive setting of group decision making. In any case, this view of communication involves thinking of communicative acts as always directed toward another person in response to the actions of that other person.

Failure to understand another person can result from a number of factors. The other person may misspeak or convey an unintended impression. You may mishear an utterance or receive some information that was not intended by the other. Or the language used by the other person may need clarification; it may be too abstract. Your response in all cases is quite similar. You should always ask for clarification. The lack of a clear understanding is frustrating. Often that frustration becomes a hidden agenda when we do not ask for clarification because we do not wish to appear foolish or stupid.

One group exhibited such a misunderstanding in its interaction because of one member's use of the jargonistic term "placebo effect." No other member responded to the term, but each continued to interact with no indication that anyone had any problem of understanding. After several moments, during which time little progress was made, one member finally asked what the speaker meant by a "placebo effect." The response was to express surprise that the other members were unfamiliar with the term. The subsequent interaction, which dealt not only with the issues at hand but also with the member's tendency to verbalize in a manner that was difficult to understand, undoubtedly led to increased effectiveness of that group process.

Because clarificaton is so significant when you are on the receiving end of the misunderstanding, you should always be prepared for the probability that other people will also misunderstand you. Consequently, you should develop the habit of checking to see whether your own expressed ideas were understood. Watch for the other person's reactions. Be prepared to restate your ideas in different ways in order to maximize mutual understanding. Realizing the fact that misunderstanding is a very common element in normal communication, you should also realize that any failure of others to understand your own communicative acts is quite normal. Their misunderstanding is not a reflection on your communication skills. In other words, be supportive rather than defensive when someone indicates a failure to understand you.

Another general rule of thumb in guiding your responses to others is, be as specific as you can. Avoid generalizing too much, particularly in responding to the other person's comments. If you are disagreeing, you should be careful to specify clearly the point of your disagreement and the reason for your disagreement. You should make your response as concrete and precise as you can. The fact that your disagreement is with a specific issue, not with the person who raised the issue, is significant to effective group decision making. It is also highly susceptible to misunderstanding.

Recalling that evaluative judgments tend to lead to defensive reactions, you might respond to others supportively by attempting to be as descriptive as possible. Some people have suggested that communicative responses should not attempt to describe the other person or the other person's ideas. Rather, the response should try to describe your own reaction. Rather than saying, "That's the most ridiculous thing I ever heard," you might say, "My first reaction to your statement is one of bewilderment. I'm not sure I agree with you." To be descriptive rather than judgmental is not to avoid disagreement on the issues. Rather, description refers to the manner in which disagreeing responses are phrased. They are directed at the idea, not the person. They describe yourself, not the other person.

Giving feedback and responding to others is important, because group members need to understand the positions of other members in order to perform their tasks adequately. Haslett and Ogilvie (1992, pp. 351–355) provide a valuable summary of suggestions for giving effective feedback:

1. *Be specific*   If you just say, "I don't agree," you are not telling the other person very much. You are being vague. But if you say, "I disagree with your point about the product liabilities because . . ." you are being more direct.

2. *Give evidence and data* People want to hear a rationale for your opinions or beliefs. Provide evidence for statements of facts, and give justifications for opinions.
3. *Separate the issues from the people* Focus your response on the task and the subject matter, not on the person. Do not tell people that they are wrong; tell them that their ideas can be improved or that there is additional evidence.
4. *Use good timing* Respond to people about immediate issues. Instead of waiting and bringing the matter up later, give feedback soon after an issue is raised.
5. *Soften negative messages* This can be most easily accomplished with language that is neither intense nor offensive. Soften the force of negative messages with such phrases as "I'm not sure about this" or "Perhaps we can improve this by . . ."

IMPROVING EFFECTIVENESS: GROUP-IDENTITY FACTORS

Up to this point we have been concerned with the individual members as related to his or her own self (attitudinal factors) and as related to other individual members (interpersonal factors). The present discussion focuses on improving effectiveness in terms of an individual's sense of relationship with the group as a single identity. We continue to assume, however, that the attitudinal, the interpersonal, and the group factors are not three different elements of communication and the group process. Rather, these three sets of factors are so interrelated that it is virtually impossible to determine where one stops and the other begins. The member who feels commitment to the group begins to refer to the group in the first person (that is, "my" or "our" group). The identity of the group stems directly from the attitudinal and interpersonal factors of the group process.

Sensitivity to the Group Process

Because of the nature of a process, the importance of timing cannot be emphasized too much. Increasing one's communicative effectiveness is more than knowing what to do and how to do it well. The most important principle of effective communication in group decision making is knowing when to communicate what.

Being sensitive to the group process enables the group member to judge fairly accurately in which phase the group is interacting. Sensitivity to the process allows the member to perceive roles and decisions as they emerge— probably before other, less sensitive members of the group are aware, and undoubtedly before the emergence process is completed. A group member who also possesses a modicum of communication skills is capable of adjusting his or her communicative behavior so as to behave appropriately in each specific phase in the process of group decision making.

Sensitivity to the group process also allows the member to pinpoint the causes of social problems and devise strategies to solve those problems. When a group is in trouble and is not functioning effectively as a group, the members generally recognize the existence of some problem. But knowing that the group is in difficulty and knowing what to do about it are two separate elements. The knowledgeable and sensitive group member becomes something of a consultant—an expert in the group process. He or she is able to discern the cause of the group's difficulties, which might, for example, be a problem member. Sensitivity to the group process does not lead the sensitive person to reject the member; rather, it establishes a desire to discover the cause of the problem member's dissatisfaction with the group and to do something to alleviate that dissatisfaction.

Commitment to the Group

Quite clearly the effective communicator in a decision-making group is a member who is deeply committed to the group and its task. In fact, active verbal participation is highly correlated with commitment. That is, committed members tend to assume a very active verbal role in the group interaction. And in true interdependent fashion, very active participants generally have a deep level of group commitment. If you feel strongly about something, you want to talk about it. Conversely, if you talk about something actively, you come to feel strongly about it.

One point must be emphasized. Effective communication in the group and low commitment of members are totally incompatible. If you feel that you are not committed to your group, you are a liability in the process of group decision making. You have but one recourse in such an untenable situation. If you are unable to perceive value in your group membership or in the group task, quit! You will undoubtedly think you are better off without the group, but don't be deceived. The group is infinitely better off without you! Without experiencing commitment to the group and the task, you cannot be an effective group member. Without your commitment as a member, the effectiveness of the group is severely curtailed.

Attitude toward Group Slowness

The member who understands the group process does not despair over the apparent inefficiency of the group's efforts. Particularly in the early stages of group interaction, the group mechanism seems excruciatingly slow. It is only normal to be somewhat frustrated and anxious. The inexperienced member will be distressed and eager to "get the show on the road." The effective member may be frustrated but will not be overly anxious. He or she will exercise patience and observe the process getting under way.

There is a sound rationale for not being overly eager for the group to increase its efficiency. What appears to be inefficiency at a snail's pace actually reflects one of the advantages of the group process of decision making.

While the group sputters and spurts in pursuit of consensus, members are allowed time to develop new ideas and reformulate earlier proposals. Too often, time is at a premium, particularly if a group operates under pressure of a deadline. Nevertheless, the importance of "mulling time" must not be underestimated. It is a crucial step in creative and high-quality decision making. And it is an integral part of the group decision-making process.

Formula Answers

A wit once remarked that you can use just one simple sentence in virtually any conversation and get excellent results. That sentence is, "Well, you know the old saying." This comment is universal and explains everything while contributing nothing. This anecdote makes the point that a cliché or an adage of conventional wisdom is available for any and every issue. Strangely enough, the cliché often commands immediate and universal acceptance, even though for every cliché there is usually another that contradicts it. If you believe that "Two heads are better than one," do you also believe that "Too many cooks spoil the broth"? "Absence makes the heart grow fonder," but "Out of sight, out of mind." It is certainly true that "Haste makes waste," but everyone knows that "A stitch in time saves nine." Tidbits of conventional wisdom are often perceived to be truer reflections than they actually are of reality.

Some group decisons are similar to clichés in that they oversimplify at the expense of realism. Groups discussing such social problems as poverty, crime, or discrimination often agree that these problems are caused by the ingrained attitudes of the society's members. The group members then decide that changing the attitudes of society with a program of education will eradicate the cause and solve the problem. The solution is true, of course, but it is unmistakably naive, simplistic, and unrealistic. How will education change society's attitudes? Who will administer this educational program? How will they do it? Are they able to do it? Is such a program possible? How long will it take? What about the influence of peer groups and opinion leaders in the society?

Groups formed in a classroom situation and discussing a policy problem have a penchant for devising formula answers. But classroom groups engaging in policy discussions are not typical of most decision-making groups in this respect. Classroom groups discussing such remote problems do little more than participate in intellectual exercises. After all, no classroom group has the power to legalize abortion or marijuana or abolish censorship laws or affect the national economy. The members engage in interaction as a classroom exercise and often discuss problems remote from their own capabilities as a realistic group. The real-life group, however, cannot afford shortcuts to realistic wisdom. Groups in the "real world" generally have the responsibility for implementing the decisions they make. They can then observe the success or failure of their consensus decisions in actual practice. Nor does their job end with the conclusion of an academic term. The formula answer is potentially a much more prevalent problem for the classroom group than for most decision-making groups in the society.

Analyzing Group Episodes

Several previous chapters have included discussions recommending that groups engage in self-analysis as a means of promoting more effective decision making. Group members who engage in analyzing themselves and the group process typically do so for several reasons. One reason is to attempt to discover and confront social problems that may be inhibiting the progress of the group's task performance. A second reason is more pedagogical. Classroom groups involved in learning about group decision-making phenomena perform self-analysis for the purpose of furthering their understanding of communication and the group process. For whatever purpose, we cannot suggest too strongly the importance of self-analysis as a means for improving the group's communication and group process.

One focus of self-analysis is the pinpointing and analysis of "critical episodes." Typically, during the process of group development, certain events occur in the group's history that later come to exert a profound impact on the development of the group's social and task dimensions. Such events typically indicate a transition, or turning point, in the group's development; that is, the event serves to precipitate some subsequent interaction that either facilitates or disrupts the group's performance as a group. A group's analysis of itself may focus on these specific episodes rather than haphazardly attempt to consider the entire process of group development. Such a focus is beneficial in allowing the members to understand their own maturation as a group.

One of the most obvious questions in analyzing critical group episodes is probably "What was going through your mind at that time?" In this case, the group member is asked to engage in some self-disclosing communication concerning the episode. Making the self-disclosures after the fact is undoubtedly more easily accomplished by the members than discussing frankly their own feelings at the time. Therefore, a successful analysis of a critical episode requires some elapsed time between the occurrence of that historical event and the time of the analysis. Typically, critical episodes bring on periods of increased social tension that further inhibit candid discussion of the episodes. An appropriate amount of time is necessary in order to allow this tension to dissipate.

A second question that may stimulate group discussion of critical episodes is to identify the critical figure or critical role in that episode. Which member of the group played the central role in either bringing about the episode or resolving the critical episode? That is, the critical episode may have involved confronting a problem member. In this case, the problem member played a central role, but an equally significant figure may be the member who initially confronted the problem member or encouraged other group members to confront him or her. After identifying these central or catalytic roles, the group may then concentrate on the reactions of those members as potentially more important than those of the other group members whose roles may have been observers more than anything else.

Another question of a more speculative nature may involve asking what the results of the critical episode were. What happened after the event? Why did those results occur? What might have occurred differently during the episode that would have led to a different outcome, either more beneficial or more disruptive? Should any action be taken at the time of analysis as a result of the retrospective analysis of the historical event? In other words, assess the significance of the effects (or results) of the critical episode.

Brown and Rothenberg (1976, p. 303) urge the use of critical episodes for group self-analysis and provide an example of their potential significance: "Although related to other components of group action—leadership, situation, the personalities of members, and social controls—the significant group episode in many ways predates all of these. The kind of person capable of coming to leadership in a group, for example, may be a function, to a greater or lesser extent, of some prior event in which another leadership style proved disastrous."

Group episodes are thus transitional events in the history of the group. They include events that led to either an acceleration or a disruption in the process of group development. Looking back on such events from the perspective of history allows the group members not only to understand "where they came from" and how they came to be what they are at that point but also to determine where the group is going. Analyses of group episodes provide valuable insights, leading to a more comprehensive understanding of communication and the group process. They may also lead to significant insights into improving communicative effectiveness during later group decision making.

Communication-Based Qualities of Effective Groups

In a series of studies, Hirokawa and his associates (Hirokawa and Pace, 1983; Hirokawa and Scheerhorn, 1986) set out to identify those qualities of groups that are most associated with effective decision making. They found a number of communication characteristics that separate effective from ineffective groups. The following are the most important characteristics of effective groups:

1. *Groups perform better when their members vigorously evaluate the validity of each other's opinions and assumptions*   Effective groups clarify, modify, and test the opinions of their members; ineffective groups gloss over the opinions of their members. Hirokawa found that whenever a member made a point in an effective group, some other group member would question the point and seek additional specificity and justification. Such communication patterns are quite prevalent in effective groups. Here is an example:

BILL: The city council will not support the building application because
    they are concerned about traffic congestion.
SUE: Really? Why do you say that?
BILL: Well, they haven't voted on it, but that's what I think.
JIM: Why do you think that? Did you read it somewhere or hear some-
    thing about it?
BILL: No, not really.

In this example we can see that Sue and Jim challenged the quality of
Bill's assertion. They did not let his statement that the city council "will
not support the application" enter the group as a fact. Groups that make
faulty decisions would not have challenged the statement, but would
have proceeded as if Bill's assumptions about the city council were true.

2. *Effective groups provide a thorough and rigorous evaluation of decison alternatives* Members of effective groups carefully test their decision alternatives. They match the alternatives against the group's preestablished
   decision criteria and critically evaluate each alternative in the same manner that they evaluate the opinions and assumptions of their fellow
   members. Forcing themselves to consider all aspects of an alternative,
   they ask whether or not it is fair, warranted, appropriate, reasonable,
   etc., to ensure that they have examined it adequately, and they analyze
   its potential consequences by asking such questions as "What is likely to
   happen if we implement this decision?" Ineffective groups do not discuss
   consequences; they go through a superficial discussion of alternatives
   and tend to settle on one alternative quickly. Here is an example of a
   superficial evaluation of a decision alternative:

JOHN: Shall we propose the parking lot to the city council?
ANN: Can we justify it?
JOHN: Yeah, we have all the data we have been collecting and it is
    possible to make the case.
PETE: How about the fairness issue? Do we think that is the best way to
    use the space?
AL: Yeah, sure.
JOHN: Sounds good to me.
AL: Let's go for it.

This group never really discussed the implications of its decision and
therefore never uncovered any problems. The decision was ineffective
and unrealistic because the members did not know enough about the
problem they were trying to solve.

3. *Decision quality depends on the accuracy of the premises the group uses*
   Hirokawa and Pace stated that this is a very important insight that
   resulted from their work. They found that high-quality groups use facts
   and inferences that are accurate and reasonable. This is easier to say than
   it is to do; many people get confused over what constitutes an accurate
   fact and an intelligent inference. Nevertheless, these skills can be

learned. And the facts and inferences improve when the group is critical and evaluative, practicing the first two characteristics of effective groups discussed above.

4. *The nature of the influential members' influence affects the quality of a group's decision*   All groups have some members who exert considerable influence over the thinking of others by moving the group in certain directions. A group becomes effective when this influence is positive and facilitative, but a negative and inhibitory influence makes a group ineffective.

Positive contributions by influential members include such communicative behaviors as asking appropriate questions, introducing important information, challenging and persuading the group to dismiss unwarranted and questionable information, and keeping the group from digressing. In the group discussing the parking lot proposal, an influencial member later asked pertinent questions about the proposal, such as "Where will it be located, what is there now, are there any other planned uses for the space, what will the community think, and are there important aesthetic issues?" These and other such questions forced the group to address many important issues, and this helped it reach a high-quality decision.

Negative contributions by influential members include introducing and supporting erroneous facts and assumptions, getting the group to accept poor information, making ridiculous suggestions, and distracting the group by leading it off in irrelevant directions. An influential member who makes negative contributions is a special problem when he or she is socially attractive. Although the members may like a person who is funny, pleasant, or otherwise appealing, these qualities alone do not make a person an effective task specialist. A group experiences the problems of ineffective groups when a socially attractive member who makes negative contributions exerts too much influence over the group's decision-making process.

SUMMARY

Developing effective communication within a group is not easy. There are no surefire principles for improving communication and group effectiveness. Such improvement ultimately requires a thorough understanding of communication and the group process. Misconceptions to be avoided include the naive assumption of human rationality and an overreliance on agendas.

Improving effectiveness depends on a number of interrelated attitudinal, interpersonal, and group-identity factors. Attitudinal factors involve each members' attitudes toward the group and toward group interaction, along with each individual member's creativity, critical ability, and honesty. Interpersonal factors include active verbal participation, communication skills, the use of supportive communication, and sensitivity when responding to others. When identifying with the group as a whole, effective members develop a sensitivity to the group process, a commitment to the group, and a reasonable attitude toward group slowness. Most important, perhaps, effective group communication often benefits from group members' engaging in interaction that is directed specifically at self-analysis, concentrating specifically on critical episodes from the group's history of past interactions.

Observing and Analyzing Small Group Communication

After reading this book it should be clear that human communication is a very complex phenomenon. Perhaps because of this complexity, scholars from Aristotle's time to the present have been interested in studying human communication, but its subtleties and difficulties continue to thwart every attempt to understand it completely. It is extraordinarily difficult to analyze and describe.

A major obstacle to understanding human communication is the tendency to think of it as someone doing something to someone else. This is a conveyor-belt concept of communication. It assumes that messages travel along channels from senders to receivers and that communication thus exists in physical space and has material components (see Fisher, 1978, pp. 98–134). Accordingly, people apply the language of spatial properties to communication. They speak, for example, of "upward" and "downward" communication, of relationships that are "close" or "far apart," and of communication "barriers" and "breakdowns" (as discussed in Chapter 3). A "breakdown" in communication implies that something is wrong with the sender or receiver, and a "barrier" to communication implies that something has deflected a message from its path—which assumes that a message has material components and is supposed to travel unimpeded in a straight line from one person to another. This concept of directional linearity leads to the assumption that the most important goal of any message or speaker is to *affect* a listener.

The structure of our English language (subject-verb-object) encourages this view of human communication. Many of our most basic sentences, such as "The child hit the ball," suggest that someone (the child) is doing something (hitting) to some object (the ball). Thus, we often describe communication as one person "persuading" another, or we say that a speaker "informs," "entertains," "dominates," or "leads" the listener. We talk about communication as a transitive action in which A leads to B, which in turn leads to C. This view of communication is at odds with our view of communication as a process—an interdependent relationship developed between communicating people who willingly engage in a system of interstructured behaviors.

283

Much communication research (and social science research in general) is conducted from a linear perspective. That is, the logic of communication experiments is formulated to establish causal relationships, such as how message A, traveling through channel B, has effect X on condition C. The experimental methods used are attempts to control environmental factors in order to note the influence of one variable on another (Bowers and Courtright, 1984, pp. 29–32). For example, researchers such as Hirokawa (1982, 1983a, 1983b) and Gouran (1983), who have been studying the influence of communication on decision quality in groups, pose their research questions in experimental language. They identify a communication variable A (which might represent the degree of high-quality communication, the amount of communication, or the inferences from communication), establish a research condition in which this variable is activated, and then note its effect X on some issue C in the group, where C might represent the quality of the group's decision. Although these procedures have led to many valuable and insightful conclusions about communication (see, for example, Hirokawa and Poole, 1986) they do not capture the communication process as we have defined it.

However, this appendix overviews some observational methods which are more consistent with our assumptions about communication and group interaction and which are better-suited to observing communicative behavior in small groups. This overview serves as a preliminary step toward understanding why the method of interaction analysis, discussed later in this appendix, is probably a superior method for observing communication in small groups as an interactive process. The procedures discussed here form the foundation for the model of decision emergence presented in Chapters 6 and 9. A specific interaction-analysis system is included here as an example of how the system may be applied to the observation and analysis of communication in ongoing decision-making groups. A second interaction analysis system is also presented.

COMMON OBSERVATIONAL METHODS

There are many different methods used to observe small group communication. Nearly every method employed in the broad spectrum of social and behavioral sciences has, at one time or another, been applied to group communication. This section reviews only a few of these methods and does not describe any single method comprehensively. (See Bowers and Courtright, 1984, pp. 91–104.) It should soon be obvious that these methods, widely used and certainly valuable for certain purposes, provide only a limited insight into communication and the group process, which naturally is our primary interest.

Self-Reports

To discover what people think or feel, undoubtedly the most simple method, and one that is thus often overlooked, is to ask them. The Gallup polls of public opinion, along with the Nielsen ratings of television programs, reflect specifically this method of social observation. Members of small groups often complete self-reports in the form of oral interviews or written questionnaires. The diary is another self-report measure. Members of classroom groups are often asked to record in such diaries their impressions and reactions immediately following each group meeting. Usually the diary does not require specific answers to specific questions, but asks only what the member thinks has happened to the group and to his or her own role in that group during that specific meeting.

Members' diaries are valuable as an observational method in that people frequently record in their diaries those feelings and thoughts which they might not wish to express during interaction with fellow group members. People are generally more willing to confide in the impersonal diary those thoughts which might otherwise escape observation. They tend to be much more frank in their diaries than in actual communication with other people, particularly in a newly formed group. Self-reports thus provide important additional information to the observer of group interaction. This information is particularly valuable in order to gain insight into the group's social dimension.

Self-report measures are typically paper-and-pencil tests in which an individual is asked to respond to a series of questions or statements. These questions or statements have been designed to identify attitudes or traits, the relatively enduring characteristics that describe a person or a situation. You might believe, for example, that a friend of yours is shy. But if you or a communication researcher designs a series of questions that ask people how they feel in certain social situations, and these questions are an attempt to measure shyness, then you have used a self-report measure to establish that someone is shy. The measures can take on numerical values that make it possible to identify people as "very shy," "very outgoing," or somewhere in the middle. McCroskey's (1977) measure of "communication apprehension," is related to shyness and has received a great deal of attention. It measures an individual's fear or anxiety about communication by asking the person the extent to which he or she agrees with such statements as "I get nervous when speaking in front of groups." In this way McCroskey has been able to establish an individual's self-report of communication apprehension. And researchers have demonstrated that shyness, or fear of communicating, has negative effects on a group (McKinney, 1982). There are many self-report measures that attempt to measure individual traits such as self-esteem, introversion, dogmatism, authoritarianism, and recently recognized traits such as interaction involvement (Cegala et al., 1982).

Despite the obvious value of the self-reporting method of observing small groups, there are problems inherent in the method itself. In many respects, the least knowledgeable source of information about any specific person is that very person. We are often unaware of how we behave, what we do, and particularly what we are thinking or feeling. Many behaviors are performed from habit, or at least without willful concentration. If it is true that people act in accordance with behavioral "rules" even though they need not be aware of those rules, then people are not necessarily aware of what they do or why they do it.

It is also extremely difficult to put thoughts and feelings into words. We just don't have the appropriate language or ability to express a feeling. Most of us find it difficult even to put our sensations into words. Try, for example, to describe the taste of an avocado or an artichoke to someone who has never tasted one. Describe the smell of some exotic cologne or perfume to someone who has never experienced that aroma.

Furthermore, self-reports often distort things. All of us have naturally developed defense mechanisms that serve to protect our ego, our personality. When the truth is harmful to our self-image or when reporting reality would embarrass us, we typically distort our perception of our true feelings, behaviors, or motives. Perceptual distortion is not necessarily conscious prevarication. In fact, we often believe the distortion to be the truth and are not even aware of having distorted anything. Under any circumstances, self-reports from group members are to be suspect. Relying on such an unreliable method as the principal means for observing group communication can easily lead to inaccurate, as well as incomplete, information. The members' degree of involvement in their group and their group task may also stimulate distorted self-reports. The overly involved member tends to idealize the group and to evaluate his or her behavior more positively than it probably merits. Conversely, the member with an extremely low level of commitment to the group tends to judge it as less effective than it is.

Finally, self-reports should be suspect because they inherently rely on the individual's memory. The human memory is quite fallible, with incomplete and distorted information typically present. You may be familiar with the classroom exercise in which one person tells a story to a second person, who in turn relays that message to a third person, who tells it to a fourth person, and so forth. After the second or third transmission, the story bears little resemblance to its original form.

Rating Scales

Rating scales are one solution to the problems inherent in self-reports, for rating scales ask an objective observer to evaluate the behavior of someone else. The rater is supposed to be more objective and less ego-involved in the evaluation. Teachers are using a form of rating scale when they test students; a student answers questions on a test, and the teacher assigns an evaluation.

In addition to their objectivity, another advantage of rating scales is that they are less disruptive of the actual communication process. If a researcher wanted to keep a running record of a group's progress toward a decision, it would be very obtrusive to stop the group every few minutes or so, ask the members to fill out self-report forms, and then tell them to continue. Rather, a rater could sit off to the side and make observations without bothering the natural development of the group.

A third advantage of rating scales is that they let the researcher control the definition of the construct. A construct is a concept that has been created specifically for a scientific purpose. It is part of a theory and usually measurable. If a researcher asks an individual to report on his or her "friendliness" or "fear of communicating," the result will be a subjective definition of the construct, which in some cases is desirable (but subject to the biases discussed above). But a rater who is evaluating the communication of others can be trained to observe things in a particular way, ignoring certain behaviors and paying particular attention to others. A researcher will provide a rater with a very specific and theoretically rigorous definition of a construct such as "fear of communicating." In this way the researcher knows that all behaviors are being evaluated the same way, according to a consistent set of principles.

A good example of a rating scale is The SYMLOG Adjective Rating Form (Figure A-1) developed by Bales and Cohen (1979) for their work in evaluating and observing group behavior. Bales and his associates explain interpersonal behavior in groups by referring to three basic dimensions:

1. *Dominant versus submissive,* or what is called upward (U) versus downward (D).
2. *Friendly versus unfriendly,* or whether a person is positive (P) or negative (N).
3. *Instrumentally controlled versus emotionally controlled,* or what is called forward (F) versus backward (B).

An observer uses the rating scale in Figure A-1 to rate individuals on the dimensions of interpersonal behavior.

As a result of using these rating scales, Bales can create what are called *directional profiles.* These are descriptions of how the group members are communicating (verbally and nonverbally) according to Bale's principles of interpersonal behavior and the three dimensions. For example, a group member named Tom might have a profile that characterizes him as upward (U). This means that his communicative behavior in the group has been described as dominant (upward). For instance, he takes the initiative in speaking, speaks loudly and firmly, and addresses the group rather than individuals. Nonverbal behaviors are also rated. In keeping with his dominant profile, Tom would be likely to sit straight, keep alert and active, and move confidently. As Figure A-1 shows, Bales's directional profiles account for multiple traits; for example, Tom might be both upward and friendly (UP), which means that in addition to his dominant behaviors he would be positive, a trait shown in his talking in a friendly way and initiating relationships.

Group Outcomes

Perhaps the method most commonly used for observing group decision making is measuring the outcome of group discussion—the quantity or quality of decisions reached by the group members. This procedure typically

Your Name_____Group_____

Name of person described_____Circle the best choice for each item:

		(0)	(1)	(2)	(3)	(4)
U	active, dominant, talks a lot	never	rarely	sometimes	often	always
UP	extroverted, outgoing, positive	never	rarely	sometimes	often	always
UPF	a purposeful democratic task leader	never	rarely	sometimes	often	always
UF	an assertive business-like manager	never	rarely	sometimes	often	always
UNF	authoritarian, controlling, disapproving	never	rarely	sometimes	often	always
UN	domineering, tough-minded, powerful	never	rarely	sometimes	often	always
UNB	provocative, egocentric, shows off	never	rarely	sometimes	often	always
UB	jokes around, expressive, dramatic	never	rarely	sometimes	often	always
UPB	entertaining, sociable, smiling, warm	never	rarely	sometimes	often	always
P	friendly, equalitarian	never	rarely	sometimes	often	always
PF	works cooperatively with others	never	rarely	sometimes	often	always
F	analytical, task-oriented, problem solving	never	rarely	sometimes	often	always
NF	legalistic, has to be right	never	rarely	sometimes	often	always
N	unfriendly, negativistic	never	rarely	sometimes	often	always
NB	irritable, cynical, won't cooperate	never	rarely	sometimes	often	always
B	shows feelings and emotions	never	rarely	sometimes	often	always
PB	affectionate, likeable, fun to be with	never	rarely	sometimes	often	always
DP	looks up to others, appreciative, trustful	never	rarely	sometimes	often	always
DPF	gentle, willing to accept responsibility	never	rarely	sometimes	often	always
DF	obedient, works submissively	never	rarely	sometimes	often	always
DNF	self-punishing, works too hard	never	rarely	sometimes	often	always
DN	depressed, sad, resentful, rejecting	never	rarely	sometimes	often	always
DNB	alienated, quits, withdraws	never	rarely	sometimes	often	always
DB	afraid to try, doubts own ability	never	rarely	sometimes	often	always
DPB	quietly happy just to be with others	never	rarely	sometimes	often	always
D	passive, introverted, says little	never	rarely	sometimes	often	always

FIGURE A-1 The SYMLOG Adjective Rating Form. (Bales and Cohen 1979).

involves determining the attributes of the group as it begins its task efforts and observing the results that accrue from the members' efforts, allegedly as a result of the particular combination of attributes. For example, a five-man group and a five-woman group may be given the same decision-making task. The decisions reached by these two groups are then observed and compared. Any difference between the decisions reached by the two groups is then attributed to their predominant structural characteristic of difference—in this case, gender.

Concentrating on the outcome from group discussion has serious short-comings. For example, the quantity of decisions that a group makes is often irrelevant. Often a group has only one decision to make, such as "guilty" or "not guilty." But the quality of decisions is also difficult to measure when no objective method outside the group interaction is available to validate the group decision. When a group decision-making task is involved, there is no externally valid decision; the sole criterion of quality is the extent to which the decision achieves group consensus. How, then, can the quality of the out-come of a group decision-making task be reliably measured? No adequate answer to this question is currently available.

Because of the difficulty involved in measuring the quality of group decisions, observers of group decision making often observe groups per-forming tasks more suited to individual decision making (Hirokawa, 1983a). Such tasks have a single "best" or "correct" answer, and their quality is objectively evident. But groups performing tasks intended for expert individ-uals are doing little more than playing games. Such tasks severely restrict the group process and encourage expert individual members to dominate other group members. At the very least, no advantage is gained from observing groups that perform tasks unsuitable to the social context. But such observa-tions unfortunately occur routinely.

Observing the group from the perspective of its outputs also assumes that structural conditions at the time of group formation determine what out-comes the group will eventually achieve. That is, a structural characteristic (for example, all males) or combination of structural characteristics causes the group to arrive at its decisions. Such an assumption denies the inherent interdependence of the members, their behaviors, the group dimensions, and so forth—interdependent relationships inherent in the nature of a process. In fact, the assumption that group structure determines group action is patently impossible in an open system, which is the perspective of small groups employed throughout this book.

Finally, observing only the group's outcomes is highly incomplete. At best, such an observational method answers only questions of *why* and *whether* group members achieve their outcomes. But it ignores the more important question of *how* groups achieve consensus. And only answers to the latter question can provide any insight into how we might increase the potential effectiveness of group decision making.

In summary, the three general types of observational methods used to analyze and describe small groups are generally unsatisfactory for our purposes. Certainly each of these methods provides highly valuable information about small groups, but that information is of a highly specialized and restricted scope. As far as communication and the group process are concerned, these observational modes are only indirectly useful and only partially relevant.

OBSERVING COMMUNICATIVE BEHAVIOR

Obviously, any method of group observation satisfactory for our purposes must directly observe the communicative behaviors of all group members. Equally obvious is the fact that observing communicative behavior is extraordinarily difficult. There are no yardsticks or microscopes with which to observe a communicative act. Communicative acts, first of all, are not physical objects that exist principally in space, such as a molecule of water. Rather, a communicative act exists only in the dimension of time. It is fleeting and transient. It ceases to exist immediately and is not permanently available for observation. And any relatively permanent record of communicative behavior, such as film or videotape, is useful but still incomplete.

Of course, not all human behavior is necessarily communicative. Although any behavior may be communicative in a given situation, some behaviors performed during group interaction are not relevant in that they do not significantly affect the group process of interaction. Thus, any observation of communicative acts must judge which behaviors are significant or relevant and which are not. No concrete guidelines are available to enable an observer to make such judgments with unquestioned validity and reliability. And authorities in communication even disagree on what communication is.

Observing all the communicative behaviors, or even just the verbal behaviors, of group members during group interaction requires that an observer be present in one form or another throughout the entire period of group interaction. The observation, of course, may not require the physical presence of an observing person. But some observational device, such as a camera or a tape recorder, must be present in order to provide a semipermanent record of the group's interaction. The question inevitably arises as to whether the presence of an observer or observational device significantly affects the behavior of group members during their interaction. That is, do members of a group behave differently because they are aware that they are being watched?

If you are a member of a group and someone is watching you with clipboard in hand, you will certainly feel some effects of that observer. And the more obtrusive the observations, the more your behavior will be affected. If, for example, an observer wanted to monitor your behavior during group interaction by wiring you to elaborate machinery and putting you in a room with all sorts of equipment and devices, you can be pretty sure that your behavior would not be very natural. On the other hand, a hidden and unobtrusive piece of equipment or an observer quietly taking notes would not dramatically disrupt group interaction. Indeed, we have witnessed classroom groups whose members concluded a meeting and left the room without turning off the tape recorder. They had simply forgotten it was there. And we also have numerous examples of classroom groups whose use of language certainly indicates that the members were not inhibited. Some authors (such as Barker and Wright, 1955) have argued that the effects of observers on group behavior are most pronounced during a brief period at the beginning of the group's development and then diminish over time.

Karl Weick, a noted psychologist and expert on observational methods, writes that the goal of an observer is "to be objective in close" (Weick, 1985, p. 567). No observer is purely objective and distanced from a group, but there are strategies and procedures for acquiring data in a useful and appropriate manner. The trained observer knows how to standardize the act of observing so that not only his procedures are understandable to others but also their impact on the subject(s) of the observation. The goal of an observer and the act of systematic observation is to organize, amplify, and impose meaning on social phenomena so that all observers gloss or reinterpret what they observe (Weick, 1981). Suppose that, as an observer, you encounter the following example of interaction:

Tom: Our marketing trend data indicate that the future looks good for VCR sales. We anticipate another fifteen percent penetration due mainly to improvements in the lower income markets.

Sue: Actually, I think the market is saturated and sales will be sluggish.

Tom: Where is the evidence of that?

Sue: Well, I don't have hard evidence, but it just seems like VCRs are so affordable now that everyone who is going to buy one has already done so.

Your goal in analyzing this communication would be to translate the natural "talk" into categories or concepts that specify the functions (or purpose) of the communicative behaviors. You might "reinterpret" the above interaction as follows:

Tom provides information in support of a desired action (selling VCRs).

Sue disagrees with Tom.

Tom questions Sue, seeking a justification for her statement.

Sue provides a subjective rationale justifying her previous statement.

The actual participants in communication do not use the above behavior-descriptive language to describe their talk. It is the observer who approaches the group armed with particular ways to interpret and understand the functioning of the group. The above interaction between Tom and Sue might be used to identify disagreement or conflict in the group, or it could mean that Tom is emerging as a dominant member of the group. In either case we can probably safely assume that the observer will not seriously distract group members and should be in a position to draw useful conclusions about the group. Below we will examine the nature and performance of interaction analysis in more detail.

INTERACTION ANALYSIS

The method of observation most pertinent to communication and the group process is interaction analysis. *Analysis* typically implies breaking down some whole into its component parts. For example, an analysis of the content of pure water reveals the presence of two units of hydrogen and one unit of oxygen. In this example of analysis, the content of water is analyzed into its compositional elements. The principle is the same for the first step in an analysis of interaction—reducing the whole of interaction into its compositional factors and the relative quantity of each.

"Now is the time for all good men to come to the aid of their party" is a familiar sentence used for a variety of purposes. The sentence may also be submitted to various systems of content analysis. One system might analyze the sentence into categories of "parts of speech" and use "words" as the units to be measured or counted. Such an analysis would reveal sixteen words analyzed as four nouns, two verbs, four adjectives, one pronoun, one adverb, and four prepositions.

Often this sentence is used to test the functional operation of a typewriter in much the same way that the prospective automobile buyer kicks the tires of an automobile. But a second content analysis of that same sentence using letters of the alphabet as units of measurement as well as analytical categories reveals that eight letters are not included in that sentence. Thus, the typewriter inspector would fail to observe the function of eight different keys. A better sentence used for the purpose of testing typewriters would be, "The quick brown fox jumps over the lazy dog." A similar content analysis of this latter sentence reveals that at least one instance of every letter of the alphabet. (Go back and check it.)

Interaction analysis, then, is a general method for analyzing the content of communicative behaviors by breaking down the whole of interaction into its component acts. Experts in many fields of study have employed numerous varieties and methods of interaction analysis, but the remainder of this section offers only a few of those varieties. This section will further emphasize one particular method of interaction analysis exemplified by two specific systems. For a more complete description of the various methods of content analysis, many books are available that describe such procedures in much greater detail. One source that focuses on various methods of content analysis and systematic observation is Weick (1985).

Characteristics of Interaction Analysis

Interaction analysis is *long-term systematic observation*. This means that a trained observer uses a measuring instrument to select and record the communicative behaviors that are occurring within a situation. *Long-term* implies prolonged and continuous observation; the emphasis is on observing a phenomenon over time in order to observe patterns and instances of connectedness. *Systematic* inquiry means that an observer works out a method of operation and adheres to it; the method of operation is theoretically and empirically sound. And *observation* is "standardized looking." When social scientists observe, they are looking for particular things in particular ways. If a communication researcher is interested in "verbal aggressiveness," for example, she will begin with a definition of the phenomenon or with some way to recognize verbal aggressiveness when she sees it. She will be armed with definitions and cues as to when verbal aggressiveness is occurring, and her observations will be controlled by these standards.

Categories   The categories (or pigeonholes) that things are classified into are perhaps the most important characteristic of interaction analysis. If the researcher's definition of a category of content (such as verbal aggressiveness) is weak or inaccurate, then the results of the research will be useless. The categories used for interaction analysis should possess three essential characteristics: When you create categories, they should be exhaustive, mutually exclusive, and sensitive to contexts.

To require that the category system be *exhaustive* means that each and every unit of behavior to be assigned can fit into some category. Some very simple category systems may have only two units: the unit of interest (e.g., "verbal aggressiveness") and a category for all other units (e.g., "not verbally aggressive"). But most category systems have more substantive categories of interest to the researcher. The system of categories is supposed to exhaust the communicative possibilities, at least in the theoretical sense. If a researcher is working with a ten-category system, then all communicative behaviors of interest must be assignable to one of the ten categories. If there are communicative behaviors that cannot be assigned, then either the category system is flawed and missing important data or there are behaviors that are not of interest to the researcher.

The categories in a system must also be *mutually exclusive*. This stipulates that a communicative behavior can fit in one and only one category. In other words, no two categories can overlap. For example, if two of a system's categories were "verbal aggressiveness" and "acts unfriendly," some behavior could be assigned to both categories. If one member of a group turned to another and said, "You never contribute much to the group," this might be both an aggressive statement and an unfriendly act, and this confusion about the function of the act would indicate a problem with the category system. The problem could be solved either by eliminating one of the categories, by refining the cateory definitions, or by making one category (such as "acts unfriendly") a subdimension of other category. However, recognizing that interaction is often multifunctional, Hewes (1979) has made a case for violating the rule of mutual exclusivity. (Although Hewes's arguments are too technical for our introductory concerns, he does offer a theoretical and statistical solution to the problem of assigning behavior to multiple categories.)

Finally, category systems should be *sensitive to contexts*. Contexts are situations; more specifically, contexts are configurations of people and things that give messages important meaning. The meanings of verbal and nonverbal utterances are not fixed; even an innocuous query such as "What is your name?" can be understood as a simple request for information (e.g., a clerk is taking information) or as a solicitous comment (e.g., asking the name of a member of the opposite sex at a party). An interaction analyst should understand the contextual constraints on a group. For instance, a corporate decision-making group is probably different from a group in the public sector, and it is often important that category systems reflect this difference. On the other hand, there may be times when a category system is relatively context-free; that is, acts representing a category are the same in one group as another. Disagreement, for example, might "look" the same in the corporate group as in the public group.

Devising a set of workable categories is not especially difficult, but it does require attention to the principles of reliability and validity. Herbert and Attridge (1975) specify thirty-three criteria for creating category systems that are reliable and valid. A *reliable* system is one that can be applied consistently across observers; that is, it ensures that there will be few judgmental errors and much agreement among observers. A *valid* system is one that is credible and yields true and useful results. Interaction researchers are always concerned with validity, for they must be able to demonstrate that their measurements are accurate. They demonstrate this by providing evidence and support for their reasoning processes (Agar, 1980) and by showing that their conclusions are plausible and can withstand the test of criticism.

Unitizing   A second important characteristic of interaction analysis is the unit of measurement—determining what should be counted and placed in a category. There is no standard unit of measurement. A unit should be inclusive enough to render the object of interest available to the researcher, but it should also be of a manageable size. Some researchers have used time intervals as the unit of analysis (Hawes, 1972); they will code every ten seconds, or thirty seconds, or however long a time metric they choose. Others have identified the "thought unit" as the unit of analysis; every time a speaker finishes a complete thought, it is coded into one of the categories. This may sound like a difficult and potentially confusing unit of analysis, but Crowell and Scheidel (1961) and Bales and Cohen (1979) developed coding systems that were specific and rigorous enough to code thought units successfully. Some researchers interested in decision making (e.g., Fisher, 1970b) have used the "decision proposal" as the unit of analysis; they are interested in tracking the various changes and modifications of decisions, so they code each time a group member modifies a decision category.

But perhaps the most common unit of analysis in communication research has been the act. An *act* is an uninterrupted verbal utterance; it is one "stand" on the floor; the act begins when a speaker starts talking and ends when he or she finishes. Most communication researchers are interested in functional category systems—systems that capture what people *do* in a communication context. People do such things as "ask questions," "act unfriendly," and "give information." An act can usually be categorized as a single function. The following example is composed of three acts (three "stands" on the floor) that are categorized according to three functions:

ROGER: What is this little venture going to cost? (*Request for information.*)
BILL: Oh, we should be able to pull it off for under a hundred thousand. I mean it depends on loan interest rates and what sort of production schedule we work on. (*Answer.*)
PETE: I don't know, I think this is a bad time to be incurring that much debt. (*Statement of opinion.*)

It is true that each of these three acts could be performing more functions than the ones indicated, but if our category system is reliable and valid, and if our theory about what we are observing is sensible, then it does not matter if these acts are multifunctional, because they are suitable for our purposes.

Contingency   After developing categories and establishing units of analysis, it is important to turn your attention to *contingent* relations. These are relations concerned with the order of events, or what follows what. The units now become *sequences of units*. The contingency level of interaction analysis is very important because it is here that elements are grouped into recognizable patterns. Without these groupings, it would be impossible to recognize interaction patterns; there would be only a series of acts, one following another with no pattern or meaning. Try to figure out the unpunctuated sentence "ilikebillbutidontcaremuchforron." Our use of spacing, punctuation, and capitalization helps us "pattern" letters in the English language and make interpretation easier. You have no trouble understanding the sentence written this way: "I like Bill, but I don't care much for Ron."

The notion of punctuation applies to communicative acts (see Chapter 4). The goal is to identify the groupings of utterances—the patterns—that recur (or repeat) over time. In the above three-act exchange between Roger, Bill, and Pete, we saw the following pattern of functional communication:

ROGER: (Request for information)
BILL: (Answer)
PETE: (Statement of opinion)

Each contingent pair of acts forms an interact. In other words, Roger performs a single act (requesting information), and Bill answers. Their two acts together are connected, or contingent, and form an interaction. Bill's answer then becomes the preceding utterance for Pete, and Bill and Pete also form an interaction. There are two interacts in the example above (Roger-Bill, Bill-Pete). Sequences such as these can go on for hundreds or thousands of utterances.

You might be wondering what use can be made of this type of interaction analysis. The following sections offer numerous examples, and many of the issues discussed in Chapter 6 and others were discovered through interaction analysis. But even in the simple example above you can see what interesting patterns might emerge. If you continued to find the above pattern, it would tell you what roles the various group members were playing. Perhaps Bill is a group expert and information source; Roger might emerge as a clarification and information seeker and be responsible for moving the group in new directions; and if Roger and Bill continued to form the same contingent pattern, it would be apparent that their relationship was responsible for stimulating this type of interaction. Moreover, it is possible to note change over time. Roger and Bill may form this relationship in the early stages of group development but change later in the group's history. Or there may be many "requests for information" during the beginning of the group's deliberations as they work to acquire information and get organized; we might see communication rich in information in the beginning and watch it dissipate later in the process. A consultant working with a group would find any of these findings valuable and would use them to improve the group's effectiveness at decision making.

In short, interaction analysis favors an evolutionary view of process. It is a technique for tracking the functional nature of communication over a group's history and identifying the patterns of interaction that characterize the group. No system of interaction analysis attempts to observe all aspects of human communicative behaviors. Rather, any analysis inherently focuses on those communicative aspects which relate to the categories. Hence, the categories are vitally important to the outcome of the analysis; they have the effect of imposing "reality" on whatever it is you are analyzing. The category system contains the meaning that you are trying to discover. Interaction analysis, unlike many other methods of observing groups, emphasizes what happens during group interaction, how it happens, and how changes occur over a period of time.

The following subsections describe two interaction-analysis systems. The detailed explanations of how these systems were developed and applied will help you understand the methods of interaction analysis and how communication researchers have discovered a number of interesting findings about the process of group decision making.

One System of Interaction Analysis: Decision Making

Since the model of decision emergence discussed in Chapter 6 results from applied interaction analysis, the system that led to discovering that model of group decision making seems appropriate to illustrate how interaction analysis might function. This system is admittedly imperfect, as are all others. It includes only verbal communication and probably places undue emphasis on the task dimension of the group process (see Chapter 4). Despite its imperfections, however, the system provides a general example of how interaction analysis might be utilized to observe group communication.

Central to this system of interaction analysis is the concept of a decision proposal. As a member presents an issue for consideration by other group members, this issue is potentially an item that will achieve group consensus—that is, the issue is a proposed decision being considered by the group members. As each member comments on this proposal, he or she implicitly attempts to influence the group's perception of it. (Naturally, a member need not be aware of attempting to influence the other members.) Thus, each comment "functions" on the proposal in some specific manner. The different functions that a member can perform on a decision proposal through an act of communication constitute the list of categories used in the analysis.

Each member's uninterrupted comment, or act, is considered a unit of communication. If an uninterrupted comment contains an instance of two functions (that is, if a single comment crosses functional categories before it is interrupted by a comment from another member), it is considered two units. During actual observation of groups, nearly all uninterrupted comments are found to contain but a single unit of communication.

These functionally defined units are quite obviously not of uniform length in either number of words or number of seconds. A single person performing a single function on the decision proposal in a single uninterrupted comment is considered to be a single unit of communication regardless of its relative length.

The categories for this system of interaction analysis are as follows (the same as presented in Chapter 4):

1. Interpretation
   f. Favorable toward the decision proposal
   u. Unfavorable toward the decision proposal
   ab. Ambiguous toward the decision proposal, containing a bivalued (both favorable and unfavorable) evaluation
   an. Ambiguous toward the decision proposal, containing a neutral evaluation
2. Substantiation
   f. Favorable toward the decision proposal
   u. Unfavorable toward the decision proposal
   ab. Ambiguous toward the decision proposal, containing a bivalued (both favorable and unfavorable) evaluation
   an. Ambiguous toward the decision proposal, containing a neutral evaluation
3. Clarification
4. Modification
5. Agreement
6. Disagreement

Several additional symbols are employed to simplify the analysis of interaction in practice. For example, the symbol O_n is used in addition to one of the categories above; it designates that an act is the one that originates a new decision proposal (identified by a subscript number) by introducing this proposal into the group discussion for the first time. Likewise, the symbol D_n represents an act that reintroduces into group discussion a decision proposal (identified by its original subscript number) that the group members had discussed previously. These two symbols do not represent categories of acts. Rather, they are used in addition to the actual analysis of interaction so that the observer may at all times keep track of which decision proposal is under consideration.

A category designated "procedural," not included in the above list, specifies acts which do not actually discuss a decision proposal and which are not substantive to the process of group decision making. Such acts coded into the "procedural" category rarely occurred during group interaction and were excluded from the final results of interaction analysis.

Although the categories are not difficult to understand, a brief explanation of each is probably necessary. The category "Interpretation" (1.) reflects a simple value judgment without evidence, reasons, or explanation offered to support the credibility of that judgment. The category "Substantiation" (2.), on the other hand, refers to an act that does include supporting evidence or reasons to enhance the believeability of the expressed value judgment. Thus, an act of substantiation may be considered more argumentative than one of interpretation.

Both "Interpretation" and "Substantiation" are subject to further classification in one of four subcategories, or dimensions of the larger category. The "Favorable" (f.) and "Unfavorable" (u.) categories should be self-explanatory. The two varieties of "Ambiguous" categories may be less clear. The comment "That seems like a good idea, but it has some flaws" is ambiguous because it includes both a favorable and an unfavorable evaluation of the proposal—hence, a bivalued evaluation and an instance of the "ab" category. The comment "That is a very interesting suggestion" is unclear because it evaluates the idea without expressing clear approval or disapproval of the suggestion—hence, a neutral evaluation and an instance of the "an" category. Both comments, of course, reflect interpretation rather than substantiation as well as both the general and the specific dimensions of the category—that is, "1.ab." and "1.an.," respectively.

The category "Clarification" (3.) indicates those acts that function to render an idea pertaining to the decision proposal more readily understandable. No evaluation is evident in such a comment. Rather, the act restates some previous act in more concrete language.

"Modification" (4.) signifies an act functioning to amend the decision proposal under consideration by direct means. The section in Chapter 6 that discusses the group process of modifying decisions notes that instances of this category rarely occur during group interaction.

"Agreement" (5.) and "Disagreement" (6.) express support or nonsupport of the immediately preceding act. A typical "5." comment, such as "Yes," "You're right," or "Okay," does not function directly on the decision proposal. But such a comment indirectly affects the members' perception of this proposal by adding weight to the act that precedes the agreement. Whatever the preceding function unit, the "5." unit assumes the functional meaning of that antecedent category and underscores it. If "5." follows a "2.f." unit, for example, it reinforces by agreement the substantiation favoring the decision proposal.

If "6." "Disagreement," follws a "2.f." act, it expresses disfavor through negatively reinforcing the favorable substantiation. The "6." unit, then, indirectly functions as a negative evaluation of the decision proposal by disfavoring the specific preceding act that favored it. An excerpt from an actual group discussion may serve to clarify how one may apply this system of interaction analysis. The following excerpt is from a management training group (all-male) discussing budget allocations for its hypothetical corporation. Decision proposal 1 might be phrased, "The corporation should seek to discover what its fixed costs will be after the proposed plant expansion has been completed." The first comment in the excerpt below initiates this proposal, and all other comments are directed toward this single proposal. The symbols that appear to the left of each communicative act indicate the classification of each unit according to the categories of the system. When in doubt, refer to the previous listing of the categories and their identifying symbols.

1.an.0_1	A: Would we want to spend \$2,000 this first quarter to find out what the cost of our plant expansion is going to be?
3.(asks for)	D: The cost of what?
3.	A: Our fixed expenses. Would we like to know how much they are going to be?
1.u.	B: No. I'm not really worried about that.
1.u.	D: No. I'm not concerned about that.
2.f.	A: But if we are concerned about production and profit, that's a factor. That is a fixed operating cost we are going to have to live with. We should know in advance what it is going to cost us.
6.	B: No.
2.u.	C: But knowing it won't influence our decision to expand or not.
2.u.	D: Why pay \$2,000 to get it if we are going to have to pay it anyway?
2.f.	A: Until we do it the first time, we've got no idea if this is going to be another \$6,000 or whether it's going to be as high as \$30,000. That might influence us considerably on our long-range goals.
2.u.	B: We are going to have to expand in spite of that, though.
2.u.	D: I don't think we are ever going to refuse to expand. So the first time that we do expand, we are going to find out the fixed operating cost.
5.	G: Yes.

2.u.   D: By rights, it shouldn't be more. By normal operating
                    procedures, it shouldn't be more than we pay right
                    now. It should be less because our main plant has al-
                    ready been built.
3.(asks for)   A: Do you mean less than $6,000?
3.(restates)   D: Yes, I do.
2.u.   A: Well, if it is anything less than $6,000, it would really
                    be silly to spend $2,000 to find it out.
2.u.   D: By just using common business sense, you have to say
                    it is $6,000 or less. It can't be more unless they have to
                    blast a hillside out of the way to get the addition to the
                    main plant in.
5.   C: Yes, I think you're right.

The above excerpt should explain by example how this system of interaction analysis may be utilized in actual practice. Note the several comments
that ask for clarification. In both cases, the comment immediately following
the request provides the clarification. Member D's "Yes, I do" might appear,
outside the context of the interaction, to be agreement. But it is really a
clarification of his preceding comment in direct response to A's request for
clarification of his intended meaning. The other coded acts appear to need no
further explanation.

After the group interaction has been analyzed into acts, the interaction is
then divided into interacts. Figure A-2 illustrates the interacts included in the
excerpt coded above. The rows of the matrix in this figure are the categories of
the interaction analysis system, which include the first (or "antecedent")
comment of each interact. The columns across the top of the matrix are the
categories of the second (or "subsequent") act of each interact. Thus, each cell
in the matrix represents an interact. The first act is the row across, and the
second act is the column down.

The nineteen acts appearing in the excerpt above translate into eighteen
interacts. The first act, "1.an.," is the antecedent of the second act, "3."
Together the two acts compose the first interact in the excerpt. The second
act, "3.," is also the antecedent of the third act in the excerpt, also "3."
Together they form the second interact in the excerpt. Thus, a sequence of
three acts includes two interacts, and the entire excerpt of nineteen single acts
contains a total of eighteen interacts.

Figure A-2 shows that during even this brief excerpt, a trend develops
regarding the group's treatment of decision proposal 1 in its interactive
patterns. Note that the only acts expressing favor of the proposal, two "2.f."
units, are immediately followed by acts that conflict with the favoring function. One of the subsequent acts is outright disagreement, "6.," and the other
argues the opposing side, "2.u." Once the argument starts, the other members "pile it on" by positively reinforcing the seven "2.u." units with additional "2.u." units a total of three times, and twice with agreement, "5."

A table such as that in Figure A-2 is called a contingency table. Such an
analysis provides the basis for analyzing possible phases of group decision

Subsequent acts

	1f	1u	1ab	1an	2f	2u	2ab	2an	3	4	5	6
1f												
1u		1			1							
1ab												
1an									1			
2f						1						1
2u					1	3			1		2	
2ab												
2an												
3		1				1			2			
4												
5						1						
6						1						

(Antecedent acts — row labels at left)

FIGURE A-2 Interacts contained in interaction analysis of decision proposals.

making. A single matrix can be used to summarize all the interacts during a specified time period; for example, if the period is five minutes, a sixty-minute group discussion will require twelve matrices (as illustrated in the figure). Each matrix can then be compared with the next, and any changes in interact patterns can be easily discerned. In this way, phase progressions during group decision making can be discovered. Chapter 6 shows in much more detail how phase progressions can be discovered.

Another System of Interaction Analysis: Relational Communication

The concept of "relational" communication was discussed in Chapter 4 and Chapter 9. The relationship dimension of communication is concerned with the ways in which verbal messages indicate how participants in an interaction "see" one another in relation to themselves. The most common relationship dimension is control, or the manner in which group members use communication to direct and dominate relationships. Chapter 4 also examined the various control modes and definitions of complementarity and symmetry. The conclusions about leadership in Chapter 7, and other issues regarding relational communication (e.g., Ellis, 1979), were arrived at using interaction analysis techniques. The control dimension of relational communication has been operationalized by a category system called REL/COM (Ellis, 1979). The system includes the following five categories:

Dominance (↑ +): An attempt to restrict severely the behavioral options of the other

Structuring (↑ −): An attempt to restrict the behavioral options of the other, but leaving a variety of options open; an attempt to control the flow of interaction

Equivalence (→): An attempt at mutual identification; an interactional mode in which one does not seek to control or submit to control

Deference (↓ −): An expressed willingness to relinquish some behavioral options to the other while retaining some choice of options; a "following" behavior in which one relinquishes control of the flow of interaction

Submissiveness (↓ +): An expressed willingness to relinquish behavioral options to the other while retaining little choice

Each communicative act—one speaker's turn—is assigned to one of the above five categories. And to remain theoretically consistent, each act receives its assignment on the basis of how it relates to the previous act. No utterance is coded in isolation from the sequence of acts, and each speaker's act acquires relational meaning by how it relates to the previous act.

Assume that member *A* makes an assertion. Member *B* challenges that assertion by demanding proof of documentation for that belief. Because *B*'s response is a challenge (an "I dare you" assertion), that demand would be coded as an attempt to control the other's behavioral options—a dominant (↑ +) act. Member *A* may respond to that challenge by providing the information or documentation that was demanded. Relationally, *A*'s response is a confrontation of the challenge and would thus be coded as another dominant (↑ +) act. If *A* fails to repond to the challenge, the action relationally submits to *B*'s control and exhibits relational submissiveness. Failing to respond to a challenge is tantamount to a retreat in the face of the enemy's attack.

The interaction coded earlier into the decision-proposal system can also be coded into the five categories of REL/COM:

```
A: (not codable; no preceding act)
D: →      (equivalence)
A: →      (equivalence)
B: ↑ −  (structuring)
D: →      (equivalence)
A: ↑ +  (dominance)
B: ↑ −  (structuring)
C: ↑ −  (structuring)
D: ↑ +  (dominance)
A: ↑ +  (dominance)
```

B: ↑ + (dominance)
D: ↑ − (structuring)
G: ↓ − (deference)
D: ↑ − (structuring)
A: → (equivalence)
D: → (equivalence)
A: ↑ − (structuring)
D: ↑ + (dominance)
C: ↓ + (deference)

Again, we can create a contingency table (Figure A-3) for the relational communication codes. Figure A-3 is an example of an interact matrix with each code as an antecedent and each as a subsequent act. If the patterns in Figure A-3 were to remain consistent over the life of the group, we could assume that competitive symmetry (↑ ↑) was a prevalent pattern and that submissive symmetry (↓ ↓) was not characteristic of the group. An even more interesting analysis would be to create an interact matrix for every relationship in the group. We could then see who was dominant, who was submissive, and what relationships each individual had with the other people in the group. This type of analysis was used to discover the leadership behaviors that are discussed in Chapter 7. For our purposes here, it is sufficient that we understand how interaction analysis works and how it is possible to observe decision making and relationship development in groups. There are, of course, much more sophisticated treatments of this subject matter (e.g., Hawes and Foley, 1976; Fisher, Glover, and Ellis, 1977; Fisher, 1977).

FIGURE A-3 Interacts contained in REL/COM analysis.

Antecedent acts \ Subsequent acts	↑ +	↑ −	→	↓ −	↓ +
↑ +	2	2		1	
↑ −	2	1	2	1	
→	1	2	2		
↓ −		1			
↓ +					

SUMMARY

It is important that you understand how to observe and analyze groups systematically. We have argued that groups are a system of interdependent communication behaviors, and it is possible to analyze groups in a manner consistent with this perspective, a perspective that preserves the importance of communication as a process. Several methods of observational research have been employed in the past. They include:

1. Self-reports, in which individuals complete paper-and-pencil questionnaires querying them about attitudes and beliefs.
2. Rating scales, which have observers rate or evaluate the behavior of others; these have the advantage of avoiding the biases of self-reports.
3. The measurement of group outcomes, which utilizes a method of manipulating some structural variable in the group and noting its effect on an outcome measure, such as decision quality or member satisfaction.

Each of these perspectives is useful, but none emphasizes the observation of communicative behaviors over time.

Interaction analysis was posed as a most effective technique for measuring the group process. This is a method for analyzing group communication by breaking it down into its component parts and classifying these parts. This type of inquiry is systematic and depends on careful preparation of methods. The analyst begins by developing categories (or pigeonholes) to classify messages. Units of analysis are also established. The categories are then placed in contingency tables, where recognizable patterns of communication emerge.

Two examples of interaction analysis were presented. The first was an example of an interaction-analysis system designed to track the various modifications on group decisions. The second example demonstrated how relational communication can be operationalized and studied as an interaction process. Conclusions about decision making (Chapter 6), leadership (Chapter 7), and communication (Chapters 4 and 9) are all dependent on the method of interaction analysis.

Glossary

Students often complain about the use of *jargon*, or language peculiar to an area of study. Most people deplore unnecessary jargon because it is cumbersome and awkward to use. Nevertheless, it is impossible to separate knowledge from language. Language is the package that ideas come in. If you are going to be knowledgeable or expert in an area of study, you must master the specialized language within that field. You may often feel overwhelmed with new terminology because as a university student you live in a virtual sea of language. It is not inaccurate to say that studying physics is to study the "language" of physics, just as studying philosophy, history, or agriculture is a matter of mastering ideas in those fields by mastering their language.

This glossary is an added effort on our part to help the student master the language associated with communication and decision-making groups. Distinctions and specialized meanings are important in any field of endeavor. The word "glossary" is a plural noun that refers to a collection of "glosses." A gloss is a brief explanatory note. It comes from the ancient practice of scholars making notes in margins or between lines explaining how a text should be interpreted. So a glossary is a list of new or specialized terms. New words are coined in order to describe new events and phenomena. Scholars assisted others with the interpretation of ancient texts by providing a list of definitions and commentary. If I told you that the computer I was working on at this very moment had a "20 meg hard drive" you would probably understand what I meant. It was not long ago that the two-word term *hard drive* would either have been gibberish or perhaps have referred to a long trip in a car. But the specialized use of those two simple words has created new meanings in the world of computer technology. You can be perfectly communicative when talking to a friend about computers and using the term *hard drive* because the term has established meaning.

This glossary is intended as a handy reference. We have tried to provide you with a manageable list of important concepts. The field of communication, particularly group communication, has more than its share of superfluous terminology. This is probably because there is no unifying theory that guides all who work in the area. So as people make new "discoveries" and identify new characteristics of groups, they create new terminology and new linguistic distinctions that perpetuate jargon. There is plenty of terminology in communication and group communication that does not appear below. This does not mean that those terms are not important or that they do not symbolize something important about groups or communication. It just means that they were not useful for our purposes. The concepts defined below are considered central to the understanding of communication and the group process.

One important warning for the reader who uses this glossary: Do not be misled by simple and overly general definitions. Definitions are easy; understanding is difficult. A brief definition is no substitute for understanding a concept. Although a single word may have a useful definition, it also implies other words. To understand a concept fully, one must understand an entire array of words and how they relate to one another. This glossary lists important concepts, but this book uses many additional terms not listed in the glossary that are necessary for a thorough appreciation of these concepts. So memorize definitions if you must, but do not confuse definitions with genuine understanding and knowledge.

Affective conflict   Emotional clashes between members of a social system, typically on procedural issues.

Assembly effect   The ability of a group to achieve collectively a level of productivity greater than the sum of the productivity of individuals when working by themselves.

Barrier or Breakdown   A cessation or blockage of communication, a concept based on the fallacious assumption that communication embodies only the structural aspects of sending and receiving messages along a channel.

Boundary spanner   A person who communicates and processes information between two or more networks.

Brainstorming   Technique to stimulate group creativity by eliminating criticism and evaluation.

Buzz groups   Technique for large groups to encourage ideas by breaking into smaller groups for discussion.

Centrality   A characteristic of a communication network indicating the position in the network in which a member requires the fewest linkages to transmit a message to every other member of the group.

Channel capacity   The number of items of information that a person can effectively process at one time.

Climate   The relatively enduring quality of the group situation that is experienced by all group members and arises from their interaction.

Coalition   A temporary alliance between two or more members of a social system, typically oriented toward a difference of opinion about the means used to achieve the group's goal.

Cohesiveness   The output of a group's socioemotional dimension; essentially, the degree to which members are attracted to one another and are personally committed to the group.

Collective structure   The repetitive pattern of behaviors that characterizes a group; when communication among group members becomes interdependent, interstructured, and predictable, a collective structure emerges.

Communication   The process of people exchanging messages, which are formulated according to the principles of a code, in a context.

Complementarity   A form of relational interaction in which a relational behavior and its response are combined to form a complete and coherent relationship; for example, question-answer, ↑↓, or ↓↑.

Conflict management   An accomplishment of the group when its members maximize the benefits of conflict and avoid the consequences of destructive conflict.

Conflict styles   Ways of handling conflict such as avoidance, compromise, competition, accommodation, and collaboration.

Conformity   Uniform behaviors exhibited by members of a social system resulting from the members choosing, from among conflicting alternatives of behavior, that alternative least subject to negative social influences.

Consensus   The degree of personal commitment the members feel toward the group's decision after it has been reached.

Content dimension   That aspect of a communication that refers to specific information or data.

Contingency model   A model of group leadership, developed by Fiedler, that incorporates general predictions of leader effectiveness in selected situations. Predictions are based on scores of group leaders on LPC (least preferred coworker) tests.

Convergent thinking   Thinking with logic, rationality, and reason.

Coorientation   The "strain toward symmetry" in which two persons (*A* and *B*) are oriented, positively or negatively, to the same object (*X*).

Decision   In a group, a choice from among available alternatives that is validated by achieving consensus among members.

Decision making   As a group task, the process of choosing among alternatives for which no "best" or "correct" answer can be validated by any means other than group consensus.

Defensive communication   When members try to manipulate and control one another. The communication is judgmental, manipulative, and insincere.

Density   The number of linkages in a network that actually exist in proportion to the number that would exist if everyone were linked directly.

Deviance   That behavior of members which is not in conformity with group norms or expectations.

Distance, communication   A characteristic of a communication network indicating the number of links required for one position in the network to transmit a message to another position.

Divergent thinking   Being highly creative and exploring unorthodox possibilities. Using imagination.

Double interact   A sequence of three contiguous acts performed by group members.

Emergence   A gradual process describing how a group develops its roles, including that of leader, and its decisions.

Encapsulation   A method used for controlling social conflict through regulating conflict by a set of rules agreed upon by all parties to the conflict.

Evolution   The characteristic of a system embodying its history; that is, the enduring changes in the system's structure and function over an extended period of time.

Feedback   A mutually causal sequence of events or acts which, self-reflexively, exerts influence on the original act or event in the sequence. Feedback, affecting a deviant act or event, serves to counteract that deviance (negative feedback) or amplify the deviance (positive feedback).

Feedback response   When one person directs a message at another in order to achieve some desired effect.

Flight   The behavioral tendency of a group to cease considering its task as a means of avoiding some unpleasant stimulus, commonly social conflict.

Focus groups   Discussion groups used to determine people's interests, values, and habits.

Formal   A term used to describe the norms, status hierarchy, communication networks, etc., of a social system sanctioned or prescribed by legitimate sources of power or authority.

Formula answer   An oversimplified and unrealistic solution to a complex problem; typically so general that it cannot be implemented.

Function   The characteristic of a system denoted by the relationships among components in time and serving to regulate the ongoing action of the system.

Functional communication   A model that illustrates how groups understand problems, establish objectives, evaluate choices, and use quality information.

Functional leadership   Perspective on leadership that emphasizes communicative behaviors performed.

Gatekeeping   The structural function of serving as an intermediary between source and receiver in the flow of messages; receiving and selectively relaying messages from the original source to the ultimate receiver.

Group   A collection of three or more persons whose behaviors are interstructured so that these persons exert a mutual and reciprocal influence on one another.

Group mind   A belief, now outmoded, in the independence of a group's manner of thinking and feeling apart from its members.

Groupthink   The phenomenon that occurs when members of a highly cohesive group disregard alternative courses of action in favor of maintaining unanimity of opinion in the group; an absence of critical idea testing and conflict, which are typical of the natural group process.

Group fantasy   The sharing of an interpretation of events that helps satisfy the group's need for organizing events and for communal bonds.

High-performance groups   Groups organized on the basis of individual work styles.

Identification   The extent to which a group member feels part of the group and has internalized its goals.

Idiosyncrasy credits   An economic model which explains the leader as both a deviant and a conformist and which illustrates the ability of a group leader to innovate after having conformed to the group norms for a period of time.

Informal   A term describing the norms, status hierarchy, communication networks, etc., developed through the emergent natural group process and not necessarily sanctioned by legitimate sources of authority or power.

Information processing   The process of using perceptions to transform data into information and then acting upon those perceptions; it may be performed by either one person or a group.

Innovative deviance   See **Verbal innovative deviance.**

Interact   A sequence of two contiguous acts performed by group members.

Interaction analysis   A method for analyzing the sequential process of communication.

Interaction management The skill involved in regulating the direction and flow of interaction in the group.

Interaction process analysis (IPA) The system of interaction analysis developed by Robert F. Bales.

Interdependence A relationship between two or more elements so that each influences, and is influenced by, the other.

Interpersonal attraction A characteristic of a relationship such that the people are drawn toward one another. Attraction usually occurs when group members hold similar attitudes.

Leader as medium Theory of leadership where information and decisions flow through a leader as he or she manages complexity.

Leaderless group discussion (LGD) A task-oriented group whose members have the capacity to determine for themselves the group's structure, function, and behavior.

Leadership A high-status position achieved in a group by performing leadership acts recognized by other group members as helping the group to perform its task; defined interdependently with followership.

Leadership styles Approach to leadership that focuses on leadership style, e.g., democratic or autocratic.

Legitimacy The principle of prescription or prior approval of norms, values, roles, or other standards imposed on a group by some person or source outside the group whose authority over it is recognized by the group members.

LGD See **Leaderless group discussion.**

Life-cycle theory of leadership The assumption that leaders should communicate with the group based on the maturity of the followers; the theory assumes that groups develop toward maturity.

Message A single communicative act.

Motivation A characteristic of group members who are stimulated to devote time, resources, and energy to the group.

Multiple-sequence models The theory of group development which argues that groups do not evolve from single phasic patterns, but interweave different patterns over time. This theory is a response to and criticism of unitary phase models.

Natural process A process of group development, nearly universal, that is based on "rules" governing behavior. Group members need not be aware of these rules.

Network The structure of channel linkages among group members that illustrates the pattern of transmitting and receiving messages.

Nominal Group Technique (NGT) A method of increasing participation in a group.

Nonsummativity A principle, inherent in any system, which stipulates that the whole is greater than, or different from, the sum of its parts because of interdependent relationships among the parts.

Norm A standard that regulates the behavior of all members of a group through feedback directed at members whose behaviors are contrary to that standard.

Open system A characteristic of a system that has a free exchange of information with its environment.

Orienting communication   Group communication that maintains the group's focus by directing the discussion through clarification, questions, answers, and relevant information.

Outcomes   What a group produces and achieves. Some outcomes are tangible, such as reports and documents, and other outcomes are personal or social, such as cohesion and satisfaction.

Partial inclusion   The notion that a person does not include all of his or her behaviors in a single role; the behaviors you are capable of are dispersed among several roles.

Persuasive arguments theory   Theory that group members are influenced by the arguments of other group members and this accounts for more polarized decisions.

PERT   Program Evaluation and Review Technique. A method of implementing solutions.

Phases   Theory that group interaction goes through cycles including different types of conflict.

Polarization   The tendency of groups to make decisions that are more extreme than the initial opinions of its members.

Political model of groups   A perspective on groups that emphasizes power relationships and how they lead to alliances, coalitions, and wheeling and dealing.

Power   The ability or right of a person to control the behavior or resources of another person.

Pragmatic perspective   A perspective on communication that emphasizes the role of contexts and relationships in determining the meaning and effects of messages.

Primary tension   The inhibitions of group members during the early period of group development; similar to the phenomenon of stage fright in an individual.

Process   A sequence of events or actions continuously changing over time in progress toward some goal.

Productivity   The output of a group's task dimension; the quality or quantity of work performed by a group.

Proxemics   The principles behind the ways in which group members use, arrange, and perceive physical space.

Punctuation   In a system, the process of organizing the sequence of acts or events in order to discover meaning and significance in the sequence.

Rating scales   A method of observing and evaluating the behavior of group members.

Reachability   The number of links in a network that it takes to connect one individual to another.

Reach-testing   The process of introducing a new idea from an anchored position of group agreement in the spiral model. Other group members test that idea through discussion and may accept it, reject it, extend it, or revise it.

Reciprocity   A norm typical of most social systems that encourages members to respond to the behaviors of others with similar behaviors.

Relationship dimension   The style dimension of a message or how a message is to be interpreted.

REL/COM   A system of analyzing interaction into categories of relational control ($\uparrow \downarrow$, $\rightarrow$).

Risky shift   The tendency of a group to make decisions involving greater risk (that is, bringing a bigger payoff but a lower probability of attainment) than individuals make.

Role   A position occupied by a group member in an interlocking network including all group members; defined in terms of the behaviors performed by the member.

Routing statements   Statements that signal the group to follow a new or potentially different path.

Satisfaction   The extent to which group members enjoy and are satisfied with the group experience.

Schismogenesis   The escalation of either symmetrical or complementary relationships to a point that the social relationship is threatened with disruption.

Secondary tension   Social discomfort typified by abrupt and abnormal departures from the routine functioning of a group; induced by interpersonal conflict, environmental pressures, feelings of frustration, etc.

Self-disclosure   Communication that informs another person about one's private self and provides information that the other person does not know and is unlikely to acquire through other means.

Self-reports   An observational method where a group members answers questions designed to identify attitudes or traits that describe a person or situation.

Social comparison   The process of evaluating characteristics of one's self-concept by comparing them with those of another person or a group, typically performed by comparison with persons having similar characteristics.

Social dimension   Relationships among group members with one another.

Sociofugal arrangements   A physical environment arranged such that it keeps people away from one another and discourages communication.

Sociopetal arrangements   A physical environment arranged in such a manner that it encourages contact and communication.

Spiral model   The process of decision making involving constant backtracking and reach-testing of ideas until the idea develops during group interaction to represent the consensus of the group members.

Status   A social class or division rank ordered in a hierarchy from high to low. Status may be ascribed, that is, given the position by some higher authority. It may also be achieved through behaviors recognized by other group members as beneficial to the group.

Structuration   The theory of how groups develop by using their resources to establish rules for processing information.

Structure   The characteristic of a system denoted by the physical or spatial arrangement of the components at any given point in time.

Substantive conflict   Intellectual clashes between members of a social system on issues pertaining to the group task.

Supportive communication   Communication which is genuine, sincere, and supportive and which is directed toward another person. This type of communication is typically nonevaluative and respectful of the other person's identity.

Symbolic convergence A theory of group communication that emphasizes the extent to which group members identify with common symbols and meanings.

Symmetry A form of relational interaction in which the response to a relational behavior is the same as the antecedent act: for example, $\uparrow \uparrow$, $\downarrow \downarrow$, or $\rightarrow \rightarrow$.

System An entity that behaves as an entity because of the interdependence of its component elements.

Task dimension Relationship between group members and the work they are to perform.

Theory The basis for explaining, describing, and understanding any set of complex phenomena: for example, communication and the group process.

Tolerance threshold The maximum degree of tension that will not prohibit a group from functioning normally. Social tension at a level above the threshold disrupts the ability of the group to function as a group.

Unitary phase models The theory of group development which suggests that all groups develop in a similar linear sequence of phases.

Verbal innovative deviance (VID) The behavior of a group member reflecting agreement with the group's goal but disagreement with the majority on the appropriate means for achieving that goal.

Wholeness A principle inherent in a system which stipulates that every component of the system affects, and is affected by, every other component and that a change in any one component inherently brings change in all other components.

References

Abelson, Robert P., and Ariel Levi. (1985) "Decision Making and Decision Theory," in G. Lindzey and Elliot Aronson (eds.), *The Handbook of Social Psychology*, 3d ed., vol. 1. New York: Random House, pp. 231–309.

Adams, J. S. (1980) "Interorganization Processes and Organization Boundary Activities," in L. Cummings and B. Staw (eds.), *Research in Organizational Behavior*, vol. 2. Greenwich, CT: JAI Press, pp. 321–355.

Agar, M. (1980) "Getting Better Quality Stuff: Methodological Competition in an Interdisciplinary Niche," *Urban Life*, 9:34–50.

Alba, R. D. (1982) "Taking Stock of Network Analysis: A Decade's Results," in S. Bacharach (ed.), *Research in the Sociology of Organizations*, vol. 1. Greenwich, CT: JAI Press, pp. 39–74.

Allison, Scott T., and David M. Messick. (1987) "From Individual Inputs to Group Outputs, and Back Again: Group Processes and Inferences About Members," in Clyde Hendrick (ed.), *Group Processes*. Beverly Hills, CA: Sage, pp. 111–143.

Alpert, M., and H. Raiffa. (1982) "A Progress Report on the Training of Probability Assessors," in D. Kahneman, P. Slovic, and A. Tversky (eds.), *Judgement Under Uncertainty: Heuristics and Biases*. Cambridge: Cambridge University Press.

Altman, Irwin, and Dalmas Taylor. (1973) *Social Penetration: The Development of Interpersonal Relationships*. New York: Holt, Rinehart & Winston.

Andersen, J. (1988) "Communication Competency in the Small Group," in Robert Cathcart and Larry Samovar (eds.), *Small Group Communication*, 5th ed. Dubuque, IA: Brown, pp. 450–458.

Andrews, Patricia H. (1988) "Group Conformity," in Robert Cathcart and Larry Samovar (eds.), *Small Group Communication*, 5th ed. Dubuque, IA: Brown, pp. 225–235.

Baird, John E., Jr., and Sanford B. Weinberg. (1977) *Communication: The Essence of Group Synergy*. Dubuque: IA: Brown.

Bales, Robert F. (1950) *Interaction Process Analysis: A Method for the Study of Small Groups*. Cambridge, MA: Addison-Wesley.

Bales, Robert F. (1953) "The Equilibrium Problem in Small Groups," in Talcott Parsons, Robert F. Bales, and Edward A. Shils (eds.), *Working Papers in the Theory of Action*. New York: Free Press, pp. 111–161.

Bales, Robert F., and Fred L. Strodtbeck. (1951) "Phases in Group Problem-Solving," *Journal of Abnormal and Social Psychology*, **46**:485–495.

313

Bales, Robert F., and Philip E. Slater. (1955) "Role Differentiation in Small Decision-Making Groups," in Talcott Parsons et al. (eds.), *The Family, Socialization, and Interaction Process.* Glencoe, IL: Free Press, pp. 259–306.

Bales, Robert F., and Stephen P. Cohen. (1979) *SYMLOG: A System for the Multiple Level Observation of Groups.* New York: Free Press.

Barker, R. G., and H. F. Wright. (1955) *Midwest and Its Children.* Evanston, IL: Row Peterson.

Bateson, Gregory. (1935) "Culture Contact and Schismogenesis," *Man,* **35:**178–183.

Bateson, Gregory. (1972) *Steps to an Ecology of Mind.* San Francisco: Chandler.

Benne, Kenneth D., and Paul Sheats. (1948) "Functional Roles of Group Members," *Journal of Social Issues,* **4:**41–49.

Bennis, Warren G., and Herbert A. Shepard. (1956) "A Theory of Group Development," *Human Relations,* **9:**415–437.

Berg, David M. (1967) "A Descriptive Analysis of the Distribution and Duration of Themes Discussed by Task-Oriented Small Groups," *Speech Monographs,* **34:**172–175.

Berger, Charles R. (1973) "Task Performance and Attributional Communication as Determinants of Interpersonal Attraction," *Speech Monographs,* **40:**280–286.

Berger, Charles R., and R. J. Calabrese. (1975) "Some Explorations in Initial Interaction and Beyond: Toward a Developmental Theory of Interpersonal Communication," *Human Communication Research,* **1:**99–112.

Berlo, David K. (1960) *The Process of Communication.* New York: Holt, Rinehart & Winston.

Birdwhistell, Ray L. (1970) *Kinesics and Context: Essays on Body Motion Communication.* Philadelphia: University of Pennsylvania Press.

Blau, Peter M. (1960) "A Theory of Social Integration," *American Journal of Sociology,* **65:**545–556.

Bochner, Arthur P. (1984) "The Functions of Human Communication in Interpersonal Bonding," in Carroll C. Arnold and John Waite Bowers (eds.), *Handbook of Rhetorical and Communication Theory.* Newton, MA: Allyn and Bacon, pp. 544–621.

Bormann, E. G. (1986) "Symbolic Convergence Theory and Communication in Group Decision-Making," in R. Y. Hirokawa and M. S. Poole (eds.), *Communication and Group Decision.* Beverly Hills, CA: Sage, pp. 219–236.

Bormann, Ernest G., and Nancy C. Bormann. (1988) *Effective Small Group Communication.* Edina, MN: Burgess.

Bowers, John W., and John A. Courtright. (1984) *Communication Research Methods.* Glenview, IL: Scott, Foresman.

Boyatzis, R. E. (1982) *The Competent Manager.* New York: Wiley.

Brilhart, John K. (1978) *Effective Group Discussion,* 3d ed. Dubuque, IA: Brown.

Brown, Steven R., and Albert Rothenberg. (1976) "The Analysis of Group Episodes," *Small Group Behavior,* **7:**287–306.

Burgoon, Judee K. (1988) "Spatial Relationships in Small Groups," in Robert Cathcart and Larry Samovar (eds.), *Small Group Communication,* 5th ed. Dubuque, IA: Brown, pp. 351–366.

Butler, D., and F. L. Geis. (1990) "Nonverbal Affect Responses to Male and Female Leaders: Implications for Leadership Evaluations," *Journal of Personality and Social Psychology,* **58:**48–59.

Canary, Daniel J., and Brian H. Spitzberg. (1987) "Appropriateness and Effectiveness Perceptions of Conflict Strategies," *Human Communication Research,* **14:**93–118.

Cartwright, Dorwin, and Alvin Zander. (1968) "Leadership and Performance of Group

Functions: Introduction," in Dorwin Cartwright and Alvin Zander (eds.), *Group Dynamics: Research and Theory*, 3d ed. New York: Harper & Row, pp. 301–317.

Cegala, D. J., et al. (1982) "An Elaboration of the Meaning of Interaction Involvement: Toward the Development of a Theoretical Concept," *Communication Monographs*, **49**:229–248.

Chemers, Martin. (1983) "Leadership Theory and Research: A System-Process Integration," in P. B. Paulus (ed.), *Basic Group Processes*. New York: Springer-Verlag.

Cline, Rebecca J. Welch. (1990) "Detecting Groupthink: Methods for Observing the Illusion of Unanimity," *Communication Quarterly*, **38**:112–126.

Coates, Jennifer. (1986) *Women, Men and Language*. London: Longman.

Collins, Barry E., and Harold Guetzkow. (1964) *A Social Psychology of Group Processes for Decision-Making*. New York: Wiley.

Coser, Lewis. (1956) *The Functions of Social Conflict*. New York: Free Press.

Cragan, John C., and David W. Wright. (1990) "Small Group Communication Research of the 1980s: A Synthesis and Critique," *Communication Studies*, **41**:212–236.

Crowell, Laura, and Thomas M. Scheidel. (1961) "Categories for Analysis of Idea Development in Discussion Groups," *Journal of Social Psychology*, **54**:155–168.

Davis, James H. (1969) *Group Performance*. Reading, MA: Addison-Wesley.

DeStephen, Rolayne S. (1977) "Leadership and Sex: Behavioral Differences in the Small Group Context." A paper presented to Western Speech Communication Association, Phoenix, AZ.

Deutsch, Morton. (1973) *The Resolution of Conflict: Constructive and Destructive Processes*. New Haven: Yale University Press.

Dewey, John. (1910) *How We Think*. New York: Heath.

Donohue, William A. (1981) "Analyzing Negotiation Tactics: Development of Negotiation Interact System," *Human Communication Research*, **7**:273–287.

Drecksel, Gay L. (1984) "Interaction Characteristics of Emergent Leadership," Ph.D. dissertation, University of Utah.

Dunphy, Dexter C. (1964) "Social Change in Self-Analytic Groups," Ph.D. dissertation, Harvard University.

Eisenberg, Eric. (1984) "Ambiguity as Strategy in Organizational Communication," *Communication Monographs*, **51**:227–242.

Ellis, Donald G. (1979) "Relational Control in Two Group Systems," *Communication Monographs*, **46**:153–166.

Ellis, Donald G., and B. Aubrey Fisher. (1975) "Phases of Conflict in Small Group Development," *Human Communication Research*, **1**:195–212.

Farris, G. F., and F. G. Lim. (1969) "Effects of Performance on Leadership, Cohesiveness, Influence, Satisfaction, and Subsequent Performance," *Journal of Applied Psychology*, **53**:490–497.

Festinger, Leon. (1950) "Informal Social Communication," *Psychological Review*, **57**:271–282.

Festinger, Leon. (1954) "A Theory of Social Comparison Processes," *Human Relations*, **7**:117–140.

Fiedler, Fred E. (1964) "A Contingency Model of Leadership Effectiveness," in Leonard Berkowitz (ed.), *Advanced in Experimental Social Psychology*, vol. 1. New York: Academic Press, pp. 149–190.

Fiedler, Fred E. (1967) *A Theory of Leadership Effectiveness*. New York: McGraw-Hill.

Filley, A. (1975) *Interpersonal Conflict Resolution*. Glenview, IL: Scott, Foresman.

Fisher, B. Aubrey. (1970a) "Decision Emergence: Phases in Group Decision Making," *Speech Monographs*, **37**:53–66.

Fisher, B. Aubrey. (1970b) "The Process of Decision Modification in Small Discussion Groups," *Journal of Communication*, **20**:51–64.

Fisher, B. Aubrey. (1977) "Interaction Analysis: An Underutilized Methodology in Communication." A paper presented to Western Speech Communication Association, Phoenix, AZ.

Fisher, B. Aubrey. (1978) *Perspectives on Human Communication*. New York: Macmillan.

Fisher, B. Aubrey. (1980) *Small Group Decision Making*. New York: McGraw-Hill.

Fisher, B. Aubrey. (1986) "Leadership: When Does the Difference Make a Difference," in R. Hirokawa and M. S. Poole (eds.), *Communication and Group Decision-Making*. Beverly Hills, CA: Sage, pp. 197–215.

Fisher, B. Aubrey, Thomas W. Glover, and Donald G. Ellis. (1977) "The Nature of Complex Communication Systems," *Communication Monographs*, **44**:231–240.

Fisher, B. Aubrey, and Randall K. Stutman. (1987) "An Assessment of Group Trajectories: Analyzing Developmental Breakpoints," *Communication Quarterly*, **35**:105–124.

Folger, Joseph P., and Marshall S. Poole. (1982) "Relational Coding Schemes: The Question of Validity," in M. Burgoon (ed.), *Communication Yearbook 5*. New Brunswick, NJ: Transaction, pp. 240–266.

Folger, Joseph P., and Marshall S. Poole. (1984) *Working Through Conflict: A Communication Perspective*. Glenview, IL: Scott, Foresman.

Gibb, Jack. (1961) "Defensive Communication," *Journal of Communication*, **11**:141–148.

Gilligan, Carol. (1982) *In a Different Voice: Psychological Theory and Women's Development*. Cambridge: Harvard University Press.

Gilstein, Kenneth W., E. Wayne Wright, and David R. Stone. (1977) "The Effects of Leadership Style on Group Interactions in Differing Socio-Political Subcultures," *Small Group Behavior*, **8**:313–332.

Goffman, Erving. (1959) *The Presentation of Self in Everyday Life*. Garden City, NY: Doubleday.

Goffman, Erving. (1961) *Encounters*. New York: Bobbs-Merrill.

Goldmann, R. B. (1980) *Round Table Justice: Case Studies in Conflict Resolution*. Boulder, CO: Westview Press.

Gouldner, Alvin W. (1960) "The Norm of Reciprocity: A Preliminary Statement," *American Sociological Review*, **25**:161–171.

Gouran, Dennis S. (1983) "Communicative Influence on Inferential Judgments in Decision-Making Groups: A Descriptive Analysis," in D. Zarefsky et al. (eds.), *Argument in Transition: Proceedings of the Third Summer Conference on Argumentation*. Annandale, VA: Speech Communication, pp. 667–684.

Gouran, Dennis S., and John E. Baird, Jr. (1972) "An Analysis of Distributional and Sequential Structure in Problem-Solving and Informal Group Discussions," *Speech Monographs*, **39**:16–22.

Gouran, Dennis S., and B. Aubrey Fisher. (1984) "The Functions of Human Communication in the Formation, Maintenance, and Performance of Small Groups," in Carroll C. Arnold and John Waite Bowers (eds.), *Handbook of Rhetorical and Communication Theory*. Newton, MA: Allyn and Bacon, pp. 622–658.

Hackman, Richard J. (1968) "Effects of Task Characteristics on Group Products," *Journal of Experimental Social Psychology*, **4**:162–187.

Hall, Edward T. (1959) *The Silent Language*. Garden City, NY: Doubleday.

Haslett, Beth, and John R. Ogilvie. (1992) "Feedback Processes in Task Groups," in Robert Cathcart and Larry Samovar (eds.), *Small Group Communication*, 6th ed. Dubuque, IA: Brown, pp. 342–356.

Hawes, Leonard C. (1972) "The Effects of Interviewer Style on Patterns of Dyadic Communication," *Speech Monographs*, **39**:114–123.

Hawes, Leonard C., and Joseph M. Foley. (1976) "Group Decisioning: Testing a Finite Stochastic Model," in Gerald R. Miller (ed.), *Explorations in Interpersonal Communication*. Beverly Hills, CA: Sage, pp. 237–254.

Hecht, Michael L., and Pat Riley. (1985) "A Three-Factor Model of Group Satisfaction and Consensus," *Communication Research Reports*, **2**:179–187.

Helgesen, S. (1990) *The Female Advantage: Women's Ways of Leadership*. New York: Doubleday.

Herbert, J., and C. Attridge. (1975) "A Guide for Developers and Users of Observation Systems and Manuals," *American Educational Research Journal*, **12**:1–20.

Hersey, P., and K. H. Blanchard. (1982) *Management of Organizational Behavior*, Englewood Cliffs, NJ: Prentice-Hall.

Heslin, Richard, and Dexter Dunphy. (1964) "Three Dimensions of Member Satisfaction in Small Groups," *Human Relations*, **17**:99–112.

Hewes, D. E. (1979) "The Sequential Analysis of Social Interaction," *Quarterly Journal of Speech*, **65**:56–73.

Hirokawa, Randy Y. (1982) "Group Communication and Problem-Solving Effectiveness I: A Critical Review of Inconsistent Findings," *Communication Quarterly*, **30**:134–141.

Hirokawa, Randy Y. (1983a) "Group Communication and Problem-Solving Effectiveness: An Investigation of Group Phases," *Human Communication Research*, **9**:291–305.

Hirokawa, Randy Y. (1983b) "Group Communication and Problem-Solving Effectiveness II," *Western Journal of Speech Communication*, **47**:59–74.

Hirokawa, Randy, Y. (1992) "Communication and Group Decision-Making Efficacy," in R. S. Cathcart and L. A. Samovar (eds.), *Small Group Communication*, Dubuque, IA: Brown, pp. 165–177.

Hirokawa, Randy Y., and R. Pace. (1983) "A Descriptive Investigation of the Possible Communication-Based Reasons for Effective and Ineffective Group Decision-Making," *Communication Monographs*, **50**:363–379.

Hirokawa, Randy Y., and Marshall Scott Poole (eds.). (1986) *Communication and Group Decision-Making*. Beverly Hills, CA: Sage.

Hirokawa, Randy Y., and Dirk R. Scheerhorn. (1986) "Communication in Faulty Group Decision-Making," in Randy Hirokawa and Marshall S. Poole (eds.), *Communication and Group Decision-Making*. Beverly Hills, CA: Sage, pp. 63–80.

Hocking, John E., Duane G. Margreiter, and Cal Hylton. (1977) "Intra-Audience Effects: A Field Test," *Human Communication Research*, **3**:243–249.

Hollander, E. P. (1983) "Women and Leadership," in H. H. Blumberg et al. (eds.), *Small Groups and Social Interaction*, vol. 1. New York: Wiley.

Hollander, E. P. (1985) "Leadership and Power," in G. Lindzey and Elliot Aronson (eds.), *The Handbook of Social Psychology*, 3d ed., vol. 2. New York: Random House, pp. 485–537.

Homans, George C. (1950) *The Human Group*. New York: Harcourt, Brace.

Homans, George C. (1961) *Social Behavior: Its Elementary Forms*. New York: Harcourt, Brace.

Horenstein, David, and Shirley J. Gilbert. (1976) "Anxiety, Likeability, and Avoidance as Responses to Self-Disclosing Communication," *Small Group Behavior*, **7**:423–432.

House, R. J., and T. R. Mitchell. (1974) "Path-Goal Theory of Leadership," *Journal of Contemporary Business*, **3**:81–97.

Hunt, Gary T. (1980) *Communication Skills in the Organization*. Englewood Cliffs, NJ: Prentice-Hall.

Janis, I. L. (1983) *Groupthink: Psychological Studies of Foreign Policy Decisions and Fiascoes*, 2d ed. Boston: Houghton Mifflin.

Janis, I. L., and L. Mann. (1944) *Decision Making: A Psychological Analysis of Conflict, Choice, and Commitment*. New York: Free Press.

Jarboe, Susan. (1988) "A Comparison of Input-Output, Process-Output, and Input-Process-Output Models of Small Group Problem-Solving Effectiveness," *Communication Monographs*, **55**:121–142.

Johnson, David W. (1986) *Reaching Out*, 3d ed. Englewood Cliffs, NJ: Prentice-Hall.

Johnson, David W., and Frank P. Johnson. (1987) *Joining Together*, 3d ed. Englewood Cliffs, NJ: Prentice-Hall.

Jourard, S. M. (1964) *The Transparent Self*. New York: D. Van Nostrand.

Knapp, Mark L. (1978) *Nonverbal Communication in Human Interaction*, New York: Holt, Rinehart & Winston.

Lewin, Kurt. (1951) *Field Theory in Social Science*. New York: Harper & Row.

Likert, Rensis, and David G. Bowers. (1972) "Conflict Strategies," in Elliott McGinnies (ed.), *Attitudes, Conflict and Social Change*. New York: Academic Press, pp. 101–122.

McCann, Dick, and Charles Margerison. (1989) "High-Performance Teams," *Training and Development Journal*, 43, 52–60.

McCroskey, J. C. (1977) "Oral Communication Apprehension: A Summary of Recent Theory and Research," *Human Communication Research*, **4**:78–96.

McKinney, B. C. (1982) "The Effects of Reticence on Group Interaction," *Communication Quarterly*, **30**:124–128.

Mansfield, E. (1973) "Empathy: Concept and Identified Psychiatric Nursing Behavior," *Nursing Research* **22**:525–530.

Marston, Peter J., and Michael L. Hecht. (1988) "Group Satisfaction," in Robert Cathcart and Larry Samovar (eds.), *Small Group Communication*, 5th ed. Dubuque, IA: Brown, pp. 236–246.

Merton, Robert K. (1957) *Social Theory and Social Structure*. New York: Free Press.

Meyers, Renée A., (1989) "Testing Persuasive Argument Theory's Predictor Model: Alternative Interactional Accounts of Group Argument and Influence," *Communication Monographs*, **56**:112–132.

Meyers, Renée A., and David R. Seibold. (1990) "Perspectives on Group Argument: A Critical Review of Persuasive Arguments Theory and Alternative Structurational View," in J. A. Anderson (ed.), *Communication Yearbook* 13, Newbury Park, CA: Sage, 268–302.

Monge, Peter R. (1987) "The Network Level of Analysis," in Charles Berger and Steven H. Chaffee (eds.), *Handbook of Communication Science*. Beverly Hills, CA: Sage, pp. 239–270.

Monge, Peter R., and Eric M. Eisenberg. (1987) "Emergent Networks," in F. Jablin, L. Putnam, K. Roberts, and L. Porter (eds.), *Handbook of Organizational Communication*. Newbury Park, CA: Sage.

Mortensen, C. David. (1966) "Should the Discussion Group Have an Assigned Leader?" *Speech Teacher*, **15**:34–41.

Mortensen, C. David. (1972) *Communication: The Study of Human Interaction*. New York: McGraw-Hill.

Moscovici, S. (1985) "Social Influence and Conformity," in G. Lindzey and Elliot Aronson (eds.), *The Handbook of Social Psychology*, 3d ed., vol. 2. New York: Random House, pp. 347–412.

Myers, D. G., and G. D. Bishop. (1971) "Enhancement of Dominant Attitudes in Group Discussion," *Journal of Personality and Social Psychology*, **20**:386–391.

Napier, Rodney W., and Matti K. Gershenfeld. (1985) *Groups: Theory and Experience.* Boston: Houghton Mifflin.

Nelson, M. W. (1988) "Women's Ways: Interactive Patterns in Predominantly Female Research Teams," in Barbara Bate and Anita Taylor (eds.), *Women Communicating: Studies of Women's Talk*, Norwood, NJ: Ablex, pp. 199–232.

Offerman, L. R. (1984) "Short-Term Supervisory Experience and LPC Score: Effects of Leader Sex and Group Sex Composition," *Journal of Social Psychology*, **123**:115–121.

Pacanowsky, Michael E., and Nicholas O'Donnell-Trujillo. (1983) "Organizational Communication as Cultural Performance," *Communication Monographs*, **50**:126–147.

Parsons, Talcott. (1951) *The Social System.* New York: Free Press.

Patton, B. R., and K. Giffin. (1988) "Conflict and Its Resolution," in Robert Cathcart and Larry Samovar (eds.), *Small Group Communication*, 5th ed. Dubuque, IA: Brown, pp. 429–441.

Pearce, W. Barnett. (1974) "Trust in Interpersonal Communication," *Speech Monographs*, **41**:236–244.

Pearce, W. Barnett, and Stuart M. Sharp. (1973) "Self-Disclosing Communications," *Journal of Communication*, **23**:409–425.

Pfeffer, J. (1981) *Power in Organizations.* Marshfield, MA: Pitman.

Phillips, Gerald M., and Eugene C. Erickson. (1970) *Interpersonal Dynamics in the Small Group.* New York: Random House.

Poole, Marshall S. (1981) "Decision Development in Small Groups I: A Comparison of Two Models," *Communication Monographs*, **48**:1–24.

Poole, Marshall S. (1983a) "Decision Development in Small Groups II: A Study of Multiple Sequences in Decision Making," *Communication Monographs*, **50**:206–232.

Poole, Marshall S. (1983b) "Decision Development in Small Groups II: A Multiple Sequence Model of Group Decision-Making," *Communication Monographs*, **50**:321–341.

Poole, Marshall S. (1992) "Group Communication and the Structuration Process," in Robert S. Cathcart and Larry A. Samovar (eds.), *Small Group Communication*, Dubuque, IA: Brown, pp. 147–157.

Poole, Marshall S., and Joel A. Doelger. (1986) "Developmental Processes in Group Decision-Making," in Randy Hirokawa and Marshall S. Poole (eds.), *Communication and Group Decision-Making*. Beverly Hills, CA: Sage, pp. 237–264.

Poole, Marshall S., David R. Siebold, and Robert D. McPhee. (1986) "A Structurational Approach to Theory-Building in Group Decision-Making Research," in Randy Hirokawa and Marshall S. Poole (eds.), *Communication and Group Decision-Making*. Beverly Hills, CA: Sage, pp. 237–264.

Poole, Marshall S., and Jonelle Roth. (1989) "Decision Development in Small Groups IV: A Typology of Group Decision Paths," *Human Communication Research*, **15**:323–356.

Putnam, L. L. (1979) "Preference for Procedural Order in Task-Oriented Small Groups," *Communication Monographs*, **46**:193–218.

Putnam, L. L. (1986) "Conflict in Group Decision-Making," in Randy Hirokawa and Marshall S. Poole (eds.), *Communication and Group Decision-Making*. Beverly Hills, CA: Sage, pp. 175–196.

Putnam, L. L., and Cynthia Stohl. (1990) "Bona Fide Groups: A Reconceptualization of Groups in Context," *Communication Studies*, **41**:248–265.

Rice, R. W., L. R. Bender, and A. G. Vitters. (1980) "Leader Sex, Follower Attitudes

Toward Women, and Leadership Effectiveness: A Laboratory Study," *Organizational Behavior and Human Performance*, **25**:46–78.

Rice, R. W., D. Instone, and J. Adams. (1984) "Leader Sex, Leader Success, and Leadership Process: Two Field Studies," *Journal of Applied Psychology*, **69**:12–31.

Rieken, Henry W. (1952) "Some Problems of Consensus Development," *Rural Sociology*, **17**:245–252.

Robert, Henry M. (1990) *Robert's Rules of Order Newly Revised*. Glenview, IL: Scott, Foresman.

Roloff, M. (1987) "Communication and Conflict," in Charles Berger and Steven Chaffee (eds.), *Handbook of Communication Science*. Beverly Hills, CA: Sage, pp. 484–534.

Rosenfeld, L. B. (1988) "Self-Disclosure and Small Group Interaction," in Robert Cathcart and Larry Samovar (eds.), *Small Group Communication*, 5th ed. Dubuque, IA: Brown, pp. 288–305.

Scheidel, Thomas M. (1986) "Divergent and Convergent Thinking in Group Decision-Making," in Randy Hirokawa and Marshall S. Poole (eds.), *Communication and Group Decision-Making*. Beverly Hills, CA: Sage, pp. 113–130.

Scheidel, Thomas M., and Laura Crowell. (1964) "Idea Development in Small Discussion Groups," *Quarterly Journal of Speech*, **50**:140–145.

Schneier, C. E., and K. M. Bartol. (1980) "Sex Differences in Emergent Leadership," *Journal of Applied Psychology*, **65**:341–345.

Seifert, C., and C. E. Miller. (1988) "Subordinates' Perceptions of Leaders in Task-Performing Dyads: Effects of Sex of Leader and Subordinate, Method of Leader Selection, and Performance Feedback," *Sex Roles*, **19**:13–28.

Shaw, Marvin E. (1976) *Group Dynamics: The Psychology of Small Group Behavior*, 2d ed. New York: McGraw-Hill.

Shaw, Marvin E. (1981) *Group Dynamics: The Psychology of Small Group Behavior*, 3d ed. New York: McGraw-Hill.

Shaw, Marvin E. (1992) "Group Composition and Group Cohesiveness," in R. S. Cathcart and L. A. Samovar (eds.), *Small Group Communication*, Dubuque, IA: Brown, pp. 214–220.

Sherif, M. (1935) "A Study of Some Social Factors in Perception," *Archives of Psychology*, **27**:(187).

Siebold, David R. (1992) "Making Meetings More Successful: Plans, Formats, and Procedures for Group Problem-Solving," in Robert Cathcart and Larry Samovar (eds.), *Small Group Communication*, 6th ed. Dubuque, IA: Brown, pp. 178–191.

Simmel, Georg. (1955) *Conflict*. New York: Free Press.

Sorensen, S. (1981) "Grouphate." A paper presented to the International Communication Association, Minneapolis, MN.

Strube, M. J., and J. E. Garcia. (1981) "A Meta-Analytic Investigation of Fiedler's Contingency Model of Leadership Effectiveness," *Psychological Bulletin*, **90**:307–321.

Taylor, R. B., and J. C. Lanni. (1981) "Territorial Dominance: The Influence of the Resident Advantage in Triadic Decision Making," *Journal of Personality and Social Psychology*, **41**:909–915.

Thibaut, John W., and Harold H. Kelley. (1959) *The Social Psychology of Groups*. New York: Wiley.

Thomas, Kenneth, W. (1976) "Conflict and Conflict Management," in M. Dunnette (ed.), *Handbook of Industrial and Organizational Psychology*, Chicago, IL: Rand McNally, pp. 890–934.

Tichy, N. M. (1981) "Networks in Organizations," in P. Nystrom and W. Starbuck (eds.), *Handbook of Organizational Design*, vol. 2. New York: Oxford University Press, pp. 225–249.

Tjosvold, D. (1982) "Effects of Approach to Controversy on Superiors' Incorporation of Subordinates' Information in Decision Making," *Journal of Applied Psychology*, **67**:189–193.

Tolar, Alexander. (1970) "The 'Natural Course' View of Conflict Resolution," *Psychological Reports*, **26**:734.

Torrance, E. Paul. (1957) "Group Decision Making and Disagreement," *Social Forces*, **35**:314–318.

Tuchman, M. L., and T. J. Scanlan. (1981) "Boundary Spanning Individuals: Their Role in Information Transfer and Their Antecedents," *Academy of Management Review*, **24**:289–305.

Tuckman, Bruce W. (1965) "Developmental Sequence in Small Groups," *Psychological Bulletin*, **63**:384–399.

Tversky, A., and D. Kahneman. (1983) "Extensional vs. Intuitive Reasoning: The Conjunction Fallacy in Probability Judgement," *Psychology Review*, **90**:293–315.

Valentine, Kristin B., and B. Aubrey Fisher. (1974) "An Interaction Analysis of Verbal Innovative Deviance in Small Groups," *Speech Monographs*, **41**:413–420.

Vroom, V. H., and P. W. Yetton. (1973) *Leadership and Decision Making*. Pittsburgh: University of Pittsburgh Press.

Watzlawick, Paul , Janet H. Beavin, and Don D. Jackson. (1967) *Pragmatics of Human Communication*. New York: Norton.

Weick, Karl E. (1978) "The Spines of Leaders," in M. McCall and M. Lombardo (eds.), *Leadership: Where Else Can We Go?* Durham, NC: Duke University Press, pp. 37–61.

Weick, Karl E. (1979) *The Social Psychology of Organizing*. Reading, MA: Addison-Wesley.

Weick, Karl E. (1981) "Psychology as Gloss," in R. Kasschau and C. N. Cofer (eds.), *Psychology's Second Century*. New York: Praeger, pp. 110–132.

Weick, Karl E. (1985) "Systematic Observational Methods," in G. Lindzey and Elliot Aronson (eds.), *The Handbook of Social Psychology*, 3d ed., vol. 1. New York: Random House, pp. 567–634.

Wood, Julia T. (1977) "Leading in Purposive Discussions: A Study of Adaptive Behavior," *Communication Monographs*, **44**:152–165.

Wood, Julia, T. (1992) "Alternative Methods of Group Decision Making," in R. S. Cathcart and L. A. Samovar (eds.), *Small Group Communication*, Dubuque, IA: Brown, pp. 158–164.

Zaleznik, Abraham, and David Moment. (1964) *The Dynamics of Interpersonal Behavior*. New York: Wiley.

Zeev, M. (1981) "The Decision to Raid Entebbe: Decision Analysis Applied to Crisis Behavior," *Journal of Conflict Resolution*, **25**:677–708.

Name Index

Subject Index

325